ELUSIVE LIVES

SOUTH ASIA IN MOTION

EDITOR
Thomas Blom Hansen

EDITORIAL BOARD
Sanjib Baruah
Anne Blackburn
Satish Despande
Faisal Devji
Christophe Jaffrelot
Naveeda Khan
Stacey Leigh Pigg
Mrinalini Sinha
Ravi Vasudevan

SIOBHAN LAMBERT-HURLEY

ELUSIVE LIVES

Gender, Autobiography, and the Self
in Muslim South Asia

STANFORD UNIVERSITY PRESS

STANFORD, CALIFORNIA

Stanford University Press
Stanford, California

© 2018 by the Board of Trustees of the Leland Stanford Junior University.
All rights reserved.

No part of this book may be reproduced or transmitted in any form or by any means, electronic or mechanical, including photocopying and recording, or in any information storage or retrieval system without the prior written permission of Stanford University Press.

Printed in the United States of America on acid-free, archival-quality paper

Library of Congress Cataloging-in-Publication Data

Names: Lambert-Hurley, Siobhan, author.

Title: Elusive lives : gender, autobiography, and the self in Muslim South Asia / Siobhan Lambert-Hurley.

Description: Stanford, California : Stanford University Press, 2018. | Includes bibliographical references and index.

Identifiers: LCCN 2017054457| ISBN 9781503604803 (cloth : alk. paper) | ISBN 9781503606517 (pbk. : alk. paper) | ISBN 9781503606524 (ebook)

Subjects: LCSH: Autobiography—Women authors. | Autobiography—Muslim authors. | Muslim women authors—South Asia—Biography—History and criticism. | Women authors, South Asian—Biography—History and criticism. | South Asian literature—History and criticism. | Women in literature. | Self in literature.

Classification: LCC CT25 .L265 2018 | DDC 920.72—dc23

LC record available at https://lccn.loc.gov/2017054457

Cover design: Rob Ehle

Cover image: Page from handwritten memoir of Safia Jabir Ali.

Typeset by Bruce Lundquist in 10.75/15 Adobe Caslon Pro

For Finn and Tess

CONTENTS

	A Note on Transliteration	ix
	Introduction: The Ultimate Unveiling	1
1	Life/History/Archive	29
2	The Sociology of Authorship	57
3	The Autobiographical Map	97
4	Staging the Self	125
5	Autobiographical Genealogies	155
	Coda: Unveiling and Its Attributes	189
	Acknowledgments	195
	Notes	199
	Bibliography	249
	Index	273

A NOTE ON TRANSLITERATION

This book considers autobiographical writing in a wide range of South Asian languages, including Urdu, Hindi, Bengali, Gujarati, Marathi, Punjabi, and Malayalam. It has proved difficult to be systematic in transliteration, but I have tried to follow some basic rules. Diacritical marks are largely omitted from the body of the text with the exception of the 'ain (') and the hamza ('). They are sometimes used, however, to make a point about pronunciation or to reflect their usage in an English title or analysis of a text. Similarly, the Persian izafat is generally denoted by -i- (as in *Zamana-i-Tahsil*), even after a vowel where –yi is often used, and the Arabic definite article, al-, as it would be pronounced (as in *Rauzat ur-Riyahin*). But these rules have been relaxed where a personal name or book title is used prominently or often in English translation with a different spelling. My guide for transliteration has been John T. Platts, *Dictionary of Urdū, Classical Hindī, and English*, on the basis that I have always used it when translating texts from Urdu. I retain English spellings for most Indian place-names in reflection of how they were used at the time (hence, Bombay and Calcutta appear more often than Mumbai and Kolkata). On the whole, words from South Asian languages have been denoted by italics, unless they are used frequently (as in the case of "purdah").

ELUSIVE LIVES

INTRODUCTION

THE ULTIMATE UNVEILING

"I was born in the time of British rule," began Jobeda Khanam. "Then, King George V was ruling." Her home was the small town of Kushtia, then in the Nadia district of central Bengal in eastern India. Her grandfather, a respected *pir*, stopped evening prayers at the neighborhood mosque to announce the birth—but did the child's piercing cry come from a boy or a girl? Dark clouds and pouring rain proved an ill omen: "when people came to know it was a girl, there was no trace of happiness left on their faces." Some women commented, "Oh God, this girl has brought such a storm, God only knows what is in store for her."[1] As Jobeda grew, she loved to eat the sweet jackfruit that grew in her family's compound. And when the annual fair came to town, she would beg her mother for money "to buy glass bangles, colored ribbons, clay toys, sweets made of sugar, puffed rice." But in those days, long before east Bengal transmuted into East Pakistan and then Bangladesh, girls were prohibited from even making sound with their shoes when they walked through the town enveloped in their black burqas. "We were in strict purdah," Jobeda explained. "Daughters or daughters-in-law were not even allowed to stand near the windows." As Jobeda grew older, her cultured father recognized an interest in music and offered to teach his daughter to sing—"Oh Bulbul of the garden, do not shake the flowering branch today"—but only with the doors and windows shut firmly so that

1

2   *The Ultimate Unveiling*

no passerby could hear her sweet voice. As she sat behind a curtain at the local mosque, Jobeda learned why she could not be seen or heard from an aged imam known for beating his child-wives: "Women are the gateway to hell. It is the responsibility of all Muslim men to keep them under strict control in purdah."[2]

Jobeda Khanam's childhood experiences, captured in the early pages of her autobiography, point to specific cultural conventions in South Asia, often encapsulated by the catch-all "purdah," by which men may exert their authority to constrain women's mobility and expression. Muslim women in particular are understood to be bound by elaborate codes of modesty defined by *sharam* and *'izzat*, shame and modesty, that inhibit any form of public articulation.[3] No wonder the renowned postcolonial theorist Gayatri Spivak was moved to assert that the South Asian woman has no real "voice" in any meaningful sense. Even if she could be heard to speak, her words were proscribed by a patriarchal discourse that defined what was appropriate for women to do and think and even feel.[4] And yet feminist scholars—myself included—have made it their life's work to find ways of recovering South Asian women's voices, however muted or enigmatic or coded they may be. To do so offers a means of restoring agency and subjectivity—even if the historical conditions under which that agency and subjectivity were constituted need to be identified, understood, and problematized.[5] Anthropologists have led the way by eliciting women's stories in oral form or interrogating their folktales, songs, and poetry for what can be read between the lines: the often subversive expressions of women less at ease with their social world than may have been assumed.[6] Historians have followed suit by employing disparate and sometimes fragmented sources—from diaries, autobiographies, and interviews to poetry, novels, architecture, and religious treatises—to consider how, despite limitations, South Asian women in the past still found ways to express a sense of self.[7]

And thus we are brought to this book. To continue the feminist project of decoding a gendered self, it focuses on autobiographical writings by South Asian Muslim women—women, like Jobeda Khanam, who refused to respect the taboo against women speaking out and instead told their life stories in the form of written autobiography. Chapter 1 explores in depth how autobiography is defined in this work, but perhaps it is sufficient to say here that contrary to some expectations, the sources are many and varied. In temporal terms, they date from the sixteenth century through the present, to give a sense of how autobiography as a literary genre has evolved over time. What soon becomes evident, however, is that beyond a few isolated texts from the Mughal period, Muslim women (and men) really began producing autobiographical writings in South Asia in greater numbers only from the late nineteenth century. This date is roughly comparable, if perhaps slightly earlier, than that proposed for women writing autobiography in other Islamicate societies. Taking the case of Egypt, Marilyn Booth notes that a few women projected the "auto" into their biographies of "friends and intellectual companions" from the 1880s, but it was only in the 1920s that "first-person book-length personal narratives" began to appear.[8] In other parts of the Arab world, and in Turkey and Iran too, Muslim women began writing travelogues and memoirs from the first decades of the twentieth century—at a point when South Asian Muslim women also became more prolific as authors.[9]

As a timeline for autobiographical production, my evidence compares favorably with that observed for South Asia as a whole and the Muslim community more specifically. The "elaboration" of life-history forms from the Middle East and Central Asia (*sira*, *tazkira*, *hayat*) is recognized in the autobiographies produced by Mughal emperors and Islamic scholars—I think of Zahiruddin Muhammad Babur's *Vaqa'i'* (Events) and Mir Muhammad Taqi's *Zikr* (Remembrance), for example—from the sixteenth century on. No doubt these early works provided autobiographical models for later South Asian authors, though as I explore in chapter 5, inspiration was more often closer at hand—from male and female exemplars within extended families in the high colonial era. Fittingly, David Arnold and Stuart Blackburn identify autobiographical writing "in the sense of a sustained narrative account of one's own life" as emerging in South Asia in the late nineteenth century and becoming more "common" only in the early twentieth century—in other words, after the establishment of colonialism proper in 1858 and the spread of a key technology for book and journal distribution in the form of the printing press.[10] As Ulrike Stark has traced in meticulous detail, print technology was well established in India by the late eighteenth century, but it remained largely in the hands of missionaries and British colonists in their coastal head-quarters at Calcutta and Madras. It was another century before the print "boom" really took off, as technological innovations and the growth of an Indian paper industry reduced the cost of printing sufficiently to make it accessible to the Indian middle classes—who could then read, write, and circulate published autobiographies alongside other genres.[11] The spread of autobiography mirrored the trajectory of print in the high noon of colonialism.

Many scholars thus characterize autobiography—like the novel and other forms of "modern" literature—as a colonial legacy. As S. P. Saksena opined in his seminal *Indian Autobiographies* as early as 1949, "self-portrayal" is of "recent origin in this country" and "essentially the result of English education."[12] What is most surprising about such Euro-centric perspectives is that they continue to be reproduced in much European and even South Asian scholarship. Writing nearly sixty years after Saksena, Udaya Kumar roots Keralan autobiography's "inhabitation of modernity" in a colonial project of education. In government schools, he explains, Malayali boys started writing diaries that, as explored in chapter 1, cultivated the "literary competence" and "disciplined survey of everyday activities" necessary for later autobiographical reflection.[13] The significance of education in providing the intellectual tools necessary to prepare autobiography will be underlined in this study also in chapter 2, but not necessarily as it was tied to colonial or "English" education. While some Muslim female authors were taught in English-language or British colonial institutions, they were hardly passive recipients of colonial knowledge or mere sitting ducks for foreign models and ideas.[14] Furthermore, just as many—and more among the early authors in this study—received a traditional education at home or attended private Muslim girls' schools intended to uphold "Islamic values" of one sort or another.

Scholarly emphasis on the autobiographies of male nationalist leaders—Gandhi, Nehru, and others—would seem to suggest that if not colonialism, it was nationalism that was responsible for autobiography becoming embedded in South Asia.[15] At that important historical juncture, "narration of self" became intertwined with "narration of the oppressed or emergent nation" to solidify the relationship between "nationalism and interiority."[16] More useful to my own context, I would argue, is to connect the growth of Muslim women's autobiographical writing from the late nineteenth century to a key development within South Asia's Muslim community: socioreligious reform. We will see in chapter 2 how *sharif* redefinition—by which I mean the reworking of elite status among Muslims after 1857—could have motivated the middle-class, aristocratic, and princely women who, in the main, wrote autobiography to assert and counter-assert their claims on nobility. But what is worth underlining here at the outset is the centrality of reformism to that process. According to Faisal Devji, Muslim reformism was little more than a *sharif* exercise in "self-creation"—and central to reformism were women.[17] Also pertinent is Francis Robinson's observation that it was under this reformist impulse from the nineteenth century that South Asian Muslims experienced the emergence of a more "this-worldly Islam" exemplified by a focus on the individual, or self. That emphasis on self-instrumentality, self-affirmation, and self-consciousness, in turn, facilitated more and different autobiographical production—including, as I show, by women.[18] This study is significant in making explicit that link between women, reformism, and autobiography in Muslim South Asia.

I thus argue that the proliferation of Muslim women writing lives was, as Barbara Metcalf observes of hajj narratives, a "modern phenomenon": one no doubt influenced by the colonial environment, but without being a European imitation.[19] Within that broad temporal frame, the timeline can be given more precision. Examples of Muslim women's autobiographical writing, I note, remain fairly evenly scattered throughout most of the twentieth century, really mushrooming only since the early 1980s. In Dhaka alone, more than forty women published life stories of various types in the 1980s and 1990s.[20] Usually born sometime between 1900 and the early 1940s, they were mature or aged women by the final decades of the twentieth century and thus—in keeping with the common practice of writing autobiography toward the end of life—ready to reflect on the many momentous changes that they had experienced, not least the growth of female education and employment outside the home, the changing nature of purdah observance, the nationalist move-

6   *The Ultimate Unveiling*

ment against British rule, Partition, the dissolution of princely states, and, depending on regional context, Indian, Pakistani, and/or Bangladeshi independence. As Khatemanara Begam (born ca. 1923–24) summarized her life's historical periodization, writing from Dhaka in 1988:

> We—I mean, people of my age group—have seen all three ages (past, present and future). The first 23/24 years of our lives were under the mighty British colonizers; our youth was spent in a lot of confusion and struggle under Pakistan; and our mature years passed in difficulty as independent citizens of Bangladesh. Today, at the end of my life when I see the past, I see we have crossed many strong waves over many years. We have seen epoch-making political changes. We have gathered many different and strange experiences. With great excitement, I have seen the great changes that have taken place in the field of women's education and her social environment.[21]

I would suggest that a new wave of women's activism from the 1970s accompanied by a growing recognition of women's history in the academy gave value to these women's stories. From that point on, as I highlight in chapter 4, publishers wanted to publish them in ever greater numbers—because there was now a market.

Shifting from time to place, I have drawn materials for this study from all parts of the Indian subcontinent, or at least those that have sported a fairly substantial Muslim population—what is now Pakistan and Bangladesh, but also Delhi, Bombay, Calcutta, Rampur, Bhopal, Hyderabad, Mysore, and many other places besides. Chapter 3 grants greater precision to this autobiographical map, but in linguistic terms it means recovering women's voices and stories in a wide range of South Asian languages, including Urdu, English, Hindi, Bengali, Gujarati, Marathi, Punjabi, and Malayalam.[22] Very often, these languages were employed with the intention of accessing specific audiences with specific interests: sometimes family and friends, but in many cases, a broader readership of elite, literate, perhaps segregated women. Like the authors themselves, they maintained links with the world outside while remaining consumed by their more immediate domestic environments. Thus, the historical world into which autobiographies by Muslim women provide a window can be one of prestigious public events and sweeping political change. But it is also one that is far more routine, sometimes even mundane: a history of the everyday. Functioning as informal ethnographies, these writings provide insight into what people ate, how they cooked, what they wore, how their homes were decorated, what they did in their gardens, how the weather changed, what made them ill, how they worshipped, what they studied, how they filled their leisure time, who it was that they loved and befriended, how they traveled and why. Of course, autobiography's association with the written word in a region of low literacy makes it a genre dominated by, though not exclusive to, the more elite.[23] But if social variation among authors is limited, the cast of characters that they depict is not. We are offered a rare view into the lives of many projected as "subaltern"—among them servants, ayahs, subjects, students, clients, viewers, and voters.

So, with these many and various sources at hand, what does it mean to write autobiography in a cultural context that idealizes women's anonymity? Reflecting on the Egyptian nationalist and feminist Huda Shaarawi (1879–1947), historian Margot Badran identifies the very feat of writing a memoir in a society in which "private life, family life, inner feelings and thoughts" were "sacrosanct" as a "feminist act." For Shaarawi to write about her "harem life" was, according to Badran, the "final unveiling."[24] In *Words, Not Swords*, literary scholar Farzaneh Milani makes a similar point that, in a "veiled society," women are not alone in being veiled: "The concrete, the specific, and the personal are also veiled. Communication is veiled. Words and feelings are veiled." To transgress the "contrived form of silence" means unveiling one's voice, even if not one's body. She thus interprets the "literary misfit" of women's autobiography in Iran as the "ultimate form of unveiling."[25] My subtitle for this introduction aims to pay tribute to Badran's and Milani's sentiments, while also pointing to the key questions asked of autobiography in this book: to what extent, and in what ways, have South Asian Muslim women revealed a sense of self in their autobiographical writings at different moments in time? Does the degree or form of self-representation reflect on how autobiography is defined as a genre? In what ways do contexts of production—historical, geographical, literary—shape the written construction of lives? And how far is it even possible to discern a gendered self in autobiographical writings from Muslim South Asia? Perhaps the first question that needs addressing, however, is why I choose to take South Asian Muslim women as a category at all.

SOUTH ASIAN MUSLIM WOMEN AS CATEGORY

So, why South Asian Muslim women in particular? Why not just South Asian women or, if that was too broad for one project, Indian women or Punjabi women or middle-class women or women writing in Urdu? Why women at all? In response to the final question first, perhaps an important clarification to make is that this book is not about women's autobiographies exclusively; rather, as I specify in my subtitle, it is about *gender, autobiography, and the self in Muslim South Asia*. In order to *gender* understandings of *autobiography* and *the self*, I examine women's autobiographies in parallel with those of men, particularly in chapter 5, where I draw many direct comparisons. Nevertheless, this study does focus primarily on autobiographical writings by *South Asian Muslim women*. Mahua Sarkar may critique this approach for producing a "separate, typically additive" history that runs the risk of simply reproducing, or "naturalizing," a discourse of difference.[26] But like Sarkar in her excellent *Visible Histories, Disappearing Women*, I do not intend to take these categories of "Muslim" and its apparent counter, "Hindu," for granted, but instead to be attentive to how they are produced and reproduced in autobiographical writings especially. "Muslim" and "woman" should also not be considered universal categories apart from the simultaneous workings of other identities—"nation," "region," "language," and "class"—to which I have alluded already. At the same time, I would argue that South Asian Muslim women have, in the modern period especially, shared certain experiences and concerns—as recorded in their life writings and analyzed within this book—that make it appropriate to consider them as a distinct group.

How, then, is this group constituted for the purpose of this study? Another point worth elucidating is that I use "Muslim" not so much as a strict religious denomination, as a fairly fluid cultural category. Certainly, some of the authors discussed here were devout in their religious practice, making at least passing mention in their autobiographical writings to daily prayers (*namaz*), fasting during Ramadan (*roza*), and ritual charity (*zakat*).[27] As Bangladeshi educator Meher Kabir wrote about her childhood in Dinajpur in the north of colonial Bengal in the 1930s: "Roza and namaz were a must."[28] Others recorded their participation in religious rituals associated with key dates in the Islamic calendar, including 'Id ul-Fitr, 'Id ul-Adha (or Baqr 'Id), and Muharram. Particularly detailed in her description of holy festivals was Jahanara Habibullah in *Remembrance of Days Past* (2001). Recalling her early life in princely Rampur, she dedicated whole sections to "Eid Festivities in Rampur" and "The Observance of Muharram at the Court of Nawab Raza Ali Khan."[29] Still others displayed a different type of Muslim religiosity by describing outings to the *dargah*, or shrines, of Sufi saints. To take one example, actress Begum Khurshid Mirza recorded multiple visits to the shrine of Makhdoom Allauddin Ali Ahmed Sabir Sahib at Kalyar Sharif near Saharanpur at a time when *piri-mureedi*, pledging allegiance to a Sufi shaikh for the purpose of spiritual guidance, was shunned openly by her reformist family and her "Westernized" husband.[30]

A few authors demonstrated their religiosity by writing whole travelogues narrating their spiritual journeys to the Hijaz for the hajj pilgrimage or, if Shia, to holy sites in Iraq, Iran, and Syria associated with the Prophet's family and later imams.[31] Many of the former are infused with a sense of religious ecstasy upon being unified with the divine at the Ka'ba at Mecca. The following entry, dated Friday, 9 Muharram [1328/1910], stands out in the hajj narrative of Ummat ul-Ghani Nurunnisa, a pilgrim from Hyderabad, for the contrast it provides to her usual matter-of-fact style:

> There was a wondrous atmosphere in the Haram tonight. There was not a single cloud to darken the deep-blue sky. The moon glittered and shone over the azure horizon. Its pure white light sacrificed itself above the Haram and the Ka'ba. Small, beautiful stars twinkled festively while the silverwork on the black curtains covering the Ka'ba glistened. The repeated calls of Allahu Akbar added to the wondrous mood. Against the light of the moon the flickering lamps were especially pleasing to the eye. White buildings, tall minarets . . . Some people performed prayers, some circled the Ka'ba, some read the

Qur'an. Others recited prayers in praise of the Prophet, while still others kissed the Black Stone. The atmosphere inside the Haram tonight filled my heart with a wonderful sense of bliss that is beyond all description, incapable of being written. Ink itself is not sufficient to record it. I pray to God that all our near and dear be given the opportunity to visit the Ka'ba. Amen.[32]

In the late 1930s, Nishatunnisa, better known as Begam Hasrat Mohani, expressed a similar depth of religious feeling—even if, reflecting her Shia piety, the emotion was different—upon being shown the exact spot where Imam Hussain was shot in a Karbala shrine: "There is a wooden board laid over the pit. I felt sick to my stomach when they lifted up that board to show me the spot . . . a strange sense of melancholy descended upon me."[33]

A couple of authors included in this study—notably educator Ghulam Fatima Shaikh and sex worker Nalini Jameela—were not born Muslim, but used their autobiographies to reflect consciously on their conversion from Hinduism to Islam. The first converted in the early twentieth century under the influence of her father after he was visited by an apparition of a local *pir*, now deceased. As she explained:

> After converting to Islam, my father increased his efforts to bring his wife and daughters into the fold. He was worried that they might be influenced by their Hindu family in whose custody they had remained. Although the offer of a job in Jacobabad made him happy, it did not offset his anxiety for his wife and daughters' spiritual well-being. In his sleep he dreamt it might be better to poison his two daughters than to let them live as Hindus. When he was overpowered by this intense emotion he saw an apparition. The late Abdur Rehman Sirhindi, who was a spiritual scholar and the grandfather of the present Hasmin Jan, appeared and advised him not to worry as by the next year his entire family would convert and would remain with him even in the life hereafter. This prophecy gave him much relief and he looked forward to that day.

In due course, Ghulam Fatima Shaikh, her mother, and her sister did become Muslim—though only after a great "tumult" in their native town of Hyderabad in Sindh resulting in "battle lines" being drawn between local Hindu and Muslim communities at odds over claiming the family as their own.[34] Nalini Jameela's conversion in the 1980s, in contrast, was, in her own telling, more practical than spiritual, and hardly contested. After moving in with one of her Muslim clients, she took the name Jameela to preserve the appearance of being his Muslim wife—despite not being convinced that she actually believed in God.[35]

Conversely, a handful of other authors discussed in this study were born into Muslim families, but chose to embrace religious practices associated with other faiths later in life. A key example here is the prostitute Piro, who, in the context of mid-nineteenth-century Punjab, was labeled a *kafir*, or unbeliever, for joining the Sikh sect led by Guru Gulabdas. The following stanza from her poetic autobiography, *Ik Sau Sath Kafian* (*One Hundred and Sixty Kafis*), gives a sense of her nebulous religious identity in a context of growing contention and conflict between Hindu and Muslim:

> Piro says, calling out, listen *qazi* to this
>
> I'm neither a Hindu nor a Musalman, how will you know?
>
> Why are you asleep in the sleep of attachment, go to the guru's feet
>
> We will be fulfilled when you awake from your slumber [?]
>
> You call out Allah but do not recognize a *murshid*
>
> Say and affirm *anal haq*, the true *kalma*.[36]

The *qazi*, or judge, responsible for interpreting Muslim jurisprudence, is taunted for not recognizing Piro's guru as a spiritual guide (*murshid*), nor his expression of absolute truth (*anal haq*) as the "true" articulation of faith (*kalma*). A link may be made with the Gandhian Raihana Tyabji, who, though nominally Muslim, became a devotee of Krishna. Of particular relevance here is her use of bhakti devotionalism as a form of self-representation in *The Heart of a Gopi*.[37] Many other authors recorded their participation in various "Hindu" or, in a Bengali context, "Brahmo" festivals, including Diwali, Dussehra, and Holi.[38]

A few authors married outside the Muslim community. An early example was Atiya Fyzee, who in 1912 wed Samuel Rahamin from the Jewish community in Pune known as the Bene Israel. Their unorthodox union was marked by the celebrated poet (and Atiya's former admirer) Maulana Shibli Nomani, with the following lines of poetry: "butan-i-

Hindi kafir kar liya karte the Muslim ko / Atiya ki ba-daulat aj ek kafir Musalman hai" (The idols of India used to make infidels out of Muslims / Today due to Atiya an infidel has become Muslim).[39] When, three decades later, Zohra Mumtaz wanted to wed Kameshwar Segal, a young artist also connected to Uday Shankar's dance company, they struggled to find a way that "a marriage between a Hindu and a Muslim need not involve a change of faith"—ultimately employing a registrar to complete the "legalities" at her sister's house in Allahabad. As she described the process by which they came to this compromise:

> My father was very upset [about our engagement]. When we went to see him in Dehra Dun, he said he understood my having made such a decision but was unable to accept the idea of his daughter marrying a Hindu. He could not help himself. At this Kameshwar said he was prepared to become a Muslim. "No!" said my father emphatically. "What would be my feelings if Zohra became a Hindu? Think of your parents." Eventually he gave his consent to the match but requested us not to have the wedding in Dehra Dun, feeling he would not be able to face his Muslim friends afterward. My elder sister Hajrah had written insisting that we have the wedding at her place in Allahabad . . .[40]

Post-Independence, these intercommunal marriages were perhaps less rare among women authors, particularly if they left the Indian subcontinent for lives and careers abroad.[41]

This final observation also raises the question of how "South Asia" is demarcated in this study—whether in geographical or ethnic terms. I have indicated already that autobiographies are drawn from all parts of the Indian subcontinent where there are significant Muslim populations, including contemporary India, Pakistan, and Bangladesh. References are also made where appropriate to materials from the peripheral territory Afghanistan, but the nature of the populations in Sri Lanka and Nepal means that they rarely, if at all, are represented in the mix. Some texts analyzed were not written in or about South Asia exclusively. Indeed, reflecting the style of other Islamic biographical forms, many authors made it a feature of their life stories to write about journeys abroad, whether for the purpose of travel, pilgrimage, education, work, or family.[42] These accounts are sometimes embedded in longer autobiographies and, at other times, stand alone in what are ostensibly travel narratives by Muslims *from* South Asia.[43] The association of autobiography with end-of-life and, more recently, diasporic reflection means that some authors included here wrote after they had left South Asia for lives elsewhere—usually Europe or North America. But in most cases their primary focus is on earlier phases of their lives: Ishvani's privileged childhood among the Khojas of Bombay, Mehrunissa Khan's youth as a "princess" of Rampur, or Sara Suleri's "meatless days" in Pakistan.[44] I have otherwise excluded those narratives belonging to the burgeoning but distinct subgenre of diasporic memoirs, particularly where authors are second-generation immigrants or more.[45] Only in those cases in which authors returned to live much of their lives in South Asia after being born elsewhere—like the Fyzee sisters, born in Istanbul but raised in Bombay—are they included in my sample.[46]

SITUATING MUSLIM AUTOBIOGRAPHY

To focus on Muslims also enables me to consider how their autobiographical writings in South Asia may relate to a long history of telling life stories in Islam. In previous work with Anshu Malhotra, I have explored how all too often autobiography as a genre is defined as the "exclusive creation of the modern West," with Jean-Jacques Rousseau's *Confessions* (1789) as its foundational text.[47] Dwight Reynolds asserts that this "fallacy" came to be promulgated by literary theorists in the years after the Second World War as cultural relativism bred fear in the context of empire's decline.[48] He quotes French philosopher Georges Gusdorf as offering the clearest articulation of this stance in his seminal "Conditions and Limits of Autobiography" (1956):

> It would seem that autobiography is not to be found outside our cultural area; one would say that it expresses a concern peculiar to Western man, a concern that had been of good use in his systematic conquest of the universe and that he had communicated to men of other cultures; but those men will thereby have been annexed by a sort of intellectual colonizing to a mentality that was not their own . . .[49]

14   *The Ultimate Unveiling*

According to this vision, autobiography is an intensely gendered phenomenon that could not appear in any non-Western context except as European imitation, thanks to a "cultural landscape where consciousness of self does not, properly speaking, exist."[50] Where "other" autobiographies were identified, they continued to be cast as "exceptions" to the rule—however many of them there may be—offering at best a "pale" or "immature" version of the European ideal.[51] Hence, Roy Pascal, in his important *Design and Truth in Autobiography*—first published just a few years after Gusdorf in 1960—could recognize the existence of the Mughal emperor Babur's lively and often frank sixteenth-century *Vaqa'i*', but still proclaim: "There remains no doubt that autobiography is essentially European."[52]

Clearly, the work of Gusdorf, Pascal, and others has cast a long shadow, for in many quarters their conclusions persisted for a long time, and in others, they still continue to do so. Even the great and the good of Middle Eastern and Islamic studies—among them, Albert Hourani, Edward Said, and Stephen Humphreys—were inclined to assess autobiography as a "very rare genre in Islamic literature" into the 1990s.[53] The same decade saw the publication of one of the few volumes dedicated to "the practice of biography and self-narrative" in the Middle East, but with many of its contributors as emphatic as before about the scarcity of autobiography in that geographical context.[54] The best example is probably the chapter by Marvin Zonis in which he judges autobiographies and biographies alike to be "few in number" and "generally lacking" in the Middle East due to "the absence of a sense of historicism and the relative underemphasis on the life of the individual in comparison with the group."[55] As there are, he concludes, few autobiographies that fulfill the "true potential of the genre" in the terms set by "Western men," the "utility" of autobiography for "illuminating Middle Eastern conceptions of the self" is limited.[56] Contemporaneous publications on South Asian literature were hardly more generous in their assessment of Muslims' propensity for self-narration. In *The History of Urdu Literature*, published by India's esteemed Sahitya Akademi in 1993, Ali Jawad Zaidi includes only one short paragraph on the "trickle" of autobiographies and memoirs appearing in "recent years," in the chapter "Literary Miscellany."[57]

"Autobiography—Urdu" attracts a few more columns in the *Encyclopedia of Indian Literature*, also published by Sahitya Akademi, as do Muslim autobiographies in other Indian languages (like Sindhi, though not in English)—but only to a total of about two dozen texts.[58] This number is comparable to that assigned to the entire corpus of Arabic autobiographies in twentieth-century studies of the genre.[59]

This circumstance in which Muslim autobiographies were considered rare, exceptional, and deficient when compared to their Western counterparts inspired Reynolds to "provoke a reevaluation of autobiography in world literature" through a detailed analysis of other autobiographical traditions.[60] Hence he dedicates part 1 of his *Interpreting the Self* to tracing "a thousand years of Arabic autobiography": from early biographical models adapted to autobiographical purposes (*sira, tarjama*) in the ninth through eleventh centuries and on to its development as a "self-conscious critical discourse" from the late fifteenth century.[61] An underlying aim is to counter the perception of Muslim autobiographies, or at least those written within the conventions of premodern literary forms, as devoid of self-reflection, as "utterly impersonal."[62] We may think here of the late Arabist Gustave E. von Grunebaum, who, as early as 1946, characterized the whole genre as consisting of "little more than confessional monologues."[63] A more recent example—actually postdating Reynolds—is provided by Stephen F. Dale in his study of Babur's *Vaqa'i'*, evocatively titled *The Garden of the Eight Paradises* (2004). In an introductory section, "Autobiography in the Islamic World," he points to various reasons why "pre-colonial" Muslims failed to write "highly personal autobiographies"—for example, Qur'anic passages discouraging acts of "self-aggrandizement"—in order to highlight the "originality" of Babur's candid text.[64] Reynolds, in contrast, argues that many Arabic autobiographies—from the eleventh century onward—demonstrate the "emotional life," "private behavior," personal evaluation, and "psychological development" of their authors in a way expected by twenty-first-century reader.[65] Even those texts at the "far end of the spectrum" in terms of their "brevity and laconic style" can be read in ways—perhaps as a "series of linked texts" or for "stylistic convention"—that reveal an inner self, a sense of individual identity or personality.[66]

16   *The Ultimate Unveiling*

His approach resonates with that taken by many of the contributors to a concurrent collection of essays, *Auto/biography and the Construction of Identity and Community in the Middle East* (2001), edited by Mary Ann Fay.[67] As historian Judith E. Tucker notes of Arab biography in chapter 1, there may not be "direct analysis of the self here," but the author does "provide the information that permits us to grasp the contours of a personality."[68] Her observation points to certain features that have been identified as characteristic of the Muslim autobiographical tradition, including in an Indo-Persian literary context. They are summed up by Barbara Metcalf under the label of "lives as lessons": the idea that autobiography had a didactic purpose by which the life stories of "exemplary" Muslims—as that of the Prophet Muhammad contained in the *Sunnah* (*Traditions*)—could be used to elucidate certain key aspects of the faith. Hence, a chronological development was often eschewed in favor of recounting anecdotes or episodes in an individual's life that offered moral instruction. Individual agency was also downplayed in order to suggest a life structured by "forces larger than one's self"—in particular, a "divine power" that found expression in the pious acts of respected elders deserving of veneration and allegiance, even after death. Related was an emphasis on relationships with others, reflected from the outset in a long and detailed genealogy of family and teachers.[69] The effect, according to Tucker, was an individual life rooted firmly in time. As she puts it, "history, not psychoanalytical theory, is what provides the context and touchstone."[70] Muslim autobiography, then, should be of special interest to historians—but is it? And, if so, what distinguishes their disciplinary approach?

HISTORICIZING AUTOBIOGRAPHY

Historians have approached autobiography in two main ways. The first, and most usual, is as a documentary source for past lives. As noted already and developed in chapter 1, gender historians in particular have embraced varying forms of personal narratives as a means of recovering suppressed or forgotten voices. But to many historians autobiography remains, in the words of Antoinette Burton, a "subspecies of evidence" for being unable to pass the "test of verifiability."[71] The memories on which autobiography relies are, as Malhotra and I have noted elsewhere, "notoriously unstable":

"sometimes telescoping time, and at others coagulating events in a given format."[72] The challenge, then, seems to be to actually turn the subjectivity of individual memory into a strength: to follow the example of those who use oral history in seeing autobiographical narratives as an "expression and representation of culture" that, in the words of historian of Italian fascism Luisa Passerini, "includes not only literal narrations but also the dimensions of memory, ideology and subconscious desires."[73] To do so can give autobiography a different "credibility."[74] Thus, a second historical approach has been to consider autobiography as a historically contingent literary form offering valuable insights into changing notions of the self, social and political discourses, and the construction of national, racial, and gender identities. A useful example here is Susan Rodgers's *Telling Lives, Telling History* (1995), in which she uses two childhood memoirs from Sumatra in Indonesia to show how reconstructing "boyhood selves" and the "remembered passage from childhood to maturity" in the final years of Dutch colonialism also reflected "much larger issues." As she explains: "Recalling the personal past, for these memoirists, becomes a witty but bitter effort of actively creating the public future, and trying to imagine an Indonesian national society of deep self-consciousness, social awareness, and religious sophistication."[75]

Arnold and Blackburn clarify these distinctions between historical approaches, while also pointing to directions for their own and future research in South Asia in the introduction to their seminal collection, *Telling Lives in India* (2004). As they write, "historians of India have generally been inclined to consider life histories as *sources*, of varying degrees of utility and trustworthiness; they have seldom paused to consider them as *genres* worthy of systematic analysis."[76] Unsurprisingly, their contributors do just that, exploring how Indian life histories may tell us as much about "wider society" as they do about the individual, while also illustrating the "power of certain cultural conventions and constraints" on variable and overlapping autobiographical forms and intents.[77] From their examples, we are given a sense of just how "pervasive" and "persistent" the practice of self-representation has been throughout the region's long history despite the common projection of South Asia as a society that privileges the social and communal over the individual.[78] Of special relevance to

18   *The Ultimate Unveiling*

this study is the chapter by the inspirational Sylvia Vatuk in which she analyzes how "an Indian Muslim woman writes her life."[79] The case she takes is Zakira Ghouse's handwritten memoir for a family magazine titled *Hamara Daur-i-Hayat* *(My Life)* about the author's childhood experiences in Hyderabad in the 1920s and early 1930s. Drawing on the work of acclaimed biographer Diane Middlebrook, Vatuk encourages the autobiographical analyst to be as attentive to silences—of reading "between" or even "against" the "narrative line"—as to "the use of genre conventions, temporal and other structuring, rhetoric, and authorial voice."[80] How pertinent this call is to Muslim South Asia, where female authors may not just *choose*, but also not be *allowed*, to write certain things.

Studies of autobiography as genre have become more common in South Asia in Arnold and Blackburn's wake. Javed Majeed, in his sagacious *Autobiography, Travel and Postnational Identity* (2007), examines the metaphor of travel in the autobiographical writings of such larger-than-life figures as Gandhi, Nehru, and Iqbal to trace the complex relationship between selfhood and the nation in formation.[81] His conclusion that their "adventure of interiority" was key to defining and grounding group identities and projects is pertinent to this study as well, particularly in chapters 2 and 5. Other scholars have sought to move beyond well-known autobiographers celebrated in nationalist discourses—whether in India or Pakistan—to explore regional contexts. Relevant here is Udaya Kumar's aforementioned analysis of early autobiographical writing in Kerala in which he seeks to draw out particular "idioms of self-articulation" in Malayalam also expressed in other literary forms, including the novel and poetry.[82] In particular, he warns against considering autobiography as a "unified genre with a distinctive identity," instead pushing the careful analyst to be attentive to the "widely varying functions" that personal narratives may perform.[83] That Kumar's interest in the "intersection of autobiography and history" has also caught hold with other scholars is evident in that several of the contributions to Vijaya Ramaswamy and Yogesh Sharma's more recent volume *Biography as History: Indian Perspectives* (2009) actually dealt with self-narration.[84] Consider Farhat Hasan's absorbing chapter in which he employs the seventeenth-century autobiography of a Jain merchant, Barnarsidas's *Ardhakathanaka* (*Half a Tale*), to show how an author could demonstrate individual agency and autonomy while still reinforcing cultural and familial norms and expectations.[85]

The importance of the autobiographical genre as a means for oppressed and marginalized groups such as women, religious converts, and dalits to "talk back" means that their narratives have garnered special attention.[86] Of these, Tanika Sarkar's analysis in *Words to Win* (1999) of the first "full-scale" autobiography written by a Bengali woman, Rassundari Debi's *Amar Jiban* (1868–97), is especially useful as a model for this study in that it reflects consciously on women's writing, religious frames, educational contexts, and the narrated self.[87] Other scholars have focused on Muslim female authors also appropriate to this study, and thus I employ their pioneering work where possible within the framework of my own analysis. We may consider, for example, Ruby Lal's 2004 study of the sixteenth-century memoir produced by Mughal princess Gulbadan (ca. 1523–1603). A main goal for Lal is to show how the princess's writing was "markedly different" from that of court chroniclers or even her own male relatives in its focus on the "everyday lives" of the royal family, including their peripatetic home life and domesticity.[88] Also seeking to theorize the relationships among gender, history, and the self in South Asia are the contributors to my own volume with Malhotra, *Speaking of the Self* (2015), from which I have already quoted. Of particular interest here, as in chapter 4 of this book, is how autobiography may be considered as a performative genre—in which conscious choices are made about form and narrative strategy or how to address an audience—to be negotiated, defined, and destabilized by primarily female authors moving beyond the "crevices" formed by nationalist and reformist agendas to craft their own subjectivity.[89] In doing so, I draw especially on Kathryn Hansen's masterful study of Indian theater autobiographies, *Stages of Life* (2011), in which she unravels the "act of self-presentation" at the core of all autobiographical writing.[90]

BEYOND AUTHORS AND TEXTS

Noticeable in many of the titles quoted in the previous section is their focus on case studies. To take one example, nearly all of the contributors to *Speaking of the Self,* myself included, provide a detailed analysis of one author or autobiographical tome.[91] The same observation may be made of much of the scholarly work on women's autobiography in Islamic or Islamicate societies. On the whole, it has been limited to the occasional article on a specific text or a scholarly introduction to a reprint or translation. I think of Margot Badran's preface and introduction to her translation of *Mudhakirrati* (*My Memoirs*) by Egyptian feminist Huda Shaarawi, to which I have referred already, or Leila Ahmed's article analyzing the same text.[92] Other examples include Hülya Adak's introduction to, and analyses of, the memoirs of Turkish nationalist Halidé Edib (1882–1964) and Abbas Amanat's lengthy contextualization of the translated memoirs of Persian princess Taj al-Saltana (1884–1914).[93] Even Nawar al-Hassan Golley's *Reading Arab Women's Autobiographies* (2003) considers the outputs of specific authors in a discrete way, among them the aforementioned Huda Shaarawi, Fadwa Tuqan, and Nawal el-Saadawi.[94] Only a few projects—for instance, by Marilyn Booth on Egypt and Farzaneh Milani on Iran—have surveyed women's life writing within specific national or cultural contexts.[95] This historiographical reality led to an interdisciplinary project in 2010–11, Women's Autobiography in Islamic Societies, that brought together many of the authors already mentioned and others besides, with the intention of amalgamating individual case studies, while also highlighting the importance of historical and geographical context.[96] Though successful in this aim, and thus highly significant to this study in offering a broad comparative framework employed throughout, most of the outputs by individual participants continued to take exemplars.[97]

I, too, began the bigger project to which this book belongs by completing close readings of individual texts that enabled me to consider specific historical, literary, and authorial contexts, while also testing theoretical and methodological constructs.[98] But I always hoped to go beyond that: to consider a broad set of autobiographical writings from Muslim South Asia—around two hundred make it into the bibliography—in order to trace patterns across time and space. So much of the theoretical consideration of gender, autobiography, and the self has been elaborated by literary scholars and historians with reference to a Euro-American context.[99] In contrast, I seek to apply, challenge, and adapt those theoretical models at the level of the Indian subcontinent, rather than at that of text or author—

even if my geographical area is narrowed by its Muslim focus. To do so makes this work part of a process by which, in the authoritative words of Sidonie Smith and Julia Watson in *Reading Autobiography* (2010), "a new, globalized history of the field might be imagined" that, I would add, is also gendered.[100] That does not mean that I disregard case studies entirely. In chapter 4, for instance, I consider four iterations of one life story by actress Begum Khurshid Mirza as an extended instance of "a performer in performance." I also hold on to the words and stories of individual authors in a conscious attempt to let the voices of the presumed voiceless resonate throughout this study. But the five main chapters that follow this introduction seek to ask a simple set of questions of my representative sample of autobiography by South Asian Muslim women—in turn, *what, who, where, how*, and *why*. Inevitably for a historian, *when* is woven throughout.[101]

So, to begin, *what*: A major concern of theorists has been to define autobiography as a genre apart from other literary forms. Applying these debates to Muslim South Asia, chapter 1, "Life/History/Archive," considers how to find and fit "real-life" historical sources into the theoretical boxes dreamt up by academics often limited to European and North American materials. In doing so, it explores the range of possible sources to be included in a "life history archive"—from autobiographical biographies and biographical autobiographies to travelogues, reformist literature, novels, devotionalism, letters, diaries, interviews, speeches, film, and ghosted narratives. Ultimately, I settle on the constructed life in written form. This definition works in tandem with my chosen nomenclature. While others before me have employed *personal narratives, life experiences*, or *life histories*, I argue for *autobiographical writing* on the basis that it fulfills three main criteria: while linking to autobiography's global canon and specifying my focus on the written word, it also frees me of certain connotations that could limit my source base. The heterogeneous practices of South Asian Muslim women—not always complete, coherent, linear, self-centered, or driven by personality—are opened to analysis. A corollary is that in South Asian languages, I am not restricted to *khud navisht*—the most common translation now for "autobiography" in Urdu—but can incorporate materials under various labels that can be historicized in terms of their usage.

22   *The Ultimate Unveiling*

I then turn to *who*—or, more specifically, who writes autobiography from the historical body of South Asian Muslim women on which I focus? In chapter 2, "The Sociology of Authorship," to disaggregate the whole, I first consider the "literacy conundrum"—the impact of South Asia's low female literacy on who writes autobiography—before turning to three key sociological categories that define authors: class, education, and occupation. Can we identify a "typical" author by her status, intellectual attainments, or employment patterns? Very simply, the answer is yes. A key inference already implied is that most authors can be described as *sharif* of one type or another. This elite social positioning opened doors to education, though the *struggle* for attainment, I show, often marked out the authors as much as the *level* did. Still, the fact that women writing autobiography in Muslim South Asia had often studied to the degree level and beyond from the early twentieth century underlines the importance to self-expression of intellectual tools garnered through education. Education also enabled pioneering careers: at court, in schools, in writing, through politics, on a stage. Creating a "constellation" of authors, time, and motivation, I conclude the chapter by tracing patterns of who writes when and why. Autobiography functions as a vehicle for *sharif* redefinition above all, but also nationalism, historicism and didacticism, literary creativity and performance are highlighted alongside a more general impulse: to narrate a life momentous for Muslim women living at a particular time and place.

Where then becomes the focus of chapter 3, "The Autobiographical Map." Geography is interpreted broadly here to allow me first to map authors in terms of region, locality, and sect before turning to language and audience. In what ways does an author's physical location, religious affiliation, linguistic choice, and (un)intended readership affect why and how South Asian Muslim women write their lives? My conclusions in terms of autobiographical motivation—the why—are various. To begin, I show how autobiography's links to *sharif* redefinition are further revealed in the reformist and princely locations that act as hubs for women's autobiographical expression. I also point to how socioeconomic, cultural, and historical specificities enabled women's autobiography to flourish within certain Muslim locations in the modern era: Jamia Nagar over

Nizamuddin in Delhi, Bangladesh over Pakistan in the north, Hyderabad over Kerala in the south. Women's associations with certain urban conurbations—Bombay, Delhi, Dhaka—also underline the city's role in offering cultural leadership to autobiographical expression and a home to religious minorities wanting to "talk back." In terms of autobiographical construction—the *how*—I use performative models to argue for the importance of specific audiences in shaping how Muslim women crafted their autobiographical outputs in terms of content, tone, and language at different historical moments: from the colonial to the postcolonial, the reformist to the nationalist, the regional to the global.

To further explore performance as a theoretical construct, I next consider *how* in more detail: how do different literary milieus—published/unpublished, magazine/book, translated/edited—shape an autobiography's form and content? Emerging from chapter 4, "Staging the Self," is the way in which different processes of production introduced new actors—editors, translators, cowriters, and publishers—that could be as complicit as the author in the construction of a gendered Muslim self. We have seen already in this introduction how autobiography in the Islamic tradition and the modern West alike is theorized in particular terms—but what if those criteria were simply being reproduced as an effect of the publication process? The four iterations of Begum Khurshid Mirza's autobiography, to which I have already referred, are especially useful here in showing how the author's identity and assumptions as a Pakistani actress, wife, and mother could be overwritten by a protective family, a feminist editor, and an Indian press keen to tailor her interests, perspectives, emotions, and sexuality to their own expectations. These conclusions, though elaborated in the context of women's autobiographical writing in Muslim South Asia, have important implications for our handling and analysis of autobiography more generally. Historians and gender scholars especially, I would argue, need to be attentive to these features of autobiographical practice when interrogating individual texts for women's agency and subjectivity.

And finally, *why*: Gender theorists have long articulated a "difference" model applicable to women's autobiography by which their self-expression was unique in form, style, and content when compared to that of men. Chapter 5, "Autobiographical Genealogies," uses the example of Bombay's Tyabji family, which produced repeated instances of autobiographical output over multiple generations, to interrogate and historicize this theoretical frame: Do women actually write their lives differently than men in Muslim South Asia do? And are the ways in which concepts of individuality are expressed in autobiographical writing changing over time? From the Tyabji case, I deduce six patterns—four of which respond to the "difference" model and two of which privilege time and location more explicitly. They may be consolidated here into a more comprehensive, if concise, argument about women writing their lives as historical selves in Muslim South Asia. In many ways, this summary foreshadows not just the content and contentions of chapter 5, but also my coda, "Unveiling and Its Attributes" in which I use unveiling as a metaphor linked to this introduction to explicate in far more detail—and thus, I hope, with greater nuance—the gendered historical phenomenon of autobiographical writing in Muslim South Asia.

And so: The first observation is that South Asian Muslim women writing autobiography do tend to focus on the domestic over a public persona, but since the home continued to structure their lives throughout my historical period, it may be counterintuitive to expect otherwise. Furthermore, if authors did have a career outside the home, they wrote about that too—just as their menfolk often wrote about their families or personal networks. A second observation, then, is that relationality is at the heart of autobiographical writing in Muslim South Asia, irrespective of gender. A third observation is that women's writing is often fragmentary, but that quality may be as much an inheritance of a longer autobiographical tradition (for example, *roznamcha* or *akhbar*), or a feature of the publication process, as a reflection of women's historical lives. A fourth observation is that while modesty is a trope in the life writings of many women (and some men too), it is not necessarily predicated on an absence of self-assertion. A fifth observation turns from "difference" to change over time. Clearly, how these authors constructed their identities, and in what language (or form of language) they did so, was contingent on historical moments defined by some of the major events and processes of the modern era, not least among them imperialism, reformism, nationalism, and feminism. As time progressed, so did women's preferred autobiographical forms and their handling of certain topics—most notably, intimacy, sexuality, and illness. Hence, a sixth and final observation is that the collectivities to which women in Muslim South Asia belonged—clan, community, country—did not undermine a sense of self so much as frame their multiple and varied expressions of interiority.

THE AUTOBIOGRAPHICAL SAMPLE

Having charted this book's course, let me conclude this introduction by making a few preliminary observations about my autobiographical sample. The first point to make is that I am under no illusion that my source base is complete, or even as comprehensive as it ought to be. Because of ongoing political instability in Pakistan, I was unable to do as much research "on the ground" there as I did in Delhi and other historically important Muslim centers in India and Bangladesh—though I did seek to take full advantage of existing contacts and communication technologies to access as much as I could from that region. Elsewhere, I found many of my materials not in mainstream archives, but instead in smaller libraries or private collections: perhaps in homes where they needed to be deemed important enough to be kept, protected, and then made available to an "outsider"—or, conversely, unimportant enough that they could molder in a forgotten corner until a foreign scholar came calling. Survival, then, is key to the sample. We can only conjecture about how many autobiographical accounts from the period before 1947 may have been lost or willfully destroyed in the tumult that was Partition. We may think here of Nazr Sajjad Hyder, who records how her own diaries and memoir were lost when the goods train carrying her belongings from Dehra Dun in India to Sialkot in Pakistan was destroyed.[102] Equally so, how many hand- or typewritten narratives kept by individual families could have perished in the subcontinent's punishing weather fluctuations? And, since these narratives can often be dismissed as "just women's words"—about the home, the family, the everyday—how many were deemed unworthy of conservation? It was a frustrating tale often heard in the course of my research, especially from struggling, once-grand families that had left family piles to move into compact city apartments from Delhi to Dhaka: "There were so many boxes of papers . . . we just couldn't keep everything."[103]

Equally key to the sample is my own necessarily haphazard research methods. As I explore in chapter 1, to recover historical materials from private collections—to make the home, the street, the market into an archive—is not a straightforward or systematic process. In chasing one source, the researcher may become known and hopefully trusted within an extended family or local area—I think, in the case of this project, of the branching Tyabji clan or the close-knit community of Jamia Nagar in Delhi. And those relationships, once established, often lead to further materials being made available within the same context: "You came to see me about an aunt's memoir, but did you know that her elder sister also wrote a kind of diary and some travel pieces? You must visit my cousin in Bombay . . ."[104] As a result, it is possible that the socioeconomic and geographical clustering that I discuss in chapters 2 and 3 may reflect research context as much as historical production. Language too must be considered as a regulating factor. Though I have some facility in South Asian languages, the subcontinent's complex linguistic map meant that in certain locations (for instance, in Bangladesh and Kerala) I had to rely on local interlocutors to assist me in recovering materials.[105] And yet, to counter too much serendipity, I also point throughout to gaps: geographical and linguistic and familial contexts in which, for all my attempts at recovery, no autobiographical materials came to light.

In terms of the research process, then, I am under no illusion that my methods are—or, in fact, could be—systematic. My sample is inevitably limited to what was available in the public archives I could access and also what I tracked down or stumbled across, sometimes quite literally. I think of a crumbling box that I tripped over on the roof of Abida Sultaan's house in Karachi in October 1995: it contained the diary/memoir of her grandmother, Nawab Sultan Jahan Begam of Bhopal, begun in the early 1870s when she was just fifteen or sixteen years old.[106] Indeed, it is a matter of great satisfaction that as the profile of this research on women's autobiographical writing grows, more and more examples continue to come to light—perhaps to bolster, perhaps to challenge my findings here. Like all history, then, this one is "partial," "unfinished"; to think otherwise would require us, as Antoinette Burton asserts, to buy in to the "total vision" of the Benthamite panopticon.[107] It also means that though I was sometimes drawn to a more quantitative approach—particularly in chapter 2, where I initially thought I could count authors by occupation or level of education, for instance—I came to a decision that the sample is too varied and the material too incomplete to enforce this kind of schematic upon it. As I note in chapter 1 and explore further in chapters 2, 3, and 5, even when Muslim women write autobiographically, they do not always offer the most basic biographical information about themselves: dates and places of birth or marriage, husbands' employment, numbers of children. Thus only in certain circumstances where I have a closed or fixed data set have I attempted this kind of statistical analysis. Otherwise, I seek to draw out overarching themes or trends relating to the two hundred or so examples of autobiographical writing by South Asian Muslim women that I consider throughout this study—among them, the autobiography by Jobeda Khanam with which I started. For a sense of the other sources, and how they were identified and defined, let us turn in chapter 1 to the archive.

CHAPTER ONE

LIFE/HISTORY/ARCHIVE

INTRODUCTION: QUESTIONS

In autumn 2005, I began researching the purposefully amorphous topic of "personal narratives of Muslim women in South Asia."[1] My intention was to look at ways in which women reconstructed their life stories in written sources. I thus placed myself, I thought, on solid historical ground—the written word—while still defining "personal narratives" broadly to include autobiographies, memoirs, journal articles, and travel narratives. I had then put together a list of primarily published autobiographical writing, the starting point for which had been those memoirs produced by women at the Bhopal royal court that I had consulted as part of my doctoral and early-career research on the last of the state's four female rulers, Nawab Sultan Jahan Begam.[2] It certainly made the project look viable, but in reality, it hid my uncertainty about what was out there to be found. When I mentioned my plans to fellow academics of Muslim or women's history in South Asia, many looked skeptical. "Is there any material?" they asked. "I mean, did Muslim women write memoirs?" This, it turned out, was a question I would face continually. The general assumption seemed to be that these silent and secluded creatures would not deign, or perhaps dare, to participate in a genre that required them, in popular parlance, to "lift the veil," to reveal something of their inner selves or even the "private" world of the zenana, or women's quarters.

29

30   *Life/History/Archive*

Other historians greeted my project with even greater suspicion. If interdisciplinarity has inspired exciting challenges to traditional historical methods on the pages of *Rethinking History*, to my colleagues at a provincial British university, it was as if Ranke and his notions of objectivity had never died. More times than I can count during my work on this project, questions have been raised of "reliability, validity and authentication."[3] As a historian of women and gender, I was all the more surprised by this response, because, as noted in the introduction, feminist scholars have been at the forefront of borrowing disciplinary techniques and seeking out new sources: ethnographies, oral traditions, life writing. These materials have transformed history by recovering voices of women and other marginalized groups whose pasts may have been unwritten or unrecorded.[4] And yet still these materials, reliant on memory, can be deemed fickle and limited, if not unreliable, by history's establishment: suitable to supplementing history, but not actually making it. As Rajeswari Sunder Rajan writes in *Real and Imagined Women*, "Women's voices from the past come to us only as ghostly visitations, not with the materiality of 'evidence.'"[5] Many historians still think of autobiography as an appropriate historical source only if it can be verified by "real" material from a "real" archive. Like Antoinette Burton in her excellent *Dwelling in the Archive*, we are left asking: "Who counts as a historical subject and what counts as an archive?"[6]

Scholars from other disciplines have asked rather different questions of autobiography. For literary theorists, the debates have often focused on defining autobiography as a genre by asking if it can be distinguished from other literary forms. As Jill Ker Conway puts it on the first page of her pithy and accessible *When Memory Speaks*: "Is autobiography just another form of fiction? A bastard form of the novel or of biography?"[7] Hayden White's persuasive interventions from *Metahistory* onward have encouraged other scholars to ask if life writers are so different from historians: are both not just aiming to "tell a story" about the past?[8] Others have looked inward, seeking to differentiate forms of personal narrative *within* the autobiographical genre. In *Design and Truth in Autobiography* (still widely consulted, though it was first published in 1960), Roy Pascal seeks to separate *memoir*—only sometimes introspective—from *autobiography*, with its necessary "driving force."[9] Significantly, both terms have been abandoned fairly recently in favor of the more inclusive *life writing* and *life narrative* by postmodern and postcolonial theorists attempting to recognize the "heterogeneity of self-referential practices."[10] And yet, for gender specialists, the question remains of whether women of all nationalities can even participate in a genre that, to borrow another of Conway's phrases, "celebrates the experiences of the atomistic Western male hero."[11]

Far from hypothetical, these questions about where to draw the line seem all the more pertinent to the historian in the field faced with the very real problem of identifying and collecting materials—for whatever the attempts on the part of academics to define and categorize, historical sources rarely sit comfortably in one theoretical box or another. The problem seems compounded when the historian's subject is Muslim women in South Asia, a group often presumed not to write autobiography at all. What I offer in this first chapter is an autobiographical narrative in itself—though, inevitably for a historian, grounded in appropriate academic literature—in which I recount my own experience of trying to find, choose, and label appropriate sources for a project on "personal narratives of Muslim women in South Asia." I do this to flag methodological and theoretical questions that this process raised in relation to the broad categories of gender, autobiography, and history itself: questions about the nature of the archive and the distinctiveness of women's writing as they relate to issues of nomenclature, structure, chronology, language, voice, and regional specificity. To justify my title, this chapter is about *life*, *history*, and the *archive*, as well as a *life history archive*.

A necessary first stage was exploration of the colonial archive par excellence, the British Library in London. In tribute to the French philosopher Jacques Derrida, I title this stage "Beginnings." For Derrida, the *arkhe* was, to quote Carolyn Steedman, "a place where things begin, where power originates."[12] This statement has resonance when working in the Oriental and India Office Collections (now, notably, renamed Asia, Pacific and Africa Collections) with all their historical associations with an imperial state's glory and authority.[13] But my beginnings here were twofold. On the one hand, my forays into the British Library marked the (frustrating, unsatisfactory) beginnings of my research process. On the other, they led to a realization that the kind of material that I uncovered here—biographies,

32   *Life/History/Archive*

reformist writings, and travelogues, but little identifiable autobiography—marked a kind of beginning for South Asian Muslim women writing lives, whether lives of others or their own or both. The second, longer section acts somewhat as an antidote to the "archive fever" of the first by charting my subsequent experience of seeking a new collection of sources outside the conventional archive. Yet this process led to problems of categorization: to "blurrings," as I title the second section. I consider the range of possibilities under the label of "personal narratives": novels, devotional literature, letters, diaries, journal articles, oral sources, film, biographies, memoirs, and ghosted narratives. I conclude this chapter by reflecting on the issue of "labeling" itself, reflected in the title of the third section.

BEGINNINGS

When I began this project, I was accustomed, as a trained historian, to thinking of the archive as a physical location: as Antoinette Burton summarizes, "an institutional site in a faraway place that requires hotel accommodation and a gruelling nine-to-five workday."[14] Admittedly, the latter had rarely been possible in the provincial Indian archive in Bhopal—with its truncated opening hours and extended tea breaks—in which I had apprenticed as a historian. But still, this description was familiar enough to my own general experience. The cultural turn has been interpreted by some imperial historians as having dealt a nearly fatal blow to the archive—such that, by the end of the twentieth century, it was "hardly dead but dissected into unrecognizability and memorialized as the victim of a veritable academic epidemic."[15] But really the hysteria seems ill-founded. Those "swirling intellectual currents" defined by the "post" prefix—"post-colonial, post-modern, post-Orientalist, and post-structural historical perspectives," to borrow an unwieldy section title from Bose and Jalal's *Modern South Asia*[16]—may have involved a robust critique of the colonial archive, but not an attempt to get rid of it entirely.[17] Most often, the British Library in London is still the first stop for British-based scholars of South Asia, and many others besides. It is hardly surprising, therefore, that I began my research by perusing bibliographical records there. In this section, I offer an extended discussion of this process of interrogating the colonial archive for South Asian Muslim women's writings.

Starting with the electronic catalogue, I came across a number of well-known historical examples of Muslim women's autobiographical writing, many of which were already in my collection. From the Mughal period was Gulbadan Banu Begam's *Ahval-i-Humayun Badshah*, usually referred to, as in Annette Beveridge's early-twentieth-century translation, as the *Humayun-nama*.[18] By this time, Ruby Lal had already probed this fascinating memoir as a source for the domestic life of the early Mughal court.[19] There was also a rather dubious little volume published in 1931 by a German linguist, Andrea Butenschon, claiming to be the translation of a handwritten memoir by the Mughal princess Jahanara, stumbled upon behind a marble slab at the Agra Fort.[20] Even if not authentic, it pointed to Jahanara's actual first-person narrative, *Risala-i-Sahibiyah* (1641), or "The Lady's Treatise," then being examined by Afshan Bokhari for her doctoral research and soon to be republished in English translation.[21] Most familiar to me, in that they related to the colonial period, were Shaista Ikramullah's *From Purdah to Parliament* (1963) and Jahan Ara Shahnawaz's *Father and Daughter* (1971), both recounting the political careers of well-known female activists in the All-India Muslim League who later became Pakistani parliamentarians.[22] There were also a few contemporary autobiographies from Pakistan—most of them the sensationalist variety, charting untold sorrows and political melodramas, but also a couple by feminist poets and even one by a blind social worker.[23]

As a historian with some facility in South Asian languages, I thought there must be more: more from the colonial period and soon after, more in Urdu. I spent some days in the Asian and African Studies Reading Room scrutinizing Blumhardt's original catalogue of Hindustani books and manuscripts from 1900, and with the generous assistance of archivist Leena Mitford, Quraishi's more recent Urdu catalogues, published and unpublished. I searched broadly—entry by entry—my eyes attuned to anything related to auto/biography and/or women (by, for, and about). The findings were revealing, if not necessarily what I thought I was looking for. What was most plentiful—with as many as twenty-eight pages of entries in Quraishi's 1991 catalogue—was biography, primarily of saints, scholars, and poets, though with some princely rulers and a few reformers thrown in. Those interested in the Muslim world will know that life history has long been a staple of Islamic scholarship, the earliest biography, or *sira*, of the Prophet Muhammad being compiled within a century of his death in 632.[24] This early example set a precedent: to narrate an exemplary life, whether of one of the Prophet's Companions, a Sufi shaikh, or a notable *'alim*, was to offer a model of Islamic practice for every "ordinary" Muslim to become, in Barbara Metcalf's phrase, "living hadith."[25] No wonder that biography and its related genre, the biographical dictionary, or *tabaqat*, were to flourish as the key mode of historical writing in the Arab world and beyond, at least from the eleventh century onward.[26]

The focus on biography in the India Office Collections, then, was not entirely surprising, reflecting as it did these "enduring Islamic patterns."[27] But a seeming proliferation in nineteenth-century South Asia also appeared indicative of a more modern trend: the spread of print culture and the religious change that accompanied it in the colonial era. Francis Robinson indicates how the acceptance of print among South Asian Muslims initiated a "process of interiorization" reflected in "the expression of a growing sense of self" or, as he puts it more poetically, "the manifold nature of the human individual."[28] As individuals became more important, biography flourished—with the effect that, as the esteemed W. C. Smith observed, "more lives of Muhammad appeared between the two World Wars than in any one of the centuries between the twelfth and the nineteenth."[29] Yet the effect was not just *more* biographies, but also *different* biographies. On the one hand, this meant the same lives told differently. To paraphrase Robinson again, even the Prophet Muhammad metamorphosed from the "Perfect Man" of the Sufi tradition to the good middle-class family man identifiable to the era's Muslim reformers.[30] On the other hand, it meant different lives told. Among the many biographies listed in the British Library catalogues were a number that recounted the lives of women. Favored were exemplars from early Islamic history—Khadijah, Aisha, Fatima—though Mughal queens and princesses, maharanis and begams, a poetess, and even a schoolteacher were also deemed appropriate subjects from the first decade of the twentieth century.[31]

These full-length biographies would have complemented the many speeches and articles being prepared around this same time by Muslim reformers on women in Islamic history. As a whole, this output is best characterized as collective biography, beginning usually with examples of women in seventh-century Arabia before moving on to female scholars and rulers at different points and places in Muslim history. South Asian examples, like Raziya Sultana in thirteenth-century Delhi and Chand Bibi in sixteenth-century Bijapur, were regularly trotted out before a survey of women at the Mughal court: always Nurjahan, but also sometimes Mumtaz Mahal of Taj Mahal fame, the scholarly Jahanara and the poetic Zaibunnisa.[32] More current examples usually filled out the list, a favorite set being the nawab begams of Bhopal—who also featured in biographical pieces in the Arabic press around the same time.[33] These columns on "famous women" soon became a regular item in women's journals in South Asia, too. An early issue of *Zill us-Sultan*, published in Bhopal from 1918, for instance, carried a lengthier piece on the grandmother of the last independent nawab of Bengal, Siraj ud-daula, in which she was described in contemporary reformist parlance as such a "helpmeet" to her husband, Nawab Ali Vardi Khan of Bengal, that she even assisted him in battle.[34] Reflecting growing nationalist sentiment, a 1934 edition of *Tahzib un-Niswan* (published in Lahore) carried an article on the French vanquisher of the English, Jeanne d'Arc.[35] Like the Egyptian examples examined so fruitfully by Marilyn Booth, these biographies of exemplary women were crafted to reflect specific reformist and political agendas.[36]

So Muslim women's lives were certainly being written in South Asia at least from the late nineteenth century, but primarily, if catalogues of Hindustani books in the British Library were anything to go by, in biographical format by male authors. That is not to say that there were no female biographers. As I already knew well, the last begam of Bhopal, Sultan Jahan, had written book-length accounts of the life of her mother, Shah Jahan, and her great-grandmother Qudsia.[37] The life of Ashrafunnisa Begam, a teacher at the Victoria Girls' High School in Lahore, was prepared by her close friend Muhammadi Begam.[38] Drawing on feminist studies of auto/biography, Booth makes the point that "biography is always autobiography."[39] What is reflected here is a charge often leveled at biography by its detractors: the idea that biography actually tells the reader more about the author than about the subject. We might consider, as an illustrative (if slightly roundabout) example, the biographer

36   *Life/History/Archive*

Richard Holmes's discussion of Samuel Johnson's biography of Richard Savage, as summarized by yet another biographer, Michael Holroyd:

> Holmes has shown how Johnson recreated the Life of Richard Savage as if it were his own buried life, a violent, dark life of the imagination. Holmes's *Dr Johnson & Mr Savage* presents us with a version of RL Stevenson's characters Dr Jekyll and Mr Hyde. Between the lines of Johnson's romantic account of Savage's early life, our modern detective Holmes reveals how the author identified with his subject. Here was the life that he never lived but that festered in his imagination.[40]

And so, according to this approach, by the very act of writing, the biographer projects himself—or, in our case, herself—into the subject, with the effect of an "interweaving of lives." As Booth explicates, "the authorial 'I' links the act of writing biography to individual and collective identity."[41]

The question is thus raised of whether these biographies by women authors were appropriate material for my study of autobiography. At the time, I did not even consider them—though, as we will see in the next section, I was forced to return to the knotty problem of auto/biography again later in my research. What I did instead was note what else in the British Library catalogues was written by or for women. At this juncture, it is perhaps worth saying that one of the underlying reasons that I had begun a project on women's personal narratives in the first place was because, after years of studying highly moralistic and often dry reformist literature (admittedly necessary for a book on women's participation in socioreligious reform movements), I wanted to read something different. Yet it was that very reformist literature that kept reappearing in my search, making it the second most inhabited of my broad categories: advice manuals for women on correct Islamic practice, home economics, housekeeping, childcare, personal hygiene, and the rest. Like the biographies, most of it was written by men, but there were a few female authors too—most prolifically, the begams of Bhopal again, but also some unknown. One of these manualists was described only as "the mother of M. Abd al-Aziz," while another, Amat al-Nasīr, had to be justified as the "daughter of Sardar Ahmed"—apparently a deputy collector, who also took responsibility for editing and publishing her text—and "wife of

Sardar Faqir Allah BA."[42] It made me consider the possibility that perhaps most women's identities were simply too relational to others in this period to participate in a genre, like autobiography, supposedly defined by its emphasis on self.

Only much later, upon revisiting Shah Jahan's *Tahzib un-Niswan wa Tarbiyat ul-Insan* (1889) for a different purpose, did I consider the manuals themselves as a form of self-representation or even life writing. Did they not contain a woman's own rules for running a household and sometimes even incidents from the author's life used to explain a particular point or justify a specific reformist stance? Perhaps the most revealing example of the latter was in a passage on sexual intercourse in the above text in which the reigning nawab asserted a woman's right to carnal pleasure using her own experiences as illustration. Apparently, she felt unfulfilled by her first husband, the older and already married Baqi Muhammad Khan, and thus her youth had been lost in "*ranj o gham*," suffering and sadness. Her controversial second husband, Siddiq Hasan, changed all that, provoking her to affirm that she had never been so happy.[43] Her daughter, Sultan Jahan, was too circumspect to discuss sexual matters in her own reformist writings (though not too circumspect to conceive five children). And yet she too used her life to illustrate her reformist stance. When discussing polygamy in her widely circulated advice manual for married couples, she suggested that women could follow her example in adding an extra clause to their marriage contracts to protect them financially should their husbands ever exercise the right to take another wife.[44] Surely there was much to be mined from reformist literature in terms of autobiographical fragments, if not more.

And yet still the question remained: were there any autobiographies proper in the British Library's Hindustani catalogues? Well, yes, a couple—but by men.[45] What I also found, though, was a goodly selection of another type of personal narrative on my list of potential sources: travel writing. Substantial academic interest has followed this literary form in recent years as, on the back of Said, scholars have sought to make explicit the links between physical travel and imaginative journey.[46] These analyses take as a starting point the idea that travel writing is not a "literal and objective record of journeys undertaken," to borrow

38   *Life/History/Archive*

the phrase of Tim Youngs, so much as it is an "ideological" undertaking that "draws on the conventions of other literary genres."[47] In a South Asian context, Barbara Metcalf has shown how even accounts of the quintessential Muslim journey, the hajj pilgrimage, became "modes of self-presentation" in the modern period—thus suggesting the crossover between travel writing and autobiography.[48] And so it felt like quite a coup to come across this stash of travelogues, several of which were written by Muslim women in the late nineteenth and early twentieth centuries. Including an Indian tour diary, pilgrimage narratives, and a European travel account, they proved to be merely representative: as my research progressed to and across the Indian subcontinent, these travel accounts continued to accrue.[49] Many women employed the regular Persian term for a book of travels, *safarnama*, while others evoked the idea of a travel diary by using *roznamcha*. Either way, by purporting to describe objective reality, the travel narrative seemed to provide women with a useful cover by which to write of personal experience, if only when in motion, in the colonial period and beyond.

And so I ended my time in the British Library with just a handful of materials, most of which I had already known about. Still, I was beginning to develop a sense of how Muslim women could have gained access to the world of life writing in colonial South Asia, how they may have found their autobiographical beginnings. I began to conjecture that the sociocultural and technological changes of the nineteenth century enabled India's Muslim women to be recognized, particularly within the context of Islamic reform, as appropriate subjects for *biography*, some of which may have had *auto*biographical content. Thus established, a few exemplars began making use of other literary genres—*reformist texts, travel literature*—to speak of the self. Good beginnings, for sure; but, like many feminist scholars before me, I still had a sense that the colonial archive had failed me. My experience of libraries and archives in South Asia— whether national, formerly princely, or university-based—was more fruitful from the perspective of conventional women's autobiography, but only partially so. The Maulana Azad Library at Aligarh Muslim University, for instance, provided access to a few fairly well-known Urdu texts, while the Nehru Memorial Museum and Library in New Delhi offered a peculiar scattering of English, Hindi, and Urdu materials. But the Rampur Raza Library—that "treasure house of Indo-Islamic learning and art"—yielded almost nothing.[50] Clearly, this project was going to require a different tack.

BLURRINGS

When I arrived in Delhi in autumn 2005, I had only a few leads—a reference to a manuscript in the Nehru Memorial Museum and Library, the possibility of an article in an early Urdu women's magazine, a name or two of people who might be able to help. Yet these one or two contacts led to meetings that led to phone calls that led to more meetings that led to more phone calls, and before long, I found myself doing historical research as I had never done it before. Whether in Delhi, Bhopal, Dhaka, Hyderabad, or Bombay, each morning saw me dashing across jagged lanes of traffic to hail an auto rickshaw to another previously unfamiliar corner of the city. Each tangled journey took me into a different woman's home or office or favorite café where she might hand over a scribbled manuscript, an old journal, or a rare publication: maybe it was her own or that of a grandmother, a famous aunt, an admired teacher. And then, over innumerable cups of tea, too many sweets, a spate of samosa folding, or an impromptu meal, I sat and listened to the stories behind the words on the page. My notebooks are revealing of the time and patience required for this kind of research, as well as the pleasures of it: relationships needed to be made, trust to be gained, goodwill to be shown. Multilingual transcriptions from books and interviews—in a scrambled mix of abbreviated English, high Urdu, everyday Hindi, and sometimes a regional language—are interspersed with recipes, children's drawings, and sketches of yoga positions. A receipt falls out for 2,000 rupees donated to a community project—an expenditure too hard to justify to my university's finance office—that facilitated access to one group of women in a Delhi neighborhood. These fragments suggest what would emerge as the main source base for my project: the home, the market, the street. To borrow Antoinette Burton's phrase, the people I met were literally "dwelling in the archive."[51]

But the problem with using the world *outside* the archive *as* an archive was that there were *blurrings*: blurrings by genre and blurrings by termi-

40   *Life/History/Archive*

nology, blurrings by others and blurrings by me. To return to the questions raised by literary theorists: How was autobiography to be identified? How was it to be defined? Let me take readers to a bright day in Dhaka in January 2006. With a friend from the Dhaka University history department, I went to a book fair. "Do you have any Muslim women's memoirs?" my friend asked in Bengali. We might note the specific phrase she employed to denote the type of writing I was looking for: *atma jibani*, one's own story. Inevitably, we were greeted with a slow shake of the head in the negative. Yet a scan of what was actually on the table often did turn up something I thought I was looking for—perhaps a piece of fiction with a lengthy autobiographical introduction or a personal travel account given the title of "guide."[52] There were even two women's accounts of their experiences of Bangladesh's war of independence in 1971.[53] My friend would check: "No memoirs? Are you sure?" Then perhaps we would be presented with a novel written by a woman—perhaps Rokeya Sakhawat Hossain's *Padmarag* (1924), described by its recent translator, Barnita Bagchi, as "resonant with autobiographical undertones."[54] I'd shake my head in refusal: "No, that's not a memoir; it's a novel, a piece of fiction." Maybe, the bookseller would shrug, but it's based on "real life."

This slippage between novel and memoir in popular parlance was raised in academic forums, too. Would I, one of my audience asked at a seminar at the lively Sarai Initiative in Delhi months later, be using what he termed so nicely "disguised autobiographical writing"? The reference was to the collected works of outstanding literary figures like Qurratulain Hyder and "partition novels," like Attia Hosain's *Sunlight on a Broken Column* (1961)—the latter, ironically, one of the first things I ever read by a South Asian Muslim woman as a student. Perhaps it is right that these materials be considered for a historical study of women's personal narratives. Qurratulain Hyder's two-volume *Kar-i-Jahan Daraz Hai*, usually translated as "The Work of the World Goes On," is sometimes described as a "family chronicle" but more often as an "autobiographical novel." Its interweaving of individual and family, past and present, fact and fiction is evoked by Ali Jawad Zaidi in his history of Urdu literature, which I discussed in the introduction—significantly, in his section on autobiography in the chapter "Literary Miscellany," not in "Modern Fiction," where the book is only listed as one of Hyder's novels. This book, he writes, "weaves autobiographical reality into the fictional stretch of centuries to show the present as an inseparable part of the past inherited through historical present."[55]

Hosain's *Sunlight*, on the other hand, was hailed by Mushirul Hasan as "one of the most compelling archives of Muslim experience before, during, and after partition" before being "counterread as a history" of house and home in Burton's aforementioned *Dwelling in the Archive*.[56] These descriptions seek to make the book admissible to history, while again raising the question of genre: that fuzzy line between novel and autobiography. On this theme, Burton points to Mulk Raj Anand's attempt to "rescue *Sunlight* from the category of autobiography" in order to give Hosain "what he viewed as the exalted and more legitimate status of novelist"[57]—thus implying that *Sunlight* needed to be rescued. Burton records Hosain's own assertion, made in an interview late in life, that *Sunlight* was "like an autobiography, but it is not one"—and yet "it's not purely fictional" either.[58]

These examples raise the important question of whether, in a cultural context like South Asia where women's voices are so often silenced, the novel becomes a preferred, if not necessary, form of self-expression. We may consider what Sukrita Paul Kumar has written of the eminent and often controversial Urdu writer, Ismat Chughtai:

> There is virtually no distinction between the actual life experience of Ismat Chughtai and the fiction she created. The members of her family, the servants of her household, and her friends, became the characters of her stories, sometimes with the same names. The episodes and relationships that she went through became the content of her fiction and the society in which she lived, the context.[59]

And yet Ismat Chughtai did also write an autobiography—alluringly titled not "Autobiographical Fragments" or "Reminiscences" or "Her Life" as in the selective translations, but instead *Kaghazi Hai Pairahan*. The title, usually translated as "My Clothes Are Made of Paper," was borrowed from a couplet by the great Urdu poet Ghalib, apparently making reference to the legend of the paper clothes worn by petitioners in Iran and thus the transience of human life as we stand before the Creator.[60] Such a title would not seem out of place as the header to one of her identifiably fictional writings. And so it is perhaps appropriate that, as critics have pointed out, not all of what she writes in her autobiography actually corroborates the known "facts of her life." As Kumar explains, "Ismat's real life gets carried into her fiction just as easily as fiction slips into the text of her life."[61]

Kumar goes on to say that we should not discount Ismat Chughtai's autobiography just because it does not appear all to be "true." As she writes: "I believe what is important is how she perceives the fact of her life, however imaginary it may be. After all, truth is what is realized, not what may get projected superficially as action. And imagination too is founded in some truth."[62] Her statement points to important questions debated routinely by literary theorists under the title of "autobiographical truth": To what extent may we assume that the life writer *is* telling the truth? And the truth of what and for whom? As Smith and Watson summarize: "Are we expecting fidelity to the facts of their biographies, to lived experience, to self-understanding, to the historical moment, to social community, to prevailing beliefs about diverse identities, to the norms of autobiography as a literary genre itself?"[63]

Whatever I presumed to be the answers to these questions was challenged further when, at the home of another gracious hostess in Delhi I was presented with a small book titled *The Heart of a Gopi*, by one of Gandhi's closest disciples, Raihana Tyabji. As noted in the introduction, this author was at least nominally Muslim, having been born into the renowned Tyabji clan at the forefront of Bombay's Sulaimani Bohra community. Yet, according to the book's introduction, she had composed this piece of bhakti devotionalism—about Sharmila, a *gopi*, or milkmaid, enraptured by Krishna in his guise as the cowherd at Vrindavan—in the following circumstances:

> Sometime in 1926, (I remember neither the month nor the date), I suddenly felt a tremendous, an irresistible urge to write—To write *what*? That I did not know . . . I sat at my desk with sheets of foolscap and poised pen, and the story of Sharmila came pouring out at the end of it almost faster than

the ink could flow. For three days I was literally possessed. And so was the heart of a Gopi revealed to my own astonished and enraptured gaze . . . To me this story was something strange, something that I had not written, and yet that no one else had written. I must risk being either smiled or sniffed at by "rationalists" if I am to speak the truth here, for the truth is that this story is not mine except in that it has been written by this hand. During the three days that it took to write I had a distinct sensation of being possessed by some force *outside* myself, and of being compelled to write even in spite of myself. I cannot explain this. I can only state the things as I experienced it.[64]

How to interpret this narration? Should we, in the tradition of Islamic life writing, breach the gap between "the miraculous and the mundane" to understand the mystical experience charted here as a kind of life writing? Even from the rationalist's perspective, should not the life of the imagination still be considered part of the life?[65]

Other attempts to use the home as an archive were fraught with similar problems of identification. Just a week after arriving in Delhi, a fellow researcher from Britain kindly offered to take me into the winding lanes of old Delhi to meet her Persian tutor. He responded generously to my request for help in finding "Muslim women's memoirs" by presenting me with a large box of dusty papers in handwritten Urdu long kept in his family's rambling *haveli*. In them, he explained, I would find his sister's "life story." What the box actually contained was the steady exchange of letters between this brother in India and his sister in Pakistan over the sixty-odd years since Partition.[66] Feminist historians especially have made excellent use of these kinds of materials to chart "changing life styles, expectations and aspirations" from the late nineteenth century—when letter writing became "increasingly common" among South Asia's elite—to the present.[67] And yet, from the perspective of a study of life writing as a genre, they seemed too immediate, not constructed enough. Like diaries and journals, they offered "raw data" instead of "synthesized memory," to quote Joanne Cooper.[68] But what if those letters were then edited for publication and even shaped into a coherent narrative? I think here of two other sources: travelogues composed by Atiya Fyzee and her sister Nazli, the begam of Janjira, during trips to Europe in 1906–7 and

1908. Both began life as regular letters to relatives in India before they were, in one case, edited by another sister, Zehra, for publication in serial form in an Urdu women's journal and, in both cases, assembled in book form as a *roznamcha*.[69]

Unfortunately, I did not have the opportunity to test this process of selection often when it came to diaries—that is, if we take a diary to refer to an individual's daily record or even "here-and-now jottings" of everyday activities not usually intended for publication.[70] My earlier work on Bhopal had suggested that the act of keeping a diary had been taken up (if not sustained) by some elite Muslim women—like the young Sultan Jahan, future nawab begam of Bhopal—as early as the 1870s.[71] She had, in turn, instilled the "habit" in her favored granddaughter, Abida, who had continued the practice from 1930 until her death in 2002—a startling seventy-two-year record![72] According to Udaya Kumar, this practice of diary writing was fostered in colonial South Asia as part of "new projects of education"; as he writes, "the diary helped in the cultivation of literary competence and a disciplined survey of everyday activities."[73] But while I had read Sultan Jahan's diary in Princess Abida's own home in Karachi, I was never given a chance to see her own log—except where portions were reproduced in her *Memoirs of a Rebel Princess*.[74] According to Burton, Attia Hosain also kept diaries "from the 1930s until her death in 1997" that were subsequently stored in a steamer trunk in her son's living room in London—but locked with a padlock![75] A notable exception to this rule of concealment—in that it was interred in an Indian national library for nationalist posterity—was the "manuscript memoir" of Badruddin Tyabji's youngest daughter, Safia Jabir Ali. Despite the title, it is really a diary written in 1926 and then again in 1942, though it does include some reminiscence on her life as a whole—which, we may conjecture, perhaps moves it into another category.[76]

What I also had a chance to consult—in that they too were deposited in an Indian national archive and a university library by the same historically conscious extended family—was a set of unusual *family* diaries known variously as "Akhbar ki Kitab," "Kitab-i-Akhbar," or "Akhbarnama," meaning literally "news books." These documents were a kind of glorified guest book kept in various homes of different branches of Bombay's Tyabji clan (after which they were named) from as early as the 1860s. They record the family's daily routines—from badminton matches and sports tournaments to picnics, club meetings, and visits to the dentist—alongside notable public events in which leading lights, like Badruddin Tyabji himself, took part.[77] Certain Tyabjis also contributed literary pieces, including poetry, extracts from speeches, travel narratives, and obituaries—many of which were written by women after they were encouraged to participate by the family matriarchs.[78] In most cases, these scattered entries have the same immediate, uncrafted quality of letters and diaries, though one might say less so of the travel accounts composed after long journeys and the occasional retrospectives on individual lives. Some of the latter even found their way into mainstream women's journals for which other Tyabji women, having cut their authorial milk teeth writing manuscripts for family circulation, also wrote short travel pieces and autobiographical fragments.[79] Several examples of this type of material are probed in chapter 5 as part of a more sustained analysis of the Tyabji family's autobiographical output from the nineteenth century onward.

My experience of perusing women's journals brought the question of oral sources to the fore. One of the first tasks I set myself in Delhi—for lack of much else to do at that point—was to survey the back issues of the feminist periodical *Manushi* (dating from 1978), in search of autobiographical fragments in the form of journal articles. There was a little of that—and in time I was to find more in other women's magazines, like *Tahzib un-Niswan* (from Lahore), *Zebunnisa* (also from Lahore), *Begum* (from Dhaka), and *Roshni* (from Delhi).[80] But what stood out more in terms of "life history" were the regular interviews, many of which were conducted by *Manushi*'s founding editors, Madhu Kishwar and Ruth Vanita, before perhaps being translated and then excerpted in article form. The careful reader will remember that right from the outset of my project, I had been clear that I intended to exclude life histories extracted through interview, somehow considering this material the purview of the anthropologist, not the historian. Yet what of the interview written down? Among the interviewees telling about their family histories, professional experiences, and political ideologies were the musician Asghari Begum Sagarwali, the writer Ismat Chughtai, and the actress Shabana Azmi.[81]

46   *Life/History/Archive*

Well-wishers directed me to other examples profiling well-known South Asian women—an important example being a lengthy interview with Attia Hosain from May 1991 published in 2004 on Harappa.com, a Pakistani website promising "glimpses of South Asia before 1947."[82] At thirty-two typed pages, it is a comprehensive document complete with wonderful photos of Attia, her family, and her contemporaries. It is told in the first person, divided into subject headings (mini-chapters, in effect), and punctuated only intermittently by the interviewer's questions. I offer, as an example, this excerpt from a section titled "Growing Up in Gadia," on Attia's childhood in the United Provinces. Here she also touches on her early political affiliations:

> Q: What did your father do?
>
> AH: My father [Shahid Hosain Kidwai] was a Taluqdar [feudal landholder of Gadia, District Bari Banki, United Provinces]. He was also one of those people who was involved in his life politically a time [in the 1910s] when it wasn't a question of confronting the British as happened later when Gandhiji came on the scene.
>
> It was when there were questions in the minds of all the people who were interested in the country's future independence, how to go about it. He was ahead of his time in many ways. . . . His friends were all people of that time who became very prominent later . . . They were all finally rather important, or part of the country's history, or fighting for independence.
>
> But I remember most of them, as we used to say "uncles". . . . Above all my hero was Panditji [Jawaharlal Nehru, India's first Prime Minister]. He was the son of father's friend, Moti Lal Nehru, a very close friend.
>
> Therefore I grew up in an atmosphere where people spoke of what to do next, how to be involved, not only in the national movements, but in the community, one had to be a part of it.[83]

Later sections moved on to her experience of living in postwar Britain, her writing, and beyond.

These published interviews, then, certainly provided a type of personal narrative, but was it the type of narrative to be included in my study of autobiographical writing? Two things made me think not. The first was their basis in conversation, a fairly unstructured medium even when punctuated by the interviewer's questions. Was it not the *constructed* life that I was interested in? But then, as those who use oral narratives know well, a story told can be as constructed as a story written, especially if it is one oft repeated.[84] At the same time, a written autobiography may well be characterized as conversational. Let me take, as an example, a text I would certainly include in my study: Hameeda Akhtar Husain Raipuri's *Hamsafar*, first published in Urdu in 1992, but translated into English fairly recently (with more connotation than was probably meant) as *My Fellow Traveller*.[85] In the preface, the author explains that she was encouraged to write her memoir by her deceased husband's friend, no less than the renowned Pakistani scholar of Urdu language and literature, Jamil Jalibi. Providing her with some pens and some registers, he advised her to "write down what you see in those films running before your mind's eye"—in other words, all those memories of the past that come to one in old age.[86] He went on: "I am not asking you to do something that is impracticable for you. All I am suggesting is to say with your pen whatever you say in your speech. Imagine when you are writing that I am sitting before you, and you are speaking to me."[87] And so she does. The book is thus in the form of an extended conversation with "Jamil Bhai"— to whom she directs her remarks and reflections explicitly in a voice that could as easily have been spoken as written. For its "chatty, conversational style," it is celebrated.[88]

To return to the published interviews, a second concern was the presence of the interviewer, setting questions and conditioning answers. Is not the crucial role played by the interviewer in shaping the story one of the "pitfalls of oral history," to quote John Tosh, against which university students are routinely warned?[89] And yet, as I explore in chapter 4, few memoirs are untarnished by outside interference. Readers, editors, and publishers—to list only the usual players—all take roles in crafting a memoir for public consumption. And what if the interviewer is still there, but just not so present? One of the bestselling recent autobiographies in Kerala—in its sixth edition when I visited in December 2005—is Nalini Jameela's account of her life as a sex worker, *Oru Laingikathozhilaliyude*

48   *Life/History/Archive*

Atmakatha, to which I referred in the introduction.[90] Again, it is worth noting the word used in the local vernacular, this time Malayalam, to denote autobiography: *atmakatha*, or one's own story. Yet, while the narrative reads fluidly (at least in the English translation kindly provided to me by J. Devika at the Centre for Development Studies in Trivandrum), the book was put together by a male reformer on the basis of taped interviews.[91] The careful reader (like my own interlocutor, Devika) may be able to discern "two voices talking"—Nalini Jameela and the interviewer—in the first editions (before the supposed author demanded that the text be rewritten to prevent "misrepresentation"), but this nuance was most probably lost on those who devoured the startling 13,000 copies sold in the first four months after publication.[92]

A linked set of questions related to the written source made oral. Not long after my arrival in Delhi, I was invited to a seminar in Aligarh hosted by the Female Education Association. The intention was to celebrate the birth centenary of the esteemed Progressive Writer, Rashid Jahan, in her hometown. Many of the talks were of an academic nature, but two nieces, Lubna Kazim and Shabnam Zafar, offered personal "recollections" of their aunt.[93] Subsequently, they provided me with copies of their scripts: an autobiographical fragment not much different from the journal articles I had set out to look for. Consider, for example, the opening to Lubna's printed speech:

> My name is Lubna Kazim, and I am Rasheed Jahan's niece and Khurshid Mirza's daughter. In 1947 my parents went to Pakistan, but we didn't lose our bonding with either Aligarh, Papa Mian, or family members. Aligarh as it is now is nothing as I used to know it then. Before 1947 it was a sleepy University town, quiet and clean. Aligarh was such a quiet city. There were no buses and only a couple of cycle rickshaws on Marris Road and no honking of traffic.[94]

We see here how her aunt gains a mention only alongside other important relationships in Lubna's own life—namely, those with her mother, actress Khurshid Mirza; her grandfather ("Papa Mian"), social reformer and educator Shaikh Abdullah; and her hometown, Aligarh. Later in the same document, Lubna did offer a number of short personal anecdotes about "Apa-bi," as Rashid Jahan was known within the family, but, again, in a way that told as much about herself as about the subject: how, as young children, Lubna and Shabnam got "new frocks and shoes" only after their aunt scolded her younger sister—their mother—for not buying a "bigger size" to replace their tight-fitting clothing and footwear.[95]

In time, other women graciously provided me with copies of speeches they had given on "personal" topics. Some of these were, like those mentioned already, a relative's account of a better-known relation—for instance, Muneeza Shamsie's dedication to her "mamou," the renowned diplomat Sahibzada Yaqub Khan, revealingly titled, "My Uncle and Me."[96] These pieces again pointed to the "interweaving of lives" that seemed to blur the boundaries between biography and autobiography. Others were more explicit in their focus on the self. To stay with Muneeza Shamsie, let me cite a speech, highly revealing and reflective in its tone, given to an audience of college girls at the British Council in Karachi in 1999 on her "experiences as a working woman":

> After my marriage, my best friend said, "Well you've always wanted to write, why don't you start?" So I did. . . . then began a long and difficult process of self-teaching, of self-discipline. Of throwing things away. Reading. Throwing away. . . . I went on writing, in secret. Most of these efforts ended up in the waste paper basket. I did not have the courage to show them to anyone, because I thought that nobody in this society was really interested in anything I had to say. Then my best friend intervened again and said, "You've got to start doing this properly, you've got to start feeling you are a writer." The next thing I knew was that my pieces started getting accepted . . . And one day, I suddenly realized that I had found what I had wanted all my life: a voice.[97]

In my previous work on Bhopal, I had pointed to the ritual of public speaking followed by publication in early women's clubs, noting that it resulted in a "linking of oral and written traditions within the new literary culture."[98] Perhaps these speeches, too, should be understood to have bridged the gap between oral traditions of life history and the written practice of memoir/autobiography.

Ultimately, I decided to consider autobiographical speeches in cases where the orator was related to an earlier author who was also included in

50 *Life/History/Archive*

my sample. My thinking was that, for instance, Shamsie's speeches could offer a productive means of considering how forms and styles of writing about the self had evolved over time when placed in juxtaposition to the autobiographical output of her own mother, Jahanara Habibullah.[99] Also deemed useful in this regard was another form of written-made-oral source: the autobiographical film. In the concluding scene of Samina Mishra's exquisite *House on Gulmohar Avenue* (2005), the filmmaker's own voice can be heard to intone: "Sometimes the story of a life is the story of a search to be at home."[100] Her brief synopsis points to how she uses the symbol of her family home in New Delhi's Okhla—the "house" of the title—to reflect on "ideas of identity and belonging" through four generations, including her own. Mishra's autobiographical reflections in film proved of special interest to my historical project in that her grandmother Sayyida Khurshid Alam also produced a personal narrative focused on previous generations: an ostensibly biographical account of her esteemed father, India's third president, Zakir Husain (1897–1969).[101] Similarly, Sabina Kidwai's film *Shadows of Freedom* was explicit in its aim to use the lives of three Indian Muslim women—the filmmaker, her mother, and her grandmother—to explore "issues of identity and gender conflicts."[102] That the filmmaker's grandmother was Anis Kidwai, author of the celebrated Partition memoir *Azadi ki Chhaon Mein* (first published in 1974, but translated recently as *In Freedom's Shade*), facilitated another comparison.[103]

The examples in the previous paragraphs also draw me back to a suggestion I made earlier: that some materials that I collected unquestioningly were not an individual's memoir so much as the interwoven life stories of a woman and a man to whom she was close. I think of another two examples mentioned already, Jahan Ara Shahnawaz's *Father and Daughter* or Hameeda Akhtar Husain Raipuri's *Hamsafar*. Far more, like Sayyida Khurshid Alam's *Zakir Husain ki Kahani*, were projected as biographies of close male relatives—husband, father, son.[104] Yet, in charting a relationship, they were often as revealing of the female author as the male subject. Examining women's accounts of social reform campaigns in Maharashtra, Jyotsna Kapur includes a section on this kind of "biography as autobiography." She points out that many "biographies" that women wrote about reforming husbands—often at their husband's request—had a special emphasis on their wedding and married life. Ramabai Ranade, in her "biography" of her famed husband, talks not of his "public role as a social reformer" but instead about "her relationship with him, how this affected her relationship with others in the family, and her own opinions about some of the public decisions that he took which affected her." Such examples lead Kapur to conclude: "The accounts, then, describe women's experiences in great detail and are really autobiographical."[105] These examples set alongside my own seemed to suggest that for women in South Asia, writing biography—or a travelogue or a novel—was another necessary strategy for writing about the self in a cultural context where women's voices were not meant to be heard.

The line between these autobiographical biographies and autobiography proper was especially blurred because many of the latter that I consulted actually seemed to be more about others in a woman's life than about the woman herself. In other words, just as the biographies would appear, to my mind at least, to be autobiographical (about the self), so some of the autobiographies would appear to be more a collection of biographies (about others). Hameeda Akhtar Husain Raipuri's aforementioned *Hamsafar*, for instance, is presented from the outset, as the title probably suggests, as being more about the author's more famous husband, the acclaimed Urdu writer Akhtar Husain Raipuri, than about herself. Hence this memoir begins not with the author's own birth, as one might expect, but instead with the moment she meets her husband for the first time.[106] And yet it is not just about him—or, perhaps better, her relationship with him—but also, as she specifies in her preface ("Dil ki Bat," or "Matters of the Heart"), all the "great personalities" that the couple had met.[107] Her focus on others is reinforced by a quick survey of the table of contents, from which we see that many of the chapters are actually named after individuals that Hameeda knew: Maulvi Abdul Haq ("Baba-i-Urdu" or "Father of Urdu"), Munir Bano, Prem Bada Devi, Khalida Adib Khanum, "My Father."[108] Other female writers proved even more explicit in their focus on others. As Hamida Rahman, a writer and educator in Bangladesh, wrote of her autobiography—notably titled *Jiban Smriti* in Bengali (*Memories of My Life*): "[This title] does not mean writing only about my own life. While walking in this event-filled world, one meets so many people. Their memories peep into the pages of one's life. I cannot but describe them."[109]

The approach taken by these authors may be viewed as reflecting some of the generic features of women's autobiography. As I have summarized elsewhere, women's autobiographical writings are often characterized—almost exclusively on a reading of those produced in Europe and North America—as being "more collective than individual, more about relationships than accomplishments."[110] What is reflected here is that while men may find it easy enough to write a "coherent, linear, narrative describing an individualized self," women are more likely to root their life stories in collective identities associated with the family, friendships, or kinship networks—though, naturally in making this statement, one should be careful of generalizations that overwrite difference of class, race, and sexual orientation.[111] The inclination to collectivity may be accentuated in a society, like South Asia, which, as noted in the introduction, is often presumed to "privilege the social and communal over the individual."[112] But the model of Islamic life story seems to be as important in the cases I discuss here. As Barbara Metcalf writes of an autobiographical narrative composed within that tradition by Maulana Muhammad Zakariyya, a Muslim scholar, or *'alim*, from the Islamic madrasa at Deoband, in northwest India, in the 1970s:

> The material is not presented as Muhammad Zakariyya's exclusive story at all, but, throughout, as the story of his relations with other people. He counts, as part of *his* life, stories of the elders he has interacted with or whom he, in turn, knows from stories recounted by others. Indeed, one might say that the "autobiography" is not much about Muhammad Zakariyya at all.[113]

No wonder I was experiencing a sense of genre instability.

Also blurring the lines between biography and autobiography was my growing realization—fostered by my informal conversations with those surrounding memoirs—that not all my sources were actually written by their proclaimed author. Returning to Delhi from Aligarh late one evening, I chatted with Lubna Kazim, the daughter of actress and later memoirist Begum Khurshid Mirza, to pass the time. In the course of our conversation, she made what seemed to me to be a surprising admission:

that, faced with a publisher's charge that her mother's memoir was too "sketchy," she had, in effect, filled in some of the bits that her mother had "left unsaid" so as to "bring things to a close." The memoir was thus written, as she put it, "as a family thing."[114] Later, I realized that Lubna had been very forthright about her contribution in print, noting in her preface to the Indian edition that "the informative chapters two, four, and five are largely mine. For reasons of preserving the continuity of the narrative, they have been included in the main text and not moved to the appendix."[115] And yet they were still written in the first person. I had come across an even more extreme example of this "ghosting" once before and had not been sure what to make of it. The preface of Bilkees Latif's *Her India* made clear that what followed was, in effect, a biography of the author's French-born mother, Alys Iffrig—later Begam Ali Yar Khan and later still Begam Ali Hydari—written on the basis of conversations with her aged mother supplemented by family papers and archival research. And yet, it too was composed in the first person: "in her own words," as the named author explained, as if this was sufficient to distinguish them from her own "author's words" that resurfaced in the final chapter to recount her mother's death and draw the narrative to a close.[116] So what makes a biography and what an autobiography? To conclude this chapter, let us consider this issue of labeling further.

CONCLUSION: LABELING

In Metcalf's aforementioned study of Muhammad Zakariyya's autobiographical writings—composed between 1970 and 1981—she notes that the Deobandi *'alim* shunned "more elevated terms" used for autobiography in favor of calling his work *Ap Biti*: the "ordinary" Hindi term for a written or spoken life story. The implication, as Metcalf points out, was of "having his own say"—perhaps appropriate, since much of this "modest, incomplete, sometimes repetitive document" was transcribed from speech.[117] But the booksellers that I encountered in Delhi's Urdu Bazaar in the shadow of the Jama Masjid—while demonstrating untold patience with my broken spoken Hindustani—only really responded to the Persianized *khud navisht*: "self-writing," or "that which is written about oneself." Their informal lessons in nomenclature suggested that this term is the more ac-

54   *Life/History/Archive*

cepted now for autobiography in Urdu. Interestingly, this phrase is not found in Platt's classic dictionary of Urdu, Hindi, and English published in 1884, though it does appear in certain Urdu publications by the early twentieth century—like the great poet Hali's fleeting account of his life up to 1901.[118] Its growing use among South Asian Muslims is also implicit in the title additions experienced by a text composed by Princess Shahr Bano Begam of Pataudi between 1885 and 1887. Originally, the manuscript was called *Bītī Kahānī*, a title that could be translated rather indelicately as a "story of incidents that one has experienced." Yet, when it was finally published in Pakistan in 1995, it also boasted a (not necessarily accurate) subtitle: *Urdu ki awwālin niswānī khud navisht* (*The First Autobiography by a Woman in the Urdu Language*).[119] Recently published again in Pakistan, but in an English translation by Tahera Aftab, it is now simply an "autobiography."[120]

Initially I identified my study as being about *personal narratives*. I had chosen this particular phrase in tribute to Malavika Karlekar's groundbreaking study of "early personal narratives" produced by (Hindu) women in Bengal, *Voices from Within* (1993). As Karlekar noted in her preface, she, too, had faced a difficulty over the "choice of texts, their availability and relevance," but had settled on those "autobiographical writings" either published or available in Calcutta's main libraries. Her sources thus included not just "the more formal, full-length, structured autobiography," but also diaries, letters, newspaper and journal articles, poems, stories, and essays.[121] Nearly two decades later, she and her coeditor, Aparna Basu, stood by this label, while also expressing a preference for the term "life experiences" in their compendium, *In So Many Words* (2008). Yet here they expanded their source base to also include "portraits from memory" and an oral interview.[122] Others working with this kind of material in the context of South Asia have preferred the term "life histories."[123] According to Arnold and Blackburn, this terminology allows contributors to their important volume, *Telling Lives in India*, already discussed in the introduction, to go beyond "clearly biographical or autobiographical texts" that could "privilege print over orality" to also include folktales, legends, and "spoken lives." Attractive in this broad definition is its attempt to avoid "artificial boundaries" that can hide the "often fragmentary or allusive nature of many life-historical forms."[124] By settling on the term "autobiographical writing" instead, I hope to recognize this instability of genre while still evoking my focus on the written life. My hope too is that by employing a derivative of the term "autobiography"—with its resonance on a global scale—my work will help disrupt the established Western canon by asserting the place of South Asian Muslim women's writings in that "new, globalized history of the field" to which I referred in the introduction.[125]

So, what actually is to be included in my life history archive? I started my fieldwork wondering if there was anything out there to be found; and, throughout, I continued to face skepticism at the idea of Muslim women writing memoirs. Without doubt, these sources can be difficult to find. While the colonial archive and its successors threw up some material, much more fruitful was the experience of getting out onto the streets and into people's homes and lives. Through this more holistic approach to research, I collected literally hundreds of books, manuscripts, articles, and words relevant to this study of autobiographical writing— whether called "autobiography" or "memoir," *ap biti, biti kahani,* or *khud navisht, atmakatha* or *atma jibani,* or, in more specific forms, *roznamcha* or *safarnama.* Yet, as I have sought to show, a constant problem was how to fit these real-life historical sources into the theoretical boxes dreamt up by academics usually within the context of a Euro-American literary tradition. In the course of this chapter, then, I have traversed from autobiographical biographies and biographical autobiographies to travelogues, reformist literature, novels, devotionalism, letters, diaries, interviews, speeches, and ghosted narratives. In the end, I draw a line—if a hazy and traversable line—at the constructed life: no novels, but more autobiographical biographies and the biographical autobiographies; the autobiographical fragment; the written-made-oral (including some film), but not the oral-made-written; the published "diary book," but not diaries or letters; the spiritual, but not the ghosted; and the travelogue where relevant. I have thus evolved a definition for autobiographical writing that emerges from the specific experience of a historian crafting a unique archive from which to study gender, autobiography, and the self in Muslim South Asia. Having done so, I now turn from *what* to *who*.

CHAPTER TWO

THE SOCIOLOGY OF AUTHORSHIP

INTRODUCTION: LITERACY AND OTHER CONUNDRUMS

At the most basic level, to write autobiography requires the facility to write—in other words, literacy. But in South Asia, literacy has been comparably low among the general population—especially among women and even more especially among Muslim women—until fairly recently. According to the 2011 census, India now boasts a functional literacy rate of 74.04 percent, up from just 12 percent at Independence in 1947, while Pakistan stood at 54.9 percent in 2009 and Bangladesh at 56.78 percent in 2010. These figures, however, hide substantial gender, regional, and social disparities. Female literacy, for instance, remains lower, at 65.46 percent in India, 40.3 percent in Pakistan, and 52.22 percent in Bangladesh for the same years.[1] Still, these figures represent a marked increase from those of the colonial period. The first comprehensive census in India was taken in 1871, and thus should give us an early marker—but, as a return column for "females" was not included in the section on education in early censuses, no reliable data on female literacy are available for the nineteenth century or before.[2] By the time female literacy came to be recorded in 1901, it stood at just 0.9 percent for India as a whole, increasing very slowly to around 8 percent in 1947.[3] On this basis alone, it may be presumed that autobiographical writing among South Asian Muslim women was a pretty elite endeavor into the late twentieth century and

57

58   *The Sociology of Authorship*

beyond. Very few women could write and, of those, only a small percentage would write autobiography. But this is a key point: just because one *can* write autobiography does not mean one *does* write autobiography.

Furthermore—and contrary to my opening gambit—to prepare an autobiography need not, strictly, require literacy. Even if a woman is able to read and write, she may choose to dictate her life story to a secretary or relative—as, indeed, did many prominent men and women in Europe and elsewhere right into the twentieth century. A well-known example relevant to this study, and thus already mentioned in the introduction, is that of the Egyptian feminist Huda Shaarawi, who did not pen her own autobiographical manuscript, "Mudhakirrati," in the school notebooks in which it was recorded in the early 1940s, but instead dictated it to her secretary, Abd al-Hamid Fahmi Mursi.[4] Dictation or some other form of collaborative writing may thus have provided a means for Muslim women with or without literacy to tell their life stories in written form. This possibility has enabled a number of less elite women—those with limited or no education and lower social status—to share the stories of their lives around the world, particularly since the "memoir boom" initiated at least partially by Frank McCourt's recollections of his quite ordinary, if harrowing, childhood in *Angela's Ashes* (first published in 1999).[5] To take an example close to the home of this study, we have seen a proliferation of autobiographies by often ill-educated Afghani women since 2001. Inspired by Euro-American political interest in the region, these texts tend to be written in English "with" a second author to record the trials and tribulations of being female under Taliban rule or influence.[6] Literacy may aid in the production of autobiographical writing, but it cannot be the only factor.

At the heart of this chapter, then, is a simple question: Who writes? Are Muslim female authors of particular social, economic, or educational backgrounds? Or is an unusual job or a degree of renown enough to motivate autobiographical production? Do particular locations and historical moments prove more likely to yield this type of personal reflection? More properly, then, my question is not just *who* writes, but, in fact, *who* writes *when*? The main body of this chapter will thus be divided into three sections defined by key sociological categories: class, education, and occupation. In each case, I seek to define these categories in relation to the specific historical moment to which they are applied, while also rooting my inevitable generalizations in real lives and real voices. By offering a multitude of historical examples, I also introduce the individual authors who populate this study as a whole. Much of my data emerges from the authors' own autobiographies, but wherever possible I have sought to supplement that information with other historical materials that allow a more complete biographical picture. By locating Muslim women's autobiography in this way, I begin a process, ongoing throughout this work, of identifying the particular historical factors that defined and facilitated gendered autobiographical production with its emphasis, greater or lesser, on the self. I thus seek to offer a more complex picture of autobiographical motivation beyond the individual—or, to pose a final question, *why* write? I develop this constellation of authors, time, and motivation in my concluding section, in which I relate *who* writes to *when* and *why*. But let me begin with class and status.

CLASS AND STATUS

Can we characterize South Asian Muslim women who have penned their life stories, or incidents within them, by social or economic status? Certainly the earliest examples—from the sixteenth century into the early twentieth century—point to the importance of elite or even royal status. The few existing texts from the Mughal period—Gulbadan's *Ahval-i-Humayun Badshah* and Jahanara's *Munis ul-arvah* and *Risala-i-Sahibiyah*—were, as is fairly well known, written by imperial princesses: daughters and sisters to emperors.[7] In the nineteenth century, too, it was nawab begams—whether rulers in their own right or wives and daughters of the court—who pioneered autobiographical writing from India's princely states. Particularly prolific were the begams of Bhopal—Sikandar (1818–68), Shah Jahan (1838–1901), and Sultan Jahan (1868–1930)—who, having established their dynasty of Muslim female rule within a small state in central India, documented their unusual life experiences in travel narratives, histories of the state, reformist literature, diaries, and multivolume autobiographies.[8] The princely state of Pataudi, not far from Delhi, also nurtured an early autobiographer in Princess Shahr Bano

60   *The Sociology of Authorship*

Begam (b. 1848). One of twelve daughters of ruler Akbar Ali Khan by his ninth wife, she was married to the heir apparent of neighboring Jhajjar state, Muhammad Nur Ali Khan, in 1853. However, he never ascended the throne, as the state's territory was confiscated by the British following the participation of her father-in-law, Nawab Abdur Rahman Khan, in the 1857 rebellion—a central event in the narrative—for which he was hanged in the same year. She remained, then, the daughter of a ruler, but never the wife of one, living out the rest of her life in reduced and unhappy circumstances in Ludhiana and Delhi.[9]

Muslim women belonging to princely houses also represent a significant proportion of those who wrote autobiography in the course of the twentieth and twenty-first centuries. Subsequent generations from Bhopal—notably, Maimoona Sultan (1900–85), a direct descendant of the Afghan ruler Ahmad Shah Abdali and married to the last nawab, Hamidullah Khan, and their daughter, Princess Abida Sultaan (1913–2002)—continued the tradition of producing travelogues, diaries, and full-fledged autobiographies. The last, Abida Sultaan's *Memoirs of a Rebel Princess*, appeared posthumously in 2004.[10] A friend of the Bhopali begams, Nazli Rafia Sultan Nawab Begam of Janjira (1874–1968), also published an early travelogue, *Sair-i-Yurop*, soon after a royal tour of Britain, Europe, and the Middle East in 1908. Though born into the extended Tyabji clan of Bombay (see below and chapter 5), she was married to Sidi Ahmad Khan Sidi Ibrahim Khan, the ruler of Janjira (also known as Habshan in reflection of his family's Abyssinian descent) in 1886.[11] Begam Qudsia Aizaz Rasul (1908–2001) and Dr. Rahmathunnisa Begam (b. 1902) were better known, as discussed below, for their own prestigious careers, documented in their full-length autobiographies. Still, it is worth noting that the first was the granddaughter of Nawab Bahadur Khan of Maler Kotla in Punjab, while the second descended from the royal families of the Carnatic and Arcot in south India.[12] Representing Hyderabad's nobility, though not as a member of the nizam's family, was Bilquis Jehan Khan (b. 1930). She devoted more than half of her autobiography, *A Song of Hyderabad* (2010), to her early life at court.[13]

A number of women connected with the ruling house of Rampur in north India also wrote autobiography. Identifying herself in terms of this princely connection on the cover of *An Extraordinary Life* (2006) was "Princess Mehrunissa of Rampur" (b. 1933), daughter of the last nawab, Raza Ali Khan, and his third wife, Talat Zamani Begum.[14] More circumspect was Salma Ahmed, who does not mention until chapter 25 of her *Cutting Free* (2002) that her grandmother Malika Husain Ara Begam, was an earlier nawab's granddaughter.[15] As noted in the introduction, Jahanara Habibullah (1915–2001) also wrote *Remembrance of Days Past* (2001) to recall her youth at the Rampur court. Though not of the ruling family, her father, Sahibzada Sir Abdus Samad Khan, was a descendant of the nawabs of Najibabad, who had lost their titles and territory as retribution for complicity in the 1857 rebellion. Her mother, Sahibzadi Aliya Sultan Begum (1888–1967), was the daughter of Nawazada Bashiruddin Mirza of the princely state of Loharu in Punjab. Their closeness to the royal court reflected her father's esteemed position as Rampur's chief minister for more than thirty years.[16] Interestingly, Jahanara's *Remembrance* also contains passages written by her mother, apparently excerpted from her diary, and her eldest sister, Rafat Zamani Begum (1907–87), wife of Rampur's last nawab, Syed Raza Ali Khan.[17] Her cousins on her father's side, Zohra Segal (1912–2014) and Hamida Saiduzzafar (1921–88), discussed below in the context of their own impressive careers, also published full-length autobiographies.[18]

Many early authors among South Asia's Muslim women, if not actually royal, belonged to what we may characterize as aristocratic families. Nawab Faizunnessa Chaudhurani (1834–1903), author of the poetic *Rupjalal* (1876) with its autobiographical introduction, was a zamindar in her own right, having inherited the estate of Pashchimgaon in Comilla district in east Bengal from her mother in the mid-1880s.[19] Others were married into or descended from zamindari or taluqdari families. Begam Qudsia Aizaz Rasul, for instance, already mentioned for her royal parentage, married the taluqdar of Jalalpur from Sandila in Hardoi district, near Lucknow, in 1929.[20] Jahanara Habibullah's mother-in-law, Begam Inam Fatima Habibullah, was, similarly, the wife of the taluqdar of Saidanpur in the United Provinces. Their comfortable circumstances are revealed by her daily account of their 1924 trip to England to visit their three sons in a British boarding school. During the trip they made a lengthy stay

62   *The Sociology of Authorship*

in Dorchester, and then, during the holidays, London.[21] One of those sons, Ali Bahadur Habibullah, subsequently married author Attia Hosain (1913–98), also of a taluqdari family, whose *Sunlight on a Broken Column* (1961) is sometimes characterized as autobiographical (see chapter 1).[22] From a similar family in a similar place was Anis Kidwai (1906–82), who is best known for her Partition memoir, *Azadi ki Chhaon Mein* (1974). A recent biographer has described her as being from "a somewhat down-at-heel zamindar family of an Awadhi qasbah" to distance her from the "ladies" of Lucknow's urban elite, but her background was still patrician.[23]

From the noble Mian family in Punjab was Jahan Ara Shahnawaz (1896–1979). Her family's links to an important kinship lineage, the Arains, were traced on the very first page of her political autobiography, *Father and Daughter* (1971).[24] A contemporaneous example from Bengal was Sufia Kamal (1911–99), one of Bangladesh's best-known feminists, poets, and activists. In her *Ekale Amader Kal* (*Our Times and This Time*) (1988), she documented how she was born into a zamindari family from Shaestabad in the coastal district of Barisal. It is worth quoting at length from her own autobiographical writings in order to get a sense of what this status meant in social, cultural, and material terms:

> In those days [during my childhood], the Shaestabad Nawab family of Barisal district was famous throughout the whole of Bengal . . . [It] was famous for its honourable reputation, riches, education and manners [*adab*]. The inner house [*antahpur*] had Mughal culture. Outside, it was Bengali and English culture—the more fashionable and modern lifestyle. My maternal uncles were a barrister, a deputy magistrate, a *diwan* of Nimak [manager of the salt stores], big officers in the police department. But they worked for six months or one year and then left their jobs to return to the traditional *zamindari* lifestyle. With elephants and horses, big boats, boat races, cars, palanquins, *nautch* [dancing] girls. They built a huge library. They lived life at leisure . . . My first memories are of lots of riches. A two-storied house of the same height as today's five-storied house. Big curved ebony doors would shine when sunlight fell on their intricate designs. On the roof, in the midst of *pankhas* [fans], were chandeliers. They made a beautiful musical sound. . . . Shadowy afternoons, a sweet-smelling breeze from the *pankhas*,

everywhere there were maidservants. . . . Some women are having *paan* [betel leaf], some are putting henna on their hands and feet, some might be doing some embroidery.[25]

Though clearly nostalgic, the author evoked a highly privileged and cultured lifestyle still linked to a "Mughal" identity and aesthetic in the late colonial period. Other female autobiographers hailing from zamindari, or "Mian," families in Bengal—and thus a similar cultural milieu in their childhoods, if not after—were educationalist Akhtar Imam, discussed below, and journalist Mafruha Chowdhury.[26]

By far the majority of Muslim women producing autobiographical writing in the twentieth century are best described simply as *sharif* or, in the plural, *ashraf*. In terms of social standing, this label—contrasted with *ajlaf*—indicated elite or noble status, though the words and means used to indicate it differed from author to author. Some used the word *sharif* itself to describe their families, while others employed *sayyid* to highlight their foreign descent.[27] Some women, like Qaisari Begam (1888–1976) in her *Kitab-i-Zindagi* (*The Book of Life*, first published in 1976), detailed their ancestry at great length—in her case, that of all four grandparents to eight generations—as evidence of sharif lineage.[28] Other women used regional terms, like *shombhranto* in Bengali, also reflecting elite status, or linguistic variants that showed they were of "good," "cultured," or "respectable" families.[29] Suggested in these latter descriptors is the way in which the very idea of "nobility" attached to sharif status was being redefined in the post-1857 period: from a characteristic of birth to one of good character. The sharif gentleman—and, by extension, his wife and daughters—were to be educated, pious, and restrained in their behavior. In financial terms, these characteristics translated into thrift as those who had belonged previously to the old Mughal "service classes" found themselves in reduced economic circumstances under British rule. Begum Khurshid Mirza (1918–89), the daughter of Aligarh educationalist Shaikh Abdullah, thus used her memoir to demonstrate her sharif status by underlining her frugality when it came to domestic economy. She went so far as to record that the table mats of Irish linen that she ordered from England in the early 1940s cost "only Rs 7 in postal charges."[30]

The elision of sharif status with class is reflected in that many Muslim female authors describe their families simply as "middle class."[31] As Sanjay Joshi has explored with reference to Lucknow, the emergence of a "new" middle class in colonial India was a "political, social, cultural phenomenon" as much a "redefinition of respectability" as wealth.[32] Still, many belonging to the middle class, broadly construed, had benefited from the educational, commercial, and administrative opportunities opened up by the British in India.[33] It is perhaps no surprise, then, that so many of the male relatives of authors discussed here attended government or mission schools and colleges before studying at universities in Calcutta, Dhaka, Allahabad, or Bombay.[34] A substantial number even traveled to Britain for further studies, usually at Cambridge, Oxford, London, or Edinburgh.[35] Others attended private or princely institutions, like Muhammadan Anglo-Oriental (MA-O) College at Aligarh (later Aligarh Muslim University) or Osmania University in Hyderabad. These institutions had been set up by Muslim reformers or princes with the intention of making boys of their religious community more competitive in the colonial or state system.[36] Having received this "modern" education, many fathers, brothers, and husbands were prepared for one of the new "middle-class" professions: allopathic medicine, education, the law.[37] Others were merchants or businessmen, sometimes trading Indian goods in Europe, the Middle East or China, or sometimes involved in India's fledgling manufacturing industry.[38]

By far the majority of fathers mentioned in the autobiographies, however, were colonial servants. We may take as a case study a volume that was published in Dhaka in 1988 to bring together the reminiscences of early female educationalists. Of the twenty-five contributors, ten gave some indication of their father's occupation, and of those ten, eight were government employees: the postmaster of a district town, a government lawyer, an officer with the police department, a teacher at a government college, a district inspector within the education department, the superintendent of a civil court.[39] This sample is, of course, small and incomplete, but where evidence is available, the pattern appears to be reproduced. Rahmat Ara Hossain, also writing about Bengal, notes that her father was the district subregistrar of Noakhali, while Jobeda Khanam (1920–90) records with some pride that her father was a school subinspector in the education department.[40] Politician and author Shaista Ikramullah (1915–2000) grew up in "Civil Lines" wherever her father was district medical officer for the East Indian Railway, as did educationalist and activist Jahanara Imam (1929–94), whose father was in the Bengal Civil Service.[41] Raised in the United Provinces, Kishwar Naheed's father was employed in a court of ward, while the aforementioned Salma Ahmed's father was district magistrate at Saharanpur.[42] The U.P. government also appointed Hamida Saiduzzafar's father as the first professor of anatomy at King George's Medical College in Lucknow in 1910.[43] In Bombay, the father of Amina Tyabji (1866–1942) and Safia Jabir Ali (1893–1962), Badruddin Tyabji, was perhaps most famous of all as the first Indian barrister and later first Muslim judge at the Bombay High Court.[44]

If not employed by the British government, the fathers and husbands of many other authors worked in princely administration in one of India's semi-autonomous states. An early and fairly well-known example is Abbas Tyabji, husband of the aforementioned Amina and father to later authors Shareefah Hamid Ali (1883–1971?) and Raihana Tyabji (1901–75). Having studied law in London, he was appointed to Baroda's judicial service during the reign of Maharaja Sayaji Rao III, eventually becoming a judge in the Baroda High Court.[45] The father of celebrated author Ismat Chughtai (1911–91) was, similarly, a magistrate in the Maharaja of Jodhpur's civil service, while educationalist Begam Zafar Ali's father rose to the post of education minister in the Dogra administration in Jammu and Kashmir.[46] More common as princely employers were Muslim-ruled states, like the nizam's Hyderabad. Many of the male relatives—fathers, grandfathers, uncles, and husbands—of the aforementioned Qaisari Begam, as well as her autobiographical contemporaries Ummat ul-Ghani Nurunnisa (1885–1915), Begam Sarbuland Jang (d. ca. 1955), Rahil Begam Sherwani (1893–1981?), Masuma Begam (1902–90), Zakira Ghouse (1921–2003), and Shaukat Kaifi (b. 1928) were employed here.[47] Perhaps best known of these men was Masuma Begam's grandfather Sayyid Husain Bilgrami (1842–1926). He was given the title of Imad ul-Mulk for his service to the nizam, first as his private secretary, then as director of public instruction for the nizam's dominions from 1887 to

1902.[48] Also awarded a title by the nizam was Begam Sarbuland Jang's husband, Muhammad Hamidullah Khan (1864–1935), who ended his esteemed career as chief justice of the High Court, Hyderabad.[49] Holding equally influential posts in Bhopal state were the fathers of Hameeda Akhtar Husain Raipuri (1920–2009) and Saeeda Bano Ahmed (d. 2001). While the first was private secretary to Sultan Jahan Begam of Bhopal, the second was tutor in English to her sons.[50]

In terms of socioeconomic status, then, most Muslim women writing autobiography in the modern period would be considered elite and often highly so. And yet there were exceptions. The surprising autobiographical narrative in verse, *Ik Sau Sath Kafian* (*One Hundred and Sixty Kafis*), composed in Punjabi probably in the second quarter of the nineteenth century, introduces its author, Piro (d. 1872)—whom we met already in the introduction—as a "low caste prostitute" (*sudar vesva*) and a "low caste woman" (*sudar nari*). Indicated here was her professional background as a prostitute or dancing girl in Lahore before she "defected" from her Muslim coreligionists to join a Sikh sect, the Gulabdasis, led by her guru and eventual lover, Gulab Das.[51] Singer Malka Pukhraj (1912–2004), author of *Song Sung True*, came from a comparably humble background in the princely state of Jammu and Kashmir. She described her maternal grandfather as a "poor, hard-working man" who, with his two brothers, cultivated a "small piece of land" by day and stitched *kurta* and *shalwar*, shirts and trousers, by night.[52] Less reputable, but perhaps more flush on occasion was her drunkard father: "gambling was his profession."[53] Still, her mother ensured that with the payouts, her daughter received an education and singing lessons—and, ultimately, Malka Pukhraj not only had a highly distinguished career, as discussed below, but also married a government officer, Syed Shabir Hussain Shah, thus joining the ranks of Pakistan's middle classes.[54]

Only much more recently have the illiterate or ill-educated in South Asia employed various forms of collaborative writing to tell their life stories in written form. A key example already discussed in the introduction and chapter 1 is Nalini Jameela's *Oru Laingikathozhilaliyude Atmakatha* (*The Autobiography of a Sex Worker*, 2005). Constructed as a written narrative by a male reformer on the basis of interviews, it offers an account of

Jameela's experiences as a sex worker and later as an activist in Kerala and Karnataka. In chapter 1, she identifies herself in socioeconomic terms as a "poor Ezhava"—indicating her birth into a caste group of lowly status in Kerala—before she later converted to Islam.[55] Though her father received a small pension in recognition of army service before Indian Independence, "not a pie of that was," according to Jameela, "offered for expenses at home."[56] The family thus relied instead on the wages brought in by her mother's employment in a thread mill—until, when her mother lost that job, nine-year-old Nalini began working "from six to six" in a clay mine.[57] We may also consider here the autobiography of Mukhtar Mai, a young Pakistani woman from a south Punjab village, who collaborated with French writer Marie-Thérèse Cuny to document her experience of being gang-raped in 2002 as punishment for her brother's alleged sexual indiscretion.[58] Growing interest from domestic and international audiences in texts like these, which give "a voice to the voiceless" suggests that proliferation may be still to come.[59]

EDUCATION AND STRUGGLE

So, we have seen that most Muslim women who wrote autobiography in South Asia were born into families of at least relative privilege. On the whole, their fathers were princes, nobles, or sharif gentlemen: well educated and gainfully employed. Can we then characterize their daughters by education too? In light of their background, it is perhaps not unexpected that most of the men so far introduced saw fit to educate their daughters. There were exceptions: fathers who, like the influential reformer Syed Ahmad Khan (1817–98), advocated Muslim education and even Western learning, but opposed girls' schooling.[60] Zakira Ghouse, for instance, made it a recurring theme in her autobiography, *Hamara Daur-i-Hayat*, written in installments in the 1950s, to comment on the "indifference or opposition" of her male relatives to girls attending school or even gaining access to books.[61] The tension appears to have been heightened for Zakira by her father's profession. Unable to secure employment in Hyderabad's civil service, he had set up a small lending library as a business venture to support his family in rented quarters close to their residence. But his daughter was permitted neither to visit nor to

68   *The Sociology of Authorship*

borrow books that he could have brought home. On only one occasion did she enter the premises so that she and some family members could watch a parade from the window: "Looking at the packed shelves of the library I felt a strange longing: 'to think that here, all around, are spread great treasures of knowledge and literature, but those who wish to benefit from them are deprived of the privilege!'"[62]

And yet she and other authors found "stratagems" to circumvent these restrictions.[63] Writing as early as 1899, Ashrafunnisa Begum (1840–1903), known as Bibi Ashraf, dedicated her entire narrative to the tortured process by which she taught herself to read and write.[64] As she explained: "[One night], it occurred to me that if I had a *salām* or a *mujrā* I could myself figure out the words and begin to read. What was so difficult about that! After all, I already knew the letters of the alphabet. What did I care if no one wanted to teach me!"[65] The young girl approached friends with the respectable request that they send her these short poems honoring the Prophet and his family (*salām, mujrā*) for copying—which they readily did. But how would she practice writing without paper and ink? Her grandmother supplied paper from the market on the claim that it was for "Uncle to copy these poems for me," but the ink had to be made with "blacking from the griddle [*tawā*]."[66] Without a teacher, it proved fruitless to continue copying words that she did not understand, so she turned to decoding an Urdu book on her own: "I would look at new words, and if I recognized any familiar letters I would put them together. Slowly, in this piecemeal manner, I would figure out whole words and read on—half right, half wrong."[67] Several books along, she began to read Urdu well enough that she could turn back to reading, then copying the poems with which she had begun until she could "write from memory." As she told herself in congratulations: "Whatever man gets, he gets it through his own efforts. By God's grace I now possess what I had so keenly sought—if not in its perfect form, then at least poorly."[68]

Others commented on how male or female relatives facilitated their education. Hamida Rahman, for instance, explained how her father, fearing the censure of society, did not want to send his daughter to school, but was overruled by her mother, who though illiterate herself, sold her ornaments to pay the fees.[69] Likewise, Saiyida Lutfunnessa and Moslema Khatun paid tribute to brothers who, while studying themselves, brought books and magazines for their secluded sisters.[70] It is worth quoting at length from Saiyida Lutfunnessa's narrative—originally published as a chapter in a Bengali collection—in order to get a sense of her brother's importance to her education and further prospects:

> After my mother came to the village [in 1932 on the death of her husband], she tried to adopt the ways of village life—so, she took care that her sons were well-educated, but she did not bother about my education . . . I could not go to school, but my education did not ever stop. Whenever my elder brother came back from Calcutta, he brought me different books written by well-known authors. He studied in Calcutta. By the time I was fifteen or sixteen, I had already read the works of Tagore, D. L. Ray, Vidyasagar, Bankim, Sarat and Saugat. I also read different magazines, like *Prabasi* . . . Even now, my brother thinks I am an extraordinary woman. He used to tell me that, in this way, one day you will become well-educated. I used to read the books very carefully. But I lacked the courage to go to school or keep a home tutor, as this would have led people to direct slander against me.[71]

The list of celebrated Bengali novelists and poets that she offered, alongside the name of a prominent literary magazine in which many of them published, points to the quality and quantity of her reading under her brother's tutelage, even within the conservative milieu of a west Bengal village. Later, this grounding enabled her to pass her matriculation before studying Bengali language and literature to the master's level at Dhaka University.[72]

Since many authors were married at a very young age, husbands could also play an important role as educational patrons. From the late nineteenth century, Muslim reformers advanced the view that educated boys required educated wives if they were not to seek solace elsewhere. Unable to find a girl to fit the bill, many chose to educate their child brides themselves.[73] An illustrative example is Jobeda Khanam's experience as told in her *Jiban Khatar Pataguli* (*Pages from My Life*, 1991). Though her father was, as noted in the introduction, the son of a respected village *pir*, he had been sent to school and then on to college to receive a "modern" education. He then landed a "very big" government job as an "Inspector Sahib" in the education department of colonial Bengal.[74]

Though he was not against girls' education himself, he did not allow Jobeda to attend school, even when he was pressured by friends, out of fear that it would upset his elder brother, who was not a college graduate. Eventually, a purdah school was opened in their town especially for Muslim girls, but as Jobeda tells it: "I was almost eleven then. Everybody thought I was of marriageable age, so I could not be sent to school."[75] Only after her marriage at the age of thirteen to a "gentleman" twenty years her senior wearing "western clothes" did she begin studying.[76] According to her account, he was so happy when she completed her matriculation examination five years later that he pronounced: "You will have to pass I.A., B.A. and M.A. You will have to get all the degrees."[77] Sadly, he died from typhoid soon after, leaving Jobeda a widow with two small children when she was just eighteen years of age. But her husband had decreed that she would study to the master's level and beyond—and so she did.

Thus, one way or another, these eventual autobiographers found, or were given, a path to education. But what kind of education did they receive? Before the twentieth century, elite Muslim girls may have expected some tutoring at home, perhaps from an *ustani*, or lady teacher, or a family member. At the least, girls needed to know how to read the Qur'an—though not necessarily understand it—so that they could say their prayers. Seldom would this zenana education have stretched to learning to write or even basic arithmetic.[78] The rare exception was in royal households, where princesses and future nawab begams may have received an education more comparable to that of their brothers. In her diary and autobiography, Sultan Jahan Begam of Bhopal detailed the rigorous routine that she followed in the early 1860s under the close eye of her grandmother Sikandar:

Before noon
From 5 o'clock to 6. Open air exercise
From 6 o'clock to 7. Morning meal
From 8 o'clock to 10. Study of the Qur'an
From 10 o'clock to 11. Breakfast with Nawab Sikandar Begam
From 11 o'clock to 12. Recreation

After noon

From 12 o'clock to 1. Handwriting lesson

From 1 o'clock to 3. English lesson

From 3 o'clock to 4. Persian lesson

From 4 o'clock to 5. Arithmetic

From 5 o'clock to 5.30. Pushtu lessons and fencing practice alternatively

From 5.30 to 6. Riding lesson

From 6 o'clock to 7. Evening meal

And so at 8 o'clock to bed.[79]

A similar regime was then followed when Sultan Jahan came to educating her daughter-in-law, Maimoona, and granddaughter, Abida, in the early decades of the twentieth century.[80] Most authors born in the 1880s and 1890s, however, received home tutoring of a type advocated by prominent Muslim reformers of the time—most famously, Qaisari Begam's own grandfather Deputy Nazir Ahmad.[81] His reformist novel *Mirat ul-'Arus* (*The Bride's Mirror*, 1869) detailed how this new program for ashraf girls would go beyond the Qur'an to include rudimentary grammar, arithmetic, and domestic training in the vernacular.[82]

Comparatively few Muslim girls born in India in the late nineteenth or early twentieth century attended school—but, significantly, many of those who went on to produce autobiographical narratives of one sort or another were among their number. In fact, it tended to be a feature of their writings to comment on the rarity of their experience. One Bangladeshi author, Moslema Khatun, born in Burdwan district in west Bengal in the early 1930s, was so insistent that she returned to the theme of how few Muslim girls attended her schools three times in the course of her short, fifteen-page survey of the "stories of my life" (*Amar Jibaner Galpa Katha*). Most revealing was her observation: "By the time I had reached class five I had already studied in quite a few schools. The strange thing is that, though I studied in so many schools, there was not a single Muslim student in any of them."[83] As Independence neared, more Muslim girls began attending primary schools, but purdah requirements and early marriage meant that their schooling was often short-lived. As Rabiya Khatun remarked of her own school near old Dhaka city in the mid-1940s: "In

Baby One and Two"—presumably the introductory classes—"there were quite a few Muslim girls. But by class four, from twenty-five, only two of us were left."[84] The situation was even more extreme in her high school. Though Rabiya started with seven other Muslim girls in her class of sixty, each year the number would drop. As she explained: "All of a sudden, one girl would stop coming. One day, two days, seven days. Later on, we would come to know that she would not attend anymore. She has got married . . ."[85] Born just after the First World War in Noakhali district in southeast Bengal, Afsarunnesa was inspired to apply a Bengali proverb to the handful of Muslim girls in her school of nearly one thousand students: "Our situation was like ducks in the midst of swans."[86]

These scattered examples raise a number of pertinent questions about the type of schooling prevalent among future authors of autobiography. What kind of schools did they attend and where were they located? And how far did they progress with their studies in light of the restrictions on Muslim girls attending school at all? Though it is a selective sample, it is worth beginning with the twenty-five women who contributed to the autobiographical collection by early Bengali educationalists already employed in the previous section.[87] The first trend—or perhaps lack of it—that is discernible here relates to location. The contributors came from all four corners of Bengal, and thus began their schooling in both rural and urban environments—most often in a village or district town, but sometimes in the important centers of Dhaka or Calcutta. Of the twenty-two women in that group, two began their studies at home, one attended a small girls' school in a neighbor's home, one went to the local *maktab*, and one was sent to a missionary school, but the other seventeen (and thus the majority) attended local government or "free" schools. Having excelled at their primary studies, many of the future authors went on to attend one of three government girls' schools treated as "model" institutions in east Bengal: Vidyamoyee in Mymensingh, Faizunnessa in Comilla, or most often, Eden in Dhaka.[88] Three others gained admission to the renowned Sakhawat Memorial Govt. Girls' High School in Calcutta, while the rest attended various high schools and colleges at the district level. Almost all of them matriculated and went on to study for their bachelor of arts degrees and, in most cases, their master's, sometimes at Bethune College in Calcutta, but usually at Dhaka University. At least two completed their doctorates.[89]

These impressive educational attainments may be interpreted as much a reflection of the sample's specificity—including only educationalists—as an illustration of the women's status as autobiographers. But the patterns appear to be reproduced among other occupational groups and in other parts of India. Muslim reformers may have deemed government and mission schools inappropriate for girls of their community on the basis of their curriculum and facilities—in particular, the prevalence of Christian teaching, the highly academic subject matter, and the lack of purdah observance.[90] But many Muslim female autobiographers still attended these types of schools, seemingly because they were the only ones available in many areas. We may consider, as an early example, Badruddin Tyabji's thirteen daughters—of whom Amina and Safia have already been mentioned—and their Fyzee cousins, Zehra (1866–1940), Nazli (1874–1968), and Atiya (1877–1967). They attended a local convent school set up by the Zenana Bible Medical Mission in 1876 as the first girls' school in Bombay—though, as supplement, they also received lessons at home in Urdu, Persian, and the Qur'an, and in most cases, drawing, painting, singing, and the piano.[91] Though a close relative of the Prince of Arcot, Rahmathunnisa Begam also attended a local mission school after the "missionary lady" who ran it visited her home to persuade her family of the benefits. In her manuscript autobiography, she notes that when the missionary left, "there was an argument at home about my being admitted into the mission school. But when all found me eager and enthusiastic about it there was not much of opposition."[92] After proving herself to be an able student, she proceeded to a government high school and, ultimately, to the Women's Christian College in Madras.[93]

Other Muslim women narrated their experiences of attending pioneering institutions for Indian girls set up by educational reformers in the first decades of the twentieth century. In north India, those mentioned most frequently are the Zenana Madrasa at Aligarh, Sayyid Karamat Husain's Muslim Girls' School in Lucknow, and Queen Mary's College in Lahore.[94] If raised in the princely states of Hyderabad or Bhopal, the authors usually attended the Nampalli Girls' School, the Mahbubiya

74   *The Sociology of Authorship*

Girls' School, or the Sultania Madrasa.[95] Befitting the authors' primarily sharif status, all of these schools were elite institutions that maintained strict purdah norms, though they were differentiated by being Urdu-medium or English-medium—a factor that perhaps affected the choice of language that these women employed for autobiographical ends later in life. To take examples from Hyderabad, Masuma Begam and Bilquis Jehan Begam both wrote their autobiographies in English after attending the English-medium Mahbubiya Girls' School, while Zakira Ghouse, educated at the vernacular-medium Nampalli Girls' School, employed Urdu.[96] And yet these schools differed in terms of curriculum, too. Female education in the early twentieth century was firmly directed toward preparing girls for their future lives as wives and mothers. To this end, these girls' schools taught academic subjects, but only alongside subjects considered appropriate for ashraf girls—namely, sewing, bookkeeping, and home economics. Still, Nampalli evolved into a more academic institution for middle-class girls entering the professions, while Mahbubiya remained more of a "finishing school" for the very elite.[97]

As in the case of authors from Bengal, most from elsewhere completed their education to the high school level and often beyond. Narrating her arrival at a teaching job in the princely state of Jaora in the mid-1930s, Ismat Chughtai recalled the response: "A woman who was a BA, and that too a Muslim woman! This was a miracle."[98] And yet Ismat was just one among many authors who completed some form of higher education. A significant number—among them Saeeda Bano Begam, Hamida Saiduzzafar, Attia Hosain, Qurratulain Hyder, and Mehrunissa Khan—accompanied her to Isabella Thoburn College in Lucknow.[99] Others, like Begum Khurshid Mirza, attended home economics colleges such as Lady Irwin College in Delhi.[100] Still others completed their BA, BT, MA, MBBS, or PhD degrees elsewhere in India or even abroad.[101] To offer two examples from south India, Iqbalunnisa Hussain (1897–1954) received her BA from the Maharani's College in Mysore in 1930 before traveling to Britain in 1933 for a two-year diploma course in education at the University of Leeds, while Zakira Ghouse studied for her BA and MA in Hyderabad before completing her PhD from the University of Madras.[102] Zohra Segal, on the hand, enrolled at Mary Wigman's Dance School at Dresden in Germany in 1933, while her cousin Hamida Saiduzzafar went to Britain for postgraduate medical studies in ophthalmology in 1947.[103] Jobeda Khanam's experience of studying first at the University of London and then at the University of Kentucky in the United States in the 1950s is illustrative of a number of female authors from Bangladesh, Pakistan, and India who undertook higher studies abroad in the post-Independence period.[104]

Like diarists and autobiographers in other places and times, Muslim women in India who produced personal narratives tended to be educated and often highly so—notably, at a time when few others were.[105] Not only did they know how to read and write, but they also possessed the ability to analyze their own experiences and use them to construct a coherent narrative, often representing an individual life. Yet what this reading of Muslim women's autobiographical writings also points to is the importance of the *struggle* for education: the ultimate desire to learn, even if it is denied. We may think here again of Nalini Jameela, who, as noted above, produced her autobiographical account of prostitution very recently and only with the help of a collaborator. She used the very first section of her first chapter to articulate her longing to attend school, even after she was withdrawn after the equivalent of third grade: "When the school emerged in sight, I'd break down. I would howl and bawl and make a big commotion. Not able to express the pain of not being able to go to school, I would put both my hands on my head and howl."[106] More dramatic was another recent and very high-profile example also applicable to this study: *I Am Malala*, by Malala Yousafzai (b. 1997). As the subtitle to her bestselling autobiography indicates, she was "the girl who stood up for education and was shot by the Taliban" in 2012. Her desire for education—not only for herself but also for other girls—was so great that it put her very life in danger in the uncertain political environs of Pakistan's Swat Valley.[107] Education in itself was not enough; rather, one had to have striven for it to justify writing autobiography.

OCCUPATION AND RENOWN

The movement for women's education among Indian Muslims may have intended to better prepare girls for future domestic roles—"to help man in his struggles, to comfort him in troubles and create a happy home," as

Sultan Jahan Begam of Bhopal told a meeting of the All-India Women's Conference in 1928.[108] But the paradoxical effect was that Muslim girls, once educated, would use their education to ends never imagined by early male and female reformers. Some would apply their literacy to writing for reformist journals or other literary outlets, while others would employ newly acquired communication skills and school networks to participate in social service organizations. Still others had the idea of entering the professions. These occupational longings were often documented by Muslim women in their autobiographies as they reflected on their childhood experiences and ambitions. Zakira Ghouse, for instance, recalling her childhood in Hyderabad in the 1920s and 1930s, remembered a small notebook given to her by her father. On the first page was the alphabet and a single sentence in bold letters: "I shall study medicine!"[109] Ultimately, her marriage to a government officer, domestic chores, and four children intervened to derail her plans of becoming a medical doctor, but Zakira did eventually fulfill a "down-scaled" goal of gaining employment as a college teacher in a girls' school in Madras.[110] This outcome reflected how cultural norms of female segregation, or purdah, were institutionalized in the early twentieth century in a way that actually facilitated increased opportunities for female employment: women needed to be served by other women.[111]

It thus becomes appropriate to categorize Muslim female authors not just by their class or education as governed by fathers, husbands, or other male relatives but also by their own occupations. As a point of comparison, reliable statistics for female employment are difficult to come by for the nineteenth century and even much of the twentieth, but sources making use of the Indian census estimate that around one-third of Indian women (of all religious denominations) were part of the paid workforce by 1921. Of these, only small percentages, or approximately 104,000 women in total, were employed as professionals in medicine, education, law, or business. By far the majority of women in paid employment worked in manufacturing, agriculture, domestic labor, or mining, though if the estimates for Bombay are anything to go by, a substantial number also participated in sex work.[112] According to a 2010 study, the numbers for female employment are not all that different for

South Asia in the twenty-first century. Still, just over one-third of Indian women of working age are working in the paid workforce, even part-time—and then largely in jobs that require little skill or education.[113] From the data presented above, we may thus presume that in the colonial period and after, most ashraf women, and many others besides, acted primarily as housewives and mothers—with all the domestic duties that those roles entail even in a society that engages outside help in the form of servants.[114] What, then, were the occupations of those Muslim women who produced autobiographical writings? Did they deviate from the norm? And, if so, was it these exceptional experiences that inspired them to write their life stories?

Courtly Women

Occupational exceptionality certainly defined many of the earliest autobiographers among South Asian Muslim women. As noted already, many of those writing from the sixteenth century into the early twentieth century were imperial princesses, ruling nawabs, and princely consorts. Aware of their key role as observers and indeed participants in major political events—from the establishment of the Mughal dynasty in the case of Gulbadan's *Ahval* to the 1857 rebellion and colonialism's triumph in later texts—they narrated their life stories against the backdrop of a larger history. As Shahr Bano Begam of Pataudi wrote in explicit terms: "This book is the narration of my story and at the same time it is a chronicle of history."[115] Some royal authors, like Shah Jahan Begam of Bhopal, saw their own careers as rulers so entwined with those of their polity that they even projected their autobiographical writings as a history of their state—in her case, *Tarikh-i-Bhopal*. In fact, this *tarikh* was divided into three parts. The first was entirely "history," chronicling in turn the reigns of those rulers of Bhopal who came before the author's birth. The second part began to merge history with autobiography as Shah Jahan narrated events of her youth, including her marriage and various journeys, against a backdrop of the reign of her mother, Sikandar. In the third part, the merger of individual and state was completed as she recorded the achievements of her own reign up to the publication of the text in 1876.[116] As Barbara Metcalf notes, by amalgamating "history, travelogue, memoir and gazetteer," this text demonstrated the "generic instability" of vernacular writing at this moment of literary transition.[117]

For Shah Jahan's daughter and successor, Sultan Jahan Begam, life history also provided a way to chronicle Bhopal's changing administration in relation to the "mighty movements" outside.[118] But, in doing so, it had three main functions. The first was to continue *tarikh*'s established function within Indo-Persianate states of bestowing symbolic authority on a reign. *Her* telling of *her* role in the history of Bhopal state as it was linked to the world beyond became a means of "setting the record" for posterity.[119] As the author explained: "When those who have witnessed these scenes have passed away, and old records have been lost or destroyed, this book may serve to remind future generations of the debt to those who have gone before them."[120] Second, Sultan Jahan portrayed her autobiography as offering "lessons" to her princely successors on the "conduct of life."[121] A third function was to spread those lessons to a wider audience. "I am not without hope," she intoned, "that the descriptions I have given of royal durbars and other State functions may be of use to my fellow Rulers in India, as well as to political officers and others to whose lot, from time to time, the arrangement of such matters may fall."[122] These examples thus serve as illustrations of how courtly women employed literary conventions associated with different genres to which they already had access—*ahval, tarikh*, "mirror for princes"—to evoke a symbiotic relationship between biography and history in Islamic life writing. As I noted in the introduction, drawing on the work of Judith Tucker, history becomes the "touchstone" when "the individual life serves to illuminate its age."[123] Their "occupation" as courtly women made this possible in the colonial era.

Educationalists

Courtly women may have been the most exceptional, but in terms of numbers, the majority of Muslim women who wrote autobiography in South Asia were educationalists of one sort or another. A number of authors were responsible themselves for founding some of India's earliest girls' schools, an achievement that they often celebrated in their writings.

I have referred already to the begams of Bhopal, Shah Jahan and Sultan Jahan, who documented the often difficult process by which they established and popularized girls' schools within their own state during their respective reigns. For example, let us consider the opening paragraphs of Sultan Jahan's chapter on the Madrasa-i-Sultania, founded in 1903, in her *Gauhar-i-Iqbal* (*The Jewel of Prosperity*, 1913):

> Female education is a subject in which I take a deep interest, and I have always resented the unjust attitude which Muslims in general have adopted towards it. In Bhopal, the popular attitude towards the problem is not as unreasonable as in other parts of the country, chiefly because the state has been ruled over by Begams for a long period of time. But the meaning attached to female education is particularly narrow everywhere. It is not understood to mean anything more than a perfunctory reading of the Qur'an and a superficial knowledge of the Urdu language.[124]

She went on to describe how, "to overcome the reluctance of the people to send their daughters to school," she held a public meeting for prominent nobles and officials at which she announced her plans for a girls' school. Some came forward in support, "but, in certain quarters, there was an ominous silence, too, and I knew what that meant."[125] As the main concern was the maintenance of adequate purdah arrangements, she addressed that issue first by providing closed conveyances and an appropriate facility, but a lack of qualified female teachers and an appropriate curriculum proved harder to overcome.[126]

In another princely context, Amina Tyabji recorded how she oversaw a Muslim girls' school established at her encouragement by Maharaja Sayaji Rao II in Baroda, in western India, in the mid-1890s. Apparently she had been dining with the princely ruler at the captain's table on a steamship to Europe in 1894 (on this journey, see chapter 5) when he had boasted to her about all that he had done for the education of Muslim boys. "What about Muslim girls?" she had asked.[127] More modest were the efforts of Nazr Sajjad Hyder (1894–1967). In her *roznamcha*, or diary, published first in the Urdu journal *Tahzib un-Niswan* in the early 1940s, she traced how she brought together women in Dehra Dun to form the Anjuman Hami-i-Talim-i-Niswan, or Association for the Support of

80 *The Sociology of Authorship*

Women's Education, with the intention of starting a small girls' primary school:

> The first gathering of our association was held at my house. Invitation cards were published and distributed throughout the city. The first meeting attracted approximately fifty women ... From the first meeting, the donations from the membership fee amounted to thirty rupees for the month ... Within a few days, consciousness about women's education had garnered such enthusiasm that members invited the association for meetings at their own homes. Then we started to hold meetings in every neighbourhood. Every meeting saw an addition of as many as twenty women members. Within a month, I had collected enough money to start a school immediately.[128]

Rahmathunnisa Begam documented a comparable effort in south India: how she established a small "madrasa" in her home sometime in the 1920s to serve "the Muslim children and the adult illiterate women" of her locality.[129] Somewhat later, but no less significant, were the efforts of Ghulam Fatima Shaikh (d. 1981). In *Footprints in Time*, it is recalled how, in 1946, she established the Madrasatul Binat, now Fatima Girls' School, in Hyderabad, Sindh, that she managed until her death, despite being only "semi-literate" herself.[130]

Many others who wrote about the period up to the mid-twentieth century pursued teaching careers at a time when few Muslim women had entered this profession. We may recall, as an early example, the case of Bibi Ashraf. When her husband died in 1870, she found herself bereft in Lahore with no way to support her two young daughters. Honoring her husband's contributions as a professor at the Government College, the director of public instruction in the Punjab offered assistance in the form of a teaching job. Bibi Ashraf initially declined, but eight years later, she accepted a post at a local primary school, Victoria Girls' School, eventually rising to become its headmistress and converting it to a middle school.[131] In *Mere Shab o Roz* (*My Night and Day*, 1987), Begam Zafar Ali similarly narrated how the dearth of educated women in Kashmir's princely state meant that she received multiple offers to teach in a local girls' school. Despite stiff opposition from her father and her own lack of qualifications, she finally accepted a teaching position in the Government

The Sociology of Authorship   81

Girls High School in Srinagar sometime after 1916. Thus began a long teaching career that saw her associated with Kashmir's department of education for most of her life.[132] The rarity of these women's experiences, even many decades later, was articulated by Jobeda Khanam when she described her appointment to Charulata Girls' School in her hometown of Kushtia in central Bengal in 1942: "In this school, the principal was a Brahmo"—indicating her adherence to socioreligious principles articulated by the reformist Brahmo Samaj—"but the rest of the teachers were Hindus. I was the only Muslim teacher there."[133]

The capacities in which these educationalists were employed were multiple and diverse. To get a sense of possible trajectories, let us follow the careers of two representative women from Bengal, as described in their autobiographies. Perhaps most celebrated in Bangladesh today for her long career, documented in innumerable autobiographies, is the aforementioned Akhtar Imam (1917–2009).[134] Having matriculated from Eden Girls' School in Dhaka in 1933 as one of just three in the "third batch of Muslim girls," she went on to complete her IA (intermediate arts) examination at the Intermediate College before enrolling for a BA at Bethune College in Calcutta in 1935.[135] Graduation from Calcutta University with an honors degree in philosophy in 1937 allowed her to join her alma mater, Eden Girls' School, in the mid-1940s as its first Muslim teacher.[136] After twelve years, she was transferred to Dhaka College, where she became its first woman lecturer and the head of the Department of Philosophy. In 1956, she also became the first permanent provost of the women's hostel, Rokeya Hall, at the University of Dhaka, a post in which she remained for twenty years.[137] Reflecting on this appointment and her later career—spanning political unrest in East Pakistan and Bangladesh's independence in 1971—she wrote:

> I was not very eager to join this post. Circumstances forced me to do so. But there is no doubt that I gained satisfaction from working with the administration . . . Under the changing political circumstances in our country during the last phase of my employment, I faced some problems . . . But I was enriched by the experience. It made me stronger as a person. So, in my retired life, I can say without hesitation, "I am happy."[138]

82   *The Sociology of Authorship*

Akhtar Imam's educational and literary achievements were recognized with many accolades, including the Begum Rokeya Padak, awarded to her by the Bangladesh government in 2002.[139]

The aforementioned Jobeda Khanam was more mobile. First employed after her husband's death in 1939 in a private school for Muslim girls in Calcutta, she moved on after only a few months to a better-paid position elsewhere in the city. When that school closed in 1941 in the midst of the Second World War, a relative helped her to find a junior post at a school in Gaibandha, in north Bengal's Rangpur district. The relative's unkind behavior toward her children motivated her to return to her father's house, then in Jessore in southwest Bengal, where she got a job at Momen Government Girls' School. A year later, as noted above, she moved to Charulata Girls' School in Kushtia, but when famine hit, she decided to continue her education. In 1946, she was admitted to David Hare Training College in Calcutta to receive formal education as a teacher. "Financial problems" meant that alongside her studies, she was forced to take a job at a Muslim girls' high school in Park Circus, while also working as a "paid caretaker" in the relief camps set up after the communal violence following Direct Action Day. Still, her qualifications meant that she was picked up by Pakistan's new Department of Education in 1947 to teach at Eden Girls' College in Dhaka, ultimately climbing in the years that followed to the post of school inspectress. That post took her to Khulna district in the southwest of East Pakistan in the 1950s, where she also was employed as an aid worker. Later, she returned to Dhaka to be appointed deputy director of East Pakistan's Bureau of National Reconstruction and, in 1976, the founding director of the Bangladesh Shishu Academy—an autonomous body under the Ministry of Women and Children's Affairs dedicated to children's welfare.[140] Today, her educational work is memorialized in the names of the academy's library and a girls' college in Khulna.[141]

A broader survey of female educationalists suggests that these occupational achievements were fairly typical of those who wrote about their experiences. For some statistical evidence, let us return to the twenty-five authors who contributed to the 1988 volume by early Bengali educationalists. Of the twelve who give details of their educational careers, five report acting as a headmistress, assistant headmistress, or principal of a school, whether in Dhaka or a regional center, while seven note that they were lecturers at a local college or Dhaka University.[142] Examples from other parts of India replicate the pattern. I have already mentioned Rahmathunnisa Begam in the context of her "home madrasa," but, in 1930, her educational career entered a new phase when the Corporation of Madras advertised for a "Muslim lady supervisor." Appointed to the position, she took responsibility for visiting and supervising all nine of the Muslim girls' schools in Madras city, a demanding role that she documented in some detail in her unpublished autobiography.[143] Shamla Mufti, on the other hand, used her autobiography, written in the 1990s, to record an esteemed educational career in Kashmir, where she served as principal of the women's college in Srinagar.[144] Elsewhere, university professors stand out for producing personal narratives. I have already mentioned Hamida Saiduzzafar for her higher education, so it is perhaps no surprise that she ended her career as a professor of ophthalmology at Aligarh Muslim University.[145] A comparable example is Suhra Mehdi (b. 1937), a professor of Urdu at Jamia Millia Islamia in Delhi, who, from the 1990s, published a number of travelogues documenting local and international journeys before turning to her own life story.[146] In a diasporic context, we may also think of noted Pakistani American memoirists Sara Suleri and Fawzia Afzal-Khan, both of whom are employed by American universities.[147]

Writers

After those employed in education, the second-largest group of authors were writers who prepared their autobiographies as an extension of existing literary careers. Used to crafting language and preparing manuscripts, they readily made the leap from journalism, poetry, short stories, and the novel to more explicit forms of self-expression. Many of the earliest writers produced travel narratives and autobiographical fragments in fulfillment of their roles as editors and contributors to reformist women's magazines. A prolific example was Sughra Humayun Mirza (1884–1958) who first edited *An-Nisa*, a monthly magazine from Hyderabad dedicated to social reform and creative writing, from 1919 until 1927. She

84   *The Sociology of Authorship*

then moved to Lahore, where she edited another journal, *Zebunnisa*, from 1934.[148] In both cases, she used the journals to serialize her many travel writings that were later brought out as books—among them, two Indian travelogues, a *Safarnama-i-Iraq* and a two-volume *Safarnama-i-Yurop* (1926).[149] Atiya and Zehra Fyzee, too, contributed travel narratives to Urdu women's journals, like *Tahzib un-Niswan*, in which they also wrote articles on female education, social customs, and other reformist topics.[150] Spanning several genres were Saliha Abid Hussain (d. 1988) and the aforementioned Nazr Sajjad Hyder. The former began writing for women's magazines in the 1930s and later published three novels, a couple of biographical works, and, finally in 1984, her autobiography, *Silsila-i-Roz o Shab* (*The Cycle of Day and Night*).[151] Nazr Sajjad Hyder, on the other hand, began her literary career by contributing articles on women's education to prominent women's magazines, like *Tahzib un-Niswan* and *'Ismat*, before turning to edit a children's publication, *Phul*, in 1909. Later, she also wrote a number of novels on reformist themes, then ultimately serialized her life story in the same magazines in which she had begun publishing many decades before.[152]

Other authors, too, fused autobiography, fiction, and social criticism. A useful early example from Bengal is Nawab Faizunnessa Chaudhurani, already introduced for her zamindari inheritance, which she sought to put to good use by establishing a pioneering girls' school in Comilla in 1873. A few years later she published the epic *Rupjalal* (1876), in which she used the autobiographical introduction to identify her "reason for writing this book" in terms of her own disastrous experience of a polygamous marriage to her distant cousin and neighboring zamindar, Muhammad Gazi, in 1860. As she explained:

> After my marriage, I enjoyed a few happy years. My husband loved me more than himself. He could not leave me even for a moment. In time, I gave birth to two daughters by God's grace. Seeing the way my husband was attracted towards me, his first wife became very jealous. She started thinking of ways to get me out of the way. Secretly, she spent a lot of money on tantrics in order to turn my husband against me. What a surprising effect sorcery had! The person who could not leave me even for a moment wanted to leave me forever.

"Oh readers!" she proclaimed. "Listening to my unhappy story, you will also feel sad."[153] To tell "what happened later," the author turned from prose to poetry. But, as it is, *Rupjalal* is a work of fiction: the gallantry and sexual exploits of the hero, Prince Jalal, are narrated in relation to two heroines, Rupbanu and Hurbanu, both of whom he is compelled to marry. A recent analyst has interpreted the text as a "manifesto of Muslim women's sexual defiance and subordination" by an author hostile to polygamy.[154] But, as polygamy is depicted more favorably in the epic than in Faizunnessa's introduction, *Rupjalal*'s message is perhaps less clear-cut. The author's ire may be directed more at the "sorcery" and a polygamous husband's neglect of one wife or another than at the practice itself.

Perhaps best known in Urdu literature for documenting women's lives as part of a wider critique of social mores is Ismat Chughtai. She wrote many collections of short stories, as well as novels, novellas, plays, essays, and film scripts, into which her autobiography, *Kaghazi Hai Pairahan*, provides insight by offering biographical and historical context.[155] We may consider, for example, the following passage in which she detailed the time and place of writing and initial responses to her controversial short story "Lihaf" ("The Quilt," 1942), for which she was eventually charged with obscenity in 1944:

> When I wrote this story I was living with my brother. I wrote it at night and read it to my sister-in-law the next day. She didn't say, "This is a filthy story," but she did recognize the protagonist in the story. Then I read it to my fourteen-year-old cousin. She said, "What have you written? I don't understand any of it." I sent the story to the journal *Adab-e Latif*. The editor made no comments and published the work immediately. About the same time, Shahid Ahmad Dehlavi included it in the collection of my stories which he was about to publish. "Lihaf" was first published in 1942, a time when my friendship with Shahid had culminated in the decision to marry him. Shahid read the story and expressed his dislike for it after which we did have an argument. But the attacks on "Lihaf" hadn't reached Bombay as yet . . . So Shahid had little reason to be worried and we got married.[156]

Elsewhere, the author narrated her first engagement as a schoolgirl in Aligarh with the short story collection, *Angarey*, which when it was first

86   *The Sociology of Authorship*

published in 1932, launched the radical Progressive Writers Movement of which she was later a part.[157] That association with a major literary movement could provide motivation to write autobiography is indicated by the fact that several wives and daughters of participants in the Progressive Writers Movement also produced narratives—among them, Hameeda Akhtar Husain Raipuri, Shaukat Kaifi, Saleema Hashmi, and Shabana Azmi.[158]

More recently, autobiographies have been written by authors characterized—by others, if not always themselves—as feminist poets and novelists. From Pakistan alone, these include Ada Jafri (1924–2015), Kishwar Naheed (b. 1940), Fahmida Riaz (b. 1946), Azra Abbas (b. 1948), and Attiya Dawood (b. 1958).[159] Three more from India and Bangladesh are Nafees Bano Shama, Sufia Kamal, and Taslima Nasreen (b. 1962).[160] As in the case of *Kaghazi Hai Pairahan*, these women's narratives belong to a recognized subgenre of literary autobiography valued as sources for literary criticism and history, and as texts for their often distinct literary qualities.[161] Of particular interest is how these skilled writers often improvised with the life history form. Exemplifying this trend is radical Urdu poetess Azra Abbas in her *Mere Bachpan* (*My Childhood*, 1994). Her memoirs have been critiqued by some reviewers for the "very laconic, almost dry language" used to record her childhood experiences. But, as other analysts have noted, her style seems to have been chosen very purposefully to "create the effect of authenticity and immediacy."[162] Using simple words and short sentences, the narrative is crafted as a series of episodes—from the author's earliest memory to her first menstruation—projected as stories (*kahani*). Some are impressionistic, while others detail interactions that dramatize the injustice meted out to Pakistani girls on a daily basis in urban, middle-class families. Consider the following episode, in which Azra gathered in the kitchen with her sisters and two brothers before school:

> My mother fills bowls of milk and places them before my brothers and the expression in her eyes mirrors her faith that they are embarking on some great enterprise. Cups of tea are placed before us sisters. I remember how before this day I had fretted as I drank my tea, but that day I don't know what

came over me. As soon as my mother placed the bowls of milk before my
brothers I stood up and with one kick overturned both bowls.[163]

The style bestows a spontaneity on her outpourings that acts as partial
cover for the author's construction of herself as the rebel child consistent
with her adult persona as the rebel poet.

Politicians

A fourth occupational group among women who wrote autobiography in
Muslim South Asia was politicians. Notably, these authors have received
the most attention in international scholarship as local embodiments of a
global phenomenon of women politicians narrating their "rise" to public
office in the face of numerous obstacles.[164] In the South Asian context,
this process was often recounted as a "purdah to parliament" narrative—
with *two* autobiographies (by Shaista Ikramullah and Begam Qudsia
Aizaz Rasul) even employing that same title.[165] These texts begin by recounting an author's privileged childhood in the zenana, or women's quarters, before documenting exceptional political circumstances that inspired
them to enter public life. For many, political motivation came in the form
of India's struggle for independence. A lesser-known example is Begam
Inam Fatima Habibullah, who recorded at the end of her European diary
written in 1924 a conversation with her husband about purdah and politics. As she had moved about freely without a veil during their travels, he
suggested that she remain out of purdah on their return from London to
Lucknow. She agreed, but only after striking a deal: "I would like to come
to an agreement: if I am to lead a life outside purdah, then it will be spent
serving nation [*qaum*] and community [*millat*]."[166] Begam Habibullah
went on to be appointed Lucknow's first female municipal commissioner
before being elected to the United Provinces' legislative assembly on an
All-India Muslim League ticket in 1937. The following year, she became a
founding member of the women's wing of the Muslim League.[167]

Other Muslim women who wrote Urdu travelogues in the early decades of the twentieth century were key players in the Khilafat Movement. Notable examples were Nishatunnisa Begam Hasrat Mohani
(d. 1937), Rahil Begam Sherwani (1894–1982), and Begam Sarbuland

Jang.[168] Begam Sarbuland Jang's *Dunya 'Aurat ki Nazar Mein* (*The World as Seen by a Woman*, 1936) points to how interactions with other Muslim women during a journey to the Middle East in 1909–10 forged her understandings of pan-Islamism.[169] More explicit about women's unique contributions to Muslim politics were Shaista Suhrawardy Ikramullah, Jahan Ara Shahnawaz, and Salma Tasadduq Husain, all three of whom wrote about the Pakistan Movement in the 1930s and 1940s.[170] A number of women who, in contrast, conceived of themselves as "nationalist Muslims," placed Gandhi and other Congress leaders at the center of their narratives. We may think here of Gandhi's close associate and fellow *brahmachari* Raihana Tyabji and her elder sister, Shareefah Hamid Ali; President Zakir Hussain's daughter, Sayyida Khurshid Alam; and Congress politicians Begam Qudsia Aizaz Rasul, Anis Kidwai, and Masuma Begam.[171] As an illustration, let us consider Raihana Tyabji's evocative account of her first meeting with Gandhi at an elegant party in Bombay in 1915: "I caught a glimpse of him in the midst of silks and brocades, frills and sparkling jewels. He was dressed in a coarse khadi dhoti and looked like a small-time tailor who'd wandered in by mistake. I lost my heart to him. He became my father, my mother, my girlfriend, my boyfriend, my daughter, my son, my teacher, my guru."[172]

Once Independence came in 1947, many of these same women found their way into the new parliaments in India and Pakistan. Begam Ikramullah and Begam Shahnawaz, for instance, acted as the two female representatives in Pakistan's first constituent assembly, while Begam Aizaz Rasul was present in India's first constituent assembly for Nehru's famous "Tryst with Destiny" speech.[173] Masuma Begam, on the other hand, did not run for office until 1952, when she contested state elections in the constituency encompassing Hyderabad's old city. During her second of two terms in office, she was appointed deputy leader of the Andhra Pradesh Congress Legislature Party and, subsequently in 1960, Andhra Pradesh's first woman cabinet minister.[174] In Bangladesh too, female politicians used autobiography to assert their political credentials and ideologies, though more often in opposition to the state. A key example is Jahanara Imam, known as Shaheed Janani, or "Mother of the Martyrs," who produced a number of autobiographical texts focusing on the 1971 conflict and her subsequent attempts to bring those who had committed war crimes to justice.[175] Similarly, both Abida Sultaan and Salma Ahmed attributed their "entry into politics" in Pakistan in the 1960s—as part of the Combined Opposition Parties—to a desire to counter Ayub Khan's imposition of martial law, though Salma Ahmed did later enter parliament on a Muslim League ticket at the height of the Zia-ul Haq era in 1985.[176] Of course, the best-known Pakistani parliamentarian to write her autobiography must be Benazir Bhutto (1953–2007). In *Daughter of the East* (1988), she elaborated, in a reversal of the dominant leitmotif, how she donned the veil in order to become the first female prime minister in the Muslim world.[177]

Performers

A fifth subset of authors was made up of performers of some sort: actresses or musicians or radio artistes. One of these, Begum Khurshid Mirza, warrants sustained analysis in chapter 4 in light of the four iterations available of her autobiography. But perhaps the best-known internationally is Zohra Segal, previously mentioned in the context of her aristocratic background, European education, and cross-religious marriage. As indicated in the introduction, she began her career in the 1930s as a dancer and teacher with the famous Uday Shankar Ballet Company—then associated with new styles of Indian modern dance—before starting to act with the leftist Indian People's Theatre Association (IPTA) in the 1940s. From the 1960s, she then starred in innumerable Hindi and English-language films, as well as in television and radio series, perhaps the most famous outside India being the British film *Bhaji on the Beach* (1992).[178] Also closely involved with IPTA before she took to the "silver screen" in the 1970s was Shaukat Kaifi. Her autobiography, *Yad ki Rahguzar* (*Memory Lane*, 2006), thus recounts not only the "love story" of her long marriage to renowned poet Kaifi Azmi, but also a performing career that spanned the early 1940s to the late 1980s.[179] Another who was drawn to the stage by "theatre activism" was Nilambur Ayisha. In 1953, her first play was Keralan playwright A. K. Ayamu's *Ijju Nalloru Manushyan Aavan Nokku*, which focused on social issues plaguing the Muslim community. From that beginning, her autobiography, *Jeevitathinte Arangu* (*The Theatre of*

90   *The Sociology of Authorship*

Life, 2005), documented a life dedicated to theater, though she also made more than fifty movies, primarily in Malayalam.[180]

A fifth example relevant here is the aforementioned Malka Pukhraj. Trained by various well-known *ustads* in music and dance, she was appointed singer at the court of the Maharaja of Jammu and Kashmir, Hari Singh, at the age of just nine. After nine years in his service, she moved to Lahore, where she continued to give private and radio performances, eventually becoming one of South Asia's most popular and celebrated singers of the classical and folk genres.[181] Also featured on radio, though in a rather different capacity, was Saeeda Bano Ahmed. As noted already, she was born and raised in princely Bhopal with close links to the ruling begam's court before completing her education in Lucknow. She was perhaps best known, however, as the first woman newsreader on All India Radio. In *Dagar se Hat Kar*, she recounted how she came to this job in 1947 after moving from Lucknow to Delhi with only her youngest son in tow to live the life of a "single individual."[182] Reflected in this description was her separation from her husband, Abbas Raza, after a stormy marriage described with great forthrightness in her autobiography.[183] That her pioneering profession enabled a less orthodox lifestyle, too, is evident from her equally candid account of a second significant relationship: a passionate extramarital affair with lawyer Nuruddin Khan begun shortly after Independence and lasting nearly twenty-seven years. As she wrote: "Today when I write this, it seems childish. But, at that time, to see his gaze, to meet him for a few minutes was a matter of life and death . . . Like the travelers of the last night, we played this youthful game until the age of 60, 65 and even 70. What strange proclivities are engendered by prohibition."[184] As an educated and financially independent woman in a new India, Saeeda Bano must have felt empowered not only to pursue this proscribed relationship, but also to write about it.

Defying society's censure in other ways was another woman on the radio, but in East Pakistan, namely, Jobeda Khanam. Her educational career has been documented already in some detail. In *Jiban Khatar Pataguli*, she also recorded how, upon arriving in Dhaka in 1947 shortly after Partition, she was picked up by the local radio station for her experience of having "[taken] part in a few radio programmes in Calcutta" before Independence.[185] With all the "Hindu" artists and technicians having left for India, the radio was desperate for new talent. But, as she explained, the profession was not an easy one for women in the conservative environs of 1940s Dhaka:

> There was danger for women. At that time, local people were spreading propaganda about Muslim women. They said that Muslim women would have to go behind the purdah. Waywardness would not be tolerated. Women had to travel in curtained rickshaws. If women travelled in open rickshaws, people would throw stones at them. The girls came to the radio office in horse carts. One had to listen to many [rude] comments. And that was not the end of it. One day, a group of people attacked the horse cart. Local people had to come and save them.[186]

As a protest to this conservativism, Jobeda wrote a "dance drama" as a fundraiser for the local branch of the All Pakistan Women's Association (APWA). It was based on the Hindi film *Pukar* (1939)—about the Mughal emperor Jahangir and his wife Nurjahan, falsely accused of killing her husband during a hunt. Jobeda also performed in this production. As she wrote with some pride: "I had never acted on a stage. I only tried it after becoming a mother to my children. My children came to see their mother perform."[187] The play's success encouraged her and a friend to open a dance and music school for local children that also faced severe opposition: "People protested. The English newspaper, *Morning News*, criticized our work very strongly. The paper asked us to stop activities that were contrary to Islamic culture. We told them that we wanted to *create* Islamic culture."[188]

Exceptional Lives

In terms of occupation, then, most Muslim women who produced autobiographical writings in the modern period and even before belonged to one (or more) of five main groupings: courtly women, educationalists, writers, politicians, or performers. A few others were difficult to categorize, but still had unusual or high-profile jobs. Representative of these "others" was Jowshan Ara Rahman (b. 1936), who spent seventeen years, from 1979 to her retirement in 1996, in the program planning department

92   *The Sociology of Authorship*

for UNICEF in Bangladesh.[189] Another was Fatima Shah (1914–2002), who, though trained as a doctor at Lady Hardinge Medical College in Delhi, was best known for establishing the Pakistan Association of the Blind in 1960, an organization of which she remained president until 1984.[190] What we may say of each of these authors is that in a context where a minority of women worked outside the home and even fewer were employed in the professions, politics, or the performing arts, they were distinguished by their occupations. As before, there were a few exceptions—for instance, two prostitutes separated by more than a century, Piro and Nalini Jameela, were perhaps representative of a broader subset of working women. But even they had career trajectories that took them beyond the norm: Piro as companion to a Sikh guru, Gulab Das, and Nalini Jameela as an activist with the organization Jwalamukhi.[191] A permanent record of one's life, or at least part of it, could thus be justified by occupational achievements that gave these women a sense of renown—of having a special story to relate—at a local, if not a national level.

CONCLUSION: AUTHORS, TIME, AND MOTIVATION

This study is limited to the autobiographical writings of South Asian Muslim women. Yet within that group, we may still start to build up a picture of *who writes*. Literacy, of course, is key when dealing with a textual tradition, but, as we have seen, not all women who *can* write *will* write autobiographically—and, furthermore, some who cannot will. Still, the majority of authors from the sixteenth century into the twenty-first century may be characterized as elite: upper or middle class, sharif of the old sort or the new. Central to the reformist project of sharif redefinition from the late nineteenth century, and the colonial project too, was female education—so it is perhaps of no surprise that these autobiographical authors were, indeed, educated. Yet the *struggle* that many underwent in order to guarantee that education and the *extent* to which they were educated—often to the degree level and beyond in the twentieth century—distinguish them from the merely literate. In most cases, their education also enabled them to pursue an occupation when few women and even fewer elite Muslim women did: at a princely court if they were so placed, but otherwise (or sometimes as well) as educationalists, writers, politicians, and performers. In sixteenth-century Florence, Benvenuto Cellini wrote that it was the duty of all men "who have done anything of excellence" to write their life stories.[192] These South Asian Muslim women, too, had exceptional life stories to tell within the specific historical and cultural context in which they wrote.

We may take this further by relating *who* writes to *when* and *why*. I have underlined that most Muslim women who produced autobiographical writings into the twenty-first century—and even then—belonged to South Asia's nobility, aristocracy, or respectable middle classes. In general, these class locations would have offered the domestic help and thus the time necessary for women to dabble in self-reflection.[193] It also meant that, with few exceptions, authors were able to access enough education to garner the intellectual skills necessary to write autobiography. In other words, they did not just know how to read and write, but they also possessed the ability to analyze their own experiences and construct them into a coherent narrative, often representing an individual life. Though I have referred to university education in the previous paragraph, I mean no facile identification here of learning with a degree, not least because this option was simply unavailable to the earliest in this study. In those times, South Asian Muslim women may have acquired education in other ways—perhaps through private reading or travel. But we may still conjecture—as Elaine McKay does of seventeenth-century England—that few autobiographical writings from "more illiterate levels of society" are out there just waiting to be found.[194] Only coauthorship has made these stories more available in very recent times.

More significant in explaining why these Muslim women wrote seems to be the redefinition of sharif status from the late nineteenth century. As indicated already, the simple distinction between nobles and commoners that had defined South Asian Muslim society before 1857 was being replaced by a new tripartite division of old nobility, ashraf, and ajlaf.[195] Sharif status was claimed from the earlier service gentry by a new middle class defined by Hamza Alavi as a "salariat": an auxiliary class of bureaucrats, military officers, lawyers, teachers, and traders that owed its existence to colonial education and economy.[196] Autobiography offered the perfect vehicle for the new middle classes to articulate their claims to

94   *The Sociology of Authorship*

nobility in opposition to the "decadent" aristocracy above and the "ignorant" commoners below. As the rearticulation of sharif patriarchy through family reform was so central to this process, it should be no surprise that ashraf women were at the heart of this exercise, producing more autobiographical writings than any other socioeconomic group.[197] In autobiography, ashraf women found a means of enacting the larger sharif project of self-creation by using descriptions of lineage, lifestyle, and behavior—tied to the "private" sphere of the family and the home—to validate their own social and moral standing.

Eager to resuscitate their reputations, nobles and aristocrats also appropriated autobiography to counter colonial and Muslim discourses that equated them with cruelty, debauchery, decadence, and decline.[198] Indian princes in particular faced a crisis of legitimacy in the high colonial period. The Queen's Proclamation of 1858 may have guaranteed their continuation as a social and political order, but as a group they still needed to justify their existence—not only to themselves and their fellow rulers but also to the British as paramount power and, increasingly, their own subjects. With "tangible power"—the ability to make war and peace—on the wane, princes had to find ways to boost their "symbolic power" instead. A court's patronage of literary production had always been vital to the "maintenance of symbolic legitimacy" in precolonial South Asia, but, according to Daniel Majchrowicz, it became even more important in this uncertain colonial context. He points to how princes utilized travel literatures especially, also touched upon here, to depict themselves as "modern, advanced and progressive."[199] This observation, I would argue, extends to other forms of autobiographical writing as well, which the old nobility employed to restore their beleaguered reputations. For their women especially, autobiography offered a context in which they could assert their transformation from the "corrupt begams" of old to the new "*sharif bibis*" by relegating aristocratic culture to the realm of nostalgic memory.[200]

These points are underscored by considering specific motivations to write. We have seen that the desire to recount one's participation in the nationalist movement or, indeed, the emergent nation, was a motivating factor for some Muslim women to write autobiography. For others, a more definably Muslim impulse could be seen in their intention to chronicle history in tandem with their lives or to honor autobiography's didactic purpose in the Islamic tradition by treating life as lesson—often to promote a reformed Islam of one sort or another or, later, a more explicitly feminist vision. Still others found in autobiography an outlet for literary creativity or performance. As elsewhere, autobiography also offered a means of recording one's thoughts and actions to attain a kind of "immortality on earth."[201] As Saliha Abid Hussain wrote in the introduction to her *Silsila-i-Roz o Shab*: "What I hope to achieve is making my name known to others."[202] This aim was especially apt, as in most cases these authors were pioneers: among them were some of the first Muslim girls to go to school, to write in periodicals, to travel abroad, to leave purdah, to get a teaching job, to be a novelist, to train as a doctor, to participate in politics, to star in a film, to be elected to public office. We may thus conclude that doing something momentous was, above all, the motivation to write autobiography—though what was deemed momentous was, at least in part, contingent on gender, religion, and historical moment.

CHAPTER THREE

THE AUTOBIOGRAPHICAL MAP

INTRODUCTION: A ROOM OF ONE'S OWN?

Missing from the triad of queries at the end of the previous chapter is an equally important fourth question: *where*? This query, I assert, warrants a separate chapter, on the basis that there are many ways in which to apply it to Muslim women's autobiographical writing. At the most basic level, it can refer to the actual space in which an author crafts her life story. Virginia Woolf famously asserted that to write fiction, a woman needed "a room of one's own."[1] It is difficult to know, in physical terms, to what extent this ideal was achieved by Muslim women writing auto-biography, if not fiction, in South Asia. Only occasionally will an author offer a glimpse into the specific space in which she crafts her life story— perhaps in a preface (*dibache* in Urdu) or at a reflective moment in the text in which she relates the narrating "I" to the one narrated.[2] Raihana Tyabji tells her readers in the introduction to *The Heart of a Gopi* that in 1926 she sat down at her desk—presumably in her own room at her parents' house, where she lived in Baroda, though we cannot be sure— "with sheets of foolscap and poised pen."[3] Safia Jabir Ali, on the other hand, chose a *takht*, a kind of sofa, in her farmhouse in Chembur, outside Bombay, on which to sit while writing her memoirs in 1942. Though her husband was away in Bombay and her son at school, the space was still shared: Mahmud was "churning the butter," and the other servants were

97

"busy about their work."[4] Hameeda Akhtar Husain Raipuri, too, reported sitting on a divan with "a few registers and a dozen pens," but in a house empty after her husband's death in 1992.[5] Though at different times and stages of life, each of these Muslim women was able to find a space, if not a whole room, in which to write, primarily because—as Woolf insisted and the previous chapter confirmed—they had the means.

A second approach would be to consider where Muslim women writing autobiography were located in geographical terms. Those scholars who have analyzed personal narratives in other times and contexts have often focused on where authors were based when they *began* their endeavors. They draw out this information on the assumption that there must have been something in that situation or environment that prompted an author to set down his or her life in print—in other words, motivation.[6] Motivation continues to be of interest here, but only alongside a second emphasis: how context relates to construction. In other words, this chapter asks how geographical, linguistic, and historical locations shaped the stories that South Asian Muslim women wrote about their lives. Inherent in this aim, and in fact in this project as a whole, is an assumption that autobiography represents *a* story—not *the* story—about a self. As Ken Plummer asserts, "The meanings of stories are never fixed but emerge out of a ceaselessly changing stream of interaction between producers and readers in shifting contexts. They may, of course, become habitualised and stable; but always and everywhere the meanings of stories shift and sway in the contexts to which they are linked."[7] The specificities of cultural milieu can thus provide some understanding of why an autobiographical narrative was not only *created* but also *crafted* in a particular way. Offering a lead is C. M. Naim in his analysis of eighteenth-century Mughal poet Mir Muhammad Taqi's *Zikr-i-Mir*. Here, Naim draws out how Mir's cultural inheritance, social expectations, and personal agendas all came together to shape his autobiography's tone and content.[8]

This chapter is thus divided into three main sections, each of which addresses autobiography's geography in a different way. In the first, I map authors in *regional*, *local*, and *religious* terms in an attempt to understand how specific locations may have stimulated autobiographical production. Distinguishing this effort is an attempt to consider where authors were located not just at the time of writing or publication but also originally, generally, or at other decisive moments in their lives. This approach seems especially suited to modern South Asia, where mobility was facilitated by a multitude of factors, many of which were beyond an author's control. Even Muslim women, often imagined to be confined within the four walls of the home, experienced various cultures of travel, colonial migrancy, and forced migration—not least Partition, which led to the displacement of more than 14 million people in 1947 alone.[9] The second section then turns to autobiography's *linguistic* geography for what it reveals about changing readerships and forms of expression. In what ways does an author's choice of language point to intended or assumed audiences at different places and times? And can we use language to identify other cultural specificities that shaped autobiographical expression? Readerships are addressed again in the third section, but with a more particular aim of identifying how *real and imagined audiences* shaped the way in which a life was written. Did Muslim women direct their autobiographical narratives at specific individuals or groups? Was it a gendered audience and thus a gendered writing as well? How did an awareness of an audience's religiously-informed cultural identities or, after Partition, national affiliations structure content and style? I conclude by considering the model of performance as a theoretical frame.

REGION, LOCALITY, AND SECT

As Sir Cyril Radcliffe discovered to India's peril in 1947, no line can be drawn on a map to neatly demarcate South Asia's Muslims from the Hindu majority. Even with Partition's disruptive effects on demography, Muslims continue to be distributed very unevenly across the Indian subcontinent. Nevertheless, it is possible to identify areas or locales in the northwest and east, but also in the north, center, and south, where there were—and usually still are—concentrations of Muslim-majority or substantial Muslim-minority populations. Most significant in terms of regional Muslim populations are those provinces now encompassed within Pakistan and Bangladesh, but certainly before 1947 and even now, that did not indicate homogeneity on either side of the border. In undivided Bengal, for instance, two-thirds of the population in the eastern divisions of Rajshahi, Dhaka, and Chittagong were Muslims, but even in Burdwan (now in west Bengal), one in seven residents proclaimed Islam. Furthermore, we should not overlook major pockets of Muslims elsewhere in the Indian subcontinent. Southern India, for instance, is often neglected as a site for Muslim history, and yet Muslims represented as many as one in four people in Malabar's western coastal districts in 1931. Similarly, central India's Muslim population was estimated at less than 5 percent in the same census, but the figure was as high as 54 percent in the nawab of Bhopal's capital city—an urban trend reproduced in other Muslim-led princely states as well. Other large conurbations at the heart of the colonial enterprise—Bombay, Delhi, Madras, and Calcutta—also boasted substantial Muslim minorities.[10] When I began this research, I expected that the autobiographical map formed when one located Muslim female authors in geographical terms would mimic this uneven but widespread distribution of Muslim populations.

But I soon found there to be gaps: areas where there are substantial Muslim populations, but few or no Muslim women's autobiographies. This trend emerged most clearly with reference to Muslim-majority localities in Delhi. Encouraged by Patricia Jeffery's influential sociological study, *Frogs in a Well*, I projected that Nizamuddin Dargah might provide an entry point for recovering Muslim women's autobiographical writings from private collections. After all, the *pirzada* women associated with this important Sufi shrine not only were literate but also played an important socioreligious function as wives and daughters to the shrine's custodians.[11] With the generous assistance of the *sajjada nashin*'s own sister, I thus negotiated access to women's homes and lives over many months—but no autobiographical writings by them or their foremothers came to light.[12] At the same time, I found myself returning again and again to Jamia Nagar—the neighborhood surrounding Delhi's national Muslim university, Jamia Millia Islamia—to meet authors or gather autobiographical materials from family collections.[13] Clearly, the sociocultural characteristics of these two Muslim localities are key: while Jamia Nagar nourishes an important educational enterprise, Nizamuddin remains focused on the shrine's business. A significant clue was in the *sajjada nashin*'s own response to my academic project. Though he responded

more than courteously to my request for help (and even offered his bless-
ings), on consecutive visits he kept offering me material on Islam, Sufism,
or the *dargah* itself. He simply could not understand why I would be interested in the life stories of his female relatives when I could be reading
some "good" Islamic literature.[14]

Also complicating autobiography's geography were regional imbalances. Pakistan has experienced its own mini memoir boom in recent
years, in part fueled by the publishing interests of Oxford University
Press's managing editor in Karachi, Ameena Saiyid. She has been responsible for commissioning new memoirs by men and women alike, while
also reissuing many previously published titles—some of which date back
to the nineteenth century.[15] Many Pakistani autobiographies were written by women who began their lives (and life stories) elsewhere in South
Asia before Partition transformed them into *mohajirs*, or migrants, most
often to Karachi in Sindh, though also to Lahore. Jahanara Habibullah,
for instance, dedicated twelve of her thirteen chapters in *Remembrance
of Days Past* (2001) to her early years in the princely state of Rampur
in north India, even though she spent the latter half of her life in independent Pakistan.[16] At the same time, Pakistan's provinces—especially
Punjab, but also Sindh and Khyber Pakhtunkhwa—have nurtured their
own female autobiographers before and after 1947. As an early example
from west Punjab, we may recall how Piro used her lyric autobiographical episode, composed sometime in the second quarter of the nineteenth
century, to narrate her move from a brothel in Lahore to her Sikh guru's
dera, or abode, at Chathianwala.[17] Later authors rooted their narratives
in particular cities and villages—from Baghanpura, Rawalpindi, Wah,
Bhera, and Meerwala in Punjab to Larkana, Hyderabad, and Kharjal in
Sindh—while tracing family, tribal, or clan lineages as far back as the
eleventh century.[18]

But for all this proliferation in the northwest, autobiographical writings by Muslim women were still far more abundant in the original
Pakistan's eastern wing. In fact, Bangladesh proved to be a gold mine of
resources for this project. By the end of a research trip in 2006, I had collected so many books and photocopies—from Dhaka University library,
bookstores, and personal collections—that I actually had to buy a new

102   *The Autobiographical Map*

suitcase (and, later, shares in Air India) to transport them all.[19] An analysis of the twenty-five authors who contributed to the autobiographical anthology *Kaler Samukh Bhela* (1988) gives a sense of the geographical spread within Bengal itself. Reflecting undivided Bengal's integrated religious map, they came from all four corners of the province: most often a village or district town, but sometimes the important centers of Dhaka or Calcutta. Authors were thus born and raised in both rural and urban environments in east and west (and north and south) Bengal, though many ended up living and working in Dhaka city for reasons of education, marriage, or resettlement following Partition.[20] This geographical concentration at the time of writing points to the "cultural leadership" offered by a capital city.[21] Nevertheless, that authors had roots throughout the province suggests that there is something about Bengal that has stimulated autobiographical production, not just by Muslim women but by women in general. After all, the first full-length Bengali autobiography— Rassundari Debi's *Amar Jiban* (1876)—was written by a woman, as were many other well-known autobiographical texts by Bengali Hindus in the twentieth century.[22] I could point to Bengal's flourishing literary tradition or longer colonial history or specific socioeconomic profile among Muslims as factors. Whatever the cause, the imbalance between the northwest and the east suggests a greater valuing of women's voices in the latter.

Another imbalance that complicates the autobiographical map is the significant number of Muslim female authors from or connected to India's princely states. I made reference in the previous chapter to the royal status of many authors, highlighting the role played by nawab begams from Bhopal, Pataudi, Janjira, and Rampur in pioneering autobiographical writing. Equally notable in my sample are the numbers of *other* Muslim women who were raised or later lived in princely states. In its analysis of fathers' employment patterns, chapter 2 pointed out how many authors were born and raised in princely Hyderabad, Bhopal, Baroda, or Jodhpur. Another example is Sughra Mehdi, who used travel writing to reflect back on her Bhopali childhood.[23] Other authors grew up in princely Jammu and Kashmir—though, since Independence, younger women have also written about their lives in this conflict-ridden state.[24] A second set of authors, including Sughra Humayun Mirza, Hameeda

Akhtar Husain Raipuri, and Begam Sarbuland Jang, were married to men employed in princely states, and thus spent part of their adult lives there.[25] They may be compared favorably with Qaisari Begam, the Fyzee sisters, and Ismat Chughtai, all of whom regularly visited or worked in Hyderabad, Bhopal, Baroda, Rampur, Janjira, and Jaora.[26] Specific explanations could be offered for individual states: the inspiration offered by Bhopal's ruling begams to their female subjects or, as Razak Khan has argued for Rampur, the usefulness of memoir as a means of articulating lineage within a small court.[27] But I would argue more generally that the preservation—or even further institutionalization—of elite zenana cultures in many princely states gave women a unique space to articulate the self, which was then translated into written form in autobiographical writing.[28] No doubt the disappearance of the princely state system after Independence also inspired many later authors to commit their "memories of a world gone by" to paper.[29]

The references to Hyderabad in the previous paragraph also point to local imbalances within south India. Clearly, Hyderabad state produced its goodly share of Muslim female autobiographers, as did certain other southern Muslim enclaves. Rahmathunnisa Begam, for instance, was introduced in the previous chapter for her long educational career in Madras, a city in which Zakira Ghouse also sometimes lived and worked.[30] Iqbalunnisa Hussain, on the other hand, was born, raised, married, and lived most of her life in Bangalore in the princely state of Mysore, though she had moved to the United Kingdom by the time of her death in 1954.[31] As indicated in chapter 2, Muslim women from Kerala also produced some autobiographical writings, but they tend to be very few in number and very recent.[32] According to my sample, Keralan Muslims are thus underrepresented, even within south India. In part, this gap could be attributed to their socioeconomic profile. Scholarly analyses of the 1921 Mappila Rebellion have made clear that most Malabar Muslims belonged to a struggling peasantry in the colonial period—not a group inclined to autobiographical production.[33] This point is underscored by actress Nilambur Ayisha's description of her own family, from Malappuram district, as "rich" with "lots of servants and an elephant"—in other words, a class apart from many of her Malabari coreligionists who, unlike

104   *The Autobiographical Map*

her, do not appear to have produced memoirs.[34] Udaya Kumar, in his important article on personal narratives from Kerala—in which there are no references, significantly, to Muslim authors—notes how the autobiographical act was linked for Brahmin women especially to a "difficult" but "desired" entry into the "public realm."[35] He offers the example of novelist Lalitambika Antarjanam, who, in *Atmakathayku Oru Amukham* (*An Introduction to [My] Autobiography*, 1979), recounted her early experiences of "stepping into the world without the protection of a veil or a shielding umbrella."[36] This transformative passage could have been experienced by only the smallest numbers of Keralan Muslim women, whether elite or not.

Local imbalances also exist within north India. Defying its size to emerge as an autobiographical nexus was the small university town of Aligarh, so associated with Islamic modernism. I noted in chapter 2 that many authors were educated at the girls' school established there by Shaikh and Begam Abdullah in 1906. A distinctive feature of this school was the supervisory role played by Begam Abdullah, who, in effect, acted as "mother" (or *ala bi*) to all pupils, and therefore made them "sisters" (*apa*) to one another.[37] Writer Ismat Chughtai was thus not actually related to the Abdullahs' daughter Begum Khurshid Mirza, and yet she was still referred to in her autobiography in a familial way as "Ismat Apa" in honor of their shared time at school.[38] Other women in this sample, including Zehra Fyzee, Sultan Jahan Begam of Bhopal, Nazli Begam of Janjira, and Nazr Sajjad Hyder, visited Aligarh on a regular basis for events connected with the girls' school, including art exhibitions or meetings of the Anjuman-i-Khawatin-i-Islam (All-India Muslim Ladies' Conference) established here in 1914.[39] On these occasions, they met the wives and daughters of the powerful group of men who acted as MA-O College trustees—among them, the husband and father of travel writers Begam Sarbuland Jang and Rahil Begam Sherwani.[40] Later, Qamar Azad Hashmi also found herself in Aligarh after her husband's business began supplying furniture to the university shortly after Partition.[41] Another set of authors, including Shamla Mufti, Sughra Mehdi, and Hamida Saiduzzafar, studied or worked at Aligarh Muslim University from the 1950s.[42] Aligarh's prominence in the life stories of Muslim female authors, particularly as the node of a fictive family network, thus reinforces the links between women, reformism, and autobiography established in chapter 2.

Another imbalance worth noting relates to autobiography's religious geography. I refer specifically to the surprising number of texts produced by Muslim women from Islam's minority sects. As specialists will know, by far the majority of South Asian Muslims belong to Islam's Sunni majority, but Shias are represented in various forms, including the Twelver majority and Ismaili minority.[43] Representing Twelver Shias in my sample are women such as Jahanara Habibullah and Mehrunissa Khan, who came from particular cities in north India associated with Shia dynasties—especially Lucknow and Rampur.[44] Others, like Nazr Sajjad Hyder, Bibi Ashraf, and Saliha Abid Hussain, emerged from Shia enclaves in Punjab or the United Provinces.[45] Jahanara Imam, on the other hand, represented the small Shia community in Bangladesh's urban centers.[46] In contrast, most authors from Bombay belonged to the Sulaimani Bohra branch of Ismaili Muslims. The prominent Tyabji clan that produced so many female writers (see chapter 5) was at the forefront of this community—though two authors, Nazli Fyzee and Shareefah Hamid Ali, were married outside the clan to Sunni Muslims.[47] Another author from Bombay, Ishvani, identified herself in *The Brocaded Sari* (1946) as a Khoja Muslim whose family had, under her grandfather's instigation, "cut loose" from the Nizari Ismailis led by the Aga Khan to become Ithna Asheri Shias—much to the Aga Khani's displeasure.[48] Also hailing from Bombay's Khoja community was educationalist and activist Kulsum Sayani, whose participation in multilingual journalism is discussed in more detail below.[49]

We can only conjecture as to why women from these minority sects were so prominent among Muslims who wrote autobiography. Clearly, their urbanity, education, and wealth set them apart, but we may refer back to a point made in the introduction: the way in which autobiography as genre has been used by religiously marginalized groups in South Asia, including converts and dalits, as a means to "talk back."[50] To draw a parallel between these elite Muslim authors and less privileged groups may seem perverse. But we should not underestimate the liminality of, for instance, Ismaili Muslims within South Asia's complex religious landscape

106   *The Autobiographical Map*

in the high colonial period. As evidence, we may consider an incident recorded in Raihana Tyabji's *Suniye Kakasahib* (*Listen Kakasahib*, 1954) in connection with her father. Apparently, having found the Jama Masjid in Baroda to be in a poor state of repair, Abbas Tyabji decided to collect donations, in part from the Muslim community and in part by securing a grant from the maharaja, for it to be renovated, perhaps sometime in the 1890s. And yet, when the mosque was renewed, he was excluded from entry. As Raihana recorded: "On the first Friday after the inauguration of the mosque, when *babajan* [father] together with some Sulamaini Bohras went to offer *namaz*, the Sunnis said, 'You cannot offer namaz here. You are not Muslims.' They drove them out with lathis [sticks]."[51] Even as Abbas asserted his Islamic credentials with a great act of piety, so he and his community were denied a place in the Muslim fold. Raihana's disgust at her father's treatment at the hands of "Sunnis" at the mosque representing organized and dominant forms of Islam is plain from how she articulated her response to this incident in her autobiography: "What shameful behavior to make such distinctions in the House of God!"[52]

Still, the many examples from Bombay in the previous paragraphs suggest the relative importance of this cosmopolitan city to a history of Muslim women's autobiographical writing. A number of other authors were not native to the city, but later found a home here. Associated with the lively film scene in particular were actresses Zohra Segal, Shaukat Kaifi, and Sultana Jafri and writer Ismat Chughtai. That Shaukat Kaifi wrote at length about the other three in her colorful evocation of life in Bombay from the late 1940s onward suggests how this city, too, acted as a node in a fictive network linking Muslim female authors.[53] Still more significant in these terms was India's national capital. Delhi's cultural vibrancy is reflected in the large numbers of women in this sample who lived and wrote there, especially in more recent times.[54] Even Attiya Dawood, though a Pakistani citizen, wrote her autobiography in Delhi while staying at Sanskriti Kendra Residency.[55] The importance of urbanism as a factor in facilitating autobiographical production—already noted with reference to Dhaka—is thus underlined. And yet authors representing city populations should not be considered undifferentiated, nor entirely separate from their rural environs. Consider, for example, Akhtar

Imam, who wrote about the distinction between refined *"khosbas"* and rustic *"kuttis"* in Dhaka during her childhood in the 1920s and 1930s: "Our neighbours were originally from Dhaka . . . According to them, Dhaka belonged to them as a birthright. It seemed as if we were entirely unwelcome. We were the rustics who had just come to Dhaka . . . We had very different kinds of social and cultural practices. We had different food habits and different clothing."[56] Mapping authors by region, locality, and sect may thus offer clues as to why Muslim women wrote (or not) about their lives, but as often as not there may be other political or personal motivations revealed by audience. To provide further insight, let us turn in the next section to autobiography's linguistic geography.

LANGUAGE, AUDIENCE, AND EXPRESSION

Throughout this project, I faced the expectation—sometimes from myself, but often from others—that the bulk of my materials would be in the Urdu language. This assumption reflects language politics in colonial South Asia by which Urdu became an integral aspect of community construction and identity formation among Muslims.[57] In the nineteenth century, Urdu had made the transition from a "highly developed language of poetry" to a "modern prose language" used by Hindus, Muslims, and Sikhs alike for communicating, in Barbara Metcalf's words, "new values and images of the person and society."[58] But by the early twentieth century, Urdu was coming to be defined as a separate language from that of Hindi with its own "script, history, literary canon and cultural orientation."[59] The adoption of Urdu as the national language of Pakistan, a country formed on the basis of its population's religion, meant that Partition only exacerbated the situation. For those born after 1947—whether in India or Pakistan—Urdu was unequivocally the language of Muslims.[60] But to privilege Urdu in this analysis would be to ignore the historical complexities of South Asia's multilingual environment: the still nebulous line between Hindi and Urdu in north Indian literary cultures in the late nineteenth and early twentieth centuries, or the dramatic effects that post-Partition language politics have had on South Asia's literary landscapes. After all, South Asian Muslims, male and female, clearly spoke and wrote in other languages too—and those languages, when used

108   *The Autobiographical Map*

to autobiographical ends, may offer useful insight into changing reader-ships and forms of expression. So, when and where did Muslim women compose and publish their life stories in different languages or registers? And what do these choices and linguistic nuances tell us about audience, motivation, and construction especially?

Many of the texts included in this study were composed initially in regional languages—most often Bengali, though also Sindhi, Kashmiri, Malayalam, and Punjabi—that would have made them fairly inaccessible to those outside that linguistic community. These language choices may have been as much about practical concerns—one's ease with a spoken or written language—as any particular awareness of regional audience. For example, it is perhaps not surprising that Ghulam Fatima Shaikh, described as only "semi-literate," originally produced *Footprints in Time* in her native Sindhi—though, ultimately, her memoirs were published in English translation in the hope of reaching a wider readership.[61] In other cases, the use of a regional language seemed more purposeful, reflecting political motivations that, in their distinct historical contexts, are reveal-ing of audience. A case in point is that of educationalist Shamla Mufti, who originally wrote her autobiography in the Kashmiri language in the 1990s, before it was also translated into Urdu. Hafsa Kanjwal argues that Shamla Mufti, against a backdrop of political instability and armed con-flict, used Kashmiri to reawaken a sense of regional identity in a younger generation by alerting them to an earlier, more peaceful history.[62] The use of Bengali by almost all of the authors from Bangladesh and west Bengal—in sharp contrast to a significant number of Urdu- and English-language texts from Pakistan and other parts of India—suggests, in turn, how a regional audience could be cast through linguistic reassertion. No wonder that so many Bangladeshi women, writing in Bengali, recalled their specific experiences of participating in the Language Movement in Pakistan's east wing in 1952.[63]

To explore the nuances of this position, it is worth returning to Jobeda Khanam's *Jiban Khatar Pataguli*, from which I have quoted already in pre-vious chapters. For her, attempts by the "central government" to enforce Urdu as Pakistan's national language from 1948 had the intention "to make us speechless."[64] A decade later, the martial-law government renewed West Pakistan's program of cultural assimilation by establishing the Bureau of National Reconstruction. Unaware of its "hidden agendas," Jobeda accepted a post as deputy director, with "responsibility for developing literature and culture" in East Pakistan. Her main aim, as she saw it, was to "encourage writers and develop new writers" to counter the dominance of Indian authors in Bengali. As she explained:

> Readers in East Pakistan were not very familiar with the writings of East Pakistani authors. Many times to feel the pulse of readers, I would go and sit in the bookshops of Bangla Bazaar and Sadar [in Dhaka]. I saw customers would scrutinise authors' names. If they were from East Pakistan, and especially Muslims, then they would reject those books. They would want to see books written by Indian writers. That is why the publishers would print Indian books in cheap newsprint editions and sell them in the market.[65]

The bureau's response was to encourage publishers to print books by East Pakistani writers by guaranteeing to buy a "certain number of copies," which would then be distributed to libraries. It also published books under its own label in "pure Bengali," which celebrated East Pakistan's history by documenting "customs, games, culture, etc."[66] To aid the cause, Jobeda also composed her own short stories, novels, and children's books for publication in Bengali in the 1960s and 1970s.[67] Writing her life story in Bengali so many years later thus represented the culmination of a lifetime's commitment to producing east Bengali literature in the Bengali language primarily for an east Bengali audience.

The implications of Hindustani or English as a language of autobiographical writing or publication are more complicated in assessing audience, but can still be revealing. The politicization of Hindi and Urdu from the nineteenth century meant that by the time Muslim women began producing autobiographical writings in greater numbers, to write in the Urdu script meant an overwhelmingly Muslim audience. As the English translator of Nawab Sultan Jahan Begam's autobiography explained in his preface to the 1912 edition: "I have endeavoured to convey to English readers the same meaning which, as far as I am able to judge, the *Urdu* original is intended to convey to *Muhammadan* readers."[68] Some families, like Bombay's Tyabji clan, that had earlier used regional languages or

110   *The Autobiographical Map*

dialects, even made a conscious effort to switch to Urdu in an attempt to build closer commercial and cultural ties with north Indian Muslims.[69] Urdu's identification with a subcontinental Muslim readership became even more pronounced after Independence in 1947. In *Kaifi and I* (2010), Shaukat Kaifi noted that in the 1960s, Urdu poetry "transcended political and geographical borders"—in other words, the India-Pakistan divide—in an observation as applicable to Urdu autobiography.[70] Still, there remained linguistic variations in autobiographical writings in Urdu that also reflected audience. Many Muslim women, for instance, produced personal narratives in what is characterized as *begamati zuban*, or women's language. Described as "pert, racy, earthy, graphic and colourful" in tone, it would have been particularly fathomable and attractive to a Muslim female readership.[71] Interestingly, this everyday speech—as adopted from the women of Delhi, Agra, and Lucknow—also seemed to encourage autobiographical reflection on everyday life: the more habitual, even quotidian events in an author's experience.[72]

To write or publish an autobiography in Hindi (using the Devanagari script), in contrast, became indicative of an attempt to reach beyond the Muslim community to an Indian audience not differentiated by religion. Consider Gandhian disciple Raihana Tyabji, who despite showing an early preference for English, Urdu, and Gujarati, later composed her book of autobiographical reflections, *Suniye Kakasahib*, in Hindi. Her choice is not surprising if one considers her involvement from the 1940s in the Hindustani Prachar Sabha, an organization intended to advance Hindustani as a national language for India in the Nagari script only. According to Gandhi's own articles and letters, Raihana rejected Urdu on the basis that it encouraged a "separatist tendency" among Indian Muslims.[73] By the final decades of the twentieth century, a generational gap had also opened. In *Guzashta Barson ki Baraf* (*The Snows of Past Years*, 2007), Qurratulain Hyder used her introduction to lament the loss of Urdu language skills, especially among the younger generation of Indian Muslims.[74] Other analysts have pointed to how Muslim elites in north India have abandoned Urdu for its Pakistani associations, with middle-class groups in particular preferring English as a mode of social mobility.[75] A shrinking Urdu readership in India, even among Muslims, has meant that certain autobiographies originally published in Urdu or even English have since been translated or at least transliterated into Hindi for an Indian audience encompassing different social and religious backgrounds.[76] At the same time, a number of texts first published in English are now being translated into Urdu to reach a broader audience in Pakistan.[77] To publish in Urdu from the late twentieth century, then, still denoted a primarily Muslim readership, but one restricted by region, age, and class, while Hindi could reach many in north India, including younger Muslims.

Other Muslim women, from the late nineteenth century onward, produced their autobiographical writings in English. Reflecting its colonial heritage, English is often portrayed as a link language for South Asia's elite, connecting peoples across regional and even national borders.[78] But for those writing in the nineteenth century, English was actually understood by too few Indians to indicate a subcontinent-wide readership. Hence, those texts that were published in English were more likely to be directed at a British—or, perhaps more correctly, British in India—audience. A useful example is Sikandar Begam's *A Pilgrimage to Mecca* (1870) that was published and then republished in English translation by British publishers in London and Calcutta, but never appeared, as far as can be determined, in the original Urdu.[79] This book advertised its intended audience from the outset by opening with a dedication to the Queen-Empress Victoria, followed by a translator's preface in which the author is celebrated for her good governance and loyalty to the British government, even during the "dark days" of the recent "Sepoy War."[80] In the accompanying image, Sikandar wears the medal bestowed on her by the British government as a Knight of the Star of India complete with its portrait of the queen-empress.[81] Conscious of a similar need to prove her reforming zeal and fidelity before British readers was Sikandar's daughter, Shah Jahan, who also published her autobiographical *History of Bhopal* in English translation (alongside Persian and Urdu editions) with Thacker, Spink & Co. in Calcutta.[82] That this press was best known for publishing the almanac *Thacker's Indian Directory*, in which government departments and commercial enterprises were listed especially for the benefit of India's European residents, gives a further indication of the intended readership.[83]

By the twentieth century, the reasons for writing in English or preparing an English edition were more varied. For many, it simply reflected a privileged English-medium education that meant English was more comfortable as a language of composition. Writing in the family *akhbar* books as early as 1898, Atiya Fyzee "beg[ged] the reader's pardon, especially dear ma's (as she prefers Urdu), for writing in English" before admitting that she found it easier.[84] The correlation is best illustrated by taking Hyderabad as a case study. As indicated in the previous chapter, those authors educated at the English-medium Mahbubiya Girls' School—Masuma Begam and Bilquis Jehan Begam—later produced their autobiographical writings in English. Those educated at home or in Urdu-medium institutions—Sughra Humayun Mirza, Zakira Ghouse, and Shaukat Kaifi—wrote in Urdu.[85] For the latter, English may not even have been an option. Shaukat Kaifi, for example, noted in *Yad ki Rahguzar* that neither she nor her husband, the Urdu poet Kaifi Azmi, knew enough English to gain entrance for their daughter, Shabana, to the English-medium Queen Mary's High School in Bombay.[86] Similarly, Shaukat's friend and mentor, Ismat Chughtai, recorded in *Kaghazi Hai Pairahan* that her command of the English language was "not felicitous enough to convey adequately what I meant to say."[87] Still, her autobiography's tribute to the poet Ghalib in its very title (see chapter 1) suggests that her choice of Urdu was more than just practical. Ismat knew and valued the Urdu literary tradition and thus wanted to claim a part in that "radical heritage."[88] The same may be assumed of Saliha Abid Hussain and her niece, Sughra Mehdi. While the first took her title, *Silsila-i-Roz o Shab*, from a poem by Iqbal, the latter, having studied Akbar Allahabadi's poetry for her PhD, reversed one of his couplets for the final chapter title in her *Hikayat-i-Hasti* (*Stories of Life*, 2006).[89] They and other authors, including Qurratulain Hyder and Nafees Bano Shama, also published their travelogues and autobiographies with presses, like Maktaba Jamia, that were geared to sustaining Urdu language and literature in independent India.[90]

Other Muslim women involved with national or international women's organizations were probably more conscious of using the English language to reach out to a national audience—though, admittedly, one of a certain class and education. A case discussed in greater depth in chapter 5 is that of Shareefah Hamid Ali, who, as a committed nationalist and leading figure in the All-India Women's Conference (AIWC), produced a series of English-language pieces for *Roshni*, the AIWC's journal, on her experiences of traveling to the United States in 1946. Other activists, including Jahan Ara Shahnawaz, Masuma Begam, Kulsum Sayani, Iqbalunnisa Hussain, and Rahmathunnisa Begam, also chose English for their autobiographical writings despite having other languages—Punjabi, Urdu, Gujarati, Persian, Arabic, Tamil—at their disposal, some of which they advocated for use in other contexts. A representative example here was the aforementioned Kulsum Sayani, who became a leading light in the AIWC as general secretary in 1944 and vice president in 1947.[91] She published a fortnightly journal directed at newly educated women in 1940s Bombay titled *Rahbar* (*A Guide*) that was unique in being printed in the Nagari script, Urdu, and Gujarati.[92] But when she published autobiographical pieces in *Roshni* on her experiences of working as a social worker or visiting local branches of the AIWC, she wrote in English.[93] Comparable is Iqbalunnisa Hussain, already mentioned for her Mysore roots, but relevant here for her national and transnational activism in the 1930s connected with the AIWC, the Girl Guide Movement, and the International Woman Suffrage Alliance.[94] Educated at home in Urdu, Persian, and Arabic, she was an outspoken advocate of vernacular schooling.[95] But when it came to documenting her own experiences of studying at the University of Leeds and traveling more widely in Europe, she too employed English.[96] That she and other AIWC women were conscious of a gendered national readership is apparent in their address to "women of India" or "our womanhood."[97]

Nonetheless, it seems significant that in a journal like *Roshni*, which was published in three languages—English, Urdu, and Hindi—by far the majority of auto/biographical pieces were in English. Much of the material in Urdu was fiction—short stories and poetry—while Hindi was used for more practical subjects, like news and conference proceedings.[98] Though a limited case study, it implies that for those Muslim women who had facility in this language, English was considered perhaps more appropriate or accessible for autobiographical reflection. This view was

114   *The Autobiographical Map*

substantiated by a number of contemporary authors to whom I spoke in the course of this project. As one woman explained it, she found it harder to express herself in an Indian vernacular because the language itself did not have the "nuances" that enabled her to articulate her "feelings."[99] Perhaps earlier authors felt the same. A possible example here is Shaista Ikramullah. She was a prolific contributor to Urdu journals before her marriage, even writing short travel pieces for the Delhi-based *Ismat* in the 1930s.[100] When she came to write her autobiography in the 1960s, however, she wrote in English. Once again, this choice could be attributed to her upbringing and education. Born in Calcutta to a highly elite family, she spoke English from an early age, thanks to nursery governesses who introduced her to Mother Goose and Beatrix Potter.[101] She also attended a private English-medium primary school in Lilloah as the only Indian child before later being sent to Loreto House in Calcutta for a convent education.[102] However, she was also taught Urdu at home, and her sustained interest in Urdu literature is evident from her subsequent PhD study of the Urdu novel and short story at the University of London.[103] Later in life, she also wrote several more books in Urdu and English, including one on women's idioms.[104] Clearly, Shaista Ikramullah had the facility to write in English or Urdu—and yet, for autobiographical reflection, she seems to have felt most at ease in English.

At the same time, we should not overlook that Shaista Ikramullah's *From Purdah to Parliament* was first published with Cressat Press in London in 1963. Her choice of a British press—where the manuscript was edited by later romance author Jilly Cooper no less—implies that the English language was used not only to facilitate autobiographical expression but also to reach beyond South Asia to an international audience.[105] I have shown already that as a marketing principle, this was understood by Muslim female authors as early as the nineteenth century.[106] But according to a 2014 article in the *Financial Times*, the "globalisation" of literature in the late twentieth century and beyond has meant that more and more Indian authors have come to feel the "pressures of English"—in other words, the demand to write in English or have their works translated to reach international markets.[107] Shaukat Kaifi makes this point explicitly in her preface to the recent English translation of her Urdu autobiography: "Publishing my book in English" meant "taking it to a wider international audience."[108] That victimized and often sexualized Muslim women have a particular currency in "the West" is evident in the way in which foreign interlocutors have been employed to make certain autobiographies—like Tehmina Durrani's *My Feudal Lord*, Mukhtar Mai's *In the Name of Honor*, and most recently, Malala Yousafzai's *I Am Malala*—available in English from British and American presses.[109] As Amina Yaqin asserts, "[These texts] help to reconfirm the idea of irreconcilable differences between a religious and secular framework and they exploit the exaggerated representation in the West of discrimination against women in an outwardly facing Islamic Republic."[110] Hence an autobiography billed as a "devastating indictment of women's role in Muslim society" becomes a "sensational European bestseller."[111] In the next section we turn to the way in which these real and imagined audiences can also shape the content of autobiographical narratives.

REAL AND IMAGINED AUDIENCES

Who were the real and imagined audiences for autobiographical writing by South Asian Muslim women? And what was the impact of those audiences on the form, tone, and manner of telling a life? Some authors, it seems, wrote for an explicit or even singular audience, although their actual readership may have ended up being different. A case in point is that of Safia Jabir Ali. When she first sat down to write her memoirs in the late 1920s, she did so as a memory aid for herself and her husband to remind them of the challenges and joys of setting up a farm in the isolated jungle of Chembur, outside Bombay. As she documented in the opening passage, "For some days now, Jabir and I have been talking about how we must start keeping some sort of diary. We've spent such delightful, such happy and good times in this enchanting place that we feel we must write it all down, every single thing, so that in later years we should have this detailed account to refresh our memories of these wonderful times."[112] But what was intended as a type of diary often ended up being written in longer sections after irregular and lengthy intervals. In fact, after a few short entries in 1926, Safia did not take up her pen again until 1942. By then, her purpose was different: "to leave my dear son"—born in the intervening years—"with some sort of memorial of us."[113] She thus began writing again as if for an outside party, but, very often, fell into directing her observations to "my dear Amir" as if in a letter.[114] The tone became chatty and informal, and family members were referred to by pet names and kinship relationships—for instance, "Khalajan" for her elder sister, Sakina, and "Chachani Saheba Begum" for an aunt—that would not necessarily be understood outside the Tyabji clan.[115] The narrative stopped and started in accordance with the author's busy schedule and commitment to the task, with some sections begun but never finished and others inserted out of order in accordance with the author's whim.[116] While this form lacks fluidity, it also offers a rare insight into the actual process of writing: how Safia would "dash off" a "few lines" while "dinner's being laid."[117]

In terms of content, Safia Jabir Ali's audience of one also left its mark on her life story. As noted in the introduction, a feature of traditional Islamic life writing is to begin with a long and detailed genealogy in order that the subject's life may be given meaning within the context of his or her relationships to family and teachers. This narrative, too, is dominated by a lengthy account of Safia's forebears, but to a rather different end. Here, three "family trees" are crafted in terms of their relationship to her son—so that "you may learn from which lines you have descended."[118] Hence, she starts with an account of the clan founder, here called Dadasaheb Tyabally, before turning to the branches headed by Amir's "Nana," Badruddin Tyabji, and his "Dada," Muizuddin Jiwabhai Abdul Ali.[119] The second major theme—that of her marriage to Jabir Ali and their life together in Bombay city, Tavoy (now Dawei) in Burma, and Chembur—is also introduced with Amir in mind. As Safia writes, "Because I used to long to know more about my parents, I feel that perhaps you will also have the same feelings and desires, so I'm going to tell you about how and when your father and I first got to know each other . . ."[120] Her subsequent account of their flirtations and courtship is suitably innocent—covert letters and hair-pulling and badminton tournaments—but, even so, one imagines that they may still have raised a flush in her adolescent son's cheeks.[121] These historic themes are otherwise interspersed with more immediate descriptions of family visits, parties, *mushairas* (poetic symposiums), and lectures, some of which seem to have been recorded on the basis that they could offer Amir a moral or political lesson. A family conversation in which Jabir asserts the importance of not condemning those who practice other religions is thus documented in some detail, as is a meeting at which Safia herself speaks about Gandhi. "Read," she instructs her son, "and learn about your mother's views!"[122] Not surprisingly, this nationalist content has made Safia Jabir Ali's memoir of special interest to the postcolonial Indian nation, with the effect that it is now kept in a national archive, the Nehru Memorial Museum and Library, in the country's capital, Delhi. No longer is the audience limited to "dear Amir" or even his offspring or extended family; rather, it is available to any scholar or researcher with sufficient credentials or purpose. Publication in English translation by one of Safia's descendants, Salima Tyabji, should make the audience even broader.[123]

Other authors used a dedication or preface to identify individuals who may have inspired their autobiographical writings. While this named audience may not necessarily have been exclusive, its influence could still be evident in the crafting of a text. Sikandar Begam of Bhopal and Shahr Bano Begam of Pataudi were two Indian princesses writing in the late nineteenth century, apparently at the request of a British individual or pair with whom they were acquainted. Sikandar began her *Narrative of a Pilgrimage to Mecca* (1870) by explaining how she had received a letter from Lady Durand and her husband, Colonel (later Major General Sir) H. M. Durand—formerly the political agent in Bhopal, but by then foreign secretary of the Government of India—encouraging her to write an account of her pilgrimage, and asking for her "impressions of Arabia generally, and Mecca in particular."[124] Apparently in response, she not only focused on the more practical elements of her journey—to the detriment of its religious content—but also included several chapters on her "impressions of Mecca and Jeddah."[125] The influence of her named readership was also evident in the parallels that she drew between Arabian and European practices in order to make them more intelligible to her British— or British in India—audience. The veils of the Sherif of Mecca's Georgian wives were thus compared to the "very small, fine handkerchiefs" that "English ladies carry in their hands," and costs were translated from Arabian currencies into more fathomable rupees and pounds.[126] Even more revealing was the way in which Sikandar portrayed herself throughout as a reformist monarch able to fulfill what Eickelman and Piscatori describe as the "British image of the good and loyal Muslim."[127] Her devastating critique of the Arab administration—the lack of "order" and "cleanliness" and "public works"—must have been, as it was surely intended to be, music to the ears of the Durands.[128]

Shahr Bano Begam of Pataudi similarly noted in a preface that she wrote her autobiography at the insistence of a Miss Gertrude Fletcher— discovered by the autobiography's recent editor, Tahera Aftab, to have been a missionary with the Baptist Zenana Mission.[129] Apparently, Shahr Bano and the "Miss Sahibah" had met by chance in Delhi, but soon struck up a friendship based on long conversations about "the past and the present."[130] Eager for some "remembrance" of their time together, Miss Fletcher encouraged her friend to write her autobiography, a request with which Shahr Bano complied only "for the sake of her happiness."[131] Like Sikandar, Shahr Bano appeared to use this anecdote to abdicate responsibility for writing, thus fulfilling what Barbara Metcalf has called a "convention of passivity" within the long tradition of writing life stories in Islam.[132] But Miss Fletcher's mark was also there upon the text, not least in the casual and conversational style that seems a continuation of their earlier chats. The language too—an idiomatic Urdu used by Delhi's women in the nineteenth century—was intended to be accessible to the Miss Sahiba who had only recently arrived in India from *vilayat*, or England.[133] One wonders if Shahr Bano's catalogue of "misfortunes"—as she billed it on the first page—was also calculated to appeal to a missionary inclined to view Indian women as victims deserving of sympathy and saving. Consider the author's original first lines: "*Bua* Miss Fletcher! What would you gain by reading my story? You will only be distressed and saddened . . ."[134]

That Shahr Bano later conceived of a wider readership beyond her missionary friend was also indicated in the preface, added two years after she wrote the main text in 1885. Here, she specified that she could see her autobiography being "read by members of my own sex and my sisters."[135] Should there be any ambiguity as to the gendered nature of her intended audience, she later referred again to her "women readers"—though it is not clear if she meant just fellow Muslims, Indians, or women from farther afield.[136] Still, in identifying her readership in this way, she anticipated a later group of authors who produced their autobiographical writings for Urdu magazines directed at a newly literate elite Muslim female audience also conceptualized as a sisterhood. A case in point is the Lahore-based publication *Tahzib un-Niswan*, founded by reformist intellectual Sayyid Mumtaz Ali with his wife, Muhammadi Begam, as editor in 1898. This journal's community of subscribers, numbering between three hundred and four hundred by 1902, was addressed directly by autobiographical contributors as "*Tahzibi bahin*," or "Tahzibi sisters."[137] No wonder, then, that their specific interests—in reformist topics like female education, women's rights, veiling, and childcare, though also food, clothes, gardens, jewelry, and servants—shaped autobiographical contributions to the journal. Writing her European travelogue in serial form for the journal in 1906–7, Atiya Fyzee even specified that she included a detailed description of the clothes and demeanor of her fellow students at a teachers' training college in London "for her *Tahzibi* sisters."[138] Her exclusion of the details of a possible affair with poet Muhammad Iqbal may also point to the way in which her content was fashioned in accordance with the proprieties of her conservative Muslim female audience.[139]

If contributors to *Tahzib un-Niswan* wrote for a fictive family network, others produced their autobiographical narratives with real family in mind. A key example here is Zakira Ghouse, who wrote her autobiography in sixteen installments for a family magazine, "Mushir un-Niswan" ("The Women's Advisor"), in the 1950s. This handwritten magazine was produced by Zakira and a female cousin in school notebooks on a nearly monthly basis from 1935—at which point Zakira would have been only fourteen—until 1956. The contributors and readers all came from the same extended family, or *khandan*, based in Hyderabad, though they included men and women, girls and boys, of all different ages.[140] As Sylvia Vatuk explains in her close analysis of this text, Zakira's awareness of a "limited audience" had a major impact on the form, style, and content of her autobiographical installments. On the one hand, it offered her a "sympathetic space" where she could express herself more freely than she could before an anonymous audience. She did not have to worry about revealing family secrets to strangers or fleshing out certain contextual de-

120   *The Autobiographical Map*

tails that would have been familiar to her readers. This "common body of historical knowledge and understanding" also enabled Zakira to skirt "painful events and situations" in her life, thus revealing less about her emotions and personality—in other words, her sense of self—on the basis that her audience could "fill in" what she had chosen not to reveal. At the same time, knowing one's audience so intimately forced Zakira to censor her content. As Vatuk explains, her text almost never presented others in a bad light and, if it did, her critique was inevitably balanced by praise or explanation of "extenuating circumstances."[141]

Women of the Tyabji clan offer a comparable example in that many of them originally produced autobiographical fragments in the family *akhbar* books. As noted in chapter 1, these books were, in effect, family diaries to which all members of the family, male and female, young and old, had access as both readers and contributors. Amina Tyabji's autobiography, first written in an *akhbar* book, reached a very different audience when it was translated into English for publication in a woman's journal, *Roshni*, in 1946. But it still bore the mark of her first audience in that, like Zakira's writing, it lacked any contextual detail that she assumed would have been known already by her readers.[142] Atiya Fyzee and her sister, Nazli, on the other hand, both specified that their book-length European and Middle Eastern travelogues, first published in the first decade of the twentieth century, began life as letters to their relations in Bombay, some of whom are even addressed by name in the script.[143] As Nazli wrote in her introduction to *Sair-i-Yurop*:

> Originally these are the letters that I wrote to my elders about my tour of Europe. In this there is neither eloquence nor poetic style; it is simple and straightforward language. I have tried to explain in my own words, as far as I was able to comprehend, the manner of living, design of places, some political matters, trade, skills, the variety of arts, culture, the way of education, courtly protocols.[144]

Her intimate readership was thus revealed not only in her content, but also in the very language she uses. Atiya's *Zamana-i-Tahsil* was similarly composed in an informal Urdu geared to a family audience in that it incorporated Gujarati vocabulary and colloquial Dakhni. This unusual mix reflected the Tyabji clan's original lingua franca—Gujarati—before it switched to Urdu in the late nineteenth century, as well as its Bombay base.[145] Let us tie together these reflections on location, language, and audience in this chapter's conclusion by relating them to the model of performance.

CONCLUSION: MOTIVATION, CONSTRUCTION, AND PERFORMANCE

I noted at the outset that this chapter had two underlying aims when considering autobiography's geography: to continue the investigation of autobiographical motivation, while also beginning to relate context to construction. In terms of the first, my analysis of region, locality, sect, language, and audience reinforces but also complicates many of the findings of the previous chapter. The link with sharif reformism among the middle classes and their aristocratic counterpoints can be mapped to autobiographical hubs in particular towns, localities, and princely states—most notably Aligarh, but also Hyderabad, Bhopal, Rampur, and elsewhere. At the same time, certain regional and local cultures seemed to facilitate autobiographical expression by Muslim women in a way that others did not—hence the uneven distribution in autobiographical output between India's northwest and east, various parts of the north or south, or even different neighborhoods in one capital city. Still, big urban conurbations—especially Delhi, Bombay, and Dhaka, but also others—emerge as nodes when charting authorial networks among Muslim women. This clustering confirms how national, regional, and princely capitals offered cultural leadership to autobiography as other literary activities, even as many authors retained their links to rural localities. In certain cases, these cities were also home to smaller Muslim sects that appear to have used autobiography to resist marginalization. Linguistic nationalism, and other political agendas could also inspire autobiographical reflection among Muslim women, as did certain personal concerns: to provide a memorial for family and friends, to catalogue misfortunes and achievements, to inform. The autobiographical map thus confounds South Asia's religious and linguistic geography to suggest multiple and varied motivations to write among Muslim women dependent not just on time—as noted in the previous chapter—but also on place.

122 *The Autobiographical Map*

The emphasis on autobiography's geography also enables a consideration of how writing for a particular audience at a particular time could shape the way in which a life story was constructed. Many Muslim women directed their autobiographical writings to specific individuals or groups: from an audience of one to an international market. Specific readerships required specific content, tone, and even language that was sometimes gendered, but as often regionally, communally, or nationally inflected. Writing in the late nineteenth century, Muslim female authors sought to fulfill or counter the differing expectations of colonial patrons: that a prince would be a benevolent autocrat, that Muslims could be loyal, that an Indian woman needed saving. Muslim reformism, too, shaped outputs by defining a set of interests for women that tied authors to audiences. To write for real or fictive families within a reformist milieu demanded attention to such topics deemed appropriate for the reformed Muslim woman, not least childbirth and childrearing, education, purdah, marriage, cooking, housekeeping, and dress. Dissemination also required appropriate forms of Urdu: *begamati zuban* or a regional dialect if practical, but a more formal variety to underline reformist credentials. Nationalism's rise galvanized other imperatives from the early twentieth century, as did regionalism in the latter half. Political lessons and messages to be transmitted through a woman's own life experiences could be best expressed, depending on the content—pro-Gandhi, pro-suffrage, pro-Pakistan, pro-Bengali, pro-peace, pro-minority—in one language or another. Global audiences in our global age also require accessible language and tropes—too often, the Muslim woman as victim.

Useful in theorizing how subjectivity was assumed for different contexts and times is the framework of performance. In her seminal article "Performativity, Autobiographical Practice, Resistance," Sidonie Smith draws our attention to how each of us constructs a story of our life—and thus our sense of self and identity—before varied and specific audiences on a daily basis. As she writes:

> Every day, in disparate venues, in response to sundry occasions, in front of precise audiences (even if an audience of one), people assemble, if only temporarily, a "life" to which they assign narrative coherence and meaning and

through which they position themselves in historically specific identities. Whatever that occasion or that audience, the autobiographical speaker becomes a performative subject.[146]

A reciprocal relationship is thus posited between the narrator and the one to whom a life is narrated: the performer and the audience. Just as the audience plays an active role in receiving and interpreting the autobiographical act, so the author, in effect, *performs* her life with a particular audience in mind. Audiences—whether overt or implicit, real or imagined—are thus key to how a gendered Muslim self is constructed at different historical moments, but so too are scribes, editors, translators, cowriters, and publishers. To further draw out the historical implications of performance as a theoretical construct, I turn in chapter 4 to these processes of production.

CHAPTER FOUR

STAGING THE SELF

INTRODUCTION: THE LIVES AND AFTERLIVES OF TEXTS

I began chapter 3 by evoking Virginia Woolf's famous assertion that to write fiction, women needed "a room of one's own." The implication, as I noted there, was that women required necessary means to be an author, but Woolf's imagery also suggested writing as a solitary act: something done alone, without the influence of the outside world. In this chapter, I probe whether this second proposition also holds true of autobiographical writing by South Asian Muslim women. In other words, is it appropriate to project autobiography as a wholly individual pursuit: a solitary crafting of one's own life story into a form that has coherence and meaning? Or, in this specific historical context at least, are there other factors at work? To address these questions, I again relate *context* to *construction*, but this time in terms of *how*: how literary milieus shaped the stories that South Asian Muslim women wrote about their lives. It is worth returning to C. M. Naim's analysis of the autobiographical writings of eighteenth-century Mughal poet Mir Muhammad Taqi for inspiration. He notes how, in later reprints of *Zikr-i-Mir*, the text was altered in its very essentials to reflect a particular historical moment. For a 1935 edition, editor Abdul Haq even excised the often vulgar "witty anecdotes" that make up the final section to allow Mir to be depicted as "sober," as may befit a Delhi poet.[1] Accordingly, though Mir displayed intentionality

125

126 *Staging the Self*

in projecting himself as a sayyid born to a Sufi master, the way in which his life story was circulated and received had the effect of transforming his self-representation.

The questions asked in this chapter also reflect methodological approaches of historians of the book. As Leah Price queries in her *How to Do Things with Books in Victorian Britain*, what are the "lives and afterlives" of books as they stretch "far beyond reading"?[2] In our age of the "vanishing book and virtual text," Antoinette Burton encourages us to "linger" on the "embodied form" of the autobiography, especially "its conditions of production, how it was handled and circulated, the practices of borrowing and annotating in which it participated, the dangers and the pleasures its embrace entailed."[3] Not all of these aims may be achieved here; my focus, after all, is on relating context to construction. But they do offer avenues for thinking about autobiographical writings as texts existing within distinct historical parameters. The framework of performance introduced in the conclusion to the previous chapter is again illuminating here. If the literary medium offers a stage for the author as performative subject, the life story is molded by the theater in which it is performed.[4] How far the Muslim female self may be refashioned can be measured against some of those theoretical constructs summarized in the introduction and chapter 1 for having been applied to autobiography by literary and gender theorists. Does circulation as a manuscript, journal, or book enable a particular form or style associated with the long history of life writing in Islam? Do editors or cowriters facilitate the casting of a unified, coherent self in the Rousseauian model? To what extent are publishers responsible for the creation of a gendered narrative that fulfills the expectation of women's autobiography?

To address these themes, this chapter is divided into just two sections. In the first, I focus on *processes of production* and, where appropriate, publication—so, in terms of literary milieu, where did Muslim women write their lives, and what impact did that context have on their style and content? Did their personal narratives remain in manuscript form, or were they published in a magazine or book? How important were scribes, editors, translators, cowriters, and publishing houses to the way in which a life story was structured and told? To underline the importance of literary and historical context, a second section then asks these questions of one detailed case study: the autobiographical writings of actress Begum Khurshid Mirza. Appearing in four manifestations over three decades and two countries, this life story offers an opportunity to consider *a performer in performance* "on stage or page," to borrow the phrase of Sherrill Grace.[5] Indicated in this description is the way in which performers used to appearing on the stage or screen then acted out their own lives in autobiographical narratives. As noted in the introduction, I draw here especially on the work of Kathryn Hansen, who has used Indian theater autobiographies to show how "the actor's self is twice-created, both as a stage performer and as a social being."[6] The concluding section then evokes Phillipe Lejeune's influential concept of the "autobiographical pact" to assess the importance of literary milieu to the construction of a Muslim female self in autobiographical writing—or, in the words of this chapter's title, "staging the self."

PROCESSES OF PRODUCTION

So, were there specific literary mediums in which Muslim women produced their autobiographical writings? Did this process of production entail publication? If so, were others involved with the text's construction? I begin with manuscripts on the basis that they may be assumed to offer the most unmediated form of autobiographical production—an assumption that, in some cases at least, may be true. Reading Safia Jabir Ali's memoir in her own hand in a timeworn notebook, it is possible to see how the literary context of a family journal has, as argued in chapter 3, left its mark on her life story in terms of its informality, indeterminacy, and selectivity. But it otherwise seems fairly free of the hand of others. Also produced by hand, though in a family magazine, Zakira Ghouse's *Hamara Daur-i-Hayat* may seem equally raw in character. But, in this instance, episodes were being read and receiving response—sometimes highly critical—from members of her extended family as her life story unfolded.[7] The author was thus engaging with her audience, not just as an imaginary act but as an embedded feature of the production process. The hand-typed sheaves that contain the autobiographies of Masuma Begam and Rahmathunnisa Begam—passed to me by a generous scholar and, in

128   *Staging the Self*

the latter case, to her by another generous scholar before that—represent more of an unknown.[8] By time they came into my hands—as photocopies of photocopies many years after the authors had died—they were so divorced from their original context as to make it impossible to know who or what may have shaped the construction of the text.

And what of the few Mughal manuscripts? Jahanara's *Risala-i-Sahibiyah* appears to have been available in the form of a Persian manuscript kept in the Apa Rao Bhola Nath Library in Ahmedabad as late as the 1950s, but it has since disappeared from that collection.[9] The only copies now available to scholars are a typed Persian version and an Urdu translation replete with errors, published in Pakistani and Indian research journals in the 1970s and 1980s.[10] Similarly, only one incomplete copy of Gulbadan's *Ahval-i-Humayun Badshah* survives today, in the British Library, but it is not known if it is her original text or a Persian translation from her native language, Turki.[11] If the latter, the influence of a court translator must be evident throughout the text—though in what ways that might be true we will likely never know. What is clear is that for those autobiographical narratives produced before the spread of printing technology, scribes and calligraphers would have had a hand in copying texts for circulation at court and beyond. As human and fallible agents, we should not underestimate their capacity to introduce errors and edits. A comparison with the later, but aforementioned *Zikr-i-Mir* is illustrative here. In the introduction and notes to his translation, Naim points to significant difference among the six extant copies, only one of which was definitely produced during Mir's own lifetime.[12] The discrepancies range from names, numbers, and dates to the exclusion or inclusion of individual words, sentences, or even whole passages—all of which are variations that can have a considerable impact on the meaning of the text and on how the author's life is interpreted.[13]

Moving from manuscripts to other mediums, as was noted in previous chapters, many of the earliest Muslim women to publish their autobiographical writings in a modern sense did so in journals or magazines. This form of publication began to proliferate in India in the nineteenth century, when it was picked up by socioreligious reformers to publicize their views on women's education and social customs especially. Urdu publications geared to newly educated Muslim women included a number of titles already mentioned: *Tahzib un-Niswan*, which was published in Lahore from 1898; *Khatun*, which was set up in Aligarh in 1904; and *Ismat*, which was founded in Delhi in 1908.[14] As the twentieth century progressed, Muslim women also contributed autobiographical writings to women's magazines in other languages, including English and Bengali, as well as to more mainstream periodicals. This literary milieu was particularly suited to short autobiographical episodes on a particular theme or incident. An early example already mentioned in chapter 2 was Ashrafunnisa Begum's account over two installments in *Tahzib un-Niswan* in March 1899 of how she learned to read and write. Many others contributed short travel pieces detailing journeys within India or even abroad. In the early twentieth century, those who wrote about their travels outside India usually went to Europe or perhaps on hajj, while later on, women's expanding horizons were revealed by visits to the United States or other parts of Asia.[15] Magazines also included letters pages that were particularly effective in preserving unsolicited personal accounts on themes deemed suitable to particular periodicals. For instance, Muslim women writing to the Delhi-based magazine *Manushi* in the 1980s reflected its feminist orientation by recording their experiences of harassment on public transport, disinheritance, and even rape.[16]

The journal form also lent itself to serialized entries. Atiya Fyzee's account of her year studying at a teachers' training college in London thus appeared in *Tahzib un-Niswan* in weekly installments throughout 1907.[17] This form allowed her to utilize the style of diary entries, or *roznamcha*, which was retained when the entries were compiled in book form some years later, in 1921.[18] Subsequent contributors of autobiography to the same magazine, including Hijab Imtiaz Ali and Nazr Sajjad Hyder, also employed this literary mode, the latter even using "Roznamcha" as a title.[19] Serialization also created gaps in publication that allowed *Tahzib*'s readers to express feedback on an author's style or content in the magazine's forum "Mahfil-i-Tahzib," to which the author could respond in subsequent entries.[20] Autobiographical writing in women's journals thus emerged out of a dialogue between the author and other contributors. A magazine's editor could be even more instrumental in crafting auto-

130   *Staging the Self*

biographical substance. In the first decade of *Tahzib*'s publication, this figure was the influential Muhammadi Begam.[21] In *Zamana-i-Tahsil*, Atiya noted that this "lady editor" had "especially asked me to inform the sisters" about specific subjects, one example given being the "way of life" in Britain.[22] Editorial influence was also apparent in the text itself when, on occasion, entries appeared to be incomplete—beginning or ending in the middle of a train of thought or offering lengthy descriptions of places never named.[23] By the 1940s, the editor was not a "lady," but Muhammadi Begam's own son, Sayyid Imtiaz Ali "Taj." Though it is harder to document his specific influence, it seems likely that he had a hand in advising his own wife, Hijab Imtiaz Ali, what to include in her serialized diary, *Lail o Nihar* (*Day and Night*, 1941–42). According to Nazr Sajjad Hyder, Imtiaz Ali was also the one who encouraged her to publish her life story in *Tahzib un-Niswan* in the 1940s, perhaps aiding her to pick and choose what incidents to include out of a lifetime of original diary entries.[24]

A later example also appropriate here is Ismat Chughtai's *Kaghazi Hai Pairahan*. Though now treated as a complete work, it was first published in the Urdu monthly *Aaj Kal*, in more than fourteen installments from March 1979 to May 1980.[25] As others have noted too, when considered as a whole, this autobiography can seem "jagged" and "fragmented."[26] There is little sense of linearity and, in chronological terms it covers only a few years of her life, from her entrance to high school until she wrote her controversial short story "Lihaf." A letter to her editor with the second installment confirms how the serialized form facilitated this episodic approach by allowing for distinct articles with separate titles:

> I'm sending the second chapter. I am trying to record from my memory the events that affected me and what I had heard from conversations in the family, the tensions inherent in every class, new questions and their resolution— all this is so complicated. I will send you whatever gets written at any point of time. Let them be published under different titles.[27]

The opening chapter, "Ghubar-i-Karawan" ("Dust of the Caravan"), was not even included in the original serialization, instead appearing with the reminiscences of other Urdu writers in a much earlier series in the same journal.[28] Ultimately, *Aaj Kal*'s editor was responsible for putting it together with the later thirteen installments to create Ismat's autobiography in book form in 1994.[29] This example thus points to the role of journal staff in crafting autobiographical form and even content in a way that came to define a text in literary terms. Ismat Chughtai's *Kaghazi Hai Pairahan* continues to be portrayed as "not a straightforward autobiography," largely because it lacks "narrative coherence."[30] But, according to a later line in the above letter to her editor, Ismat apparently intended for the text to be put in "sequence" when it was converted from journal articles to book-length autobiography. Poor health and "other preoccupations" meant that she was not able to fulfill this intention, but had her editor done so rather than simply putting the entries together in the original order, the fragmentary nature of this autobiography that so defined it as "women's writing" according to literary theory would have been lost.[31]

A parallel may be drawn with Qaisari Begam's *Kitab-i-Zindagi* in that it too has been described as "disconnected and fragmentary" in fulfillment of the established criteria for women's autobiographical writing.[32] But to understand how the structure, if not the content, of this autobiography's final form came to be defined, the process of production is again key. According to the preface (written by a relative, not the author), Qaisari Begam never intended to write an autobiography or even a book. Rather, her narrative began life as 260 separate essays written over many years on whatever topic came to mind. Sometimes these vignettes related to incidents in her own life, including her fractious marriage, the birth of her children (the first of whom died as an infant), or, very often, the protracted deaths of family members.[33] On other occasions, she described customs and ceremonies within her household or extended family grouping in Delhi and Hyderabad. Publication seemed not to have been a consideration for the author, who instead wrote for her own satisfaction—not just prose but also poetry—or the benefit of future generations within her family: her daughter and her daughter's daughter, as well as nieces, nephews, and their children. However, when a younger relative, Shan ul-Haq Haqqi, himself a scholar and teacher, heard about the manuscript, he pushed for publication. The result was the serializa-

132 *Staging the Self*

tion of some of these essays in *Urdu Nama*, an Urdu literary magazine associated with the Urdu Dictionary Board, in the early 1970s, to acclaim from appreciative readers and critics.[34] When the magazine ceased publication in 1976 and the author died the same year, the remaining essays then languished until 2003, when the full set was brought together by Qaisari Begam's granddaughter—the named "editor," Zahra Masrur Ahmad—for publication with a Pakistani press. Only at this point was it arranged into twenty-seven chapters that totaled more than a whopping 661 printed pages.[35]

When Nazr Sajjad Hyder's autobiography was compiled in book form from her journal entries, an external editor also had a major role to play. But in this case, the editor was even more invested in the process because she was the author's own daughter and a writer herself. I refer to the highly influential Urdu novelist Qurratulain Hyder. In 2007, she published her mother's autobiography as *Guzashta Barson ki Baraf.* As Asiya Alam has explored in some depth in a recent article, Qurratulain's mark is all over this later text. First of all, there is the title. As noted already, Nazr titled her *Tahzib* diary very simply as "Roznamcha." Post-1947, she continued her autobiographical production in another journal, *Ismat*, retaining "Roznamcha" as her title at first. Then, at the instigation of her new editor, Rashid ul-Khairi, she changed it to "Ayyam-i-Guzashta," meaning "Past Days," to reflect a more retrospective approach necessitated by the destruction of her original diary during Partition (see introduction). For the book, Qurratulain chose a new title entirely. It reflected her "sensibility as a fiction writer," to quote Alam, by borrowing from an old French ballad that lamented the demise of great queens and other formidable women. A title was also inserted for each entry, though in the original magazines there had been none. Furthermore, Qurratulain was selective in what she included in the book: only some of Nazr's original diary entries in *Tahzib un-Niswan* (about fifty pages are missing) appear, more of her *Ismat* memoir is preserved, but none of her equally self-reflective letters that were published with them made the cut. In a few cases, the content was even changed. Qurratulain was also responsible for contextualizing her mother's autobiographical output in familial, historical, and literary terms in a substantial introduction. As Alam concludes, it is simply not appropriate to think of this later incarnation of Nazr's autobiographical writing as "framed and shaped" by the author alone.[36]

Those Muslim women who first wrote their autobiographies as booklength compositions also experienced editorial interference. While it can be difficult to trace the editorial process, some authors chose to reflect upon it in a preface to their longer narrative. Particularly illuminative was novelist Saliha Abid Hussain in *Silsila-i-Roz o Shab*. She noted that for a "year or so" in the late 1970s, she dedicated herself almost entirely to writing her autobiography. Once that first draft was complete, she then revised and rewrote it herself, as was her established writing practice. By the beginning of 1980, she was ready to hand over that draft to an editor, Shahid Ali Khan, expressing that it was then "up to him to do the rest." It seems that he then edited the text in a fairly superficial way—perhaps clarifying sentence structure and language—before coming back to Saliha to report that the book was "too large." As she was opposed to publishing it in two parts, she first removed all of the sections—approximately 150 pages—relating to travel. Apparently, these sections were then grouped in a separate book titled *Safar Zindagi ke liye Soj o Saj* that was published first in 1982.[37] But her autobiography was still too long. Saliha conjectured that her proclivity to write long sentences was partly to blame, but so too was her comprehensive approach to autobiographical content. As she explained, this earlier draft was not just her story, but also mentioned "relatives, elders, friends and servants," while also detailing many long-standing customs and cultural activities. By placing relationships and history at its heart, she must have adhered to certain characteristics that were theorized to define Islamic life writing (see chapter 1). And yet, encouraged by her editor, she continued to strip back her narrative, removing another two hundred pages. What she was left with, in her own words, was a "simple straightforward autobiography": something more reminiscent of those texts written in a Western autobiographical tradition.[38]

An editor's role in shaping autobiographical reflection was also evident in those contexts where they had solicited material for a particular volume or purpose. I made use in the previous chapters of a volume edited by Bengali educationalist Nurunnahar Faizunnessa (1932–2004), for

134   *Staging the Self*

publication with Dhaka-based press Muktodhara in 1988. Clearly, her intention was to pull together an experiential record by those women who were some of the earliest Muslim girls to attend school and make a career in education in Bengal. Their contributions thus follow a fairly standard format exemplified by her own chapter—though admittedly with some variations. Most began by discussing their parents and other relatives in terms of their impact on their own schooling: how was it that they managed to receive an education when so many other Muslim girls in early twentieth-century Bengal were denied? That education was then recalled, often with reference to circumstances, curriculum, and fellow pupils. Some women chose to reflect on changing social mores, while others used major political events as historical markers in their own lives. A brief description of their own careers as teachers or perhaps university lecturers justified their inclusion in the volume. In short, they were asked to contribute because of a particular aspect of their life story, on which they then focused in their chapter.[39] When one contributor, Noorjehan Murshid (1924–2003), wrote an autobiographical piece for a different edited volume—this time on Bangladesh's literary scene—she focused on a later aspect of her working life not even mentioned in her chapter in *Kaler Samukh Bhela*: her six years as editor of the Bengali periodical *Edesh Ekal*.[40] In neither volume did the author dwell on other topics of life, like marriage, husband, or children—though many other Bengali Muslim women did so in their autobiographical writings—presumably because that was not deemed part of the task set by their editor. Focusing almost exclusively on family relationships, in contrast, were those women chosen by playwright Saif Hyder Hasan to contribute to a book of memoirs on leading Indian writers, filmmakers, and musicians. Though often celebrated as actresses in their own right, these women wrote chapters that were tailored to concentrate on their more-famous husbands or fathers.[41] Their autobiographical output thus displayed what has been identified as a gendered proclivity to focus on others that may not have been present without the intervention of the editor.

Translators, as much as editors, have played a major role in crafting Muslim women's autobiographical writing for public consumption. As has been well documented, translation itself is a process that can shape and even transform self-expression: what is captured of human experience in one language may not always transpose to another.[42] Ruby Lal offers a relevant case study by examining how Gulbadan's *Ahval-i-Humayun Badshah* was translated from Persian into English by scholar Annette Beveridge for publication in 1902. She asserts that the "self-confident colonial context" in which Beveridge worked led to a "slanting" of the narrative. As she writes, "numerous interesting nuances are lost and what appears before the reader is a flattened picture," in which "early Mughal society and mores" are assimilated into "something more recognizably Victorian."[43] And yet most translators of Muslim women's autobiographical writing, from the nineteenth century through the present, have sought to play down their interpretive role by claiming that they "adhere to the literal meaning" of the original language as much as possible or, conversely, that they retain the "tenor" or "flavour" of the author's prose even if their translation is not exact.[44] To facilitate "accuracy," translators often retained some of the original language in one way or another. Translating Sikandar's hajj narrative from Urdu to English in the late nineteenth century, Emma Willoughby-Osborne sometimes included literal translations in brackets or even lines of transliterated Urdu text.[45] More recently, Nasreen Rehman went to some length in her preface to Shaukat Kaifi's *Kaifi and I* to explain why she did not translate honorifics and kinship terms, nor those words relating to embroidery, food, flowers, or clothing. As she writes:

> A gharara, a shalwar and a churidar pyjama are trousers or pantaloons of sorts, but they are very different from each other; qaliya and qorma are both meat curries but this is where the similarity ends; and a mogra flower is not simply a jasmine. For the reader familiar with these words, the terms will evoke a picture very close to the one that the author intended.[46]

Still, as Shahr Bano Begam of Pataudi's most recent translator, Tahera Aftab, recognizes: "Translations, even the most accurate ones, are not what the original texts are."[47]

Another way in which translators have shaped autobiographical expression is through selection and addition.[48] Quite recently, Safia Jabir Ali's memoir—previously available, as noted in the previous section, only

136 *Staging the Self*

as a handwritten Urdu manuscript—was published in English translation by one of her descendants, Salima Tyabji. Clearly, she did not deem Safia's particularly lengthy accounts of kinship relationships to be of interest outside the family—for whom they had been composed originally—because she either dropped them or moved them into notes.[49] A characteristic feature of Islamic auto/biography—beginning with a long and detailed genealogy intended to contextualize a life within family and scholarly networks—was thus expunged.[50] Salima also inserted an account of the missing years, 1926 to 1942, by Safia's son, Amiruddin Ali, seemingly to make the book more accessible and appealing to general readers. Particularly interesting in terms of narrative content was the way in which Amiruddin Ali emphasized his parents' contributions to the nationalist struggle: Jabir Ali's three spells in jail between 1929 and 1935, their attendance at two open sessions of the Indian National Congress in 1930 and 1931, Safia's participation in the Salt Satyagraha, Jabir's presidency of the Bombay Suburban District Board as a Congress member, and their constructive work spinning, selling handspun, handwoven *khadi* cloth, and picketing liquor stores.[51] Writing her narrative in the 1940s, Safia must already have been aware of a potential interest in Gandhi, as evidenced by her dedication of a number of pages to documenting their friendship during shared time in Tavoy in Burma.[52] But Salima, as her translator, took further steps to draw out this nationalist aspect of her autobiographical writing by commissioning the new section. The English translation, published many years after the original was written, thus underlined a particular aspect of the author's identity.[53]

Playing an even more transformative role in the writing of life stories were cowriters. While it can be difficult to assess their full impact on an autobiography's style, form, and content, the mere inclusion of their names in an attribution recognizes that their contributions were extensive.[54] When reading some of these texts—Tehmina Durrani's *My Feudal Lord* with William and Marilyn Hoffer, Mukhtar Mai's *In the Name of Honor* with Marie-Thérèse Cuny, and Malala Yousafzai's *I Am Malala* with Christina Lamb, for example—one can speculate as to questions asked and gaps filled.[55] But offering more concrete evidence was cowriter Joan Erdman in her foreword to *Stages: The Art and Adventures of Zohra*

Segal. Here, she explained that some years before the book was published in 1997, actress Zohra Segal composed a 160-page memoir that she circulated among family and friends. Many of them suggested "revisions and rewritings," but, fully aware that she was an actress and not a writer, she did not feel able to incorporate them. However, she did make the manuscript available to Erdman in 1983 when the latter was completing a research project on dancer-choreographer Uday Shankar with whom Segal had worked in the late 1930s and early 1940s.[56] A year or more later, Erdman suggested to Segal that they "co-author" the book. Erdman would interview her and others for necessary "contextualization" to her story, while also prompting Segal to provide "more detailed written descriptions of certain episodes in her life."[57] From her acknowledgments, we know that esteemed professor C. M. Naim also collected family sources from Lahore that he then translated from Urdu for her use.[58] Erdman justified her role as coauthor by explaining: "The task of turning this material into the story of Zohra's art and adventures was mine, and what follows is thus a joint effort."[59] And yet, aware of the need for autobiographical authenticity, Erdman retained the first person and even claimed to have preserved Zohra's voice. As she concluded, "Zohra's voice, in this volume, resonates for all who have heard her, with the inflections and syntax of her English and her sophistication as an actress and woman of the world."[60]

Interestingly, this book—unlike many others cowritten with international authors—was published by a Delhi-based publishing house, Kali for Women. Founded in 1984, this press was India's first to focus exclusively on writings by and for women—and, as such, had a particular feminist agenda that went beyond individual writers, editors, or translators. Exemplifying the role that a publisher can play in crafting the shape and tone of a narrative is Shaukat Kaifi's autobiographical writing. Her memoir was first published in Urdu as *Yad ki Rahguzar*, translated as *Memory Lane*, with Delhi-based Star Publications in 2006. But when it was picked up by Kali for Women offshoot Zubaan, for an English translation, it underwent a number of changes and additions. The adoption of a new title, *Kaifi and I*, already packaged the narrative rather differently by placing emphasis on the author's famous husband, the

138   *Staging the Self*

renowned poet Kaifi Azmi, or at least her relationship with him. The treatment of her memoir as a "love story," to quote the translator's note, was further augmented within the text by the addition of some new passages, apparently at the instigation of Zubaan's well-known founder and director, Urvashi Butalia, in which the author further explicated her feelings.[61] According to translator Nasreen Rehman, she also restored the end to an earlier Urdu draft, in which the author addressed her now-deceased beloved directly in a grief-stricken lament.[62] While this strand was already present in the Urdu original—perhaps showing the influence of the romantic *afsana* tradition within Urdu literature—it was thus heightened in Zubaan's English translation. In other words, the later version showed the publisher's mark in fulfilling, even more than the original, the gendered expectation that women's autobiography will be different from that of men in its usage of relationality and raw emotion.[63] No doubt the power of Kaifi Azmi's name and a memoir packaged as love story were also calculated to produce better sales figures, whatever the ideological convictions of the author, her deceased husband, and the press itself.

If publishers shaped individual narratives, they also crafted the autobiographical canon as a whole through what they chose to publish. A pertinent example from the early twentieth century is Mufid-i-'Am in Agra, which advanced a reformist agenda by publishing books by and for Muslim women.[64] Accordingly, the publisher's catalogue included autobiographical writings by a number of well-known female reformers, including Atiya and Zehra Fyzee, as well as their sometimes patron, Nawab Sultan Jahan Begam of Bhopal.[65] The link between reformism and autobiography outlined in the introduction and chapter 2 may thus have been forged, at least in part, by partisan presses. Linda Peterson has developed this idea in the context of nineteenth-century England by exploring the role of editorial staff in "institutionalizing" women's autobiography as a separate autobiographical tradition distinct from that of men. In particular, she points to the way in which Victorian presses published domestic memoirs originally written by women in the seventeenth century as a "model for female subjectivity and self-representation" in their own time. The earlier texts were thus validated as the origins of a separate, "appropriately feminine" form of autobiography in the Victorian present.[66] A parallel could be drawn here with various contemporary presses in South Asia that simultaneously publish autobiographies written in the nineteenth, twentieth, and twenty-first centuries. As noted already, Oxford University Press in Pakistan has been particularly prolific in publishing and republishing autobiographical writings by Muslim women.[67] The earlier texts can set a precedent for women's autobiographical expression in a troubled present where the rights of women to education and representation are constantly being eroded. Also committed to the publication of women's autobiographies, past and present, is Zubaan in Delhi. It is to one of that publisher's books that I now turn to offer a more sustained analysis of audience and production in Muslim women's autobiographical writing.

A PERFORMER IN PERFORMANCE

As a case study of context and construction, this section considers the autobiographical narratives of Begum Khurshid Mirza (1918–89). I chose this specific example on the basis that, unusually, I was able to gain access to four separate versions of her one life story. In the early 1980s, she wrote an account of her varied and sometimes unconventional life in manuscript form.[68] This typed original complete with later editorial markings was sent to me by her daughter, Lubna Kazim. She did so after we and other members of her family, including her sister Shabnam Zafar and cousin Shahla Haidar, met on several occasions in Delhi and even traveled to their family home in Aligarh together for a two-day conference on the birth centenary of their aunt Rashid Jahan.[69] Begum Khurshid Mirza's autobiography, as contained in the manuscript, had been first published as a nine-part serial in the *Herald*, a monthly English-language publication from Karachi, in 1982–83.[70] In 2003, the entries were brought together in a poorly circulated Pakistani book edition attributed to Lubna Kazim.[71] This work provided the basis for the most recent edition, which was edited by Lubna Kazim and published by the Delhi-based feminist publisher Zubaan, in 2004.[72] These four separate incarnations of one life story, bolstered by conversations with the author's family and other contributors, offer a unique opportunity to consider the

140   *Staging the Self*

importance of editorial influence, literary medium, audience, and processes of production on the construction of a written life.

But first, let us consider the author as an agent of her own life/story. As indicated in chapter 2, Begum Khurshid Mirza was born in Aligarh in north India to a well-known family associated with Muslim reform and girls' education. Her parents, Shaikh Abdullah and Waheed Jahan, are perhaps best known as the founders of Aligarh Girls' School in 1906, though her father, as a lawyer and contemporary of Syed Ahmad Khan, also participated in the Muhammadan Educational Conference, established the Urdu women's journal *Khatun*, and acted as a trustee of the Muhammadan Anglo-Oriental College.[73] Buoyed by her formative education at her parents' school, where she had acted in school plays, Begum Khurshid Mirza distinguished herself in early adulthood as one of India's first film stars under the screen name Renuka Devi. Her adoption of a Hindu screen name was meant as a foil to save herself and her family from the "social consequences" of her association with a "disreputable" film industry, but it proved unsuccessful in masking her real identity and she was targeted in the Muslim press.[74] Still, she continued to pursue her chosen career, citing her "enthusiasm for dramatic art" as a driver.[75] In turn, she acted in a number of hits (and not-so hits) filmed in Bombay, Lahore, and Poona, including the "super hit" *Bhabi* (1939), the "lively" *Naya Sansar* (1941), the "moderate success" *Sahara* (1943), the historical "extravaganza" *Samrat Chandragupta* (1945), and the "publicity film" *Ghulami* (1945).[76] Though not the only Muslim woman in films at this time—her contemporaries included her brother Mohsin's wife, Shahida, as well as leading ladies Naseem Banu and Sardar Akhtar—Begum Khurshid Mirza was certainly a pioneer.[77]

To defend her foray into the Bombay talkies, the author underlined how she continued to fulfill the roles of a good wife and mother alongside her acting career. For instance, she explained how the wages from her first film, the aforementioned *Bhabi*, were spent on clothes and a perambulator for her young children.[78] Yet, in 1944, Begum Khurshid Mirza "said goodbye to films forever," apparently under pressure from her husband, Akbar, who was growing impatient with her long absences and neglect of wifely duties. The following passage is worth quoting at length for its frank discussion of the particular challenges that the author experienced as a working woman—many of which will no doubt sound familiar to contemporary readers too:

> How does one explain the selfishness of a beloved husband who has to be reassured all the time that he has the priority in his wife's life, despite her professional commitments? . . . Akbar maintained a strange attitude towards my work. He enjoyed the benefits the money brought us, such as a new car, expensive game-hunts, and pleasure trips to fashionable Mussoorie in summer and excellent schooling for our children. And, yet, he treated my work as a hobby, instead of giving it its due importance. Although he was supportive of my work in cinema even in the face of opposition from his family and mine, I sensed that Akbar would not mind in the least if some of my films flopped because that would mean an end to my career.

When her films did not "flop," Akbar took more direct action and ordered his wife to come home. After Partition and their move to Karachi in 1947, Begum Khurshid Mirza diversified her public activities. She became known as a social welfare activist with the All Pakistan Women's Association (APWA), a radio artiste with Radio Pakistan, and an author of short stories for the "prestigious" Urdu literary magazine *Saqi*, while also making and remaking several homes and raising a family.[79] Bringing her the greatest fame, however, were her acting roles in plays and long-running serials for Pakistan Television in the 1970s and 1980s. These included *Kiran Kahani*, *Zer Zabar Pesh* (during which she became synonymous with her character Akka Bua), *Parchain*, *Uncle Urfi*, *Roomi*, *Shama*, *Aagahi*, *Afshan*, *Shosha*, and *Ana*, as well as the plays *Moments Will Live*, *Dhund*, *Khizar Khan*, *Nadir Shah*, and *Pannah*.[80] For her performances, she won many acting awards, including the Prize of Performance Award presented by Pakistan's president, General Zia ul-Haq, in 1985.[81]

Performance, then, is at the heart of Begum Khurshid Mirza's life story. As such, it belongs to an autobiographical subgenre in South Asia introduced in chapter 2 for its associations with actors, actresses, musicians, and theater personnel. On the whole—and in contrast to the example given here—these narratives tended to be written in Indian vernaculars (rather than English) and produced by small publishers for a

142   *Staging the Self*

reading public used to consuming the products of a burgeoning popular press.[82] It is significant for my focus on female authors that this subgenre was, in effect, initiated by a woman, when the celebrated Bengali theater actress Binodini Dasi (1863–1941) published her *Abhinetrir Atmakatha* (*Autobiography of an Actress*) in 1910.[83] For Muslim female performers especially, the autobiographical form seemed to offer a way of challenging societal stereotypes about a closed and conservative Islam by asserting their connections to the public and often flamboyant existence of an actress or singer, while at the same time justifying their transgression by asserting their domestic credentials as wife and mother. A distinctive feature of this subgenre, then, is what Hansen has labeled a "doubled performativity"—or, as I word it in my section title, "a performer in performance."[84]

As a point of entry, let me observe first that the material forms of the four versions are very different. While the actual written content differs little between the original manuscript and the first published edition, the *Herald* edition still reflects the magazine's distinct literary milieu. Rather than one continuous narrative, Khurshid's life story is serialized in nine installments over as many months—from August 1982 to April 1983. While this structure may suggest a disjointed or fragmented form— comparable to Ismat Chughtai's serialized autobiography in *Aaj Kal* that has already been discussed—in fact the magazine version follows a largely sequential organization. It may move, in the middle installments particularly, from Khurshid's marriage to hunting outings to her acting career, but the structure is coherent in terms of the periodization of her own life—even if the dates are sometimes missing.[85] The organization of the book versions, on the other hand, is substantially altered. By her own admission, this reorganization was undertaken by the proclaimed author/ editor Lubna Kazim, at the encouragement of "publishers."[86] While the actual text begins with the same material on the author's birth and childhood, the bulk is rearranged around specific topics. For example, what made up the fourth and fifth installments (November and December 1982) in the *Herald* on Khurshid's life generally in the 1930s and 1940s is reorganized into three thematic chapters on her marriage (chapter 7: "An Early Marriage"), her hunting adventures (chapter 8: "On Shikar with Akbar"), and her film career (chapter 9: "Renuka Devi: My Celluloid Identity").[87] The fragmented form associated with women's autobiography is thus discarded in favor of a more thematic organization, highlighting the development of personality.

Also distinguishing the magazine publication in its embodied form are the many photographs interspersed throughout the text. All of these and more find their way into the richly illustrated Pakistani book edition (if in poorly produced reproductions), but only some of them are included in the Zubaan publication, presumably because of production costs. Marianne Hirsch and Linda Haverty Rugg have noted the way in which photographs in an autobiography can "tell" a subjective story apart from and sometimes even in conflict with the textual narrative.[88] The inclusion or exclusion of photographs is not simply about illustration, but again highlights the significance of editorial decision and literary form on the crafting of a life story. In this specific case, the photographs suggest a very different packaging of the narrative for the Pakistani and Indian audiences. The first installment in the *Herald* (August 1982) begins with a collage of photographs of Khurshid Mirza at different points in her life, of which three out of seven show her as an actress.[89] Similarly, the cover of the Pakistani book edition features the author in her most famous role, as Akka Bua in the television serial *Zer Zabar Pesh*.[90] The Zubaan volume, on the other hand, contains just a handful of photos of her film and later television career and none of her radio performances. Instead, it foregrounds her Aligarh connections by including several pictures of her father, Abdullah Lodge, Waheedia Hostel, and even a meeting of the Old Girls' Association. The emphasis is also placed on Khurshid as a girl or young woman before she left for Pakistan. Even the cover features an image of her from 1941 with her *Naya Sansar* costar, Ashok Kumar. There are a few photos of her on her own or with her husband in the 1950s and 1960s, as well as a couple of the "proud grandmother" later on, but on the whole, the images from her Pakistan years are few, small, and cramped in their layout.[91] Perhaps unsurprisingly, this phase is illustrated much more fully in the two Pakistani publications—magazine and book—with the exception of the last six years of the author's life, which fell after the *Herald*'s publication date.[92]

144   *Staging the Self*

The flexibility of the magazine format is reflected in that certain passages are extracted from the main text and highlighted in dark, italicized type. The *Herald*'s editor at the time, Razia Bhatti, must have considered these passages especially significant and thus employed a special design treatment that could draw the casual reader's eye, thereby emphasizing some of the more controversial or recognizable elements of Khurshid's narrative: her "boyish mannerisms" as a child or a first meeting with prominent stateswoman Begum Liaquat Ali Khan.[93] Another unique visual design element is a ruled box that encloses a three-paragraph introduction in which Khurshid offers her own explanations of why she decided to write her life story. As with the photographs, she begins with "the showbiz side" of her life. As she explains, autobiography offers a means of narrating how that "star" came to be by offering insight into her family, upbringing, and early experiences. As she describes it: "A record of nostalgia for the old and a source of wonder for the young."[94] In contrast, the book versions published after her death do not begin with her own words, but instead are bolstered by family reminiscence and academic apparatus. For Zubaan, a foreword by feminist historian Gail Minault contextualizes Khurshid's life, not within the performance tradition highlighted in the *Herald*, but instead with reference to a "movement for women's education among Indian Muslims"—in other words, her Aligarh connections.[95] Her nephew, renowned Indian politician Salman Haidar, also offers a portrait of "Appi and Daddy"—a foreword to the Pakistan version and an afterword to the Indian version—that fuses his aunt to her husband in a way often resisted in Khurshid's own account.[96] These other elements are flanked in both books by a preface and an afterword by her daughter Lubna Kazim as author/editor, the prefaces explaining the book's evolution and the afterwords describing Khurshid's final illness and death.[97]

In terms of the book's form, the fourteen chapter titles were also chosen and inserted by Lubna Kazim. They emphasize certain connections and relationships in Khurshid Mirza's life that only sometimes seem intended by the original manuscript. For instance, chapter 6 is titled "My Sister, Rashid Jahan 1905–1952."[98] Indicated here is a focus on Khurshid Jahan's eldest sister, who was a doctor and an even more celebrated writer closely affiliated with the radical Progressive Writers Movement and now a feminist icon.[99] In the original, she appears at various points, usually involved in some sort of prank, educational endeavor, or nationalist activity—but so do Khurshid Jahan's other sisters, Khatoon, Mumtaz, and Birjees, for whom no separate chapters are named. That an external figure was responsible for this significant alteration in form and thus autobiographical focus is suggested by penciled marginalia on the original manuscript. Next to one particular sentence about Rashid Jahan's new bobbed haircut adopted in the early 1930s is scribbled: "*more* on Rashid Jahan's education and emancipated attitude."[100] It was not clear to me at first who made these editorial marks that resulted in a whole separate chapter, but that person's identity seemed paramount to the reconstruction of Khurshid Mirza's life story in a more explicitly feminist vein. Was it the editor of the first book version, Samina Choonara? According to Lubna's two prefaces, this writer, editor, and feminist activist from Karachi "ably edited" the *Herald* installments, suggesting a number of "additions and deletions."[101] Or was it perhaps her Indian cousin Shahla Haidar, also named in the prefaces for having helped Lubna to "develop and complete the manuscript"?[102] Or was it someone else again? Recalling an earlier conversation with Lubna, I eventually recognized the handwriting as that of the aforementioned feminist historian Gail Minault, who confirmed her role as an early reader of the book manuscript.[103]

Encouraged by Minault, Lubna Kazim also made other changes to the autobiography's form and content. I noted in chapter 1 that according to Kazim's own admission in interview and the preface, the "informative chapters"—identified as chapter 2 ("Papa Mian"), chapter 4 ("The Struggle for Female Education"), and chapter 5 ("Abdullah Lodge, Aligarh")—were added to address publishers' critiques and thus were "largely" Lubna's own.[104] Her claim is belied in the case of chapter 2 by the large amount of material incorporated from Khurshid's second installment, but still it is clear that the three chapters have been bolstered by material from biographies, the journal *Khatun*, and even Minault's academic work.[105] As noted of the photographs and introduction already, these specific additions have the effect of reorienting the autobiography around Khurshid's Aligarh connections and her early life in India—with only the last four of

146 *Staging the Self*

fourteen chapters covering her forty-two years in Pakistan. Academic influence—if not from Minault, then from the publisher's editorial staff—is also evident in the variations in language used in the book editions to address nationalist episodes. References to "cunning firangi" and "red-faced devils" give way to more measured descriptions of a "patriotic army" seeking to "eject" certain "foreigners" from India.[106] Phraseology that worked for a Pakistani magazine could not have been deemed acceptable by the more academically oriented Karachi editor or a Delhi press. At a more prosaic level, the Urdu poetry published in the original script in the *Herald* was also transliterated into Latin script and usually translated into English in the book versions.[107]

The impact of editorial influence on the book versions is perhaps even more noticeable in the different titles. The *Herald* publication was titled "The Uprooted Sapling" without any further differentiation between installments. This title appears to have been chosen very deliberately by Khurshid Mirza in tribute to her father, Shaikh Abdullah. In the aforementioned introduction not included in the manuscript or later books, he is portrayed as a "young sapling uprooted from a green hilly Bhantani hamlet and transplanted in the fertile soil of Aligarh."[108] This description points to his physical and intellectual move from the Kashmiri village where he was born into the Hindu Brahmin caste as Thakur Das to the Muslim reformist center of Aligarh in the United Provinces after his conversion to Islam. Khurshid refers to her father as an "uprooted sapling" again in the final paragraphs of the final installment in a section also deleted from the book versions.[109] When her autobiography was first published as a book in Pakistan, however, it had a new title that emphasized her over her father: *The Making of a Modern Muslim Woman: Begum Khurshid Mirza, 1918–1989.*[110] Clearly, this title played to the religiously informed cultural identity that gave rise to Pakistan's formation and national identity, while also emphasizing the author's progressive qualities in terms that were resonant with an earlier reformist discourse. Khurshid's impressive achievements must have made her life story attractive to Zubaan as a feminist press, but equally so, it could not have been considered politic in early twenty-first-century India to highlight her Muslim identity. Hence, her narrative was renamed for the Indian audience with the autobiographical element clarified to: *A Woman of Substance: The Memoirs of Begum Khurshid Mirza*.[111]

Moving from form to content, other changes and exclusions also illustrate the way in which later editions of Khurshid Mirza's life story were crafted for a more religiously mixed South Asian audience. For instance, in the original manuscript and *Herald* installment, she explains her father's project for Muslim women's education in the following terms: "over the centuries, [Muslim women] had lost their legal rights because of the impact of Hindu culture, in which a woman had no identity of her own."[112] The penciled marginalia, attentive to the derogatory implications of this overgeneralized statement, suggested: "You may want to soften the import of this sentence."[113] In fact, the passage disappears entirely from the book versions. Elsewhere, similar assumptions of religious difference are also eradicated, even where the incident remains. For instance, in a particularly poignant passage, Khurshid recounts how, early in her marriage, her husband developed the "distressing habit" of avoiding evenings with her at their club in favor of "playing bridge and poker with a group of friends."[114] In the early versions, these friends are described as "government officers like him," but "all Hindus."[115] As she writes:

> They were nice people really, but their way of life was quite different from ours. Most of them had got married while at college and their mothers, sisters and wives were completely illiterate. They accepted the joint family system as a way of life in which the male members could do what they liked and the women had no further rights than to be fed, clothed and given a roof over their heads. It was inevitable that the company in which Akbar spent most of his evening had its influence and probably gave him the idea that he was giving in too much to me. It was not at all acceptable for a girl of my nature to wait till three in the morning, hungry and resentful, for her lord and master's pleasure.[116]

While much of this latter passage is reproduced in the book versions, the telling references to "Hindu" identity—including the husband's depiction as "lord and master"—are not.[117] A passage that is communally inflected thus appears more as a gendered critique appropriate both to an expanded audience and to the ideological interests of a feminist editor or press.

148   *Staging the Self*

The handling of Partition's violence, migration, and resettlement is similarly neutralized in the book versions. It is no longer "a very large number of Muslims" who were forced to migrate as a result of the "conditions that would arise from Partition," but instead a "mass migration of Muslims from India, *and Hindus and Sikhs from Pakistan*."[118] With a pan–South Asian audience in mind, Khurshid's focus on Muslim experience—a telltale sign of her sense of self and identity—was broadened by editors to incorporate experiences from both sides of Partition's divide. Even a reference in the original to "Hindu refugee property" in Lahore—deemed unacceptable for occupation by the Mirza family on account of being available only because of "other people's misfortunes"—is made religiously indeterminate in the book versions as "someone else's belongings."[119] At the same time, Khurshid's familial and sometimes patronizing attitude toward Pakistan as a new nation is also expunged. In the original manuscript and a *Herald* installment, she writes rather evocatively: "For me Pakistan was like a husband acquired through an arranged marriage, one with whom I fell in love as time went by. Pakistan was also like a child that needed devoted care and the right upbringing to enable it to reach the pride of its manhood."[120] The implication and meaning are quite different from the one that remains in the abbreviated and somewhat sanitized book versions: "as time went by, I fell in love with Pakistan."[121] Authorial intention in the crafting of a life story seems to have been lost through an editorial process attentive to political sensitivities in India and Pakistan alike.

Also particularly noticeable in the editing is the different handling of the mystical or supernatural. In her manuscript, Khurshid displays an ease with otherworldly phenomena that is often expunged, toned down, or treated with suspicion in the book versions. Whether these changes are attributable to her daughter's judicious editing or to the influence of a secular press is unknown, but they certainly suggest a very different relationship to the unseen in the author's life. One example comes early in the narrative when, in all four versions, Khurshid writes about her first "mystic" experience (changed to "supernatural" in the Zubaan version), at the age of four.[122] According to her description, she felt what she thought were her mother's hands on her feverish head during an illness, and she began to heal. Realizing that no human could have been there, her mother explained with a "wondering look" (changed to "faraway expression" in the book versions) that she had been visited by angels, of whom she should not be afraid, as they had been sent by Allah so that she would not feel alone. In the original and the magazine installment, Khurshid goes on to narrate other "unexplainable things" that occurred in the same room before reflecting:

> Cynics do not believe in the supernatural and would undoubtedly scoff at these incidents but I believe that there was—maybe still is—a benevolent Presence there . . . For me that experience has been a source of great strength all through my life; more than anything else, it gave me the firm conviction that Allah was always near and I was never alone.[123]

Not only do these omitted or truncated passages offer important insights into Khurshid's sense of self as a resolute believer in mystic phenomena, but they also situate her narrative within the long Urdu-Persianate tradition of life writing with its "expanded sense of reality."[124] As Barbara Metcalf writes of this literary tradition, "magic is on the loose."[125]

The mark of a skeptical editor on Khurshid's life story, then, is also evident elsewhere in the book versions. In chapter 8, an incident is related in which Khurshid rubs mango blossoms onto her hands in an attempt to bring "curative powers" to one of their orderlies who had been stung by a black scorpion while on shikar, hunting in the jungle. In all four versions, she recognizes that her proposal to use "old prescriptions" from a tattered volume in Urdu found in a secondhand bookshop could make her an "object of ridicule" in the eyes of her husband and his brother, but only in the book versions does she make the suggestion "sheepishly"—as if she herself is embarrassed by it, rather than perhaps her editors, who must have inserted the adverb.[126] Khurshid's brother-in-law continues to deride her, but in the original manuscript and the *Herald* installment, it is as if she has been overcome by a higher force: "oblivious to his words, I stared into space as if I was afloat and had nothing to do with the shackles of this earthly life."[127] Compare this description with the edited book versions in which, cleansed of the mystical element, she only "stared into space and prayed for the poor man's health."[128] Either way, he is cured. Khurshid's acknowledgment of the supernatural resurfaces later in the manuscript when she records various "inexplicable phenomena" at their house, Kenfield Cottage, in Naini Tal in the mid-1940s: bolts turning of their own accord, lights flipping on, and even ghosts. But for the book, her opening words are edited to achieve almost the opposite meaning: from "I did not know our house was haunted" to "I still refuse to believe that this house was haunted."[129]

One might imagine that an audience of cosmopolitan urbanites—as may read an English-language publication from Lahore or Delhi—may also not be entirely at ease with Khurshid Mirza's lengthy descriptions of her hunting exploits in accompaniment of her husband, Akbar. Clearly, these sections—grouped into one chapter in the book editions—were deemed too lengthy and significant in the original narrative to be left out altogether, but they still display the mark of an editor sensitive to her audience's historical location. For example, let us consider the subtle change in meaning imported to the passage in which Akbar shoots his "first tiger"—by the early twenty-first century, a somewhat cringeworthy topic in light of the species' threatened status. In the manuscript, the incident is portrayed as game hunting, as indeed it would have been at the time, but in final book versions a subtle attempt at justification is made by the insertion of an additional description of the tiger as a "declared man-eater."[130] The implication is that Akbar was providing a service, not just having fun. Khurshid's overarching description of her many shikar outings as "thrilling experiences" that represented her husband's "favourite sport" is also toned down to the far less gung-ho "stories of adventures and misadventures."[131] The use of this Kipling-esque phrase seems intended to relegate this section of her autobiography to the imperial past while at the same time demonstrating necessary sensitivity to contemporary animal ethics.

Other changes seem to have been made less in response to audience than to the editor's specific concerns. In one conversation that I had with Lubna Kazim about her mother's autobiography, she specified that she had felt particularly uncomfortable that an episode that had "shattered" her mother was not covered in sufficient depth in the original manuscript.[132] She referred to the untimely death of her youngest sister, Sumbul, in 1954 at the age of just fifteen, probably resulting from complications connected with her disabilities attributable to Down syndrome—a genetic disorder not named in the original, where Sumbul is described, in the language of the day, only as "mildly retarded."[133] While there are many references to this child, her special care, and her unique contributions to the family in the first versions, her death is treated rather perfunctorily: "She returned to her Maker in 1954 after a brief illness."[134] Having been with her mother at the time, Lubna clearly felt able to capture her mother's feelings on this occasion for the later versions. As she must have written (for her mother apparently did not): "I was numb with shock, unable to grasp the terrible truth that she was gone. For several years I was unable to function normally since Sumbul had been the focus of my life. After her death, I felt there was nothing I could do that was worthwhile and my family worried for my sanity."[135] This type of emotional introspection is often identified as a feature of the fully realized modern autobiography, so to include it even where the author did not could be to change the very character of the autobiographical narrative in terms of the sense of self that it projects.[136]

Nowhere is this more evident than in the handling of intimacy and sexuality. As I have explored elsewhere, a sharp distinction is often made in terms of autobiographical writing between a "West" that "reveals all" and Islamicate societies that do not.[137] The general assumption seems to be that Muslim authors, in South Asia especially, are too inhibited by "cultural codes of modesty" as defined by *sharam* and *'izzat*, shame and honor, to discuss love, lust, or the sexual act.[138] Reading the book versions of Begum Khurshid Mirza's autobiography seems to offer support for this position. Marriage begets children, and Khurshid's daughters appear one after another with little reference to her husband—beyond her desire to begin accompanying him once again on hunting trips or to the tennis court as soon as possible after birth.[139] However, a careful reading of the original manuscript, and, notably, the first Pakistani edition too, reveals that this omission is actually attributable to later editorial interference. Consider, for example, the following passage in which Khurshid narrates the events leading to her first child's conception:

> Marriage opened many enchanting vistas for me. I would dress up in all sorts
> of clothes to please Akbar and I had an unlimited supply of new clothes

152   *Staging the Self*

> to choose from including some alluring nightdresses from England. I was
> in love with my husband, but that love was mostly an idealistic sort of
> emotion—the kind which inspires worship, rather than physical union. But
> he was a man after all, poor darling. I could not blame him for his passion,
> and soon after I conceived my first child.[140]

We may presume that Lubna Kazim was responsible for removing this
passage, not considering her mother's seduction and her father's lust
appropriate for public consumption. But ultimately, its exclusion—like
other changes in the book editions—has important implications for how
Begum Khurshid Mirza's autobiography is framed and read.

CONCLUSION: IN DIALOGUE WITH OTHERS

I began this chapter, as the last, with Virginia Woolf on the basis that she
raises important questions of autobiography in evoking "a room of one's
own." As I queried in this chapter's introduction: is it really appropriate
to project autobiographical writing by Muslim women in South Asia as a
wholly personal act? The idea of autobiography as an individual crafting
of an autonomous self has long been central to its definition in the West.
We may recall Phillipe Lejeune's influential assertion in his oft-quoted
L'autobiographie en France (1971): "We call autobiography the retrospective narrative in prose that *someone* makes of his own existence when *he*
puts the principal accent upon *his life*, especially upon the story of *his own*
personality."[141] In the intervening years, Black American and feminist
critiques have largely dismantled the idea of the "sovereign self" as a myth
that ignores more "relational aspects": individual lives circumscribed as
much by cultural norms as the modern state's "technologies of power."[142]
And yet Lejeune's concept of the "autobiographical pact" between author
and reader remains salient. The reader assumes that by the affixing of an
authorial signature, a "contract of identity" will be honored: the author
and the narrative's protagonist are accepted to be one and the same. A
publisher may play a role in attesting to the "truth" of the "signature"—
guaranteeing that a narrative is indeed "self-reflexive or autobiographical" by agreeing to publish it—but the publisher's influence on a text is
otherwise imagined to be minimal. Hence, we read autobiography differ-

ently than we do fiction or even biography. We presume that an author is responsible for writing an essential truth about her life.[143]

But as this and the previous chapter have shown, the autobiographical act is actually far more complicated than a woman sitting alone to craft an unmediated story about her life. We saw in chapter 3 that South Asia's Muslim women produced autobiographical narratives with specific audiences in mind—from an audience of one to international distribution—with varying consequences for style and content. Gendered audiences inspired gendered narratives, their topics chosen to satisfy the domesticated interests of a fictionalized sisterhood. An autobiography for real family, on the other hand, could inspire intimacy and self-censorship in equal measures. This chapter develops that argument by showing that literary milieu was as influential in shaping a narrative's form and content, whether that narrative was circulated as a manuscript, a journal article, or a book. In each case, the process of production introduced new actors—editors, translators, cowriters, and publishers—who were complicit in the construction of the autobiography. The four iterations of Begum Khurshid Mirza's life story illustrate in particular how structure, illustrations, titles, and even individual passages could be shaped by editors, audiences, and publishers. The very characteristics theorized as representative of men or women in Islamicate societies or the West may be defined by the production process. These examples thus point to just how central the "narrator-reader-publisher relationship," as Smith and Watson call it, is to understanding how the Muslim female self has been constructed in autobiographical writing.[144]

The framework of performance offers an effective means of theorizing this relationship by underlining how concepts of selfhood may be "staged" in autobiographical writings. By regarding the author as a performative subject—an artiste acting out her life story on the page—this approach enables an appreciation of how each rendition of a life story may be tailored *to* and *by* audience, literary milieu, or historical moment. At the same time, my historical materials attributed to South Asian Muslim women encourage an extension of the theoretical model of autobiography as a performative act in a way that may also be appropriate to other contexts. Clearly, it is not just the author who is acting out her life on the page when the construction of her life story is also affected by a variety of other theatrical players: the publisher as director, coauthors as scriptwriters, editors and translators as stagehands, the audience as reviewer. The very stage, or in fact stages, on which she performs her life story may be multiple, malleable, or even revolving. Autobiography thus emerges from this chapter less as an individual act of the self in performance than as a full theatrical production on tour: a fluid and sometimes even scripted narrative constructed in dialogue with others. To recover the Muslim female self from autobiographical writings, I contend, offers a challenge beyond interrogating a given text in isolation for individuality or emotionality. Accordingly, chapter 5 seeks to minimize cultural variation when assessing representation and identity as a gendered and historicized articulation by comparing self-narratives within families—or autobiographical genealogies.

CHAPTER FIVE

AUTOBIOGRAPHICAL GENEALOGIES

INTRODUCTION: KITH AND KIN

Particularly striking when considering autobiographical writings in Muslim South Asia as a body of literature are the kinship links between authors. In chapter 2, I made the point that many authors from Bhopal and Rampur were related through ruling families. The Bhopal case is especially pronounced, since it includes five generations of royal women—Sikandar, Shah Jahan, Sultan Jahan, Maimoona Sultan, and Abida Sultaan—who produced autobiographical writings of various sorts over nearly a century and a half.[1] With regard to Rampur, I noted that Jahanara Habibullah included autobiographical extracts by her mother and sister in her own *Remembrance of Days Past*. Jahanara and her distant relative Mehrunissa Khan also recorded the same court life at roughly the same time in their respective autobiographies, though from very different positions within the zenana hierarchy: Jahanara as sister to the nawab's first wife and Mehrunissa as daughter of the nawab's third wife.[2] Less removed were Jahanara's two cousins on her father's side, Zohra Segal and Hamida Saiduzzafar, both of whom published full-length autobiographies. Even her mother-in-law, Inam Fatima Habibullah, prepared a European travelogue (see chapter 2). More recently, Jahanara's daughter Muneeza Shamsie has written shorter autobiographical pieces for Pakistani newspapers and other forums, as has Muneeza's daughter, novelist Kamila Shamsie, in the British press.[3]

155

156   *Autobiographical Genealogies*

Taking kinship in a different direction, Hamida Saiduzzafar's brother (and thus Jahanara's cousin), Mahmuduzzafar Khan, was married to the same Rashid Jahan who, as noted in chapter 4, featured in her sister Khurshid Mirza's autobiography.[4] Another notable link is that between Saliha Abid Hussain and her niece, Sughra Mehdi—the former dedicated her *Silsila-i-Roz o Shab* to the latter in tribute to her inspiration and support.[5] In other cases, the autobiographical links were between women and their male relatives. Perhaps the best-known cases come from the Mughal court, where Gulbadan and Jahanara participated in an autobiographical culture exemplified by Babur's *Vaqa'i'* and Jahangir's *Tuzuk*.[6] In the modern era, a parallel could be drawn with Saliha Abid Hussain, who, as noted in chapter 2, followed in the footsteps of her great-grandfather, reformer and poet Altaf Husain Hali, in writing an autobiography.[7] Hamida Saiduzzafar and Shaista Ikramullah, on the other hand, may have been inspired by brothers and cousins who penned autobiographies and travel narratives before their own—I think of Mahmuduzzafar Khan's *Quest for Life* (1954) and Huseyn Shaheed Suhrawardy's *Memoirs* (1963).[8]

There are also a surprising number of autobiographical couples. In her introduction, Saliha Abid Hussain informed her readers that her husband, Sayyid Abid Hussain, had begun writing a life story but died before he was able to take it beyond an account of his first trip abroad to study in Oxford and Berlin.[9] Still, that he and other male relatives had *not* completed their autobiographies acted as a stimulus for her to persist with her own.[10] Though Jahanara Habibullah's husband, Isha'at, did write a memoir, as yet it remains unpublished beyond a few short excerpts in a Pakistani newspaper.[11] More explicit in following her husband's autobiographical example was Hameeda Akhtar Husain Raipuri. As she explained in the preface to her *Hamsafar*, it was only after reading Akhtar's celebrated literary autobiography, *Gard-i-Rah* (1984)—translated recently as *The Dust of the Road*—that she was inspired to "fill in the things that he had left unsaid": all those details about the "great personalities" from whom they had received "affection and kindness" over the years.[12] Clearly, a shared life need not make for a shared life story.

These autobiographical genealogies thus reflect back on motivation by suggesting how family models could inspire but also structure autobiographical output. At the same time, they offer a unique context in which to consider autobiography as an evolving literary form that is gendered in its construction. Accordingly, the aim of this chapter is to use a closed case study—of one extended family in which the cultural milieu was largely shared—to examine how autobiography's form, style, and content may have been contingent on gender and time. Chosen for analysis is Bombay's Tyabji clan on account of its many and varied contributions to the autobiographical genre—family diaries, travelogues, speeches, memoirs, autobiographies, and articles—that date from the mid-nineteenth century to the near present. By examining how Tyabji men and women of multiple generations narrated their lives, or at least fragments of them, I indicate how articulations of a Muslim female self could be transformed by history. Underlying this analysis is an emphasis on representation and identity. In three chronological sections, I compare various themes and sub-themes in this set of autobiographical writings: from shifting nationality and regional identity to motherhood, the home, and sexuality. As evidence of how an author chose to present herself—intentionally or otherwise—these autobiographical motifs prove key to the project of gendering and historicizing interiority. Theoretical models of autobiographical difference summarized in the introduction and chapter 1 will thus be interrogated throughout, and especially in the concluding section, for their applicability to Muslim South Asia.

The Tyabjis, it should be noted, encompass a bewilderingly large and complex extended family, referred to as the *qabila* or *khandan*, traced to an eponymous founder, Tyabjee Bhoymeeah (1803–63).[13] According to a family biographer, he began life as a "penniless urchin" in Cambay, but "did odd jobs, repaired umbrellas, sold onions, hawked old goods, became a pedlar, sold millinery and toys" until he rose to the status of a "merchant prince of Bombay."[14] His commercial success enabled him to send his sons to England for a foreign education that guaranteed their access to the upper echelons of Bombay's colonial society. Perhaps most illustrious was his second-youngest son, Badruddin Tyabji (1844–1906), already introduced in chapter 2. Having trained as a barrister, he rose to become the first Muslim judge, then the first Indian chief justice of the Bombay High Court. His parallel career as a politician and reformer—notably, as

158   *Autobiographical Genealogies*

president of the third Indian National Congress in 1887—ensured him a celebrated place in Indian nationalist history.[15] Later male descendants of Tyabjee Bhoymeeah, including nationalist Abbas Tyabji (1854–1936), tennis player A. H. Fyzee (1879–1962), legal scholar Asaf A. A. Fyzee (1899–1981), and ornithologist Sálim Ali (1896–1987), also achieved national and international fame.[16] So did a number of female Tyabjis featured in this chapter—among them, author and patron of the arts Atiya Fyzee, social activist Shareefah Hamid Ali, and craft campaigner Laila Tyabji. Other Tyabji women achieving renown were food writer Surayya Tyabji (1919–78) and lawyer and campaigner Kamila Tyabji (1918–2004).[17]

Members of the *khandan* thus fulfill the authorial criteria laid out in chapters 2 and 3 of belonging to a highly educated and urban elite with exceptional occupational achievements appropriate to justifying autobiographical expression. An effect in the colonial era and after was an anglicized lifestyle—to which descriptions in this chapter of private clubs, English drawing rooms, European furniture, and foreign travel attest. The Tyabjis were thus far from typical—and may even have been perceived as different, exotic, or aspirational by those outside the clan who consumed their life stories. At the same time, they remained rooted in South Asian Muslim culture, supplementing the convent education given to girls, for instance, with lessons at home in Urdu, Persian, and the Qur'an (see chapter 2). Nazir Ahmad's seminal reformist novel, *Mirat ul-'Arus*, with its overt message that Muslim women should be educated and hardworking, but also pious, modest, and well mannered, also remained required reading for Tyabji girls.[18] Still, as leading figures in Bombay's Sulaimani Bohra community, the Tyabjis retained a liminal status as part of a minority Ismaili sect (see chapter 3) that was not entirely mitigated by their adoption of Urdu (over Gujarati) or their patronage of Islamic organizations from the late nineteenth century.[19] The clan thus remained apart at least until the mid-twentieth century—in a way pertinent to the aims of this chapter—from the more dominant north Indian ashraf with whom they, like many Gujarati Muslims, declined to intermarry beyond a few isolated instances.[20] Cousin marriages made for complicated kinship relations that underlie the autobiographical genealogies that we now explore.

LIFE, DEATH, AND TRAVEL
IN THE HIGH NOON OF IMPERIALISM

The progenitor of the Tyabji autobiographical tradition appears to have been Tyabjee Bhoymeeah himself, who sometime before May 1862 wrote a first rough draft of his life story: twelve pages in his own hand on a few sheaves of paper. That initial draft was then corrected and expanded into twenty-three pages written mostly in his own hand (with the exception of the last six pages) in a larger family notebook titled "Kitab-i-Akhbar-i-Qabila Tyab Ali." Both are described as "Sawanih Tyab Ali bin Bhai Miyan Baqalam Khud," or "Incidents in the life of Tyab Ali bin Bhai Miyan as written by himself."[21] The narrative is chronological in form, starting with his year of birth in 1803, but ending abruptly in 1829 in his twenty-fifth year. As he died at the age of sixty, in 1863, the bulk of his life, including the years during which he achieved real success as a merchant, is not addressed. Nevertheless, the existing narrative represented a clear attempt to chart how the author's enterprising nature enabled him to rise from penury to commercial success. This central theme, or leitmotif, is introduced early in the narrative through an anecdote. According to Tyabjee, his father sometimes cursed him as a baby for having been born shortly after his entire fortune was lost to a great fire in Bombay that consumed his shop that sold European and Chinese goods. Tyabjee's grandfather Haji Bhai apparently retorted: "O foolish fellow, never speak such words about this boy. This son of yours will be very blessed [*mabruk*]; he will be clever, fortunate and sit in a *palkhi* [palanquin]."[22] His ultimate fate, and the means of achieving it, were thus forecast nearly from the outset.

The indeterminacy attributed by Pascal to the best autobiographers in the Western tradition is apparent here too in that Tyabjee goes on to dismiss his grandfather's predictions as "wishful thinking" on the part of an indulgent parent.[23] He also intersperses his tale of upward mobility with sketches of failed business ventures that resulted in sometimes disastrous loss.[24] When an eventual turn of fortune does come, however, it is attributed not to Tyabjee's efforts but to a number of strokes of "good luck": finding two apparently deserted bundles of indigo worth several hundred rupees, purchasing a cartload of liquidated goods that turned out to be boot polish (an item that was in demand with soldiers), gaining ac-

160   *Autobiographical Genealogies*

cess to several trunks of women's hats that he hawked to European ladies at great profit.[25] The passivity identified with the Islamic autobiographical tradition—by which events just happen to the author, rather than being instigated by the protagonist—was thus displayed here on occasion.[26] And yet this short autobiography left little doubt that it was Tyabjee's own personality traits—his ingenuity, his enterprise, his fight—that enabled him to succeed in the fluid commercial environment that characterized Bombay in the early nineteenth century. In "Sawanih," we are thus introduced to a tangible and engaging individual who was often frank in his self-reflection. That his written language evoked the spoken Hindustani of that era's commercial classes—interspersed with Gujarati vocabulary and expressions, erroneous pronunciations, grammatical errors, and even spelling mistakes not common to more standardized Urdu—perhaps heightens his character's authenticity.[27] His everyday language also facilitates an everyday discussion of his domestic circumstances—for instance, the delicate and unsatisfactory negotiations that led to his pitiable marriage celebrations, and also the births of his first two children—that ensures that this autobiography is not limited to Tyabjee's public persona.[28]

Possibly predating Tyabjee Bhoymeeah's autobiography by a few years were the family notebooks already remarked upon for having contained the revised draft of his text. As explained in chapter 1, these were known variously as the "Akhbar ki Kitab," "Kitab-i-Akhbar," and "Akhbarnama," all titles that indicated their status as "news books." At family functions in the early 1940s, Asaf A. A. Fyzee gave talks on this *akhbar* tradition in which he explained that it was started by Tyabjee's third son, Camruddin, soon after he returned to India from studying in England in 1858. It is not clear why he decided to adopt the practice—if he was adapting a model that he had come across in British homes or, as Fyzee suggested, he was reinvigorating an old Arab custom.[29] Irrespective of the reasons, the seriousness with which the *khandan* took up the enterprise is indicated by the production of five initial volumes between 1860 and 1878.[30] From the 1870s, a number of Tyabjee's sons and a couple of his daughters also started volumes in their own homes that were first named after individual family patriarchs, then particular residences.[31] The formal dedication with which each book began emphasized its purpose in recording "interesting" and "fun" happenings within the family for the sake of posterity.[32] These newsworthy incidents sometimes were notable public events—for instance, Badruddin Tyabji's account of his Congress presidency in Madras in 1887 or Surayya Tyabji's summary of debates held at the Muhammadan Educational Conference in Bombay in 1903.[33] But more usually they described quotidian activities within the family: picnics, parties, horse-riding, badminton matches, sporting tournaments, poetry readings, and even trips to the dentist.[34]

The *akhbar* books, then, are more family diary than autobiography in that they rarely contain a retrospective or constructed life story. Nevertheless, they offer a useful means by which to consider the gendered contributions of one extended family to a distinct proto-autobiographical genre. As suggested by the examples already given, Tyabji women wrote in the *akhbar* books on a very regular basis—perhaps even more regularly than their menfolk. Many of the opening dedications, in fact, emphasized women's participation by encouraging "our young ladies" especially to "work hard at their pieces."[35] Yet a clear distinction between the entries made by Tyabji men and women is not immediately apparent: both sexes demonstrated their commitment to a reformist milieu associated with Islamic modernity through their focus on education, physical activity, music, literature, and the Urdu language. The family's positioning in relation to the colonial state was also apparent in that men and women alike recorded their visits to British homes in Bombay, where they met English officials or their wives in cordial circumstances. In these sections, Tyabji girls were more likely to comment on the elegance of English drawing rooms by recording at some length their impressions of furniture, paintings, carpets, and other domestic interiors.[36] Their older female relatives, on the other hand, were more inclined than their menfolk to reflect on changing social customs within the clan in terms of marriage, dress, and veiling practices. A number of women chose to write at length, for instance, on the aforementioned Muhammadan Educational Conference in 1903 that saw Badruddin Tyabji speak out against purdah as a social convention not imposed by the Islamic faith. While men had their say in a public forum, Tyabji women expressed their opinions in the family's *akhbar* books.[37]

162   *Autobiographical Genealogies*

The final illness and death of a family member could also inspire poignant entries in the *akhbar* books by Tyabji men and women keen to memorialize a loved one. Two such passages appropriate for comparison here in that they offer particular insight into language, emotionality, and introspection appeared in the "Chabooka" and "Mahableshwar" chronicles. In the first entry, Badruddin Tyabji's third daughter, Sakina (1871–1960), described the final days of her mother, Rahat, in August 1905, while in the second, Hadi Camruddin Tyabji (1871–1960), recorded the passing of his wife, Jamila, in April 1906.[38] Not only were the dates very close, but the family relationships were as well: Jamila was the sister of Sakina and the daughter of Rahat. A first distinction may be made in terms of language: Sakina wrote in Urdu, while her brother-in-law chose English. But it would be inappropriate to generalize from these examples, as, on the whole, the language of composition within the *akhbar* books was more reflective of paternity. While Badruddin's branch took pride in their use of Urdu, the children of Camruddin, of which Hadi was one, were more likely to write in English.[39] The form and style of these two entries, on the other hand, are almost identical. Both are several pages long, tracing the heart-rending process by which Rahat and Jamila first became ill, then rallied enough to give hope for recovery, then declined to their ultimate end. The language used is highly emotive, leaving little doubt as to the author's anguish. As Sakina opened with reference to their family home: "Poor poor Somerset has been orphaned, left desolate, hopeless. Oh God, why did dearest Mother all of a sudden go away from us?"[40] A few months later, Hadi addressed the deceased Jamila directly before reflecting upon his own loss: "What recollections and associations does your name wake up! What happy days of the past which are to return no more! Who'd have thought that we were to part company so soon, and that only 5 years, 4 months and 10 days of married life were allotted to us . . . It is dreadful to think what a void her departure has created in my life."[41] For Tyabji men and women to reveal their feelings so completely distinguished their respective contributions to the *akhbar* books, not from each other but from traditional Islamic life stories deemed devoid of this type of self-expression.[42]

As family members were cornered to contribute to the *akhbar* books upon arrival or departure, another feature was that they often documented journeys of one type or another. Particularly notable among these journeys was an eight-month trip to Europe made by Badruddin Tyabji's eldest daughter, Amina Tyabji (1866–1942), accompanying the Maharani of Baroda in 1893–94. Upon her return, Amina was cajoled into recording her impressions of Britain, France, Switzerland, and Italy in the Badruddin and Amiruddin *akhbar* books.[43] These two separate travel pieces, composed nearly a year apart, are remarkably similar in that in both cases, the author demurred from writing in any detail on the basis that she was too short on time or just "too lazy" to offer anything more than a "fragmentary account."[44] As she elaborated in the Amiruddin entry: "France, Italy, Switzerland—in all those places we saw all sorts of wonderful things, natural and man-made, and it would be a huge task even to give a short description of it all . . . Just thinking about it overwhelms me."[45] It can thus prove difficult to draw out her sense of self, but a glimpse of individual interests was perceptible in Amina's occasional attention to clothes, café culture, and crowded streets. Consider, for example, the following few lines on her time in Paris: "We would spend half the night looking at the shop windows, so beautifully dressed with wonderful things, and then we would watch absolutely mesmerized, people drinking coffee in the cafés, in their elegant clothes."[46] Otherwise, Amina provided brief and somewhat impressionistic accounts of "dark smoking" London, "delicate, bridelike" Paris, and "historic" Rome before reflecting on the joys of meeting family and friends in Britain and France.[47]

More florid in her description of travel was Atiya Fyzee (1877–1967) when she wrote in the Yali *akhbar* a few years later in May 1898. A "hazardous" trip in high winds by steamer and paddleboat from her sister Nazli's home in Murud to the family's beach house in Kihim, a resort south of Bombay, inspired her short account of a "never-to-be-forgotten voyage."[48] To get a sense of her style and inspiration, it is worth quoting the second paragraph in full:

> Yesterday at the usual time in the early morn, the steamer that was to convey us was signalled as in view. The previous day the sea was somewhat calmer although the wind continued to blow, while yester morn the sun had risen through a bank of reddened clouds, tinging with its crimson rays the crests

164   *Autobiographical Genealogies*

> of the black waves. The sea kept roaring & ran so high that the speed of our steamer (by the way it was unusually swift thanks to the Captain, a worthy fellow!) was nothing compared to the rolling of the billows, in which our vessel & fast plunging first in one direction & then the other.[49]

Composed in impeccable, if rather ornate, English, the passage suggested an imagination fueled more by Victorian romance novels than by the reformist or historical texts preferred by many Tyabji women.[50] Still more expansive, if less colorful, was Badruddin Tyabji's sixth daughter, Halima (1881–1969), when recounting a family expedition to Jog Falls (also known as Gersoppa Falls), now in Karnataka, a few years later in 1905. Over a number of pages in Urdu in the Badruddin *akhbar*, she demonstrated her family's appreciation of the natural environment, physical fitness, and a good adventure.[51] As she narrated their journey by cart and bicycle along the "road from Kamsi": "For about five or six miles we went through a huge bamboo jungle, and it is quite impossible to convey the beauty of their shapes, the denseness, the different forms, and then, the majesty of that jungle in the evening light—it is truly a wonderful sight. . . . The forests were so dense that one couldn't see anything inside at all—who knows what sorts of animals lurk inside them!"[52] While reflective of individual personalities, these increasingly lengthy and detailed mini-travelogues point to how women's capacity for self-expression was evolving on the cusp of the twentieth century.

Having written these travel narratives for family consumption in the *akhbar* books, several Tyabji women turned to publishing longer pieces in the Urdu press in the early twentieth century. While some of these articles traced journeys within India, others followed Amina Tyabji's lead in documenting travel abroad.[53] Two notable book-length works were produced by the Fyzee sisters, Atiya and Nazli, between 1906 and 1908. In terms of style, they demonstrated their debt to the *akhbar* tradition by taking the form of a *roznamcha*, or travel diary. The relationality associated with Muslim and women's autobiography alike was also manifest in their attention to others—with more than 150 individuals being named or described in Atiya's account alone. At the same time, Nazli's *Sair-i-Yurop* displayed a formality in its structure and language eschewed by the short entries in colloquial Urdu in Atiya's *Zamana-i-Tahsil*. As evidence, we may compare the following two entries in which the sisters depicted their arrival in London. The first, by Atiya in September 1906, was exuberant: "How can London be described and how can it be imagined without seeing it! Ofo! Such streets and what a grand city, and the shops! It appears very nice when it is lit up at night. The way each shop is decorated—it's truly a skill."[54] Nazli, in comparison, was staid as she narrated the journey with precision:

> [W]e set off from Paris for Calais which we reached around 1:15. Then a short steamer voyage was again before us. We were afraid that this portion of the trip would be problematic but fortunately the sea was calm as a lake. In an hour and fifteen minutes we stepped foot on English soil. The train was ready. There was a big crowd in the carriage but we managed and set off for London reaching Charing Cross Station in two hours.[55]

Atiya's *Zamana*—with its everyday observations in everyday language—thus displayed characteristics more comparable to Tyab Ali's foundational autobiography than to its sister narrative, Nazli's *Sair*.

Still, Atiya and Nazli both exhibited typical Tyabji traits in focusing on education, gardens, the natural environment, and physical activity alongside more gendered preoccupations with food, dress, servants, and domestic interiors. A useful example of the latter is Atiya's description of a visit to her old friend Navajbai Tata at her new home, the stately York House, in Twickenham, outside London, in June 1907:

> The entire drawing room was decorated in pink, and [Navajbai] was wearing agreeable clothes. Right now they have twenty-one servants. A haughty and cunning doorman of long service—how many revolutions he must have seen—opened the door; the well-built and tall gardeners; the boys serving at the table with such well-bred manners, dressed in dark blue and gold uniforms; the cook's manner is unique; and there are four maids. . . . The sensibility, politeness and propriety of the servants are perfect. None of them is visible, but whenever one is needed, they are present . . . I don't know where the maids hide for if you go in your room ten times and mess everything up, even then everything is always in its place.[56]

166   *Autobiographical Genealogies*

The two travelogues thus conveyed the "vivid and plausible individuality" associated with modern European autobiographies, but not always the introspection.[57] Atiya, for instance, revealed only in one of her final entries the "health problems"—very likely a type of depression—that forced her to leave London one year into her two-year program.[58] Nazli likewise admitted that she was too "depressed" to do more than "sleep" in her room in her first days in London, but she did not say why.[59] Troubled circumstances in their personal lives—Atiya's now infamous relationship with Iqbal and Nazli's childlessness—suggest that their inhibition masked intimacies not deemed appropriaste for public revelation.[60]

As well as contributing short travel pieces to the *akhbar* books and Urdu press, Tyabji women also wrote speeches. Two that have been preserved in manuscript form in family collections deserve close attention here in that they too recounted trips to Europe, but nearly three decades apart. The first was composed by Amina Tyabji soon after her return to India for presentation at the family ladies' club, Akdé Suraya, in August 1894, so even before she contributed to the *akhbar* books. As in those entries, she evoked the strange and wonderful (*'aja'ib*) things that she had seen in Europe: beautiful scenery, historic buildings, sporting occasions, and the workings of government. She thus registered her debt to the *'aja'ib* genre—summarized by Sunil Sharma as a "catalogue of wonders and curiosities"—in using descriptions of travel to reveal "configurations of knowledge created and revealed by god."[61] But she offered few particulars of her transforming experience, seemingly unable to express herself even before her "sisters" in the *khandan*. As she explained: "Dear sisters, I felt like telling you about some of my experiences, but I don't know what to say. What am I to explain? Everything was new and wondrous [*'aja'ib*] to me. . . . If I start describing all these wonders and beauties, the hearers' capacity of listening and my own talent of describing will both be put to the test."[62] The effect was a speech limited to just four short paragraphs—of which the first was introduction, the second was dedicated to the begam of Awadh as Amina's precursor in traveling to Europe, the third contained the list of wonders detailed above, and the final paid tribute to the *khandan* and their club for giving her the opportunity to speak.

The second speech was delivered by Amina's youngest sister, Safia Jabir Ali, to a group of women in Rangoon around 1920.[63] That it was written in English probably reflected her mixed audience—Indians and Burmese from different regions and religious communities—as she usually wrote in Urdu. Still, it began on an equally modest note: "I feel very diffident about interesting you sufficiently, but what cannot be cured must be endured, so I hope you will have the patience to bear with me!"[64] She then went on to describe over eight pages her experience of traveling alone by steamship to Europe, where she joined her husband to visit many places in England, Scotland, and Germany—not just London, Edinburgh, and Hamburg, but also Bournemouth, Cambridge, Birmingham, Manchester, Liverpool, Sheffield, Glasgow, Rosyth, and Leipzig. About each town or city, she recorded what had left the "best most vivid impression," whether it be a sight, an activity, or an encounter after her often solitary sightseeing. The natural environment was, as in many Tyabji writings, a recurrent theme that evoked intense emotion, as were Safia's impressions of the local people and the local people's impressions of her. We may consider the following extract as an example of the latter:

> One thing that surprised me was the ignorance even educated people showed towards India. One would naturally expect them to know a good deal about us. We read so much about them, and have adopted so many of their customs, are so familiar with their literature, thought, art, ways of living that it is quite easy for us to live with them, there, without having to learn anything extraordinary about them. But they, on the contrary, seem to be ignorant of everything connected with us! There were many who were awfully surprised to find an Indian woman of a good well-to-do family, being able to walk about, and go about in their moving staircases and lifts etc. without being scared to death! Also they are under the impression that Indian ladies generally lie on durwans [divans] in gorgeous apparel, waited on by women, and dream away their days surrounded by wealth and luxury! I had to tell them that, though we did not work half as hard as they did, still we were not anything like what they imagined![65]

Her bold nature thus shone through in her determination to travel soon after the First World War against advice, her independence in exploring

168   *Autobiographical Genealogies*

new cities alone, and her willingness to challenge her hosts' preconceptions about Indians. Thirty years on, Safia was far less inhibited than her sister Amina in representing self and other.

NARRATING LIVES IN A NATIONALIST AGE

Interestingly, both sisters—Amina and Safia—moved on from travel writing to produce memoirs representative of more full-fledged autobiographical writing in the interwar years. Both of these examples have been employed in previous chapters when discussing authors, audiences, and literary milieus, but it is worth revisiting them here to consider their comparative representation of self and identity. As noted in chapter 3, Amina's short piece of just five pages, packaged as "extracts" from a "diary," was published in the journal *Roshni* in 1946—a few years after the author's death in 1942. According to an editor's note, the journal acquired these extracts from Amina's daughter Shareefah Hamid Ali after they had been translated by Amina's husband, Abbas, in the 1930s. Various historical references in the text—to new legislative councils, the Maternity and Child Welfare Association, and a current civil disobedience movement—suggest that the narrative was actually written around 1920. According to her own account, Amina was inspired to prepare a "short sketch" of her educational, social, and political activities over thirty years as a response to the "malignant propaganda" being circulated by English women about their "Indian sisters." She thus began by detailing her role in establishing a Muslim girls' school in Baroda shortly after her return from Europe in 1894, then turned to a description of her involvement with various ladies' clubs, a reformatory for juvenile offenders, and the Indian National Congress. Her nationalist affiliations were expressed in terms of her "wholehearted" support for a civil disobedience movement intended to attain "full Swaraj for my Motherland." A religiously informed communal identity could be discerned in her description of projects for Muslim girls involving instruction in Urdu and Qur'anic studies. But far more prevalent was her conscious evocation of "we Indian women"—a phrase repeated throughout the short article with the explicit aim of including both "city women" and "our village women."[66]

As explained in chapter 3, Safia's much longer memoir—more than three hundred pages of handwritten Urdu in a tattered notebook—was started a few years after her elder sister's endeavor in 1926, but not really elaborated until the early 1940s. It, too, revealed the author's nationalist affiliations, not least in her description of meetings with and for "Gandhiji" in Burma and Bombay. At the same time, a stronger Muslim identity surfaced in the distinctions that Safia sometimes made between the "Muslim community," or *qaum*, and "other Indians"—though clearly she did not consider religious and national identities to be mutually exclusive.[67] Nowhere did she refer to her family's specific attachment to the minority Sulaimani Bohra sect, despite dedicating large sections of her narrative to Tyabji genealogy. Being a member of the *khandan*—descended from "Dadasaheb" Tyab Ali via the great Badruddin Tyabji—was far more crucial. That the latter sections of the memoir were addressed explicitly to her beloved son, Amiruddin (see chapter 3) points to his singular importance within her life (and life story) as the fruit of her apparently perfect union with her husband, Jabir Ali. As she began the second, longer section of her memoir in 1942:

> Our son Amiruddin was born on 23 June 1928, and is now 14 years old, and sitting for the Cambridge exams from the Gwalior Scindia school. We feel his absence sorely . . . But we feel that our dear son's health and education are of paramount importance, and we bear up with fortitude. . . . When this book was started we had no child—indeed, we'd borne the grief of losing two children, and resigned ourselves to God not wishing to bless us with children. Yet in spite of this deep sorrow that lay hidden in our hearts, we were so happy together that life held much joy for us. For me to have such a good, amiable, eager man for a husband, one who was so loved by all, was cause enough for happiness.[68]

Her gendered identity as mother and wife within the family collective was thus couched in terms of basic human emotions—"joy" and "grief," "fortitude" and "happiness"—nowhere apparent in her sister's more matter-of-fact account of career and politics.

Closely related to these two female authors was the aforementioned ornithologist, Sálim Ali. His autobiography, *The Fall of a Sparrow*, was not

170   *Autobiographical Genealogies*

published until 1985, by which time the author was nearly ninety years old.[69] He was, however, a contemporary of Safia Jabir Ali, having been born just three years after her, in 1896. Her husband, Jabir, was also his brother, while Amina Tyabji was his aunt. Like them, he touched on many themes recurrent in Tyabji writings, not least travel and transport, gardens, poetry, language, and the natural environment. But, unsurprisingly, his main focus was birds. In fact, Sálim proved himself to be as singular in his autobiographical intentions as the clan's founder, Tyab Ali. While the latter charted his rise to mercantile success, Sálim traced the often convoluted path by which he became a world-class ornithologist—or, as he phrased it simply in the first line of the first chapter, "how my interest in birds originated."[70] His narrative also retained the indeterminacy that distinguished Tyab Ali's "Sawanih" in that Sálim was self-deprecating of his abilities at school and, on a number of occasions, described himself as an "unemployed and unsuccessful job hunter."[71] But ultimately that indeterminacy was resolved through a recognition of his own achievements, not least many bestselling books—perhaps the best known of which is *The Book of Indian Birds* (first published in 1941, but now in its fourteenth edition)—and a raft of national and international prizes.[72] His use of autobiography to justify his then unusual career to various "doubting" elders is revealed at various points in the final chapters. As he wrote of his maternal uncle, Abbas Tyabji: "Abbas remained the most caustic critic among my elders of my ornithological activities, which he thoroughly disapproved. He considered I was merely a shirker and a waster, and that ornithology was just a cover for my indolence and reluctance to do honest and gainful work. It is a pity he did not live to see that the indolence has paid dividends!"[73]

While retaining a central theme, or leitmotif, Sálim Ali's *The Fall of a Sparrow* also implied a debt to the Rousseauian model in providing insight into the personality or characteristics that facilitated ornithological success. At various points throughout the narrative, the author recalled anecdotes that pointed to the practical, dogged, and adventurous spirit that enabled his birding career. Indeed, Sálim was often explicit about his own "congenital unbelief in all forms of spiritualism, occultism, astrology and ultra sensory 'magic,'" which led him to find rational and scientific explanations for the world around him.[74] While he may have begun life as a "god-fearing Muslim child," by adulthood he identified himself as an "upper middle-class Indian" with a "Muslim name," but presumably little or no faith.[75] At the same time, Sálim's sense of self was often revealed best through his descriptions of others, specifically the qualities in them that he admired. Embracing the relationality associated with Islamic life stories, his autobiography—like others produced by Tyabji men and women before him—was populated throughout with perceptive and meticulous biographies of family, friends, and the "characters that ornithology introduced me to."[76] For example, he often held up his brother Hamid Ali as a model, including in an eponymous chapter, of a "rational, this-worldly human being" displaying "unostentatious generosity and humanism."[77] In describing himself as an "inferior imitation" of this "favourite brother," Sálim demonstrated characteristic modesty—though deference and self-effacement are more often identified with the "feminine" in autobiographical theory and practice.[78] That he used this modesty as a strategy to counter the common association of autobiography with egoism and self-justification was revealed in the epilogue. Here, he quoted Victorian novelist Samuel Butler as justification to resist the "temptation" of "laying it on too thick."[79]

A gendered reading of Sálim Ali's autobiography is perhaps best facilitated by comparison with the memoirs of his Tyabji contemporary and sister-in-law, Safia Jabir Ali. Particularly revealing are sections in which the authors recounted their experiences of living—often together in the same house headed by Safia's husband, Jabir—in Tavoy (now Dawei) and Rangoon (now Yangon) in Burma in the 1910s and 1920s. While Sálim's coverage of this period is contained in two separate chapters (chapter 3, "Burma 1914–17," and chapter 5, "Memories of Burma"), Safia's more random reminiscences returned to this period of her life on half a dozen different occasions. Comparing their form suggests that Safia's memoirs were less systematic than those of her brother-in-law, thus fulfilling the gendered expectation, outlined in chapter 1 of this volume, that women's autobiographies are more fragmentary than linear. But this portrayal may have more to do with the published status of Sálim's autobiography than with his original intention. According to the prologue, his writings too

172   *Autobiographical Genealogies*

began life as "random recollections and reminiscences jotted down lackadaisically in bits and pieces, as the spirit moved" until a friend, R. E. Hawkins, stepped in to "sort out the jumbled narrative and reduce the chaos to some semblance of order."[80] This writing process may be compared favorably with that articulated by Safia to her son, Amiruddin, fairly early in her narrative: "Dear Amir, this isn't a connected account or tale—I write about whatever I feel like. So today I feel like telling you about your aunts Rafia and Akhtar . . ."[81] Even so, the published version of Sálim's autobiography still resisted chronology and construction, with anecdotes often connected by theme, rather than timing, and the text interspersed with his own and others' diary entries, interviews, and letters.[82]

In other ways, the pair's approaches to recounting this period during which the Ali brothers pursued business ventures in Burma—primarily mining and hardware—were strikingly different. While both focused on other people known in Burma, Sálim emphasized business and birding associates, while Safia told about servants and "wonderful friends" that they met through "the club" and other avenues.[83] Both wrote about their family dwellings, Safia from the perspective of domestic interiors and Sálim from the point of view of location and construction. Consider, for example, his description of the house shared with his wife, Tehmina, while living in Tavoy in the mid-1920s: "A couple of years after Jabir and Safia had left Tavoy to settle in Rangoon my wife and I found and moved into a pleasant and more comfortable cottage with a large compound and some shady cashew trees, in a more 'genteel' locality known as the Civil Lines on the outskirts of the town. The cottage was pretty and well-designed, but of a semi *pukka* nature, raised off the ground on posts to fight the damp, with the walls of asbestos-cement sheets and roof wooden-shingled."[84] Later in his narrative, he fell back on quoting a letter that Tehmina had written to his sister Kamoo to evoke the *inside* of the flat in which the couple lived in Bombay's Byculla in the late 1920s. Here, Tehmina followed the lead of Safia and other Tyabji women in describing with evocative detail not only the rooms and their formation, but also details of the furniture—from a "gun almirah" designed by Sálim himself to the "mats and d'oyleys" on their well-polished, oval dining table.[85] A gendered thematic is also discernible in Sálim's close attention to weapons and hunting—though, as noted in chapter 3, shikar did appear in certain Muslim women's autobiographies too.[86] Still, female authors were unlikely to offer, as Sálim did, a comprehensive schematic of various firearms used to shoot tigers, panthers, sloth bear, sambar, cheetal, nilgai, blackbuck, and innumerable birds over half a century.[87]

Safia's emotive account of her isolation and homesickness in Burma may also be contrasted with Sálim's more dispassionate account of the family business—about which there is valuable detail in *The Fall of a Sparrow*, but only a cursory summary in Safia's memoirs.[88] This distinction could, of course, be attributed to their respective duties during the Burma interregnum—Sálim working with his brother, while Safia maintained their home and social life. As she specified, "it was during the day, when I was alone, and saw nothing familiar around me at all, that I found it very difficult to bear. Slowly I got accustomed to the house, the surroundings, the people, made friends, took an interest in the house, but I still missed Bombay very very much, and it took me a long time to settle down. This may be difficult for a man to understand, but I think most women would immediately feel for me."[89] And yet elsewhere his narrative, Sálim also proved unwilling to reveal his feelings even in response to the most tragic of events. At the start of a chapter titled "Dehra Dun and Bahawalpur," Sálim abruptly described, then left, his wife's sudden death: "These good times [in Dehra Dun] were cut short by a great personal tragedy in my life. After a comparatively unrisky surgical operation Tehmina developed blood poisoning and died in July 1939. Now that she was gone I had a hard decision to face: to stay on or to migrate . . ."[90] Only from a consolation letter written by ornithologist friend Hugh Whistler to Sálim Ali and included in an appendix (tellingly titled "Ragbag") do we get a sense of the "desolation and heartbreak" that he must have experienced on this occasion.[91] The handling of this tragedy is thus entirely at odds with the poignant memorials by Tyabji men and women alike already quoted from the *akhbar* books. Still, that Sálim felt unable to explore his grief within the public forum of a published autobiography perhaps offers as great an insight into the man as any more introspective narrative would have done.

Moving to the next generation, several grandchildren of the great Badruddin Tyabji also produced autobiographical narratives of one sort

174 *Autobiographical Genealogies*

or another. Most senior among them—on account of being the eldest daughter of Badruddin's eldest daughter—was Shareefah Hamid Ali (1883–1971). As the daughter of Abbas and Amina Tyabji and the wife of the aforementioned Hamid Ali, she was also sister-in-law to Sálim Ali and niece to Safia Jabir Ali. Having made her mother's "diary" available to the journal *Roshni* in 1946, Shareefah contributed a series of her own travel writings from July through November 1947. As indicated in chapter 3, her choice of this particular journal reflected her long-term involvement with its parent organization, the All-India Women's Conference, of which she served as president in 1935.[92] Displaying none of the reticence that her mother evidenced upon her return from Europe in the 1890s, Shareefah published four separate articles about her "visit to America" to act as India's representative to the first sessions of the Commission on the Status of Women at the newly formed United Nations in New York. Indeed, the series would have been much longer had her two-year appointment not been interrupted by Partition violence in her hometown of Mussoorie. The four articles varied widely in content and style. While the first was focused entirely on the author's "extraordinary" three-day plane journey from Bombay to New York, the second provided a more formal and less personal account of the work of the commission.[93] The third and fourth pieces were more typical fare for a travelogue: recounting a visit to Washington, DC—ostensibly to attend a reception honoring India's newly appointed ambassador, Asaf Ali, but also including a day of sightseeing—and another to George Washington's home at Mount Vernon.[94]

Tying the entries together, and offering a clear indication of the author's sense of self in the process, was Shareefah Hamid Ali's close attention to social discrimination of different types. Her feminist standpoint was apparent from the outset in her scathing response to reflections on her husband's Indian dress during a stopover in Greece: "Any man who wears Indian clothes is supposed to be a Maharaja but the same does not hold good for a women [*sic*] dressed in Indian clothes. Sad, isn't it? I don't think that sex-discrimination llke [*sic*] this should be tolerated."[95] The second article was more reasoned in its argument, detailing how the Commission on the Status of Women responded to the "usual imperial dope" advanced by male critics—that education was necessary before franchise—by passing a "strongly worded resolution" in favor of universal adult suffrage.[96] This prioritizing of women's political rights was justified by relevant statistical evidence from member countries. As Shareefah explained the situation in India: "In India so far (under the Act of 1935) over 60 lakhs of women have the vote as against 290 lakhs of men who are entitled to vote. Comment is needless."[97] At the same time, she recognized that, in the United States particularly, it was not just women for whom universal suffrage existed "only in name": "Jim Crow Laws" and "Indian camps and reserved areas" also placed restrictions on "American Indians" and "negroes."[98] Particularly revealing was a conversation with a "mixed bload [sic], half American-Indian" bus driver, which she recounted at the end of her final article:

> He described many of the hardships negroes and his people had to suffer on account of race discrimination. According to him the coloured people are "segregated" practically in the same manner as our ill-treated Harijans were in the past. I was greatly pained to hear him, and over and over again I regretted bitterly when I remembered that our poor long-suffering "bhangis" and depressed class people were ostracised in almost the same manner that he was describing. Thank God, those days are passing away for us in India.[99]

Her assumption of an Indian identity to relegate untouchability (undeservedly) to history confirmed her affinity with the Gandhian nationalism advanced by most of the Tyabji clan.

In light of her nationalist affiliations, it is perhaps unsurprising that it was symbols of freedom that evoked the greatest feeling in Shareefah Hamid Ali. As she narrated her experience of viewing the American Declaration of Independence in the Library of Congress: "[A] little thrill of emotion went through our hearts. We put up a silent prayer that God grant. [sic] the time should soon come, when our own country also would be writing its Charter of Independence in letters of gold."[100] Otherwise, the last two articles tend to rehearse visits to fairly standard tourist attractions—historical monuments honoring Lincoln, Washington, and Jefferson, Arlington House, the Pentagon, the aforementioned Mount Vernon—in the impersonal style of a guidebook. This "formulaic" quality,

176   *Autobiographical Genealogies*

to quote Antoinette Burton, makes Shareefah's writings about the United States highly reminiscent of those travelogues written by Indian men, particularly about London, from the late nineteenth century.[101] Only in the first article—on her lengthy plane journey from Bombay to New York—does she offer a more colloquial account calling to mind those *roznamcha* produced by her Tyabji cousins, the Fyzee sisters, nearly half a century before. By the end of six pages, Shareefah had initiated her readers into what she packed, what she ate, the ways of air hostesses, the formalities of airports, her opinions on fellow travelers, the inconveniences of "never hop[ing] to have a decent wash," and her initial impressions of New York ("neither attractive nor artistic").[102] Her travel writings are thus difficult to characterize in terms of their representation of a gendered self. While they are sometimes introspective, individual, and even definably feminine, at other times they are quite the opposite.

A few years later, in 1964, Shareefah's younger sister Raihana Tyabji (1901–75) published a more full-fledged autobiography. Titled *Suniye Kakasaheb*, it took the form of conversations with Raihana's fellow Gandhian disciple D. B. Kalelkar (popularly known as Kaka Kalelkar or Kakasaheb, as in her title), with whom she was closely associated at the Sabarmati Ashram in Wardha.[103] As highlighted in chapter 3, this book was published in Hindi (using the Devanagari script) by an organization intended to advance Hindustani as the national language of India, the Hindustani Prachar Sabha. The conversational form imposed a disjointed quality already recognized in the memoirs of her aunt Safia Jabir Ali, but associated more generally with women's autobiography. Still, it must have established her reputation with interviewers interested in Gandhi, since subsequently, her narrated experiences as one of his "apostles" appeared in other books as well.[104] As noted in the introduction and developed in chapter 1, Raihana had already played with the autobiographical form several decades before by employing bhakti devotionalism in *The Heart of a Gopi*, written in the mid-1920s, but not published until 1936. *Suniye Kakasaheb* was somewhat more conventional in that, though based in conversation, it contained first-person anecdotes about her family and life. In many, she reflected on what it meant to her to be born into a well-heeled Muslim family belonging to the sometimes ostracized sect of

Sulaimani Bohras (see chapter 3), at ease with English ways and manners but committed to Gandhian nationalism. As she wrote of Tyabji patriotism: "The Partition of India broke our hearts. I can't bear to look at the truncated map of India."[105]

CONTEMPORARY ARTICULATIONS OF CAREER, COURTSHIP, AND CRISIS

Not until the 1980s did Raihana's male relatives produce what were to become the most widely circulated examples of Tyabji autobiography. Sálim Ali's *The Fall of a Sparrow* (1985) has already been discussed at length, but two other texts relevant here are Badruddin Tyabji's *Memoirs of an Egoist* (1988) and *More Memoirs of an Egoist* (1994).[106] This Badruddin (1907–95) was a younger child of the great Badruddin's third son, Faiz Hasan Tyabji, and his wife, Salima (1885–1939)—and thus the nephew of Amina and Safia. His two-volume memoir differed from most Tyabji models, male and female, in that it was almost exclusively a public document tracing the author's illustrious career, first in the Indian Civil Service and then, after Independence, in the Indian Foreign Service. Occasionally, his family, including his wife, Surayya, their four children, and various Tyabji relatives, did appear, but usually only as a flank to his official persona.[107] Though the two volumes are divided by chronology—the first covering 1907–56 and the second 1956–67— they otherwise act as a continuous narrative, *More Memoirs* picking up where *Memoirs* left off with only a paragraph-long preface as introduction. Chronology also defined their internal structure, with individual parts labeled by dates and place. For instance, in the second volume, "Part I: 1956–58: Iran" gave way to "Part II: 1958–60: Germany" and then "Part III: 1960–62: External Affairs," and so on. This format may reveal a debt to the family's *akhbar* tradition as it was translated into published *roznamcha* by the Fyzee sisters, especially in the early twentieth century. Indeed, one often gets the sense from the memoir's episodic nature, arranged by date and sometimes even time, that the author may have done little more than write up his personal diary.[108] But as a retrospective narrative, Badruddin's text displayed none of the randomness or, in fact, humility identified in Safia's handwritten memoirs or Sálim's

178   *Autobiographical Genealogies*

published autobiography—though it did take up some themes similar to those of the latter, not least shikar, motorcycles, and gardens.[109] Overall, then, it reads as a fairly typical example of male autobiography within the subgenre of political memoir.[110]

It seems likely that the publication of Badruddin's *Memoirs* in the late 1980s may have inspired his cousin Najmuddin S. Tyabji (1912–2001), known as Najm—the son of the great Badruddin's fourth son, Salman (1885–1962)—to begin writing his own "Random Reminiscences" around the same time.[111] This memoir was composed in Canada, where the author had moved to live with his children and grandchildren upon his retirement. In an introduction to the text, the author's grandson Mark Devereux explained that Najm had always hoped to publish his life story "so that his family could understand better where they'd come from," but circumstances did not allow him to do so before his death. Six years on, Devereux thus decided to liberate his grandfather's memories from a "dusty binder" by publishing them online as a "retroblog."[112] This digital archive includes twenty posts—in effect, mini-chapters apparently inserted by Devereux as editor—made available between November 2008 and August 2010. The posts are roughly chronological, beginning with an account of the author's birth and family before skipping over most of his childhood to recount in some detail three fateful years spent as an engineering student in England in the mid-1930s. He then related his return to India and marriage before turning to his working life. That the last post, "The Railway Beginnings," discusses only the start of Najm's career with the Bengal Nagpur Railway suggests that the series remains incomplete.[113] Still, it offers more than seventy printed pages of text and pictures to which readers, including Tyabji relatives, can (and do) respond with comments.[114] In a small way, the Tyabji tradition of writing and receiving response in the *akhbar* books is thus re-created through a digital medium—though admittedly without the participation of the now deceased author.

Most striking about Najmuddin's "Random Reminiscences" is their resemblance to the autobiographical writings of earlier Tyabji women. As noted already, his narrative began by placing his own life story within the context of the Tyabji clan's history. This introduction could be compared with the opening genealogy in traditional Islamic life writing except that here the aim was to celebrate the author's extraordinary family to ensure "reflected glory."[115] Like Safia Jabir Ali, Najm thus began by introducing various family personalities—though, a generation removed, he was perhaps more selective and less elaborate in his descriptions. Still, he followed the established family narrative in evoking Bhoymeeah Hajeebhoy and Tyab Ali—described unambiguously as "Sulaimani Muslim (Shia)"—as the clan's founders before turning to Camruddin and his own grandfather Badruddin as exemplars of that generation's "England returned."[116] With their prestigious degrees, exalted government careers, and love of Shakespeare, they are represented as setting the bar for Najm's father and his five brothers—introduced in turn in potted biographies—as well as Tyabji women. As Najm wrote: "What about the women folk? Even though born into a Muslim family of that era, they were not backward in any way!"[117] Like his aunt Amina in her *Roshni* diary, he thus countered gendered preconceptions by narrating his female relative's achievements in terms of education, unveiling, nationalist politics, and in the case of Raihana (to whom he devoted the most words), social work and singing.[118] The subsequent posts on Najm's journey to England and his experiences there as a student then compared favorably with Atiya Fyzee's *roznamcha* for their informal style and everyday content—presumably feminine qualities in travel writing.[119] Downplaying museums and monuments, Najm too enticed his reader with meals enjoyed, clothes worn, games played, people met, topics studied, speeches heard, transport taken, places visited, and an ongoing commentary on the weather.[120]

Where Najm's account differed from that of Atiya and her sister Nazli, too, was in his handling of love and sexual intimacy. I have noted already that Atiya and Nazli did little more than hint at their convoluted personal lives in their respective *roznamcha*. But, eighty years on, Najm chose to write at length about his courtship and marriage to his Scottish wife, Mona. Initially, this reminiscence took the form of chaste descriptions of their first meetings and growing friendship: evenings at the cinema, weekly outings to Hyde Park, day trips on his motorcycle in the sunny summer of '33 to the countryside then surrounding London.[121]

180   *Autobiographical Genealogies*

A gentle story of love blossoming, it encourages parallels with Safia Jabir Ali's equally innocent account of a flirtatious courtship and then happy marriage to her cousin, Jabir Ali. As she wrote of the early stages:

> I began to think like my dear brother, that there was no one to compare with Jabir. He was the King, the leader! I didn't notice or pay any attention to any of the others. We were of course on friendly terms with all the other boys in Hatoo's group, but Jabir was someone special . . . I'd keep up a great pretence of being quite indifferent to Jabir in front of others and quarrel and fight with him, pull his hair (which was very curly), pinch him, smear his face or nose with soap—all that kind of thing. Then he came and spent the summer with us in Matheran. We'd be together all day, and keep on teasing each other. I'd begun to guess from Jabir's manner—his expression, how he'd begun to feel about me.[122]

Jabir's brother Sálim also dedicated part of a chapter in his *The Fall of a Sparrow* to his engagement to Tehmina. Though less protracted, it laid the foundations for his affectionate account of their apparently companionable marriage.[123] Najm, on the other hand, turned from early courtship to what might have been: an earlier attachment to his cousin Hamida that, after meeting Mona, he ignominiously put in "second place." His reflections on this "first love" were highly revelatory and introspective: "I still was fond of [Hamida] to the extent that I was half in love! In fact, whenever we met, I could not but feel, with a sense of guilt, 'if things had been different' . . . She had been my 'first love' and, looking back, I find that there is something in the feelings one has when one finds oneself in love for the first time which is missing on subsequent occasions."[124]

Still, Najm continued his relationship with Mona, and by the next "romantic" summer, they were finding themselves in compromising situations that necessitated sharing rooms—at a time when, according to his own admission, "it was not common for 'boyfriends' to be so intimate in public."[125] The first occasion came about when they were late back from one of their day trips out of London, making it impossible for Mona to get back into her hostel after curfew. According to Najm's telling, Mona was the one who initiated staying in his room and then, when he did the gentlemanly thing and slept on the floor, "came over and snuggled down with me." And yet, as he explained, "That was very nice and cosy and, after some talking, both of us went to sleep—not what the sophisticated youngsters of today would think!"[126] A week or so later, Najm took the initiative by riding his motorcycle down to Torquay, where Mona was on holiday for a week—only to find that Mona's boardinghouse was "fully booked." Once again—though against the landlady's protestations—Mona agreed for him to share her room. As Najm told it: "The room was very small—about 9 feet by 11 feet, with a small single bed and no room for even a mattress for the floor. That, however, did not worry Mona as she said we would share the bed. And so . . . we had a very cosy and romantic week. The sophisticated youngsters of today would have been justified in their conclusions!"[127] Though not explicit, his meaning was clear. From then on, when they traveled together even as an unmarried couple, it was decided that it would be "more enjoyable and economical if we stayed together in a double room."[128] To be so open about a censured subject like premarital sexual relations certainly distinguished Najm's "Reminiscences" from the autobiographical writings produced by his Tyabji predecessors and contemporaries, whether male or female. The author's diasporic location in a comparatively uninhibited late twentieth-century Canada may offer some explanation.

Saying that, the next Tyabji generation—the great Badruddin's great-grandchildren—were even less reserved when it came to autobiographical content. Let me take, as a first example, a purportedly biographical piece written by the craft campaigner Laila Tyabji about her mother, Surayya Tyabji—wife of the "egoist" Badruddin—for a Delhi quarterly in 1996. Titled "Amma—Recipes for a Family" in tribute to her mother's renown as a food writer, it offered an intimate portrayal of her parents, their relationship, and her personal interactions with them.[129] Continuities with earlier Tyabji writings are evident in Laila's attention to family inheritances, the "unconventional ways" of women in "our *khandaan,*" a "proudly Indian" identity, aesthetics, travel, and the everyday as represented in clothes and domestic interiors.[130] At the same time, she was often shockingly frank about sex, infidelity, mental illness, menstruation, and rape. On two separate occasions, she addressed her parents' conjugal intimacy by identifying the specific locations of her brothers' conceptions.[131] She also sought to unravel her mother's sexuality in a passage worth quoting at length:

> It is always difficult for children to encompass their parents' sexuality; so much easier to assume that they only did "it" four times in the disinterested cause of our own procreation! Knowing my mother's adolescent growing pains, her reticence about sex, her distress at extra-marital infidelity, her determination that I should grow up without hangups or traumas, I assumed she herself was rather inhibited. I'd wondered how my father, with his rather sexy past, but a notoriously faithful husband, had coped. Asking him once, I was charmed and reassured by his reply, "She was delightful; shy but very passionate—but always frightfully jealous!" It was awareness of the importance of sexuality in a relationship, not prudery, that made her find adultery so messy.[132]

Laila's willingness to write about this most private aspect of her parents' relationship may have been an inheritance from her father, whom she portrayed as "matter-of-factly forthright about sex"—and yet, as indicated already, sexual intimacy was certainly not a feature of his own memoir.[133]

Laila was equally candid about her mother's mental illness. Anxiety and depression seem to have been afflictions that touched many within the Tyabji clan, including all three Fyzee sisters and their father, too—and yet, as noted already, they were oblique at best in their autobiographical references to the problems.[134] In contrast, Laila referred twice in a short article to a "breakdown" during which her mother saw "demons and tragedy" everywhere.[135] Challenging even more deeply entrenched taboos was her discussion of menstruation. Laila explained her mother's handling of this delicate topic in the following terms:

> Since she herself had been taken unawares by the onset of adolescence and sexuality, she took great pains to make mine fun. She made even the messy, bloody business of menstruation seem like a deliciously adult, feminine joke and adventure—wrapping up my first sanitary belt and Kotex pack in lace, pink frills and roses, and later conspiratorially initiating me into the discreet advantages of tampons.[136]

In its explicitness, this passage was perhaps surpassed only by Laila's telling of her own near-rape while staying in Kutch in the late 1970s. Here, she recounted how, while walking back to her rented room after dinner out, she was "jumped on and thrown in a ditch" by a "lecherous" sergeant in India's Border Security Force. She described him as "sweaty and slobbering" as he "panted" on top of her: "trying to pull my saree while I fought him." According to her recollection, it was in the midst of this terrifying scene that she suddenly remembered her brother's advice, given while she was a teenager in Delhi: "If the worst comes to the worst she can always knee him in the balls." And so she did, enabling her escape with only a "shredded sari." Rape's depiction, even in her own account, as a "fate worse than death" for the dishonor associated with the "loss of a girl's most precious jewel" underlines the significance of her disclosure.[137]

Rape also featured in the autobiographical output of another Tyabji woman of this generation, Sohaila Abdulali (b. 1963). She came to international attention early in 2013 when, in the wake of protests following the "Delhi gang rape case," an article that she had published thirty years before in the feminist magazine *Manushi* went viral on the Internet. In the original two-page piece, she had employed a confessional mode—complete with a picture captioned with her own name—to write about her experience of being gang-raped three years before, near her home in the Bombay suburb of Chembur.[138] As she told it, she and a friend, Rashid, had gone for a walk up a nearby mountainside when they were ambushed by four men armed with a sickle. The couple were then held for two terrifying hours during which Sohaila was raped perhaps ten times—though she was in "so much pain" that she "lost track of what was going on after a while."[139] Her intensely emotive and evocative personal account narrated not only the horrific circumstances of that captivity but also the flagrant mishandling of her case by the police afterward and the emotional scars that she continued to bear. As she wrote: "It has been almost three years now, but there has not been even one day, when I have not been haunted by what happened. Insecurity, vulnerability, fear, anger, helplessness—I fight these constantly."[140] At the time, her autobiographical fragment apparently caused a small "stir" in the Indian women's movement and, more immediately, among her own family before it "quietly disappeared."[141] However, the high-profile events of December 2012 brought it back to the fore, and Sohaila was invited to write her story again, including what had happened since, first in an opinion piece for the *New York Times* and then on the comment pages of the *Guardian*.[142] These commissions suggest how, by the twenty-first century, the autobiographical mode was deemed especially appropriate for Muslim women contributing to political debates.[143]

It seems significant that beyond these few articles, Tyabji women have hardly produced autobiographies and travelogues for nearly half a century.[144] During the same period, the *akhbar* books to which they were such frequent contributors have been given away to library collections in Bombay, Delhi, and Karachi or have begun to molder on dusty bookshelves in family homes. That is not to say that Tyabji women have not written at all in the contemporary era. On the contrary, they have remained prolific as journalists, academics, novelists, children's authors, and food writers.[145] Others contribute to new semi-autobiographical media, like the Tyabji family's website, Twitter, and Facebook, or they repackage the Tyabji legacy for wider audiences by editing earlier family writings.[146] But the historical moment for them to narrate their pioneering experiences as travelers, reformers, nationalists, and professionals seems to have long ago passed—and, interestingly, before it did for their menfolk. Offering a useful comparison here are Najmuddin Tyabji and his sister Rafia Abdul Ali. The latter explained to me that many members of her family, including her brother, wrote daily diaries that they later turned into memoirs. But she was never interested in this autobiographical project. Her explanation was that unlike her younger brother, she did not enjoy talking about herself or discussing her feelings. Instead, she preferred to read about "great people, saints and prophets" who gave her a sense of being "at the bottom" of a spiritual hierarchy. Having achieved this realization, she asked, "What are you going to write about yourself?"[147] While her personality and interests may be individual to her, they suggest a gendered and historicized understanding of self that finds expression in autobiographical writings. In conclusion, let us trace those patterns.

CONCLUSION: INTERROGATING THEORIES OF DIFFERENCE

The Tyabji case offers a unique opportunity to interrogate theoretical frames applied by gender theorists to autobiographical writing. Estelle Jelinek was an early proponent of contrasting female and male narratives, and her influential anthology, *Women's Autobiography: Essays in Criticism* (1980), still offers one of the clearest articulations of the "difference" model.[148] A first claim was that men wrote "success stories" that focused on their professional lives, while women emphasized personal and domestic details.[149] Accordingly, several Tyabji men wrote autobiographies that traced their path to esteemed careers: how they became a successful merchant, a renowned ornithologist, or an influential diplomat. Tyabji women, on the other hand, writing first in the *akhbar* books, then in travelogues or memoirs, were more likely to comment on domestic routines and interiors that structured their lives—and, notably, the reformist discourse in the late nineteenth and early twentieth centuries too. But, equally so, if they had a public role or employment outside the home—as the founder of a girls' school, a UN commissioner, or a Gandhian apostle—they would write about that. Moreover, while a few of the clan's men prepared entirely or primarily public documents, most incorporated their home life into their life stories by discussing their wives, children, families, servants, and friends. Jelinek's claim that only women describe their connections to other people is thus not sustained in a cultural context, like Muslim South Asia, where all selves are considered definable in relational terms, and relationality is thus identified as central to regional forms of autobiographical expression.[150]

Jelinek also identifies a "disconnected" and "fragmentary" quality in women's lives that translates into their autobiographical writings. Men, on the other hand, are claimed to reconstruct their past in a selective and purposeful way that suggests linearity and cohesion in their construction of self.[151] If one were to read some Tyabji women's travelogues and memoirs in isolation, one might be convinced of the applicability of this frame. Female authors were often, though certainly not always, episodic in their approach, writing about one thing and then another as the spirit took them. But then, so it seems, so were a number of their

186   *Autobiographical Genealogies*

male relatives—or at least before an editor stepped in to bring some kind of order to a published output. The diary-like quality of the *akhbar* and *roznamcha* traditions, as they were employed or developed by many within the clan, probably encouraged this less systematic approach to life writing, as did the practice of publishing autobiographical fragments as individual or serialized articles in journals and magazines. Also found in speeches, memoirs, and autobiographies composed by Tyabji men and women alike were the self-deprecation and understatement that Jelinek associates with women's writings alone.[152] And yet tropes of modesty or passivity, so often identified with South Asian women but as apparent in traditional Islamic life stories, need not denote a lack of agency, nor self-effacement a lack of self.[153] Indeed, most of the clan's women, if not as aggrandizing as some of their male relatives, still represented themselves as capable, dynamic, and effective in fulfilling their chosen and socially determined roles: as reformers, nationalists, and feminists or as daughters, wives, and mothers.

Jelinek's model for theorizing women's autobiography in terms of gender difference thus falls short when applied to the Tyabji case. By essentializing women (and men too) across cultures and time, it fails to recover the specific subjectivities associated with different global locations at particular historical moments. A case in point is the multiple and varied ways in which the Tyabjis constructed their religious and national identities from the colonial era to the postcolonial: often erasing or playing down their Bohra associations when their liminality was a threat to Islamic orthodoxies or, in nationalist contexts, situating their sense of belonging to a Muslim community, or *qaum*, within a broader Indian whole. Also changing over time were the topics considered appropriate for autobiographical reflection. Raised on Victorian romance novels and a reformist model of companionate marriage, a Tyabji generation born in the final decades of the nineteenth century may have written of more innocent intimacies within courtship or marriage. But the overt sexuality of the most recent writings—referencing premarital sex, adultery, conjugal intimacy, menstruation, and rape—would have been anathema. Similarly, mental illness seems to have moved from the realm of the oblique to a challenged taboo—at least within the privileged confines of an elite urban family. Also relevant here may be a shift in language: as a conversational Urdu stippled with Gujarati and Marathi gave way to a more "correct" form of the language that coexisted with English until the latter came to dominate Tyabji autobiographical expression almost entirely by the late twentieth century.

Still, what defined the available autobiographical canon of this extended family throughout was a strong sense of identification with the Tyabji clan itself: a collectivity that certainly did not erase or even subsume the self, but actually provided a framework within which to articulate individual expression. How that interiority was achieved differed depending on the author. Some Tyabjis, male and female, revealed their feelings so completely—on the death of a loved one, on undertaking a journey, on falling in love, on moving to a new country, on the birth of a child, on the aftermath of rape—that their emotions seem to be an open book to the reader. Their personalities were on show, to be analyzed and interpreted in terms of how they acted as the "driving force," in Pascal's phrase, to their life story.[154] Others were more circumspect. Certain Tyabji men and women alike skirted painful moments or failed to analyze how they felt on a momentous or life-changing occasion. And yet they recounted anecdotes in which they revealed their behavior in a particular context or situation, thus allowing the reader to, in Judith Tucker's words, "sense a personality."[155] Many Tyabjis also wrote about their contemporaries in such a way as to reveal admired or repugnant qualities that tell as much about the self as about the other. Any sharp distinction between the individual and the collective, the self and society, thus gives way to an active dialogue between what Arnold and Blackburn call the "life of the individual" and the "life of others"—or, more simply put, the "self-in-society."[156] Let us now turn, in this book's coda, to these differing notions of the self as exemplified by the concept of unveiling.

CODA

UNVEILING AND ITS ATTRIBUTES

To unveil suggests a dramatic and daring act. It evokes iconic episodes in the established historical narrative of Muslim women's feminism—most famously, Egyptian activist Huda Shaarawi's audacious gesture of casting her long black veil into the sea after attending a meeting of the International Alliance of Women in Rome in 1923.[1] Upon her return to Cairo, she and fellow Egyptian delegate Saiza Nabarawi stepped out onto the running board of their train and, in turn, pulled the black cloth back from their faces before a crowd of cheering women. Recounting this incident in the opening paragraph of her introduction to Shaarawi's memoir, Margot Badran identifies it as a pivotal moment for Egyptian women: as signaling the end, no less, of "the harem system in Egypt."[2] We may be reminded, too, of Afghanistan's Queen Soraya, who, in 1928, appeared beside her husband and king, Amanullah Khan, at a public event with her face uncovered for the first time. So enraged were more-conservative elements of Afghan society at the couple's flagrant betrayal of "Afghan cultural values and concept of honour," that they were forced from the throne by a tribal rebellion and banished to exile.[3] Authoritarian rulers of other primarily Muslim polities were not deterred. Perhaps most bold was Reza Khan's legal abolition of the chador in 1936 that forced Iran's urban elite at the least to abandon their heavy black veils under threat of "brutal enforcement."[4]

190   *Unveiling and Its Attributes*

What it meant to unveil in the historical context of Muslim South Asia was rather more ambiguous than what is suggested by these emblematic stories from Egypt, Afghanistan, and Iran. As I have documented elsewhere, no reformist debate was more divided by the early twentieth century than that on veiling and seclusion. The battle lines were firmly drawn between those who opposed the purdah system in its entirety, those who wanted to diminish its severity, and those who wanted to maintain it in its customary form.[5] And yet even those identified with the first camp—we may think of leading South Asian Muslim families, like the Shafis of Lahore and the Tyabjis of Bombay—showed delicacy in their negotiation of purdah norms. The emphasis among the Shafis was on facilitating participation by Muslim couples in the mixed society of the colonial capital or women's role in nation-building. As Jahan Ara Shahnawaz narrated her family's unveiling in 1920:

> It was in that city [Calcutta] that Father asked us to discard the veil and we went out to the New Market without *burqas* for the first time in our lives . . . Shafi was used to spending his life with his women-folk, and he did not like the idea of attending and arranging mixed functions without his wife and daughters. Moreover, he had been carefully watching the progress of Hindu women and had felt for some time that Muslim women must give up *purdah* and take their place in the building of the nation.[6]

Challenged by her father for her indiscretion, Jahan Ara's mother explained that she was only following his own advice to "heed" her husband's wishes in order to be a good Muslim wife.[7]

The Tyabji case was even less clear-cut. A cousin, Zubeida Futehally, was considered to have initiated the family practice of women appearing in public unveiled when during a trip to England with her husband, she was received by the Queen-Empress Victoria at a mixed gathering at Windsor Castle in 1894. This celebrated event saw her hailed, alongside two of her cousins, Amina Tyabji and Atiya Fyzee—both of whom have been met already in this book—as the first elite Indian Muslim women to unveil.[8] However, when Atiya wrote about her attire when in England studying to be a teacher in 1906, she stressed, "I have been meaning to write for a while that I have continued wearing my Indian clothes and do not intend to ever give them up. When I go out I cover my head, etc. with a gauze cloth. Everything is covered except the face."[9] Her means of mobile modesty was to wear what she referred to as the Fyzee *charshaf*— a Turkish-style burqa first adopted, according to her sister Nazli's later travelogue, by their elder sister Zehra from their country of birth sometime in the early 1890s.[10] Atiya admitted that in the English context she had "modified [it] a bit," wearing the burqa in the style of a cloak with gloves, umbrella, and "good walking shoes on the feet."[11] Photographs taken then and later in England and India confirm that at the least, she wore a voluminous sari over a long-sleeved and high-necked blouse with her head always covered.[12] The unveiling was thus only partial at best, suggesting continued restraint and concealment.

Atiya's sister Nazli did not "come out of purdah" at all until two years later, in 1908, when undertaking an official tour of Britain, Europe, and the Ottoman Empire with her princely husband, the nawab of Janjira. In her travelogue, she reflected on a number of conversations inspired by her recent unveiling, during which she was often quizzed as to her level of discomfort on appearing in mixed company. As she recorded an exchange with the princess of Wales at a royal ball in London in June 1908:

> Then she said: you have just come out of purdah, so does it feel strange to you? I gave a casual response that it was very difficult, but I am now becoming habituated to it. Then she said: now tell me, when you go to India, will you go back into purdah? I said: perhaps I won't observe such strict seclusion because, after being out like this, that, too, would be difficult. But the fact is that it is not proper to give it up altogether because such things are not customary in India yet. There is great disapprobation there for those women giving up purdah, so why would a person make herself a target of censure?[13]

Nazli thus articulated the notion of a "vacation from purdah," an idea also documented by other South Asian Muslim women. To take another example, Princess Abida Sultaan of Bhopal recorded with some relish how her mother, Maimoona, crucially with the approval of her father, "abandoned her *burqa* and started to sneak out" to explore London by the Underground with her three young daughters while on a state visit in 1925–26—only for the burqa to reappear shortly before they disembarked

192   *Unveiling and Its Attributes*

in Bombay on their return journey.[14] Clearly, public exposure could wax and wane depending on circumstance.

The ambiguity of real-life experience makes unveiling perhaps all the more appropriate as a concept to capture the gendered historical phenomenon of autobiographical writing in Muslim South Asia. Clearly, not all of the authors discussed in this book were veiled women, or *purdah-nashin* in local dialects, but, as Milani notes of Iran, Muslim South Asia still denotes a "veiled society": a cultural context in which privacy equates to concealment and exposure to transgression.[15] As I indicated in the introduction, words may be veiled even when bodies are not. To write autobiography—to narrate childhood, marriage, domestic life, everyday rituals, trials, and tribulations, perhaps even one's thoughts and feelings—is thus to transcend the most severe limits on bodies and voices alike: to break the silences, to move beyond the boundaries of permitted discourse, to make the unseen visible. It is, as I flagged in the introduction, *the ultimate unveiling.* But, as in the above examples, the unveiling may not be total or straightforward. It may be symbolic, convoluted, partial, or paradoxical. It may be undertaken only by particular individuals or groups for particular purposes at particular moments. Moreover, the parameters—when and where, but also how and why—are crucial to understanding how this bold act was constructed and construed. Simply put, unveiling does not occur in isolation, and thus we must be attentive to historical processes that enabled it to occur as it did.

In seeking to historicize interiority, I have resisted a model of tracing the *emergence* of an autonomous self in Muslim South Asia as "impersonal" autobiographical narratives written in the Islamic tradition gave way to "proper" European models disseminated in colonial contexts and after. Rather, I have come to take for granted Muslim autobiography's ongoing function as self-representation—in other words, and in direct challenge to Zonis and others invoked in the introduction, its usefulness as a means of illuminating conceptions of self. I have recognized that, in women's writing especially, the self may be elusive. More often than not, in South Asian autobiography the story of the self is one of self-deprecation over self-aggrandizement, with individual lives told in relational terms.[16] And women, it seems, have a special propensity for employing "collective voice."[17] But, as Kathryn Hansen emphasizes, a self that is told with modesty or deference to others need not denote an "absent" or "weak" self somehow at odds with "Western" notions of a "sovereign" or even "fractured" self.[18] On the contrary, just as South Asian scholarship has moved to recognize the individual agency still present alongside and within paradigms of collectivity, so Black American and feminist critiques have intersected with postmodernism to reveal the West's claim to a unitary and unified self as a myth.[19] In short, to essentialize notions of selfhood as "culture-specific" only obscures more-complex subjectivities.[20]

My preoccupation in this book has thus been to recover, decipher, and unravel the specific codes and contexts that have enabled and structured articulations of a gendered self in Muslim South Asia. As noted in the introduction, there is a tendency to project autobiographical writing in South Asia, as in other colonized societies, as a European import during the "high noon" of imperialism—but clearly, South Asian Muslim women participated in a much longer tradition of telling life stories within Islam. Even when they adopted more evidently "Western" forms, conventions often persisted, if not always to the same ends. Commencing with a long and detailed genealogy, for instance, may no longer have been to assert Islamic credentials or justify a life being used as a model for others.[21] Thus, as Muslim life writing grew exponentially in South Asia in the modern period, it also changed or, perhaps better, variegated: partly in response to colonial and postcolonial frameworks, but also in recognition of reformist imperatives that dictated a very particular (and gendered) set of social relationships. The effect was that many Muslim women wrote autobiography differently than Muslim men did, thus perpetuating assumptions made about "women's texts" from the nineteenth century onward. But it only really makes sense to think how they *wrote* their lives as women if we think how they *lived* their lives as women too: undoubtedly constrained by multiple patriarchies, but still in different places, times, and settings. The sheer diversity of women's lives within the same cultural frame means that patterns and commonalities discernible in their life writing still resist easy categorization.

And that brings me back full circle to where I began this book: with Jobeda Khanam writing about a childhood sharply defined by elaborate patriarchal norms understood to define Muslim South Asia. Even if she does not always appear to write consciously as a woman—her constitutive identities as a Muslim and a Bangladeshi shine out in as sharp relief—her specific lived experience as a middle-class Muslim girl in a small town in early twentieth-century Bengal shaped the way she later narrated her life. I noted in chapter 2 that when a school for Muslim girls opened in her town, she was not permitted to attend since, at nearly eleven, she was considered of marriageable age. The first two bridegrooms' families brought to see Jobeda rejected her for her dark skin and lack of shame: Did she not lift her eyes to "stare straight at their faces"? Was she not known for "cycling on the rooftop" and "climbing trees in the garden" to claim mangoes and guavas? When a third bridegroom came himself from Calcutta, did she not meet him in person, sharing stories and poems already published in local magazines before playing the harmonium and even singing one of those sweet songs learned from her father with the doors and windows firmly shut? Her family and neighbors asked how this could happen: "When did Muslim men start seeing their would-be brides? Is there no purdah left?"[22] When Jobeda *actually* left purdah is not recorded: there is no dramatic account of unveiling here.[23] But her autobiography is emblematic of the autobiographical writings analyzed throughout this book in being an unveiling nevertheless: an intimate portrayal of how the daring and curiosity that scuppered her early marriage chances later enabled her to find a way for her voice to be heard.

ACKNOWLEDGMENTS

At the close of a lengthy and immersing project, it is a pleasure to be able to recognize the many individuals and institutions that have helped and sustained me along the way.

I describe in chapter 1 how my main archive was "the home, the market, the street." This kind of research necessitated lengthy periods in South Asia, during which my project progressed only thanks to the overwhelming generosity of so many individuals. In Delhi: Jaya Bhattacharji Rose and Shobhana Bhattacharji, Urvashi Butalia (at Zubaan), Indira Chandrasekhar (at Tulika), Mahmood Farooqui and Anusha Rizvi, Emma Flatt and Yunus Jaffrey, Kai Friese, S. Gautham, Shohini Ghosh, Sarmistha Gupta, Shabnam Hashmi and Qamar Hashmi (at ANHAD), Malavika Karlekar, Sabina Kidwai and Ambarien Alqadar (at A.J.K. Mass Communication Research Centre), Shahla Haidar, Sakina Hasan, and Sabiha Hussain (at the Centre for Women's Development Studies), Lubna Kazim and Shabnam Zafar, Sughra Mehdi, Ritu Menon (at Women Unlimited), Samina Mishra, Nazneen Nizami, Neeraj Pathania, Biswamoy Pati, Rani Ray, Sumit Roy and Nusrat Jafri, Shikha Sen, Yogi Sikand, Anand Vivek Taneja, Laila Tyabji, Salima Tyabji. In Aligarh: Farhat Hasan and Shadab Bano. In Bhopal: V. K. Juneja. In Bombay: Rafia Abdul Ali and Amiruddin Jabir Ali. In Thiruvananthapuram: J. Devika. In Dhaka: Asha Islam Nayeem, Sonia Nishat Amin and Hameeda Hossain. In Karachi: Muneeza Shamsie and Shaharyar M. Khan. I know I have missed mentioning some by name, but your mark remains. For their munificence in funding my South Asian sojourns (2005–7), I thank the British Academy and the Higher Education Funding Council for England.

I used many "real" archives too. In Britain: the Asia and African Studies collections at the British Library. In India: the Nehru Memorial Museum and Library and the library of the All India Women's Conference in Delhi, the Maulana Azad Library and the library of the Women's College at Aligarh Muslim University, the National Archives of India, Bhopal, and Sundarayya Vignana Kendram in Hyderabad. In Bangladesh: Dhaka University Library and the library of Bangla Academy in Dhaka. Materials were also received from the University of Mumbai archives, the Fyzee-Rahamin archives in Karachi, the Rampur Raza Library, and the Khuda Bakhsh Oriental Public Library in Patna. Without the diligent and helpful staff at all of these institutions, nothing could have been achieved.

Particularly enriching to this project was the experience of leading the international research network, Women's Autobiography in Islamic Societies, http://www.waiis.org. Funded by the Arts and Humanities Research Council (2010–11), it enabled the most exciting and enjoyable workshops in Austin, Texas (January 2010), Delhi, India (Decem-

196   *Acknowledgments*

ber 2010), and Sharjah, UAE (November 2011). There were also conference panels at the European Conference of Modern Asian Studies, University of Bonn (July 26–29, 2010), the 40th Annual Conference on South Asia, University of Wisconsin-Madison (October 21–23, 2011), and the Berkshire Conference of Women Historians, University of Toronto (May 22–25, 2014). Every member of this group deserves special mention for contributing intellectual sustenance and enduring friendship: Hülya Adak, Asiya Alam, Sonia Nishat Amin, Kathryn Babayan, Margot Badran, Afshan Bokhari, Marilyn Booth, miriam cooke, Nawar al-Hassan Golley, Kathryn Hansen, Sadaf Jaffer, Ruby Lal, Anshu Malhotra, Ellen McLarney, Roberta Micallef, Farzaneh Milani, Gail Minault, Mimi Mortimer, Sunil Sharma, Sylvia Vatuk, and Amina Yaqin.

Four from this list must be singled out:

Marilyn Booth always kindles inspiration. She was also outstanding as guest editor of a special issue titled "Women's Autobiography in South Asia and the Middle East" for the *Journal of Women's History* 25, no. 2 (Summer 2013), that showcased some of our network's research. A first draft of chapter 1 appeared in this special issue as: "Life/History/ Archive: Identifying Autobiographical Writing by Muslim Women in South Asia," 61–84. Together, we also received funding from the Islamic Studies Network of the Higher Education Academy (2011–12) to set up a digital archive of autobiographical writing in translation, "Accessing Muslim Lives," http://www.accessingmuslimlives.org.

Farzaneh Milani is a guiding light. She also hosted a fabulous conference, "Unveiling the Self: Women's Life Narratives in the Middle East and North Africa," at the University of Virginia at Charlottesville (October 29–30, 2012), which acted as a follow-on to our network gatherings.

Anshu Malhotra makes every scholarly meeting the happiest reunion. Our long friendship began as doctoral students working under the wonderful Avril A. Powell at SOAS in the 1990s. A mutual interest in autobiographical writing brought us together again for rich collaboration through the network and beyond. Our edited volume, *Speaking of the Self: Gender, Performance, and Autobiography in South Asia* (Duke University Press, 2015), enabled me to think through the theoretical grounding for this project. As I wrote *Elusive Lives*, she completed *Piro and the Gulabdasis: Gender, Sect, and Society in Punjab* (Oxford University Press, 2017). What next?

Sunil Sharma represents the best of academia. His boundless generosity led to our coauthored *Atiya's Journeys: A Muslim Woman from Colonial Bombay to Edwardian Britain* (Oxford University Press, 2010), in which I tried out many ideas that come into greater focus here. He also extended a kind invitation to Boston University in April 2014, during which I presented on this project to a particularly thought-provoking audience. More recently, we have joined with Daniel Majchrowicz for a collaborative research project on Muslim women travelers from Asia and the Middle East funded by the Leverhulme Trust (2015–18). This newest triangular alliance has offered much fresh insight in the final stages of revision.

Additionally, I thank Antoinette Burton, Geraldine Forbes, Barbara Metcalf, and Barbara Ramusack for their interest in this work at various points. Padma Anagol, Paula Banerjee, and Swapna Banerjee made fruitful suggestions on an article adapted from the second half of chapter 4 as "A Performer in Performance: The Multiple Constructions of Begum Khurshid Mirza's Written Life" for their forthcoming volume, *New Horizons in Women's History: Recovery, Agency, and Activism* (Oxford University Press, 2019). I also benefited from the fertile discussion at a workshop organized by Monika Browarczyk, Nora Melnikova, and Tara Puri, "Opening Up Intimate Spaces: Women's Writing and Autobiography in India," at Adam Mickiewicz University, in Poznań, Poland (May 19–20, 2016). The Gendered Lives Research Group, chaired by Jennifer Cooke at Loughborough University offered valuable feedback at its inaugural event in December 2015.

Remarkably, I have held posts at three separate universities in the course of this project. My colleagues and students at each of them have been invaluable in offering inspiration, encouragement, and a sounding board for ideas. My particular thanks to Mary Vincent, Julia Hillner, Dina Gusejnova, Anthony Milton, Phil Withington, and Saurabh Mishra at the University of Sheffield; Thoralf Klein, Marcus Collins, Max Drephal, Helen Drake, Phil Parvin, and Alex Christoyannopoulos at Loughborough University; and Nick Hayes, Ian Inkster, and Nayala Rehmat at Nottingham Trent University.

There was also the joy of returning to my alma mater, the University of British Columbia in Vancouver, Canada, for two separate spells as a visiting professor in the Department of History (2013–14, 2017). Most generously, the first was funded by a research fellowship from the Leverhulme Trust and the second by a project grant also from the Leverhulme Trust. John Roosa, Leslie Paris, Jessica Wang, and the late Allen Sinel were especially welcoming to the Department of History, as were Mandakranta Bose and Anne Murphy to the Centre for India and South Asia Research.

At Stanford University Press, the team is unsurpassed. A special mention goes to Marcela Maxfield, the acquisitions editor for Sociology and Asian Studies, for her enthusiasm, remarkable effort, and patience. Thomas Blom Hansen has been great as series editor for South Asia in Motion. My two anonymous reviewers offered particular suggestions that enriched the manuscript to no end.

And, of course, there are my family and friends to thank for their untold patience, understanding, and fun. My parents, John Hurley and Evelyn Hiscock, are always there and always curious. My uncle Lionel and aunt Donalene took a special interest in this project throughout. The Fisher family make the world go round. And my husband, Josh, is the rock at the center of everything. But this book is dedicated to our children, Finn and Tess: always bright and energetic and astonishing. Both were born after this project was begun, and thus they have never known life without it. Motherhood has made the experience of completing this book so much harder, but also so much richer—and so it is for them.

NOTES

INTRODUCTION

1. This paragraph draws on the opening paragraphs of Jobeda Khanam's *Jiban Khatar Pataguli* (Dhaka: Kathamala Prakashani, 1991). Nadia district was partitioned in 1947, with the name being applied to a smaller administrative territory in West Bengal and Kushtia being formed into its own district in East Pakistan. On Nadia's "demographic contours" as a "border district," see Subhasri Ghosh, "Population Movement in West Bengal: A Case Study of Nadia District, 1947–1951," *South Asia Research* 34, no. 2 (2014): 113–32.

2. This paragraph summarizes Jobeda Khanam's own reflections on her childhood in *Jiban Khatar Pataguli*, 15–28. It also draws on Saiyida Lutfunnessa's "Bangali Muslim Narir Cromobikash," in *Kaler Samukh Bhela*, ed. Nurunnahar Faizunnessa (Dhaka: Muktodhara, 1988), 80–87.

3. A classic study is Hannah Papanek's "Purdah: Separate Worlds and Symbolic Shelter," *Comparatives Studies in Society and History* 15, no. 3 (June 1973): 289–325.

4. See Gayatri Chakravorty Spivak, "Can the Subaltern Speak?" in *Colonial Discourse and Postcolonial Theory: A Reader*, ed. Patrick Williams and Laura Chrisman (New York: Harvester Wheatsheaf, 1993), 66–111, esp. 90.

5. On this, see Anindita Ghosh, ed., *Behind the Veil: Resistance, Women, and the Everyday in Colonial South Asia* (Ranikhet: Permanent Black, 2006), esp. 3.

6. See, for example, Gloria Goodwin Raheja and Ann Grodzins Gold, *Listen to the Heron's Words: Reimagining Gender and Kinship in North India* (Berkeley: University of California Press, 1994).

7. For further explication of this idea and many examples, see Anshu Malhotra and Siobhan Lambert-Hurley, eds., *Speaking of the Self: Gender, Performance, and Autobiography in South Asia* (Durham, NC: Duke University Press, 2015). Also see Malavika Karlekar, *Voices from Within: Early Personal Narratives of Bengali Women* (Delhi: Oxford University Press, 1993); Tanika Sarkar, *Words to Win: The Making of* Amar Jiban—*A Modern Autobiography* (New Delhi: Kali for Women, 1999); Myththily Sivaraman, *Fragments of a Life: A Family Archive* (New Delhi: Zubaan, 2006); and Aparna Basu and Malavika Karlekar, *In So Many Words: Women's Life Experiences from Western and Eastern India* (Delhi: Routledge, 2008).

8. Marilyn Booth, "Locating Women's Autobiographical Writing in Colonial Egypt," *Journal of Women's History* 25, no. 2 (2013): 39, 49.

9. Nawar Al-Hassan Golley, *Reading Arab Women's Autobiographies: Shahrazad Tells*

200   *Notes to Introduction*

Her Story (Austin: University of Texas Press, 2003), 79; Roberta Micallef, "Identities in Motion: Reading Two Ottoman Travel Narratives as Life Writing," *Journal of Women's History* 25, no. 2 (2013), 85; Farzaneh Milani, "Iranian Women's Life Narratives," *Journal of Women's History* 23, no. 2 (Summer 2013), 131.

10. David Arnold and Stuart Blackburn, introduction to *Telling Lives in India: Biography, Autobiography, and Life History*, ed. David Arnold and Stuart Blackburn (Delhi: Permanent Black, 2004), 7–9.

11. Ulrike Stark, *An Empire of Books: The Naval Kishore Press and the Diffusion of the Printed Word in Colonial India* (Ranikhet: Permanent Black, 2007). Also see Francesca Orsini, *Print and Pleasure: Popular Literature and Entertaining Fictions in Colonial North India* (Ranikhet: Permanent Black, 2009).

12. S. P. Saksena, ed., *Indian Autobiographies* (Calcutta: Oxford University Press, 1949), v, vii.

13. Udaya Kumar, "Autobiography as a Way of Writing History: Personal Narratives from Kerala and the Inhabitation of Modernity," in *History in the Vernacular*, ed. Partha Chatterjee and Raziuddin Aquil (Delhi: Permanent Black, 2008), 418–19. For another example, see A. R. Venkatachalapathy, "Making a Modern Self in Colonial Tamil Nadu," in *Biography as History: Indian Perspectives*, ed. Vijaya Ramaswamy and Yogesh Sharma (Hyderabad: Orient Blackswan, 2009), 30–52.

14. On Indian agency in colonial knowledge production, see Indra Sengupta and Daud Ali, *Knowledge Production, Pedagogy, and Institutions in Colonial India* (Abingdon: Palgrave Macmillan, 2011).

15. See, for example, David Arnold, "The Self and the Cell: Indian Prison Narratives as Life Histories," in Arnold and Blackburn's edited volume, *Telling Lives in India*; and Javed Majeed, *Autobiography, Travel and Postnational Identity: Gandhi, Nehru, and Iqbal* (Basingstoke: Palgrave Macmillan, 2007).

16. Arnold and Blackburn, *Telling Lives in India*, 9; Majeed, *Autobiography, Travel and Postnational Identity*, 2–3.

17. Faisal Devji, "Gender and the Politics of Space: The Movement for Women's Reform in Muslim India, 1857–1900," *South Asia* 14, no. 1 (1991): 141–53.

18. Francis Robinson, "Religious Change and the Self in Muslim South Asia," in his *Islam and Muslim History in South Asia* (Delhi: Oxford University Press, 2000), 105–21.

19. Barbara Metcalf, "The Pilgrimage Remembered: South Asian Accounts of the Hajj," in *Muslim Travellers: Pilgrimage, Migration and the Religious Imagination*, ed. Dale Eickelman and James Piscatori (London: Routledge, 1990), 87, 101.

20. See the bibliography for details.

21. Khatemanara Begam, "Nari Shiksha: Ami Ja Dekhechhi," in Nurunnahar Faizunnessa, *Kaler Samukh Bhela*, 70.

22. My own linguistic training in Hindi-Urdu alongside my native language, English, allowed me to consult many sources in their original languages, but in other cases I worked closely with regional specialists—sometimes even translating line by line to appreciate nuance and inflection—to include other materials. I am particularly grateful to Sarmistha Gupta, who displayed untold patience in working through many Bengali sources with me.

Notes to Introduction 201

23. For more detailed reflection on "the literacy conundrum," see chapter 2.

24. Margot Badran, preface to Huda Shaarawi, *Harem Years: The Memoirs of an Egyptian Feminist*, translated and with an introduction by Margot Badran (London: Virago, 1986), 1.

25. Farzaneh Milani, *Words, Not Swords: Iranian Women Writers and the Freedom of Movement* (Syracuse, NY: Syracuse University Press, 2011), xix.

26. Mahua Sarkar, *Visible Histories, Disappearing Women: Producing Muslim Womanhood in Late Colonial India* (New Delhi: Zubaan, 2008), 13.

27. See, for example, Jobeda Khanam, *Jiban Khatar Pataguli*, 100; Safia Jabir Ali, "Manuscript Memoirs of Mrs. Safia Jabir Ali," Badruddin Tyabji Family Papers 6, Nehru Memorial Museum and Library, New Delhi, India, entry for October 21, 1942; Abida Sultaan, *Memoirs of a Rebel Princess* (Karachi: Oxford University Press, 2004), 127–28.

28. Meher Kabir, "Amader Kal," in Nurunnahar Faizunnessa, *Kaler Samukh Bhela*, 62.

29. Jahanara Habibullah, *Remembrance of Days Past: Glimpses of a Princely State during the Raj* (Karachi: Oxford University Press, 2001), 45–47, 85–89. For another example, see Sufia Kamal, *Ekale Amader Kal* (Dhaka: Gyan Prakashani, 1988), 3–4.

30. Lubna Kazim, ed., *A Woman of Substance: The Memoirs of Begum Khurshid Mirza* (Delhi: Zubaan, 2005), 142.

31. For two early examples, see Nawab Sikandar Begam of Bhopal, *A Pilgrimage to Mecca*, trans. Mrs. Willoughby-Osborne (London: Wm H. Allen, 1870); and Sultan Jahan Begam, *Rauzat ur-riyahin* (Bhopal: Matba'-i-Sultani, 1909). The latter was published in English translation as: Sultan Jahan Begam of Bhopal, *The Story of a Pilgrimage to Hijaz* (London: Thacker, Spink, 1909).

32. Ummat ul-Ghani Nurunnisa, *Safarnama-i-Hijaz, Sham o Misr* (Hyderabad: N.p., 1996). This translation has been prepared for a chapter by Daniel Majchrowicz in our *Anthology of Muslim Women Travelers* (Bloomington: Indiana University Press, forthcoming).

33. The original source is a letter from the author to her daughter Na'imah, dated February 25, 1936, in *Nishatunnisa Begam, Begam Hasrat Mohani aur unke Khutut va Safarnama* (Delhi: Maulana Hasrat Mohani Foundation, 2015), 117–22. This translation has been prepared for a chapter by Daniel Majchrowicz in our forthcoming *Anthology of Muslim Women Travelers*.

34. Ghulam Fatima Shaikh, *Footprints in Time: Reminiscences of a Sindhi Matriarch*, trans. Rasheeda Husain (Karachi: Oxford University Press, 2011), 6. This passage was reprinted as Ghulam Fatima Shaikh, "The Changing Faith," *Friday Times* (Lahore) 22, no. 49 (January 21–27, 2011), http://www.thefridaytimes.com/21012011/page26.shtml.

35. Nalini Jameela, *Oru Laingikathozhilaliyude Atmakatha*, chapters 3 and 5.

36. I rely here on Anshu Malhotra's excellent analysis and translation of Piro's poetic autobiography, "Ik Sau Sath Kafian" [One hundred and sixty kafis], at "Accessing Muslim Lives," http://www.accessingmuslimlives.org/images/pdfs/Piro%20160%20Kafis.pdf. The stanza quoted is the thirtieth *kafi*. The question mark denotes where the meaning is unclear. I have added commas for greater clarity. For a fuller study, see Anshu Malhotra's *Piro and the Gulabdasis: Gender, Sect, and Society in Punjab* (Delhi: Oxford University Press, 2017).

202   *Notes to Introduction*

37. For the original text, see Raihana Tyabji, *The Heart of a Gopi* (Poona: Miss R. Tyabji, n.d.). For my analysis of this text as self-representation, see Siobhan Lambert-Hurley, "The Heart of a Gopi: Raihana Tyabji's Bhakti Devotionalism as Self-Representation," *Modern Asian Studies* 48, no. 3 (May 2014): 569–95.

38. See, for example, Abida Sultaan, *Memoirs of a Rebel Princess*, 150; Begum Khurshid Mirza, *A Woman of Substance*, 144; Raihana Tyabji, *Suniye Kakasahib* (Wardha: Hindustani Pracher Sabha, 1954); and Akhtar Imam, "Amader Shikal," in Nurunnahar Faizunnessa, *Kaler Samukh Bhela*, 30.

39. The original is printed in Letter 1, February 17, 1908, in Muhammad Amin Zuberi, *Khutut-i-Shibli ba-nam-i-muhtarma Zahra Begum sahiba Faizi va 'Atiya Begum sahiba Faizi* (Bhopal: Zill us-sultan Buk Ejansi, 1930), 29. For a full translation, see Siobhan Lambert-Hurley and Sunil Sharma, *Atiya's Journeys: A Muslim Woman from Colonial Bombay to Edwardian Britain* (Delhi: Oxford University Press, 2010), 33–34.

40. Joan L. Erdman with Zohra Segal, *Stages: The Art and Adventure of Zohra Segal* (Delhi: Kali for Women, 1997), 109.

41. I think here of diasporic authors, like Sara Suleri Goodyear.

42. See Dwight F. Reynolds on the *tarjama*, or biographical notice, in his *Interpreting the Self: Autobiography in the Arabic Literary Tradition* (Berkeley: University of California Press, 2001), 42.

43. Including a significant component on life abroad within a longer narrative is Safia Jabir Ali's "Manuscript Memoirs," (Badruddin Tyabji Family Papers 6, Nehru Memorial Museum and Library, New Delhi, India), in which she records her life in Burma in the early 1920s (see chapter 5). Similarly, Hameeda Akhtar Husain Raipuri dedicates a chapter of *Hamsafar* (Karachi: Daniyal, 1992) to life in Paris in the 1930s, while Abida Sultaan describes her diplomatic assignments to the United States, China, and Brazil in the 1950s and a later stay in Jordan in *Memoirs of a Rebel Princess*, 217–25, 253–55. An autobiography dominated by foreign travel is Ghulam Fatima Shaikh's *Footprints in Time* with four out of seven chapters dedicated to the eight years she spent living in the Ottoman Empire during the First World War and the Khilafat Movement. There are many more examples in Muslim women's autobiographical writing of long stays in the United Kingdom, especially. On the inclusion of travel narratives in this study, see chapter 1.

44. Ishvani, *The Brocaded Sari* (New York: John Day, 1947); Princess Mehrunissa of Rampur, *An Extraordinary Life* (Noida: Brijbasi Art Press, 2006); and Sara Suleri, *Meatless Days* (Chicago: University of Chicago Press, 1987). It is worth noting that despite writing in the United States, where she had lived for nearly three decades, Mehrunissa Khan still styled herself as "Princess Mehrunissa of Rampur" on the cover. Also relevant here is Fawzia Afzal-Khan's *Lahore with Love: Growing Up with Girlfriends Pakistani-Style* (Syracuse, NY: Syracuse University Press, 2010).

45. Examples include Yasmin Hai's *The Making of Mr Hai's Daughter: Becoming British: A Memoir* (London: Virago, 2008); and Sadia Shepard's *The Girl from Foreign: A Search for Shipwrecked Ancestors, Forgotten Histories, and a Sense of Home* (New York: Penguin, 2008).

46. On the Fyzees' Turkish links, see Lambert-Hurley and Sharma, *Atiya's Journeys*, 18–20.

Notes to Introduction   203

47. Anshu Malhotra and Siobhan Lambert-Hurley, "Introduction: Gender, Performance, and Autobiography," in our *Speaking of the Self*, 2–3.

48. Reynolds, *Interpreting the Self*, 17.

49. Georges Gusdorf, "Conditions and Limits of Autobiography," trans. James Olney, in James Olney, ed., *Autobiography: Essays Theoretical and Critical* (Princeton: Princeton University Press, 1980), 29.

50. Ibid., 30.

51. Reynolds, *Interpreting the Self*, 19. For examples of this type of analysis, see Marvin Zonis, "Autobiography and Biography in the Middle East: A Plea for Psychopolitical Studies," in *Middle Eastern Lives: The Practices of Biography and Self-Narrative*, ed. Martin Kramer (Syracuse: Syracuse University Press, 1991), 61; Stephen Frederic Dale, "Steppe Humanism: The Autobiographical Writings of Zahir al-Din Muhammad Babur, 1483–1530," *International Journal of Middle East Studies* 22 (1990): 39.

52. Roy Pascal, *Design and Truth in Autobiography* (New York and London: Garland, 1985), 22.

53. The quotation is from R. Stephen Humphreys, *Islamic History: A Framework for Inquiry*, rev. ed. (Princeton: Princeton University Press, 1991), 194. For other examples, see Albert Hourani, *Arabic Thought in the Liberal Age: 1798–1939* (Oxford: Oxford University Press, 1962), 224; and Edward Said, *Beginnings* (Baltimore: Johns Hopkins University Press, 1987), 81.

54. Kramer, *Middle Eastern Lives*.

55. Zonis, "Autobiography and Biography in the Middle East," 61, 63.

56. Ibid., 60–61.

57. Ali Jawad Zaidi, *A History of Urdu Literature* (Delhi: Sahitya Akademi, 1993), 434–35.

58. Amaresh Datta, *Encyclopedia of Indian Literature* (Delhi: Sahitya Akademi, 1988), 285, 287–89. It is worth noting that rather more—over fifty texts—are discussed in a full-length study of the genre in Urdu: Wahhaj al-Din Alvi, *Urdu Khud Navisht* (New Delhi: Maktaba Jamia, 1989).

59. See Reynolds, *Interpreting the Self*, 27. Scholars of Persian and Turkish literature suggest that numbers in those languages were also low. Milani, "Iranian Women's Life Narratives," 130; and Olcay Akyildiz, Halim Kara, and Börte Sagaster, *Autobiographical Themes in Turkish Literature: Theoretical and Comparative Perspectives* (Würtzburg: Orient-Institute Istanbul, 2007), 10.

60. Reynolds, *Interpreting the Self*, 31.

61. Ibid., part 1. The quotation is on 72.

62. Ibid., 82.

63. Gustave E. von Grunebaum, "Self-Expression: Literature and History," in *Medieval Islam*, 2nd ed. (Chicago: University of Chicago Press, 1952), 275.

64. Dale, *The Garden of the Eight Paradises: Bābur and the Culture of Empire in Central Asia, Afghanistan, and India (1483–1530)* (Leiden: Brill, 2004), 28–36.

65. Reynolds, *Interpreting the Self*, 74.

66. Ibid., 82, 87–88.

204   *Notes to Introduction*

67. Mary Ann Fay, ed., *Auto/biography and the Construction of Identity and Community in the Middle East* (New York: Palgrave, 2001).

68. Judith E. Tucker, "Biography as History: The Exemplary Life of Khayr al-Din al-Ramli," in Fay, *Auto/biography*, 11.

69. This summary is based on Barbara D. Metcalf, "The Past in the Present: Instruction, Pleasure, and Blessing in Maulana Muhamad Zakariyya's *Aap Biitii'*, in Arnold and Blackburn, *Telling Lives in India*, 119–21.

70. Tucker, "Biography as History," 11.

71. Antoinette Burton, *Dwelling in the Archive: Women Writing House, Home, and History in Late Colonial India* (Delhi: Oxford University Press, 2003), 139.

72. Malhotra and Lambert-Hurley, introduction to *Speaking of the Self*, 17–18. There is now a vast literature labeled as "memory studies." Some works on which we draw are A. K. Ramanujan, "The Ring of Memory: Remembering and Forgetting in Indian Literatures," in *A. K. Ramanujan: Uncollected Poems and Prose*, ed. Molly Daniels-Ramanujan and Keith Harrison (New Delhi: Oxford University Press, 2001), 83–100; Urvashi Butalia, *The Other Side of Silence: Voices from the Partition of India* (New Delhi: Penguin, 1998); and Jill Ker Conway, *When Memory Speaks: Exploring the Art of Autobiography* (New York: Vintage, 1998).

73. Luisa Passerini, *Fascism in Popular Memory: The Cultural Experience of the Turin Working Class* (Cambridge: Cambridge University Press, 1987), 20–21.

74. Anna Green and Kathleen Troup, *The Houses of History: A Critical Reader in Twentieth-Century History and Theory* (Manchester: Manchester University Press, 1999), 236.

75. Susan Rodgers, ed. *Telling Lives, Telling History: Autobiography and Historical Imagination in Modern Indonesia* (Berkeley: University of California Press, 1995), 4.

76. Arnold and Blackburn, introduction to *Telling Lives in India*, 3–4.

77. Ibid., 6.

78. On "life histories in India," see ibid., 6–9.

79. Sylvia Vatuk, "Hamara Daur-i Hayat: An Indian Muslim Woman Writes Her Life," in Arnold and Blackburn, *Telling Lives in India*, 144–74. Also see her "Dr Zakira Ghouse: A Memoir," in *Muslim Portraits: Everyday Lives in India*, ed. Mukulika Banerjee (New Delhi: Yoda Press, 2008), 109–27.

80. Vatuk quotes from Diane Wood Middlebrook, "Postmodernism and the Biographer," in *Revealing Lives: Autobiography, Biography, and Gender*, ed. Susan Groag Bell and Marilyn Yalom (Albany: State University of New York Press, 1990), 155.

81. Majeed, *Autobiography, Travel and Postnational Identity*.

82. Kumar, "Autobiography as a Way of Writing History," 418–48. Also see his faculty website for a summary of the bigger project, accessed July 1, 2015, http://www.englishdu.ac.in/index.php?page=udaya-kumar.

83. Kumar, "Autobiography," 420.

84. Ramaswamy and Sharma, *Biography as History*.

85. Farhat Hasan, "Presenting the Self: Norms and Emotions in Ardhakathanaka," in ibid., 105–22. In the same volume, also see A. R. Venkatachalapathy, "Making a Modern Self in Colonial Tamil Nadu," 30–52; and Vijaya Ramaswamy, "Muffled Narratives: The Life and Times of Neelambakai Ammaiyar," 123–51.

Notes to Introduction   205

86. See, for example, Uma Chakravarti, *Rewriting History: The Life and Times of Pandita Ramabai* (Delhi: Kali for Women, 1998); Sharmila Rege, *Writing Caste/Writing Gender: Narrating Dalit Women's Testimonios* (New Delhi: Zubaan, 2006); and Raj Kumar, *Dalit Personal Narratives: Reading Caste, Nation and Identity* (New Delhi: Orient Blackswan, 2010). Sidonie Smith offers a theoretical discussion of how autobiography may be used by those "excluded from official discourse" to "embody subjectivity" or, as I have noted here, "talk back," in her *Subjectivity, Identity, and the Body: Women's Autobiographical Practices in the Twentieth Century* (Bloomington: Indiana University Press, 1993).

87. Sarkar, *Words to Win*.

88. Ruby Lal, "Historicizing the Harem: The Challenge of a Princess's Memoir," *Feminist Studies* 30, no. 3 (Fall/Winter 2004): 590–616. Other studies relevant here include: Anshu Malhotra's nuanced analysis of the aforementioned Piro's autobiographical narrative in verse, "Telling Her Tale? Unravelling a Life in Conflict in Peero's *Ik Sau Saṭh Kāfiaṅ* [One hundred and sixty *kafis*]," *Indian Economic and Social History Review* 46, no. 4 (2009): 572–73; Amina Yaqin's dissertation, "Intertextuality of Women in Urdu Literature: A Study of Fahmida Riaz and Kishwar Naheed," University of London, 2001; and Afshan Bokhari's ongoing work on the autobiographical articulations of later Mughal princess Jahanara, including "Between Patron and Piety: Jahan Ara Begum's Sufi Affiliations and Articulations in Seventeenth-Century Mughal India," in *Sufism and Society: Arrangements of the Mystical in the Muslim World, 1200–1800*, ed. John J. Curry and Erik S. Ohlander (Abingdon: Routledge, 2012), 120–42.

89. Malhotra and Lambert-Hurley, introduction to *Speaking of the Self*, 2.

90. Kathryn Hansen, *Stages of Life: Indian Theatre Autobiographies* (Ranikhet: Permanent Black, 2011), xiii.

91. For example, Asiya Alam writes on Nazr Sajjiad Hyder, Shubhra Ray on Kailashbashini Debi, Ritu Menon on Nayantara Sahgal, Afshan Bokhari on Jahanara Begam, and Anshu Malhotra on Piro. My own chapter is on Raihana Tyabji. See Malhotra and Lambert-Hurley, *Speaking of the Self*, 33–280.

92. Margot Badran, preface and introduction to *Harem Years*, 1–22; Leila Ahmed, "Between Two Worlds: The Formation of a Turn-of-the-Century Egyptian Feminist," in *Life/Lines: Theorizing Women's Autobiography*, ed. Bella Brodzki and Celeste Schenck (Ithaca: Cornell University Press, 1989), 154–74. More-recent studies of Huda Shaarawi's memoirs include: S. Asha, "The Intersection of the Personal and the Political: Huda Shaarawi's *Harem Years* and Leila Ahmed's *A Border Passage*," *IUP Journal of English Studies* 7, no. 2 (June 2012): 31–38; and Julia Lisiecka, "Re-reading Huda Shaarawi's *Harem Years*—Bargaining with Patriarchy in Changing Egypt," *SOAS Journal of Postgraduate Research* (2015): 46–58.

93. Hülya Adak, "An Epic for Peace," in *Memoirs of Halidé Edib* (Piscataway, NJ: Gorgias Press, 2005), v–xxvii; Hülya Adak, "Suffragettes of the Empire, Daughters of the Republic: Women Auto/biographers Narrate National History (1918–1935)," in "Literature and the Nation," special issue, *New Perspectives on Turkey* 36 (May 2007): 27–51; Hülya Adak, "National Myths and Self Na:(rra)tions: Mustafa Kemal's *Nutuk* and Halide Edib's *Memoirs* and *The Turkish Ordeal*," *South Atlantic Quarterly* 102, nos. 2/3 (January 2003): 509–28; Abbas Amanat, "The Changing World of Taj al-Saltana," in *Crowning Anguish: Memoirs of*

206   *Notes to Introduction*

a Persian Princess from the Harem to Modernity (Washington, DC: Mage Publishers, 2003), 9–102. Also on Taj al-Saltana's memoirs is Afsaneh Najmabadi's "A Different Voice: Taj os-Saltaneh," in *Women's Autobiographies in Contemporary Iran*, ed. William Hanaway, Michael Hillman, and Farzaneh Milani (Cambridge: Center for Middle Eastern Studies, Harvard University, 1990), 17–32. Comparable studies of individual texts include: Margot Badran, "Expressing Feminism and Nationalism in Autobiography: The Memoirs of an Egyptian Educator," in *De/Colonizing the Subject: The Politics of Gender in Women's Autobiography*, ed. Sidonie Smith and Julia Watson (Minneapolis: University of Minnesota Press, 1992), 270–93; miriam cooke, "*Ayyam min Hayati*: The Prison Memoirs of a Muslim Sister," *Journal of Arabic Literature* 26, nos. 1–2 (1995): 121–39; Mildred Mortimer, "Assia Djebar's Algerian Quartet: A Study in Fragmented Autobiography," *Research in African Literatures* 28, no. 22 (Summer 1997): 102–17; and Kathryn Babayan, "In Spirit We Ate of Each Other's Sorrow: Female Companionship in Seventeenth Century Safavi Iran," in *Islamicate Sexualities: Translations Across Temporal Geographies of Desire*, ed. Kathryn Babayan and Afsaneh Najmabadi (Cambridge: Harvard Middle Eastern Monographs, 2008), 239–74.

94. Golley, *Reading Arab Women's Autobiographies*. Also see her edited volume, *Arab Women's Lives Retold: Exploring Identity through Writing* (Syracuse: Syracuse University Press, 2003).

95. Marilyn Booth, *May Her Likes Be Multiplied: Biography and Gender Politics in Egypt* (Berkeley: University of California Press, 2003); and Farzaneh Milani, "Veiled Voices: Women's Autobiographies in Iran," in *Women's Autobiographies in Contemporary Iran*, 1–16. Also by Booth, see "Who Gets to Become the Liberal Subject? Ventriloquized Memoirs and the Individual in 1920s Egypt," in *Liberal Thought in the Eastern Mediterranean: Late 19th Century until the 1960s*, ed. Christoph Schumann (Leiden: Brill, 2008), 267–92; and "Reflections on Recent Autobiographical Writing in an Arab Feminist Vein," *Middle East Women's Studies Review* 15, no. 4/16, no. 1 (Winter/Spring 2001): 8–11. Also by Milani, see *Veils and Words: The Emerging Voices of Iranian Women Writers* (Syracuse: Syracuse University Press, 1992); and *Words, Not Swords*.

96. See the website of this project at http://www.waiis.org.

97. A major collective output of this project was "Women's Autobiography in South Asia and the Middle East," a special issue of *Journal of Women's History* 25, no. 2 (Summer 2013), guest-edited by Marilyn Booth. Contributors Anshu Malhotra, Marilyn Booth, Roberta Micallef, Mildred Mortimer, and Margot Badran each offered a close examination of one to three autobiographical narratives in her respective chapter. Also see miriam cooke's *Nazira Zeineddine: A Pioneer of Islamic Feminism* (Oxford: Oneworld, 2010), and future publications from this group still to come.

98. See my "Introduction: A Princess Revealed" to Abida Sultaan's *Memoirs of a Rebel Princess*; *A Princess's Pilgrimage: Nawab Sikandar Begum's "A Pilgrimage to Mecca"* (New Delhi: Kali for Women, 2007); *Atiya's Journeys* (with Sharma); "Forging Global Networks in the Imperial Era: Atiya Fyzee in Edwardian London," in *India in Britain: South Asian Networks and Connections, 1858–1950*, ed. Susheila Nasta (Basingstoke: Palgrave Macmillan, 2013), 64–79; and "The Heart of a Gopi."

99. There is a vast theoretical and historical literature on autobiography in Europe and

North America. Some texts that have proven especially useful to this study (in alphabetical order) are: Shari Benstock, ed., *The Private Self: Theory and Practice of Women's Autobiographical Writings* (Chapel Hill: University of North Carolina Press, 1988); Bella Brodzki and Celeste Schenk, eds., *Life/Lines: Theorizing Women's Autobiography* (Ithaca: Cornell University Press, 1988); Conway, *When Memory Speaks*; Margo Culley, ed., *American Women's Autobiography: Fea(s)ts of Memory* (Madison: University of Wisconsin Press, 1992); Robert Folkenflik, ed., *The Culture of Autobiography: Constructions of Self-Representation* (Stanford: Stanford University Press, 1993); Carolyn G. Heilbrun, *Writing a Woman's Life* (New York: Ballantine Books, 1988); Estelle Jelinek, ed., *Women's Autobiography: Essays in Criticism* (Bloomington: Indiana University Press, 1980); Shirley Neuman, ed., *Autobiography and Questions of Gender* (London: Frank Cass, 1991); Linda H. Peterson, *Traditions of Victorian Women's Autobiography: The Poetics and Politics of Life Writing* (Charlottesville: University Press of Virginia, 1991); Sidonie Smith and Julia Watson, *Reading Autobiography: A Guide for Interpreting Life Narratives*, 2nd ed. (Minneapolis: University of Minnesota Press, 2010); Sidonie Smith and Julia Watson, eds., *Women, Autobiography, Theory: A Reader* (Madison: University of Wisconsin Press, 1998); Smith, *Subjectivity, Identity, and the Body*; Liz Stanley, *The Auto/biographical I* (Manchester and New York: Manchester University Press, 1992); Johnnie M. Stover, *Rhetoric and Resistance in Black Women's Autobiography* (Gainesville: University Press of Florida, 2003); Gillian Whitlock, *The Intimate Empire: Reading Women's Autobiography* (London: Cassell, 2000). An important exception in that it seeks to theorize women's autobiography with reference to multiple global locations is Sidonie Smith and Julia Watson, eds., *De/Colonizing the Subject: The Politics of Gender in Women's Autobiography* (Minneapolis: University of Minnesota Press, 1992).

100. Smith and Watson, *Reading Autobiography*, 4–5.

101. As the great Annalist Marc Bloch observed, the historian is charged with never losing from sight that time is "the plasm in which events are immersed, and the environment from which they derive their meaning." See his *Apologie pour l'histoire ou métier d'historien* (Paris: Colin, 1974), 36.

102. Asiya Alam, "Interrupted Stories: Self-Narratives of Nazr Sajjad Hyder," in Malhotra and Lambert-Hurley, *Speaking of the Self*, 74.

103. I think, for example, of my conversation with Sakina Hassan in her apartment near Connaught Place in Delhi, on February 13, 2006. The situation was even more acute when families moved abroad—but occasionally I benefited from that process. A case in point relates to Begum Khurshid Mirza's manuscript employed in chapter 4. It was gifted to me by her daughter, Lubna Kazim, when she moved from Lahore to the United States to be closer to her children and grandchildren.

104. I summarize a conversation with Salima Tyabji at her flat in Delhi, on November 29, 2005.

105. On the process of translation, see n. 22.

106. This document is hereafter referred to as the "Diary of Sultan Jahan Begam." It consists of just sixteen pages written in Urdu, though with extensive Persian and Arabic vocabulary.

107. Burton, *Dwelling in the Archive*, 144.

208   *Notes to Chapter 1*

CHAPTER 1

1. The British Academy and Higher Education Funding Council for England (HEFCE) funded this early stage of the project (2005–6); I acknowledge their support with gratitude.

2. See, for example, Siobhan Lambert-Hurley, *Muslim Women, Reform and Princely Patronage: Nawab Sultan Jahan Begam of Bhopal* (London: Routledge, 2007).

3. I quote a review of Suvir Kaul's *The Partitions of Memory*, cited in Burton, *Dwelling in the Archive*, 21.

4. For a useful summary of these developments, see Vatuk, "Hamara Daur-i Hayat," 147.

5. Rajeswari Sunder Rajan, *Real and Imagined Women: Gender, Culture and Postcolonialism* (London: Routledge, 1993), 91.

6. Burton, *Dwelling in the Archive*, 141.

7. Conway, *When Memory Speaks*. For a fuller discussion of these questions, see Smith and Watson, *Reading Autobiography*, 5–12.

8. Smith and Watson, *Reading Autobiography*, 13–15.

9. Pascal, *Design and Truth in Autobiography*, 5.

10. Smith and Watson, *Reading Autobiography*, 4.

11. Conway, *When Memory Speaks*, 3.

12. Carolyn Steedman, *Dust* (Manchester: Manchester University Press, 2001), 1.

13. On a related theme, see Ann Laura Stoler, "Colonial Archives and the Arts of Governance," *Archival Science* 2, nos. 1–2 (March 2002): 87–109.

14. Burton, *Dwelling* in the Archive, 139.

15. Ibid., 141.

16. Sugata Bose and Ayesha Jalal, *Modern South Asia: History, Culture, Political Economy*, 1st ed. (London: Routledge, 1997), 7.

17. See, for example, Gayatri Chakravorty Spivak, "The Rani of Sirmur: An Essay in Reading the Archives," *History and Theory* 24, no. 3 (1985): 247–72.

18. Gulbadan Begam, *The History of Humāyūn-Humāyūn-nāma*, trans. Annette S. Beveridge (London, 1902). For the Persian original, see MS.Or 166.

19. Lal, "Historicizing the Harem." Also see her *Domesticity and Power in the Early Mughal World* (Cambridge: Cambridge University Press, 2005).

20. Andrea Butenschon, *The Life of a Mogul Princess* (London: George Routledge and Sons, 1931). It has since been reprinted by Sang-e-Meel Publications in Lahore (2004). Contemporary reviewers seem to take Butenschon's claim at face value. See Mohsin Maqbool Elahi, "Review: A Princess with Taste," *Dawn*, July 18, 2004.

21. Afshan Bokhari's doctoral thesis will appear as *Imperial Women in Mughal India: The Piety and Patronage of Jahanara Begum* (London: I. B. Tauris, forthcoming). Sunil Sharma is preparing a full translation of Jahanara's *Risala-i-Sahibiyah* for publication. An extract from his translation is available at "Accessing Muslim Lives," http://www.accessing muslimlives.org.

22. Shaista Ikramullah, *From Purdah to Parliament* (London: Cressat Press, 1963); and Jahan Ara Shahnawaz, *Father and Daughter: A Political Autobiography* (Lahore: Nigarishat,

1971). More recently, both of these texts have been republished by Oxford University Press in Karachi (1998 and 2002).

23. Tehmina Durrani, *My Feudal Lord* (London: Bantam Press, 1994); Salma Ahmed, *Cutting Free* (Karachi: Sama, 2002); Kishwar Naheed, *Buri 'aurat ki Katha: Khudnavisht* (New Delhi: Adab Publications, 1995); Azra Abbas, *Mere Bachpan* (Karachi: Jadid Klasik Pablisharz, 1994); and Fatima Shah, *Sunshine and Shadows: The Autobiography of Dr. Fatima Shah* (Lahore: Ferozsons, 1999).

24. Ira M. Lapidus, *A History of Islamic Societies*, 2nd ed. (Cambridge: Cambridge University Press, 2002), 22.

25. Metcalf, "The Past in the Present," 119.

26. On the relationship between biography and history in the Arab world, see Tucker, "Biography as History," 9–10.

27. Metcalf, "The Past in the Present," 119.

28. Robinson, "Islam and the Impact of Print in South Asia," in his *Islam and Muslim History in South Asia*, 95.

29. W. C. Smith, quoted in ibid.

30. Robinson, "Islam and the Impact of Print," 96.

31. See, for example, Sayyid Asghar Husain, *Nurjahan Badshah Begam ki Sawanih-i-'Umri* (Agra: Agra Akhbar, 1903); Muhammad Husain Mahvi Siddiqi, *Azvaj ul-Anboya* (Bhopal: Nawab of Bhopal, 1916); Inayat Allah, *Panc Mashhur Begamat* (Lahore: Nur Il-lahi, 1928); and Muhammad 'Ilm al-Din Salih, *Dukhtaran-i-Hind* (Lahore: Malik House, 1935).

32. A typical example of this type of writing is Ameer Ali's "The Influence of Women in Islam," reprinted from *The Nineteenth Century* (May 1899), in K. K. Aziz, *Ameer Ali: His Life and Work* (Lahore: Publishers United, 1968), 172–76.

33. For example, see Abdullah Yusuf Ali, "The Indian Muhammedans: Their Past, Present and Future," *Journal of the Society of Arts* 55, no. 2825 (January 4, 1907). For comparison, see Booth, *May Her Likes Be Multiplied*, 91–92, 136, 150, 165, 228, 270, 272.

34. "Nawab Ali Vardi ki Begam," *Zill us-Sultan*, February 1918, 20–23.

35. *Tahzib un-Niswan*, January 6, 1934, 33–36.

36. Booth, *May Her Likes Be Multiplied*, esp. xiv.

37. Sultan Jahan Begam, *Hayat-i-Shahjahani* (Agra: Mufid-i-'Am, 1914); and *Hayat-i-Qudsi* (Bhopal: Matba'-i-Sultani, 1917). These biographies are available in English translation as: *Hayat-i-Shahjehani: Life of Her Highness the Late Nawab Shahjehan Begum of Bhopal*, trans. B. Ghosal (Bombay: Times Press, 1926); and *Hayat-i-Qudsi: Life of the Nawab Gauhar Begum alias the Nawab Begum Qudsia of Bhopal*, trans. W. S. Davis (London: Kegan Paul, Trench, Trubner, 1918).

38. Muhammadi Begam, *Hayat-i-Ashraf* (Lahore: Rifah-i-'Am Press, 1904).

39. Booth, *May Her Likes Be Multiplied*, xvi. For examples of the wider literature on which she draws, see Stanley, *The Auto/biographical I*; and Blanche Weisen Cook, "Biographer and Subject: A Critical Connection," in *Between Women: Biographers, Novelists, Critics, Teachers, and Artists Write about Their Work on Women*, ed. Carol Ascher, Louise de Salvo, and Sara Ruddick (Boston: Beacon Press, 1984).

210   *Notes to Chapter 1*

40. Michael Holroyd, "Our Friends the Dead," *Guardian* (June 1, 2002). For the original study, see Richard Holmes, *Dr Johnson and Mr Savage: A Biographical Mystery* (London: Flamingo, 2004).

41. Booth, *May Her Likes Be Multiplied*, xvi.

42. The Mother of M. Abd al-Aziz, *Mu'avvin-i-Mashurat* (Hardoi: Matba'-i-Muraqqa'i 'Alam, 1905).

43. Shah Jahan Begam, *Tahzib un-Niswan wa Tarbiyat ul-Insan* (Delhi: Matba'i-Ansari, 1889). I develop this theme in my "To Write of the Conjugal Act: Intimacy and Sexuality in Muslim Women's Autobiographical Writing in South Asia," *Journal of the History of Sexuality* 23, no. 2 (May 2014): 155–81.

44. Sultan Jahan Begam, *Hadiyat uz-Zaujain* (Madras: Weekly Newspaper Press, 1917), 22–25. This work was translated into English as *Muslim Home, Part 1: Present to the Married Couple* (Calcutta: Thacker, Spink, 1916).

45. M. Abd al-Qadir, *Sirat ul-Mamduh*, ed. Maulavi Hidayat Muhayy al-Din (Agra: Mufid-i-'Am, 1906); and Khwaja Altaf Husain Hali, *Bayan-i-Hali* (Panipat: Shaikh M. Ismail Panipati, 1939). The latter appears to be a reprint of "Maulana Hali ki Khud-navisht Sawanih-i-'Umri," *Ma'arif* 19: no. 5 (May 1927): 344–51.

46. A useful compendium is Peter Hulme and Tim Youngs, eds., *The Cambridge Companion to Travel Writing* (Cambridge: Cambridge University Press, 2002).

47. Tim Youngs, "Introduction: Filling the Blank Spaces," in Tim Youngs, ed., *Travel Writing in the Nineteenth Century: Filling the Blank Spaces* (London: Anthem, 2006), 2–3.

48. Metcalf, "The Pilgrimage Remembered," 85.

49. See Siobhan Lambert-Hurley, "Muslim Women Write Their Journeys Abroad: A Bibliographical Essay," in *Travel Writing in India*, ed. Shobhana Bhattacharji (Delhi: Sahitya Akademi, 2008), 28–39. Three dedicated studies of this material, spin-offs and follow-ons to the larger project, are: Lambert-Hurley, *A Princess's Pilgrimage*; Lambert-Hurley and Sharma, *Atiya's Journeys*; and Lambert-Hurley with Sharma and Majchrowicz, *Anthology of Muslim Women Travelers*.

50. See the website of the Rampur Raza Library, accessed June 29, 2011, http://raza library.gov.in/index.asp.

51. Burton, *Dwelling* in the Archive.

52. Nawab Faizunnessa Chaudhurani, *Rupjalal*, ed. Mohammad Abdul Kuddus (originally published Dhaka, 1876; reprint Dhaka: Bangla Academy, 2004); and Dr. Sabrina Q Rashid, *Hajj: A Wonderful Experience: With a Guide to Hajj* (Dhaka: Islamic Foundation Bangladesh, 2005). Bangladesh proved to be a mine of resources, a geographical clustering discussed in chapter 3.

53. Jahanara Imam, *Of Blood and Fire: The Untold Story of Bangladesh's War of Independence*, trans. Mustafizur Rahman (Dhaka: The University Press, 1998); Farida Huq, *Journey Through 1971: My Story* (Dhaka: Academic Press and Publishers, 2004).

54. Rokeya Sakhawat Hossain, *Sultana's Dream and Padmarag*, trans. Barnita Bagchi (New Delhi: Penguin, 2005), back cover.

55. Zaidi, *A History of Urdu Literature*, 435.

56. Burton, *Dwelling in the Archive*, 106.

Notes to Chapter 1   211

57. Ibid., 117.

58. Ibid.

59. Sukrita Paul Kumar, "Introducing Ismat," in Kumar and Sadique, *Ismat: Her Life, Her Times* (Delhi: Katha, 2000), 9.

60. Ibid., 18. A very recent translation has simplified the title to *The Paper Attire*. See Ismat Chughtai, *Kaghazi Hai Pairahan* [The paper attire], trans. Noor Zaheer (Karachi: Oxford University Press, 2016).

61. Kumar, "Introducing Ismat," 10.

62. Ibid., 10.

63. Smith and Watson, *Reading Autobiography*, 15.

64. Raihana Tyabji, *The Heart of a Gopi*, v–vi.

65. The questions are transposed from my "The Heart of a Gopi," 569.

66. This meeting occurred on November 21, 2005.

67. Karlekar, *Voices from Within*, 19.

68. Joanne E. Cooper, "Shaping Meaning: Women's Diaries, Journals, and Letters— The Old and the New," *Women's Studies International Forum* 10, no. 1 (1987): 95.

69. Atiya Fyzee's *Zamana-i-Tahsil* (Agra: Mufid-i-'Am, 1921), originally published in the Lahore women's weekly *Tahzib un-Niswan* (see issues dated January 26, 1907–November 30, 1907); and Nazli Rafia Sultan Nawab Begam Sahiba, *Sair-i-Yurop* (Lahore: Union Steam Press, n.d.). For a detailed analysis of the first, see Lambert-Hurley and Sharma, *Atiya's Journeys*.

70. I borrow the latter phrase from Karlekar, *Voices from Within*, 18.

71. As indicated in chapter 1, I came across this brief sixteen-page document among the possessions of Princess Abida Sultaan at her home in Karachi, Pakistan. Written in Urdu, it contains extensive Persian and Arabic vocabulary.

72. Abida Sultaan, *Memoirs of a Rebel Princess*, 132.

73. Kumar, "Autobiography as a Way of Writing History," 418–19.

74. For example, see Abida Sultaan, *Memoirs of a Rebel Princess*, 244.

75. Burton, *Dwelling in the Archive*, 135.

76. "Manuscript Memoirs of Mrs. Safia Jabir Ali," Badruddin Tyabji Family Papers 6. Also blurring the lines around the diary form are various autobiographical acts on the Internet, including blogs and social media posts—but as a historian, I choose to leave those to scholars more interested in the contemporary. For example, see Zainab Bawa's Twitter feed @zainabbawa and blog, *A Writer Runs*, https://writerruns.wordpress.com/. For an analysis of the blog as a "new autobiographical genre," see Gillian Whitlock, *Soft Weapons: Autobiography in Transit* (Chicago: University of Chicago Press, 2007), chapter 1, "Arablish: The Baghdad Blogger."

77. This summary is based on my consultation of the "Akhbar ki Kitab" from Matheran and Mahabaleshwar relating to the period from 1894 to 1907 at the Nehru Memorial Museum and Library in New Delhi. Some notebooks, like the "Kitab-i-Akhbar-i-Kihim-Yali," are kept in the archives of the University of Mumbai; others, labeled "Akhbarnama-i-Qabila-i-Shujauddin Tyabji," are in the Fyzee-Rahamin archives in Karachi. Still others remain in the private collections of Tyabji descendants.

212   *Notes to Chapter 1*

78. See, for example, Durrat al-Vali's entry for June 1, 1892, "Kitab-i-Akhbar-i-Kihim-Yali," University of Mumbai.

79. See, for example, "A Page from the Past: Extracts from the Diary of Amina Binte Badruddin Tyabji," *Roshni*, special issue (1946): 69–73; and Shareefah Hamid Ali, "My Journey to America by Air," *Roshni* 2, no. 6 (July 1947): 23–28; "My Visit to America II," *Roshni* 2, no. 7 (August 1947): 16–22; "Washington Diary III," *Roshni* 2, no. 8 (October 1947): 23–26; and "Excursion to Mount Vernon," *Roshni* 2, no. 9 (November 1947): 5–7.

80. I consulted *Tahzib un-Niswan* and *Zebunnisa* at the Maulana Azad Library of Aligarh Muslim University and/or the Sundarayya Vignana Kendram in Hyderabad, *Roshni* at the All India Women's Conference Library in Delhi, and *Begum* at the Bangla Academy in Dhaka. My thanks to my generous hostess, Asha Islam, for her assistance with Bengali translation. Perhaps the best known of this type of material is Bibi Ashraf's "How I Learned to Read and Write," first published in *Tahzib un-Niswan* in two installments (March 23 and 30, 1899), then reproduced in Muhammadi Begam's *Hayat-i-Ashraf*, 5–20, then translated in C. M. Naim's "How Bibi Ashraf Learned to Read and Write," *Annual of Urdu Studies* 6 (1987): 99–115.

81. "A Grand Old Lady of Music—An Interview with Asghari Begum Sagarwali," *Manushi* (March–April 1983): 8–10; "An Irrepressible Spirit—An Interview with Ismat Chughtai," *Manushi* 19, no. 4 (November–December 1983): 2–7; "The Final Goal Is Justice . . . ," *Manushi* 36, no. 6 (September–October 1986): 2–6.

82. See the opening page, accessed January 10, 2010, http://www.harappa.com/.

83. I consulted "Attia Hosain—Interview," accessed January 10, 2010, http://www.harappa.com/attia/growingup.html. It is now available here, accessed April 20, 2017: http://old.harappa.com/attia/growingup.html. I have corrected some punctuation, but the material in square brackets is original to the document.

84. For a fascinating study of the "literary qualities" of Texan oral narratives, see Richard Bauman's *Story, Performance, and Event: Contextual Studies of Oral Narrative* (Cambridge: Cambridge University Press, 1986).

85. Hameeda Akhtar Husain Raipuri, *Hamsafar* (Karachi: Daniyal, 1992). For the translation, see Hameeda Akhtar Husain Raipuri, *My Fellow Traveller: A Translation of Humsafar* (Karachi: Oxford University Press, 2006). I refer to the use of the phrase "fellow traveller" to denote Communists. Doubt as to the appropriateness of this translated title was raised by the author's son, Irfan Husain, who generously invited me to the book's release in the UK at the Pakistan High Commission in London on September 12, 2006.

86. Raipuri, *Hamsafar*, 9. For the translation, see Raipuri, *Fellow Traveller*, xiii.

87. Quoted in Mushfiq Khwaja's foreword to Raipuri, *Fellow Traveller*, ix–x.

88. Asif Farrukhi, introduction to Raipuri, *Fellow Traveller*, xxvii. Similar descriptors have been applied to other autobiographical writings by South Asian Muslim women. For example, Mehr Afshan Farooqi, in her "translator's note," admires Qaisari Begam's *Kitab-i-Zindagi* for its "refreshing, animated, conversational style." See Qaisari Begam, "Excerpts from *Kitab-e Zindagi*," *Annual of Urdu Studies* 20 (2005): 232–41.

89. John Tosh, *The Pursuit of History*, 5th ed. (Harlow: Pearson, 2010), 319.

90. Nalini Jameela, *Oru Laingikathozhilaliyude Atmakatha*.

Notes to Chapter 1 213

91. J. Devika's translation of Nalini Jameela's autobiography was later published as *The Autobiography of a Sex Worker* (Chennai: Westland, 2007).

92. This discussion is based on a wonderful conversation with J. Devika at her office and elsewhere in Trivandrum on Christmas Eve 2005.

93. Speeches by Shabnam Zafar and Lubna Kazim at the conference to celebrate Rashid Jahan's birth centenary, Aligarh, November 27–28, 2005.

94. Speech by Lubna Kazim, 1.

95. Ibid., 2.

96. Muneeza Shamsie, "My Uncle and Me" (unpublished manuscript). A condensed version was subsequently published in *Strategy, Diplomacy, Humanity: Life and Work of Sahabzada Yaqub-Khan*, ed. Anwar Dil (San Diego and Islamabad: Intercultural Forum, Takshila Research University, 2005), 361.

97. Muneeza Shamsie, "Women's Day speech, March 1999" (unpublished manuscript).

98. Lambert-Hurley, *Muslim Women, Reform and Princely Patronage*, 114.

99. Habibullah, *Remembrance*. For application of this method, see chapter 5.

100. *The House on Gulmohar Avenue*, dir. Samina Mishra (Public Service Broadcasting Trust, New Delhi, 2005). I am particularly grateful to the filmmaker for sharing her film, time, and memories in situ at the family's Okhla home. The film is now also available online at https://www.youtube.com/watch?v=cjvd6bvj2YA.

101. Sayyida Khurshid Alam, *Zakir Sahib ki Kahani: ap ki beti ke zubani* (Delhi: National Book Trust, 1975).

102. *Shadows of Freedom*, dir. Sabina Kidwai (Public Service Broadcasting Trust, New Delhi, 2004). Again, I am grateful to the filmmaker for presenting me with a copy of this film.

103. I used a reprint of the original: Begam Anis Kidwai, *Azadi ki Chhaon Mein* (New Delhi: National Book Trust, 1980). In translation, see Anis Kidwai, *In Freedom's Shade*, trans. Ayesha Kidwai (Delhi: Penguin, 2011).

104. Other examples include: Qamar Azad Hashmi, *Panchwan Chirag* (New Delhi: Safdar Hashmi Memorial Trust, 1995), trans. Madhu Prasad and Sohail Hashmi as *The Fifth Flame: The Story of Safdar Hashmi* (New Delhi: Penguin, 1997); Zakia Sultana Nayyar, *Bite Lamhe: Yadon ke Chiragh* (New Delhi: Modern Publishing House, 1995); and Sara Suleri Goodyear, *Boys Will Be Boys: A Daughter's Elegy* (Chicago: University of Chicago Press, 2003). There are also a number of shorter examples in Saif Hyder Hasan, ed., *One Yesterday* (New Delhi: Rupa, 2004).

105. Jyotsna Kapur, "Putting Herself into the Picture: Women's Accounts of the Social Reform Campaign in Maharashtra, Mid Nineteenth to Early Twentieth Centuries," *Manushi* 56 (1990): 28–30.

106. Raipuri, *Hamsafar*, 16.

107. Ibid., 11.

108. Ibid., ii.

109. Hamida Rahman, *Jiban Smriti* (Dhaka: Naoroze Kitabistan, 1990), 84.

110. Siobhan Lambert-Hurley, "Introduction: A Princess Revealed," in Abida Sultaan, *Memoirs of a Rebel Princess*, xxiii.

214   *Notes to Chapters 1 and 2*

111. Shirley Neuman, "Autobiography and Questions of Gender: An Introduction," in her *Autobiography and Questions of Gender*, 1–11.

112. Malhotra and Lambert-Hurley, introduction to *Speaking of the Self*, 7.

113. Metcalf, "The Past in the Present," 116–17.

114. Conversation with Lubna Kazim, between Aligarh and Delhi, November 28, 2005.

115. Kazim, A Woman of Substance, viii.

116. Bilkees Latif, *Her India: The Fragrance of Forgotten Years* (New Delhi: Arnold-Heinemann Publishers, 1984), esp. 8, 254. A parallel could be drawn here with Abida Sultaan's *Memoirs of a Rebel Princess*. It, too, includes an "epilogue" by her son, Shaharyar M. Khan, in which he recounts her death and also how he was responsible for producing the "draft of the final chapters" while she lay bedridden during her last days. Distinguishing his effort, however, was his mother's continued involvement in the process: "She would meticulously go through the drafts and make corrections where I had recorded her thoughts inaccurately." Ibid., 285–86.

117. Metcalf, "The Past in the Present," 116–17.

118. "Maulana Hali ki Khud-navisht Sawanih-i-'Umri."

119. Shahr Bano Begam, *Bītī Kahānī, Urdu ki Awwālin Niswānī Khud Navisht*, ed. Moinuddin Aqeel (Hyderabad, Pakistan: Allied Printing Corporation, 1995). My thanks to Barbara Metcalf for directing me to this text.

120. Tahera Aftab, trans. and ed., *A Story of Days Gone By: A Translation of Bītī Kahānī: An Autobiography of Princess Shahr Bano Begam of Pataudi* (Karachi: Oxford University Press, 2012).

121. Karlekar, *Voices from Within*, 2, 12, 18–19.

122. Basu and Karlekar, introduction to their *In So Many Words*, viii.

123. For a recent exploration of this term, see Judith M. Brown, "'Life Histories' and the History of Modern South Asia," *American Historical Review* 114, no. 3 (June 2009): 587–95.

124. Arnold and Blackburn, "Introduction: Life Histories in India," to their edited volume, *Telling Lives in India*, 9.

125. Smith and Watson, *Reading Autobiography*, 5.

CHAPTER 2

1. "Census of India," accessed January 8, 2013, http://www.censusindia.gov.in/; "UNESCO Institute for Statistics," accessed September 16, 2013, http://stats.uis.unesco .org/; "Index Mundi," accessed September 16, 2013, http://www.indexmundi.com/facts/ bangladesh/literacy-rate.

2. Henry Waterfield, *Memorandum on the Census of British India, 1871–72* (London: Eyre and Spottiswoode, 1875), 37.

3. *Towards Equality: Report of the Committee on the Status of Women in India* (Delhi: Ministry of Education and Social Welfare, 1974), 94.

4. Shaarawi, *Harem Years*, 1.

5. The phrase "memoir boom" was coined by Leigh Gilmore in "Limit-Cases: Trauma, Self-Representation, and the Jurisdictions of Identity," *Biography* 24, no. 1 (Winter 2001):

Notes to Chapter 2 215

128–39. On the significance of this text to "ordinary" people writing lives, see Smith and Watson, *Reading Autobiography*, 75.

6. See, for examples, Zoya, with John Follain and Rita Cristofari, *Zoya's Story: An Afghan Woman's Struggle for Freedom* (London: Review, 2002); Fawzia Koofi with Nadene Ghouri, *The Favored Daughter: One Woman's Fight to Lead Afghanistan into the Future* (Basingstoke: Palgrave Macmillan, 2012); and Sulima and Hala as told to Batya Swift Yasgur, *Behind the Burqa: Our Life in Afghanistan and How We Escaped to Freedom* (Hoboken: Wiley, 2002).

7. For short biographies of these two figures, see Lal, *Domesticity and Power in the Early Mughal World*, 57; and Afshan Bokhari's introduction to translated extracts from the *Risala-i-Sahibiyah* and the *Munis al-Arvah* at "Accessing Muslim Lives," http://www .accessingmuslimlives.org.

8. For a full list of the Bhopali begams' many publications, see Siobhan Lambert-Hurley, *Muslim Women, Reform and Princely Patronage: Nawab Sultan Jahan Begam of Bhopal* (London: Routledge, 2007).

9. Tahera Aftab, "An Introduction to Shahr Bano Begam's *Bītī Kahānī*," in *A Story of Days Gone By*, 13, 20, 24, 39.

10. Maimoona Sultan, *Siyahat-i-Sultani* (Agra: Muhammad Qadir Ali Khan, n.d.); Abida Sultaan, *Memoirs of a Rebel Princess*.

11. On the ruling family of Janjira, see John McLeod, "Marriage and Identity among the Sidis of Janjira and Sachin," in *India in Africa, Africa in India: Indian Ocean Cosmopolitans*, ed. John C. Hawley (Bloomington: Indiana University Press, 2008), 253–72.

12. Begam Qudsia Aizaz Rasul, *From Purdah to Parliament* (Delhi: Ajanta, 2001), 2; "The Autobiography of Dr. Rahmathunnisa Begam" (unpublished manuscript), 1.

13. Bilquis Jehan Khan, *A Song of Hyderabad: Memories of a World Gone By* (Karachi: Oxford University Press, 2010), 3–168.

14. Princess Mehrunissa of Rampur, *An Extraordinary Life*.

15. Salma Ahmed, *Cutting Free*, 208.

16. Jahanara Habibullah, *Remembrance of Days Past*, 3, 11, 16.

17. Ibid., 18–19, 23–26.

18. Joan L. Erdman, with Zohra Segal, *Stages*; Hamida Saiduzzafar, *Autobiography*, ed. Lola Chatterji (Delhi: Trianka, 1996).

19. Nawab Faizunnessa Chaudhurani, *Rupjalal*, ed. Mohammad Abdul Kuddus (Dhaka: Bangla Academy, 2004), 13.

20. Begam Qudsia Aizaz Rasul, *From Purdah to Parliament*, 20.

21. Inam Fatima Habibullah, *Tasirat-i-Safar-i-Yurop* (n.p., n.d.). My thanks to the author's granddaughter, Muneeza Shamsie, for presenting me with a copy of this text.

22. "Attia Hosain," accessed September 18, 2013, http://www.open.ac.uk/research projects/makingbritain/content/attia-hosain.

23. "Begum Anis Kidwai: Fragments of a Life," in Anis Kidwai, *In Freedom's Shade*, 347.

24. Jahan Ara Shahnawaz, *Father and Daughter*, 1–2.

25. Sufia Kamal, *Ekale Amader Kal*, 1–3. Curiously, the Shaestabad Nawab family now

216   *Notes to Chapter 2*

has its own family website, accessed April 24, 2017, https://sites.google.com/site/shaesta bad/.

26. Akhtar Imam, "Amader Shikal" and Mafruha Chowdhury, "Smriti Katha," in *Kaler Samukh Bhela*, ed. Nurunnahar Faizunnessa, 26, 186.

27. See, for example, Kishwar Naheed, *Buri 'Aurat ki Katha*, 14.

28. I rely here on the analysis of Sylvia Vatuk in her paper "The Book of Life: A Collection of Family and Personal Reminiscences by a North Indian Muslim Woman" (presented at the Women's Autobiography in Islamic Societies: Representation and Identity conference, American University Sharjah, October 29–31, 2011). For the original source, see Qaisari Begam, *Kitab-i-Zindagi*, ed. Zahra Masrur Ahmad (Karachi: Fazli Sons, 2003).

29. See the chapters authored by Begam Azizun Nessa and Afsarunnesa in Nurunnahar Faizunnessa, *Kaler Samukh Bhela*, 33, 54, 195.

30. Kazim, *Woman of Substance*, 145.

31. For five examples, see the chapters authored by Begam Azizun Nessa, Nurunnahar Faizunnessa, Rabeya Khatun, Hamida Rahman, and Nazma Jasmine Chowdhury in Nurunnahar Faizunnessa's edited collection, *Kaler Samukh Bhela*, 33, 130, 167, 187, 212. For an example from outside Bengal, see Saeeda Bano Ahmed, *Dagar se hat kar* (New Delhi: Sajad Publishing House, 1996), 13.

32. Sanjay Joshi, *Fractured Modernity: Making of a Middle Class in Colonial North India* (Delhi: Oxford University Press, 2001), 23, 48.

33. Swapna Banerjee develops this point with reference to Bengal in *Men, Women, Domestics: Articulating Middle-Class Identity in Colonial Bengal* (Delhi: Oxford University Press, 2004), 4–7.

34. See, for example, Shahnawaz, *Father and Daughter*, 2; Saeeda Bano Ahmed, *Dagar se hat kar*, 11; and Begam Makshuda, "Smritir Jhinuk Theke," in Nurunnahar Faiunnessa, *Kaler Samukh Bhela*, 216.

35. See, for example, Masuma Begam, "From Behind the Veil—Into the Mainstream" (unpublished manuscript); Saiduzzafar, *Autobiography*, 2.

36. See, for example, Hameeda Akhtar Husain Raipuri, *Hamsafar*, 18; Kazim, *A Woman of Substance*, 103; and Vatuk, "Hamara Daur-i Hayat," 154. On MA-O College, see David Lelyveld, *Aligarh's First Generation: Muslim Solidarity in British India* (Delhi: Oxford University Press, 1996). On Osmania University, see Kavita Datla, *The Language of Secular Islam: Urdu Nationalism and Colonial India* (Honolulu: University of Hawai'i Press, 2013).

37. See, for example, Humayun Mirza, *Meri Kahani Meri Zubani* (Hyderabad: Privately published, 1939); Maliha Khatun, "Smritir Parday," in Nurunnahar Faizunnessa, *Kaler Samukh Bhela*, 89; and Shahnawaz, *Father and Daughter*, 3.

38. See, for example, Maulana Shibli Nomani, *Safarnama-i-Rum o Misr o Sham* (Lucknow: Anvar al-Matabi', n.d.), 97–98 (on Hasanally Feyzhyder, father of the Fyzee sisters); Jahanara Habibullah, *Remembrance of Days Past*, 107.

39. See the chapters authored by Mehrunnessa Islam, Meher Kabir, Khatemonara Begam, Maliha Khatun, Moslema Khatun, Noorjehan Murshid, Hamida Rahman, Afsa-

runnesa, Makshuda Begam, and Malika Begam in Nurunnahar Faizunnessa's edited collection, *Kaler Samukh Bhela*.

40. Rahmat Ara Hossain, *Smriti* (Dhaka: Usha Art Press, 1996); Jobeda Khanam, *Jiban Khatar Pataguli*, 7.

41. Shaista Ikramullah, *From Purdah to Parliament*, 14; Jahanara Imam, *Anya Jiban* (Dhaka: Dana, 1985).

42. Kishwar Naheed, *Buri 'Aurat ki Katha*, 15; Salma Ahmed, *Cutting Free*, 2.

43. Hamida Saiduzzafar, *Autobiography*, 3.

44. For a biographical introduction to Badruddin Tyabji, see F. H. Brown, revised by Jim Masselos, "Tyabji, Badruddin (1844–1906)," in *Oxford Dictionary of National Biography*, accessed June 23, 2006, http://www.oxforddnb.com/view/article/36600.

45. On Abbas's judicial career, see Aparna Basu, *Abbas Tyabji* (New Delhi: National Book Trust, India, 2007), 24–42.

46. "Family Tree," in Ismat Chughtai, *A Life in Words: Memoirs*, trans. M. Asaduddin (Delhi: Penguin Books, 2012), 279; Farida Abdulla Khan, "Other Communities, Other Histories: A Study of Muslim Women and Education in Kashmir," in *In a Minority: Essays on Muslim Women in India*, ed. Zoya Hasan and Ritu Menon (Delhi: Oxford University Press, 2005), 161.

47. "Hameed Ullah Khan, M., Al-Haj ul-Ulma Nawab Sarbuland Jang Bahadur" entry in C. Hayavando Rao, *The Indian Biographical Dictionary* (Madras: Pillar, 1915), 175; Ummat ul-Ghani Nurunnisa, *Safarnama-i-Hijaz, Sham o Misr* (Hyderabad: N.p., 1996); Rahil Begam Sherwani, *Zad us-Sabil* (1923); Vatuk, "The Book of Life"; Masuma Begam, "From Behind the Veil—Into the Mainstream" (unpublished manuscript), 1–2; Vatuk, "Hamara Daur-i Hayat," 153–54; and Shaukat Kaifi, *Yad ki Rahguzar* (New Delhi: Star Publications, 2006), 28.

48. On his career, see Gail Minault, *Secluded Scholars: Women's Education and Muslim Social Reform in Colonial India* (Delhi: Oxford University Press, 1998), 201–4.

49. On his career, see "Hameed Ullah Khan, M., Al-Haj ul-Ulma Nawab Sarbuland Jang Bahadur" entry in Rao, *Indian Biographical Dictionary*, 175.

50. Hameeda Akhtar Husain Raipuri, *My Fellow Traveller*, 13; Saeeda Bano Ahmed, *Dagar se hat kar*, 11.

51. I rely here on Anshu Malhotra's excellent commentary and translation of Piro's text at "Accessing Muslim Lives," www.accessingmuslimlives.org.

52. Malka Pukhraj, *Song Sung True: A Memoir*, trans. Saleem Kidwai (Delhi: Kali for Women, 2003), 6.

53. Ibid., 12.

54. Ibid., 290.

55. Nalini Jameela, "The Autobiography of a Sex-Worker" (unpublished manuscript), trans. J. Devika, chapter 1, p. 11. On her conversion, see chapter 5, pp. 6–9. This translation was later published as Nalini Jameela, *The Autobiography of a Sex Worker*.

56. Ibid., 4.

57. Ibid., 3, 7.

58. Mukhtar Mai with Marie-Thérèse Cuny, *In the Name of Honor: A Memoir* (New York: Washington Square Press, 2006).

59. Nilanjana S. Roy, "Giving a Voice to the Voiceless in India," *New York Times*, July 6, 2010. http://www.nytimes.com/2010/07/07/world/asia/07iht-letter.html.

60. On Sayyid Ahmad Khan's stance on female education, see Lambert-Hurley, *Muslim Women, Reform and Princely Patronage*, 22–23.

61. Vatuk, "Hamara Daur-i Hayat," 158. Also see Sylvia Vatuk, "A Passion for Reading: The Role of Early Twentieth-Century Urdu Novels in the Construction of an Individual Female Identity in 1930s Hyderabad," in Malhotra and Lambert-Hurley, *Speaking of the Self*.

62. Vatuk, "A Passion for Reading," 40–41.

63. Vatuk, "Hamara Daur-i Hayat," 161; Vatuk, "A Passion for Reading," 41–42.

64. As indicated in chapter 1, this narrative was first published in *Tahzib un-Niswan* in two installments in the issues dated March 23 and 30, 1899. It then appeared in Muhammadi Begam's biography of Ashrafunnisa, *Hayat-i-Ashraf*, 5–20. More recently it has been translated by C. M. Naim in "How Bibi Ashraf Learned to Read and Write," 99–115.

65. Ibid., 106–7.

66. Ibid., 107.

67. Ibid., 108–9.

68. Ibid., 109.

69. See the chapter authored by Hamida Rehman in Nurunnahar Faizunnessa, *Kaler Samukh Bhela*, 188.

70. Saiyida Lutfunnessa, "Bangali Muslim Narir Cromobikash," and Moslema Khatun, "Amar Jibaner Galpa Katha," in Nurunnahar Faizunnessa, *Kaler Samukh Bhela*, 82, 106.

71. Saiyida Lutfunnessa, "Bangali Muslim Narir Cromobikash," 82.

72. Ibid., 84.

73. Minault, *Secluded Scholars*, 112.

74. Jobeda Khanam, *Jiban Khatar Pataguli*, 18.

75. Ibid., 22.

76. Ibid., 27.

77. Ibid., 43.

78. This summary is based on women's own accounts. See, for instance, Naim, "How Bibi Ashraf Learned to Read and Write," 102; Khatemanara Begam, "Nari Shiksha: Ami Ja Dekhechhi," in Nurunnahar Faizunnessa, *Kaler Samukh Bhela*, 71; and "An Excerpt from Ammajan's Diary," in Habibullah, *Remembrance*, 18.

79. "Diary of Sultan Jahan Begam"; Sultan Jahan Begam of Bhopal, *An Account of My Life*, vol. 1, trans. C. H. Payne (London: John Murray, 1910), 32.

80. Abida Sultaan, *Memoirs of a Rebel Princess*, 16–18, 23–27.

81. Vatuk, "The Book of Life." For other examples, see Minault, *Secluded Scholars*, 196, and Asiya Alam, introduction to Nazr Sajjad Hyder, *Roz-namcha* (1942), at "Accessing Muslim Lives," http://www.accessingmuslimlives.org.

82. Minault, *Secluded Scholars*, 34–36.

83. Moslema Khatun, "Amar Jibaner Galpa Katha," in Nurunnahar Faizunnessa, *Kaler Samukh Bhela*, 105.

84. Rabeya Khatun, "Sonali Atit," in ibid., 164.

85. Ibid.

86. See the chapter authored by Afsarunnesa in ibid., 199.

87. The summary that follows relies on data from all twenty-five chapters in ibid.

88. On these "model" girls' schools, see Shahla Rahman Young, "Changing Women's Lives: A Study of Government Schools for Girls in Late Colonial Bengal" (PhD diss., University of London, 2012). For a dedicated account of studying at Eden in the 1930s, see Akhtar Imam, *Eden theke Bethun* (Dhaka: Akhtar Imam, 1990). Rahmat Ara Hossain recalls her experience of studying at Vidyamoyee in Mymensingh in her *Smriti*, as does Lulu Rahman in "Jibaner Sarbattam Dinguli," in *Biddamoyee School Praktan Chatri Purnamilan Utsab 1999*, ed. Selina Bahar (Mymensingh: Vidyamoyee School Prakton Chatri Samiti, 1999), 9.

89. I refer here to Dr. Nilima Ibrahim and Dr. Nurunnahar Faizunnessa.

90. Lambert-Hurley, *Muslim Women, Reform and Princely Patronage*, 81.

91. Salima Tyabji, *The Changing World of a Bombay Muslim Community, 1870–1945* (Margao: CinnamonTeal Publishing, 2013), 16; and Safia Jabir Ali, "Manuscript Memoirs of Mrs. Safia Jabir Ali," 59–60.

92. Rahmathunnisa Begam, "The Autobiography of Dr Rahmathunnisa Begam" (unpublished manuscript), 2.

93. Ibid., 3.

94. For examples at Aligarh Zenana Madrasa, see Kazim, *A Woman of Substance*, 108. For examples at Karamat Husain Muslim Girls' School, see Saeeda Bano Ahmed, *Dagar se hat kar*, 21; and Hamida Akhtar Husain Raipuri, *Hamsafar*, 35. For examples at Queen Mary's College, see Qudsia Aizaz Rasul, *From Purdah to Parliament*, 7; Jahan Ara Shahnawaz, *Father and Daughter*, 23; Hamida Saiduzzafar, *Autobiography*, 20; and Joan Erdman with Zohra Segal, *Stages*, 1.

95. For examples, see Vatuk, "Hamara Daur-i Hayat," 166; Masuma Begam, "From Behind the Veil—Into the Mainstream"; Bilquis Jehan Khan, *A Song of Hyderabad*, 64; and Saeeda Bano Ahmed, *Dagar se hat kar*, 20.

96. Masuma Begam, "From Behind the Veil—Into the Mainstream"; Bilquis Jehan Khan, *A Song of Hyderabad*, 64; Vatuk, "Hamara Daur-i Hayat," 166

97. Minault, *Secluded Scholars*, 206.

98. Ismat Chughtai, *A Life in Words*, 94.

99. Hamida Saiduzzafar, *Autobiography*, 35; Saeeda Bano Ahmed, *Dagar se hat kar*, 29–30; Mehrunissa, *An Extraordinary Life*, 86.

100. Kazim, *A Woman of Substance*, 109.

101. I refer here to the bachelor of arts, bachelor of education, master of arts, bachelor of medicine, bachelor of surgery, and doctor of philosophy.

102. Iqbalunnisa Hussain, *Changing India: A Moslem Woman Speaks* (Bangalore: Hossali Press, 1940), ii; Vatuk, "Hamara Daur-i Hayat," 144, 166.

103. Erdman with Zohra Segal, *Stages*, 9; Hamida Saiduzzafar, *Autobiography*, 67.

104. Jobeda Khanam, *Jiban Khatar Pataguli*, 88–89. For a contemporaneous example from East Pakistan, see Rahmat Ara Hossain's *Smriti*, in which she narrates her experi-

220 *Notes to Chapter 2*

ence of studying mathematics at Imperial College, London, in the 1950s. Akhtar Imam also studied in Britain, completing an MPhil in philosophy at University College London in the early 1950s before returning as a research fellow at the University of Nottingham in the early 1960s. These experiences are highlighted in Fayza Haq, "A Trailblazer, An Exemplary Mother," *Daily Star*, January 13, 2012, http://archive.thedailystar.net/maga zine/2012/01/02/tribute.htm. Hamida Saiduzzafar also returned to Britain from 1967 to 1970 to complete a PhD in ophthalmology from the University of London (*Autobiography*, 74). For two later examples from Pakistan, see Sara Suleri, *Meatless Days*; and Fawzia Afzal-Khan, *Lahore with Love*.

105. For comparison, see Elaine McKay, "English Diarists: Gender, Geography, and Occupation, 1500–1700," *History* 90, no. 298 (April 2005), 205.

106. Nalini Jameela, *The Autobiography of a Sex Worker*, 3.

107. See Malala Yousafzai with Christina Lamb, *I Am Malala: The Girl Who Stood Up for Education and Was Shot by the Taliban* (London: W&N, 2013).

108. Quoted in Lambert-Hurley, *Muslim Women, Reform and Princely Patronage*, 78.

109. Vatuk, "Hamara Daur-i Hayat," 165.

110. Ibid., 167.

111. In this paragraph, I summarize arguments articulated in my *Muslim Women, Reform and Princely Patronage*, 98–99, 122.

112. I summarize data presented in the chapter "Women's Work in Colonial India," in Geraldine Forbes, *Women in Modern India* (Cambridge: Cambridge University Press, 2008), 157–58.

113. Tripti Lahiri, "By the Numbers: Where Indian Women Work," *IndiaRealTime: Wall Street Journal*, November 14, 2012, http://blogs.wsj.com/indiarealtime/2012/11/14/by-the-numbers-where-indian-women-work/.

114. According to a 2010 report, just over one-third of Indian women of working age were working outside the home, even part-time. Ibid.

115. Aftab, *A Story of Days Gone By*, 33.

116. Shah Jahan Begam of Bhopal, *Taj ul Ikbal Tarikh-i-Bhopal or The History of Bhopal*, trans. H. C. Barstow (Calcutta: Thacker, Spink, 1876).

117. Barbara Metcalf, "Islam and Power in Colonial India: The Making and Unmaking of a Muslim Princess," *American Historical Review* 116, no. 1 (February 1, 2011), 15n.47.

118. *An Account of My Life (Gohur-i-Ikbal)*, trans. C. H. Payne (London: John Murray, 1912), 1.

119. On how *tarikh* functioned in relation to the state, see Blain Auer, "Persian Historiography in India," in *Persian Prose outside Iran: The Indian Subcontinent, Anatolia, and Central Asia after Timur*, ed. John Perry and Sunil Sharma (London: I. B. Tauris, forthcoming), 37. I also draw here on Daniel Majchrowicz's analysis of how travel writing was not a "discrete genre" apart from *tarikh* during this period; see his PhD dissertation, "Travel, Travel Writing, and the 'Means to Victory' in Modern South Asia," 31, 107–8 (Harvard University, 2015).

Notes to Chapter 2 221

120. Sultan Jahan Begam, *Account of My Life*, 1.

121. Ibid., 1.

122. Ibid., 2.

123. Tucker, "Biography as History," 11. On "mirror for princes" and how these literary conventions were also employed by the Mughal princess Jahanara in her autobiographical treatise, *Risala-i-Sahibiyah*, see Afshan Bokhari, "Masculine Modes of Female Subjectivity: The Case of Jahanara Begam (1614–1681)," in Malhotra and Lambert-Hurley's edited volume, *Speaking of the Self*, 179.

124. Sultan Jahan Begam, *Gauhar-i-Iqbal* (Bhopal: Matba'-i-Sultani, 1913), 166. For two different contemporary translations of this passage, see Sultan Jahan, *Account of My Life*, 323; and Sultan Jahan Begam of Bhopal, *An Account of My Life*, vol. 2, trans. Abdus Samad Khan (Bombay: Times Press, 1922), 150.

125. Sultan Jahan Begam, *Gauhar-i-Iqbal*, 167.

126. I discuss how Sultan Jahan addressed these various problems to make the school a success in my *Muslim Women, Reform and Princely Patronage*, 82–86.

127. "A Page from the Past: Extracts from the Diary of Amina Binte Badruddin Tyabji," *Roshni*, special number 1946, 69–73. On this school, also see Basu, *Abbas Tyabji*, 34–36.

128. Nazr Sajjad Hyder, *Guzashta Barson ki Baraf*, ed. Qurratulain Hyder (Delhi: Educational Publishing House, 2007), 45–46. A longer translation from this passage with introduction by Asiya Alam is available at "Accessing Muslim Lives," http://www.access ingmuslimlives.org/images/pdfs/Nazr%20Sajjad%20Hyder%20Guzashta%20Barson%20 ki%20Baraf.pdf. For a fuller discussion of her educational contributions, see Alam, "Interrupted Stories," 82–83.

129. "The Autobiography of Dr. Rahmathunnisa Begam," 4–5.

130. Ghulam Fatima Shaikh, *Footprints in Time*, xxi.

131. Naim, "How Bibi Ashraf Learned to Read and Write," 100.

132. Begam Zafar Ali, *Mere Shab o Roz* (Srinagar: n.p., 1987). As I have been unable to locate this text, I rely here on a summary in Farida Abdulla Khan, "Other Communities, Other Histories," 161–62.

133. Jobeda Khanam, *Jiban Khatar Pataguli*, 47.

134. For an example of these tributes, see Mohsin Shastrapani, ed., *Professor Akhtar Imam Reception Volume* (Dhaka: Professor Akhtar Imam Reception Committee, 2001).

135. Akhtar Imam, "Amader Shikal," in Nurunnahar Faizunnessa, *Kaler Samukh Bhela*, 18–32.

136. On this early phase of her life, see Akhtar Imam, *Amar Jiban Katha* (Dhaka: Unmesh Prakashan, 1993).

137. On this period of her life, see Akhtar Imam, *Rokeya Halle Bis Bochhor* (Dhaka: Akhtar Imam, 1986).

138. Akhtar Imam, "Amader Shikal," in Nurunnahar Faizunnessa, *Kaler Samukh Bhela*, 32.

139. On these accolades, see Rawsan Ara Firoz, "Imam, Akhter," in *Banglapedia*, accessed April 26, 2017, http://en.banglapedia.org/index.php?title=Imam,_Akhter.

140. Jobeda Khanam, *Jiban Khatar Pataguli*, 44, 46–47, 60, 67, 85, 90–91, 105.

222 *Notes to Chapter 2*

141. See, in *Banglapedia*, the entries for "Bangladesh Shishu Academy," http://en.banglapedia.org/index.php?title=Bangladesh_Shishu_Academy and "Koyra Upazila," http://en.banglapedia.org/index.php?title=Koyra_Upazila.

142. This summary is based on the essays in Nurunnahar Faizunnessa's edited collection, *Kaler Samukh Bhela*.

143. "The Autobiography of Dr. Rahmathunnisa Begam," 5ff.

144. Hafsa Kanjwal, "Placing Kashmir: Gender, Social Status, and Mobility in a Kashmiri Woman's Autobiography" (paper presented at the Feminist South Asia Pre-conference, 41st Annual Conference on South Asia, University of Madison at Wisconsin, October 2012).

145. Hamida Saiduzzafar, *Autobiography*, 75.

146. Sughra Mehdi, *Sair Kar Dunya ki Ghafil . . . (Safarnama)* (New Delhi: Nayi Awaz, 1994); Sughra Mehdi, *Mekhanon ka Pata (Safarnama)* (Bhopal: Urdu Akademi, 2005); and Sughra Mehdi, *Hikayat-i-Hasti: Ap Biti* (New Delhi: Modern Publishing House, 2006). I am grateful to the author for providing me with copies of these books.

147. Sara Suleri, *Meatless Days*; Sara Suleri Goodyear, *Boys Will Be Boys: A Daughter's Elegy* (Chicago: University of Chicago Press, 2003; and Afzal-Khan, *Lahore with Love*.

148. Minault, *Secluded Scholars*, 151–52. Another journal editor who published her diary, or *roznamcha*, in serial form in *Tahzib un-Niswan* was Hijab Imtiaz Ali. It was published under the title "Lail o Nihar" [Day and night] in 1941–42. On her literary contributions, see Shaista Akhtar Banu Suhrawardy, *A Critical Survey of the Development of the Urdu Novel and Short Story* (London: Longmans Green, 1945), 283–90.

149. Sughra Humayun Mirza, *Sair-i-Bhopal o Bengal* (1914); Sughra Humayun Mirza, *Safarnama-i-Iraq* (1915); Sughra Humayun Mirza, *Roznamcha-i-Safar-i-Bhopal* (Hyderabad: al-Nisa monthly, 1924); and Sughra Humayun Mirza, *Safarnama-i-Yurop*, 2 vols. (Hyderabad: 'Azim Press, 1926).

150. Zehra Fyzee's articles, including her travel writing, are collected in *Mazamin* (Agra: Mufid-i-'Am, 1921). As indicated in chapter 1, Atiya Fyzee's European travelogue was first serialized in *Tahzib un-niswan* in issues dated January 26, 1907–November 30, 1907, before appearing as a book titled *Zamana-i-Tahsil*.

151. Saliha Abid Hussain, *Silsila-i-Roz o Shab: Khudnavisht* (New Delhi: Maktaba Jamia, 1984).

152. For a concise summary of her career, see Asiya Alam, introduction to Nazr Sajjad Hyder, *Roz-namcha* (1942) at "Accessing Muslim Lives," http://www.accessingmuslimlives.org.

153. Nawab Faizunnessa Chaudhurani, *Rupjalal*, 7.

154. Fayeza S. Hasanat, *Nawab Faizunnesa's* Rupjalal (Leiden: Brill, 2008), 2.

155. M. Asaduddin develops this point in his introduction to Chughtai's *A Life in Words*, xv–xvii. For a more detailed overview of her career, see Tahira Naqvi, "Ismat Chughtai—A Tribute," *Annual of Urdu Studies* 8 (1993): 37–42.

156. This passage is from a separate chapter, "The 'Lihaf' Trial," in *Kaghazi Hai Pairahan*. It was translated by Tahira Naqvi and Muhammad Umar Memon for *Annual of Urdu Studies* 15 (2000): 429–43. This quotation is from 433.

Notes to Chapter 2   223

157. This section is translated by M. Asaduddin at "Accessing Muslim Lives," http://www.accessingmuslimlives.org/images/pdfs/ismat%20chughtai%20extracts.pdf. On the Progressive Writers Movement, see Talat Ahmed, *Literature and Politics in the Age of Nationalism: The Progressive Episode in South Asia, 1932–56* (Delhi: Routledge, 2009).

158. Two key examples are Hameeda Akhtar Husain Raipuri's *Hamsafar* and Shaukat Kaifi's *Yad ki Rahguzar*. Also see Sultana Jafri, "52 Years in Togetherness"; Saleema Hashmi, "His Heart Was in His Homeland"; Shaukat Azmi, "55 Years Were Too Little"; and Shabana Azmi, "He Rose above the Personal" and "You Are Always with Me Abba," in *One Yesterday*, ed. Saif Hyder Hasan (New Delhi: Rupa, 2004), 15–20, 39–45, 81–101.

159. Ada Jafri, *Jo Rehi so Bekhabar Rehi: Khudnavisht* (Karachi: Daniyal, 1995); Kishwar Naheed, *Buri 'Aurat ki Katha*; Fahmida Riaz, *Reflections in a Cracked Mirror*, trans. Aquila Ismail (Karachi: City Press, 2001); and Azra Abbas, *Mere Bachpan*; Attiya Dawood, *Aine ke Samne: Khudnavisht* (Karachi: Oxford University Press, 2009).

160. Nafees Bano Shama, *Jannat se Nikali hui Hawwa: Ap Biti* (New Delhi: Abshar Publications, 1998); and Sufia Kamal, *Ekale Amader Kal*. The four parts of Taslima Nasreen's autobiography are *Amar Meyebela* (Kolkata: People's Book Society, 1999); *Utal Hawa* (Kolkata: People's Book Society, 2002); *Ko* (Dhaka: Chardik, 2003); and *Sei Sob Ondhokar Din guli* (Kolkata: People's Book Society, 2004).

161. On literary autobiography, see Brian Finney, *The Inner I: British Literary Autobiography of the Twentieth Century* (London: Faber, 1985). For an analysis of two of these writers, see Amina Yaqin, "Intertextuality of Women in Urdu Literature: A Study of Fahmida Riaz and Kishwar Naheed" (PhD diss., University of London, 2001).

162. See Christina Oesterheld's book review of *Mere Bachpan* in *Annual of Urdu Studies* 18 (2003): 599.

163. The translation is taken from Azra Abbas, *Kicking Up Dust*, trans. Samina Rehman (Lahore: ASR Publications, 1996), 13.

164. See, for example, Smith and Watson, *Reading Autobiography*, 131.

165. Ikramullah, *From Purdah to Parliament*; Rasul, *From Purdah to Parliament*.

166. Begam Inam Fatima Habibullah, *Tasirat-i-Safar-i-Yurop* (N.p., n.d.), 316.

167. Muneeza Shamsie, "Discovering the Matrix," in *Critical Muslim 04: Pakistan?*, ed. Ziauddin Sardar and Robin Yassin Kassab (London: Hurst, 2012), 165–76.

168. As noted in the introduction, Nishatunnisa Begam's *Iraq ka Safarnama* (1936) was republished very recently in *Begam Hasrat Mohani aur unke Khutut va Safarnama*. Rahil Begam Sherwani's travelogues include *Zad us-Sabil* (1923) and *Safarnama-i-Bilad-i-Muqaddas* (1929). Begam Sarbuland Jang wrote *Dunya 'Aurat ki Nazar Mein* (Delhi: Khwaja Baruqi Press, 1910).

169. Daniel Majchrowicz, "Learning Arabic in a Hammam: Cultivating Islamic Sisterhood between Hyderabad and Syria" (paper presented at Annual Conference on South Asia, University of Wisconsin at Madison, October 22, 2016).

170. Shaista Ikramullah, *From Purdah to Parliament*, chapters 10–17; Jahan Ara Shahnawaz, *Father and Daughter*, chapters 2–3; Salma Tasadduq Husain, *Azadi ki Safar: Tahrik-i-Pakistan aur Muslim Khawatin* (Lahore: Pakistan Study Centre, Punjab University, 1987), chapters 3–6.

171. Raihana Tyabji, *Suniye Kakasaheb*; Sayyida Khurshid Alam, *Zakir Sahib ki Kahani*; Begam Qudsia Aizaz Rasul, *From Purdah to Parliament*, xiii–xviii; Begam Anis Kidwai, *Azadi ki Chhaon Mein*, 11; Masuma Begam, "From behind the Veil—Into the Mainstream," 3.

172. Quoted in Ved Mehta, *Mahatma Gandhi and His Apostles* (Harmondsworth, Middlesex: Penquin Books, 1976), 211.

173. Shaista Ikramullah, *From Purdah to Parliament*, chapter 19; Jahan Ara Shahnawaz, *Father and Daughter*, chapter 4; Begam Qudsia Aizaz Rasul, *From Purdah to Parliament*, chapter 17.

174. Masuma Begam, "From behind the Veil—Into the Mainstream," 5–6. On her career, also see Gouri Srivastava, *The Legend Makers: Some Eminent Muslim Women of India* (Delhi: Concept Publishing, 2003), chapter 20.

175. Jahanara Imam's most celebrated autobiographical work is *Ekattorer Dingulee*, on "The Days of '71." It was first published in 1986, but quickly went into multiple editions, including an English translation titled *Of Blood and Fire*. Her other autobiographical and literary works include: *Anya Jiban* (1985); *Jiban Mrityu* (1988); *Buker Bhitare Agun* (1990); *Nataker Abasan* (1990); *Dui Meru* (1990); *Cancer-er Sanger Bosobas* (1991); and *Prabaser Dinalipi* (1992). See "Tribute to Shaheed Janani," *Daily Star*, May 4, 2012. For another example of autobiographical writing by a sometimes dissident Bangladeshi politician, see Matia Chowdhury's prison diary, *Dayal Diye Ghera* (Dhaka: Agami Prakashoni, 1995).

176. Abida Sultaan, *Memoirs of a Rebel Princess*, 236; Salma Ahmed, *Cutting Free*, 121, 215.

177. Benazir Bhutto, *Daughter of the East* (London: Simon and Schuster, 1988).

178. For a useful summary of her career, see "Zohra Segal: A Chronology," in her *Stages*, xv–xix.

179. Shaukat Kaifi, *Yad ki Rahguzar*, esp. chapters 7 and 8.

180. Nilambur Ayisha, *Jeevitathinte Arangu* (Trivandrum: Women's Imprint, 2005).

181. Malka Pukhraj, especially chapters 16, 46, and 50. Also see her many obituaries in the South Asian and international press, including "Malika Takes a Final Bow," *Dawn*, February 15, 2004.

182. Saeeda Bano Ahmed, *Dagar se hat kar*, 136. I am indebted to Asiya Alam for her dedicated analysis of this text in "Intimacy against Convention: Marriage and Romance in Syeda Bano's *Dagar se hat kar*," (paper presented at the 40th Annual Conference on South Asia, University of Wisconsin–Madison, October 21–23, 2011).

183. See, for example, Saeeda Bano Ahmed, *Dagar se hat kar*, 38.

184. Ibid., 226.

185. Jobeda Khanam, *Jiban Khatar Pataguli*, 70.

186. Ibid., 70–71.

187. Ibid., 78.

188. Ibid., 79. Italics added.

189. Jowshan Ara Rahman, *Smritikatha: Ekti Ajana Meye* (Dhaka: Nabajuga Prokashani, 2005).

190. Fatima Shah, *Sunshine and Shadows*; and "Dr. Fatima Shah Passes Away," *Dawn*, October 13, 2002.

191. Malhotra's introduction to Piro's text, at "Accessing Muslim Lives," accessingmus limlives.org; and Nalini Jameela, *Autobiography of a Sex Worker*, chapter 4.

192. Quoted in Smith and Watson, *Reading Autobiography*, 107.

193. I am grateful to Patricia Jeffery for encouraging me to make this point explicit.

194. McKay, "English Diarists," 211.

195. On these transformations, see Margrit Pernau, *Ashraf into Middle Classes: Muslims in Nineteenth-Century Delhi* (Delhi: Oxford University Press, 2013).

196. Hamza Alavi, "Pakistan and Islam: Ethnicity and Ideology," in *State and Ideology in the Middle East and Pakistan*, ed. Fred Halliday and Hamza Alavi (New York: Monthly Review Press, 1988), 67.

197. On the rearticulation of sharif patriarchy, see Faisal Devji, "Gender and the Politics of Space."

198. For insight into colonial discourses, see Indrani Sen, "'Cruel, Oriental Despots': Representations in Nineteenth-Century British Colonial Fiction, 1858–1900," in *India's Princely States: People, Princes, and Colonialism*, ed. Waltraud Ernst and Biswamoy Pati (London: Routledge, 2007), 30–49.

199. Daniel Majchrowicz, "Travel, Travel Writing, and the 'Means to Victory' in Modern South Asia" (PhD diss., Harvard University, 2015), chapter 3, "Strategy, Legitimacy, and Travel Writing in the Princely States."

200. I draw here on a draft chapter titled "Re-forming 'Muslim Culture': Rampur under Nawab Hamid Ali Khan (1889–1930)," from Razak Khan's "Minority Pasts: The Other Histories of a 'Muslim Locality,' Rampur, 1889–1949" (PhD diss., Freie Universität Berlin, 2014).

201. Michael Mascuch, *Origins of the Individualist Self: Autobiography and Self-Identity in England, 1591–1791* (Stanford, CA: Stanford University Press, 1997), 73.

202. Saliha Abid Hussain, S*ilsila-i-Roz o Shab*, 9.

CHAPTER 3

1. Virginia Woolf, *A Room of One's Own* (London: Penguin Classics, 2000), 6. I am grateful to John Roosa, my "neighbor" in the Department of History at the University of British Columbia in 2013–14, for encouraging me to relate my own study to this literary maxim.

2. On this concept, see Francoise Lionnet, *Autobiographical Voices: Race, Gender, Self-Portraiture* (Ithaca: Cornell University Press, 1989), 193.

3. Raihana Tyabji, *The Heart of a Gopi*, v–vi.

4. "Manuscript Memoirs of Mrs. Safia Jabir Ali," entry for October 5, 1942.

5. Hameeda Akhtar Husain Raipuri, *My Fellow Traveller*, xiv.

6. See, for example, McKay, *English Diarists*, 206.

7. Ken Plumber, *Telling Sexual Stories: Power, Change, and Social Worlds* (London: Routledge, 1995), 21–22.

8. C. M. Naim, introduction to *Zikr-i-Mir: The Autobiography of the Eighteenth Cen-*

226   *Notes to Chapter 3*

tury Mughal Poet: Mir Muhammad Taqi "Mir," trans. C. M. Naim (Delhi: Oxford University Press, 1999), 1–21.

9. Lambert-Hurley, *A Princess's Pilgrimage*, xiii–xiv.

10. This overview summarizes Peter Hardy's *Muslims of British India* (Cambridge: Cambridge University Press, 1972), 2–11.

11. Patricia Jeffery, *Frogs in a Well: Indian Women in Purdah* (London: Zed Books, 1979).

12. Personal communication from Nazneen Nizami, December 9, 2005. *Sajjada nashin* refers to the main caretaker, or spiritual custodian, of the Sufi shrine.

13. I think, for example, of meetings with Samina Misra, November 22, 2005, and Sughra Mehdi, February 18, 2006, at their family homes in Jamia Nagar.

14. Our first meeting was November 21, 2005.

15. For an overview of OUP Karachi's publishing output in this area, see the "Biographies/Memoirs" section of the press's website, accessed December 4, 2013, http://www.oup.com.pk/. As noted in chapter 1, an example is Princess Shahr Bano Begam of Pataudi's *Biti Kahani* (1885), which was republished as *A Story of Days Gone By*. On the role of feminist publishers especially in creating an "archive" of women's writing in South Asia, see Burton, *Dwelling in the Archive*, 25.

16. Habibullah, *Remembrance of Days Past*, chapters 1–12. Also see Shaista Ikramullah, *From Purdah to Parliament*; Ada Jafri, *Jo Rehi So Bekhabar Rehi*; Abida Sultaan, *Memoirs of a Rebel Princess*; Salma Ahmed, *Cutting Free*; Nazr S. Hyder, *Guzashta Barson ki Baraf*; and Bilquis Jehan Khan, *A Song of Hyderabad*. Also describable as *mohajirs,* since they were the children of migrants, are Kishwar Naheed, author of *Buri 'Aurat ki Katha*; Fahmida Riaz, author of *Reflections in a Cracked Mirror*; Azra Abbas, author of *Mere Bachpan*; and Sara Suleri, author of *Meatless Days*.

17. See extracts from Piro's *Ik Sau Sath Kafian* at "Accessing Muslim Lives," accessed December 4, 2013, http://www.accessingmuslimlives.org/images/pdfs/Piro%20160%20Kafis.pdf.

18. Jahanara Shah Nawaz, *Father and Daughter*, 1; Salma Tasadduq Husain, *Azadi ki Safar*; Tehmina Durrani, *My Feudal Lord*, 22; Fatima Shah, *Sunshine and Shadows*; Mukhtar Mai, *In the Name of Honor*; Benazir Bhutto, *Daughter of Destiny: An Autobiography* (New York: Simon and Schuster, 1989), 38–9; Ghulam Fatima Sheikh, *Footprints in Time*, 3; Attiya Dawood, *Aine ke Samne*, chapter 3, "Kharjal gaon mein." Also see Malala Yousafzai, *I Am Malala*, 15–19.

19. My haul included: Akhtar Imam's *Jemon Bhebechhi, Jemon Dekhechhi* (Dhaka: Akhtar Imam, 1981), *Rokeya Halle Bis Bochhor, Eden theke Bethun, Amar Jiban Katha*, and *Bileter Din Ghulo* (Dhaka: Umbesh Prakashan, 1997); Nawab Faizunnessa Chaudhurani, *Rupjalal*; Umratul Fazl, *Smritikatha Priyadiner Smriti* (Dhaka: Muktadhara, 1987); Sufia Kamal, *Ekale Amader Kal*; Jobeda Khanam, *Jiban Khatar Pataguli*; Zubaida Mirza, *Sei Je Amar Nana Ranger Dinguli* (Dhaka: Muktadhara, 1984); Hamida Rahman, *Jiban Smriti*; Saiyida Lutfunnessa, *Bibortoner Smirticharan* (Dhaka: Unmesh Prakashan, 1994); Taslima Nasreen, *Ko*; Jowshan Ara Rahman, *Smritikatha*; Farida Huq, *Journey through 1971: My Story*; Matia Chowdhury, *Dayal Diye Ghera*; Jahanara Imam, *Of Blood and Fire*; Sabrina Q. Rashid, *Hajj*; Rahmat Ara Hossain, *Smriti*; Hamida Khanam, *Johora Bokuler Gondho* (Dhaka: Shahitya

Prakash, 2001); Jahanara Haq, *Aparahner Sanglap* (Dhaka: Agami Prakashani, 1996); Sufia Khatun, *Jiban Nadir Banke Banke* (Dhaka: Papyrus, 2005); Nurunnahar Faizunnessa, *Kaler Samukh Bhela*; Shamsun Nahar Khan, *Ekti Nimesh* (Dhaka: Anwar Ali Khan, 1985).

20. This summary is based on the twenty-five autobiographical essays in Nurunnahar Faizunnessa's edited volume, *Kaler Samukh Bhela*.

21. I draw here on McKay, *English Diarists*, 207.

22. Sarkar, *Words to Win*. Other examples include: Binodini Dasi's *Abhinetrir Atmakatha* (1910), translated recently as *My Story and My Life as an Actress*, ed. Rimli Bhattacharya (Delhi: Kali for Women, 1998); Sarala Debi Chaudhurani's *Jibaner Jhara Pata* (1944–45), translated recently as *The Scattered Leaves of My Life: An Indian Nationalist Remembers*, trans. Sikata Banerjee (Delhi: Women Unlimited, 2009); and *The Memoirs of Haimabati Sen: From Child Widow to Lady Doctor*, ed. Geraldine Forbes and Tapan Raychaudhuri (Delhi: Roli Books, 2000).

23. Sughra Mehdi, *Sair Kar Dunya ki Ghafil . . .*, 88–107.

24. Among the former, I refer to Begam Zafar Ali, Shamla Mufti, and Malka Pukhraj. As examples of the latter, see Hameeda Bano, "A View from Kashmir," in *Speaking Peace: Women's Voices from Kashmir*, ed. Urvashi Butalia (Delhi: Kali for Women), 2002), 171–77, and Farida Abdulla, "A Life of Peace and Dignity," also in *Speaking Peace*, 262–67; Anjum Zamrud Habib, *Prisoner No. 100: An Account of My Days and Nights in an Indian Prison* (Delhi: Zubaan, 2011).

25. Minault, *Secluded Scholars*, 196; Hameeda Akhtar Husain, *Hamsafar*, chapter 5, "Hyderabad"; Rao, *Indian Biographical Dictionary*, 175. Marriage was also a link for Salma Ahmed to the Hyderabad and Bhopal royal families. See Salma Ahmed, *Cutting Free*, 12.

26. Qaisari Begam, *Kitab-i-Zindagi*; Zehra Fyzee, "Safarnama-i-Bhopal" and "Safar-i-Badauda" in *Mazamin*, 46–55, 114–30; Jahanara Habibullah, *Remembrance of Days Past*, 35–36 (on Atiya Fyzee's visit to Rampur); Chughtai, *A Life in Words*, 94.

27. Razak Khan, "Purdah Politics: Rethinking Gender and Power in Princely India" (paper presented at the South Asia Conference, University of Wisconsin at Madison, October 20, 2013).

28. For further development of this argument, see my "To Write of the Conjugal Act," 155–81.

29. I borrow this phrase from Bilquis Jehan Khan's subtitle to *A Song of Hyderabad*.

30. Vatuk, "Hamara Daur-i Hayat," 166–67.

31. Iqbalunnisa Hussain, *Changing India*, iii; personal communication from her grandson, Arif Zaman, April 27, 2007.

32. Nalini Jameela, *Oru Laingikathozhilaliyude Atmakatha*; Nilambur Ayisha, *Jeevitathinte Arangu*; Ayesha Bibi, unpublished manuscript.

33. See, as an example, K. N. Panikkar, *Against Lord and State: Religion and Peasant Uprising in Malabar, 1836–1921* (Delhi: Oxford University Press, 1989).

34. I take this quote from an interview with Nilambur Ayisha. See Anasuya Menon, "Courageous Act," *Hindu*, May 31, 2013, http://www.thehindu.com/features/friday-re view/theatre/courageous-act/article4765841.ece. Also see her autobiography, *Jeevitathinte Arangu*.

228   *Notes to Chapter 3*

35. Kumar, "Autobiography as a Way of Writing History," 440.

36. Ibid. Also see Lalitambika Antarjanam, *Atmakathayku Oru Amukham* (Kottayam: Sahitya Pravarthaka Co-operative Society, 1979). For other examples of autobiographical writing by Keralan women, see J. Devika, ed., *Her-Self: Gender and Early Writings of Malayalee Women* (Kolkata: Stree, 2005), in which a number of essays from early women's magazines are translated, including pieces by Nayar, Christian, and Muslim authors—though the contributions from Muslim women are not autobiographical.

37. Gail Minault, "Shaikh Abdullah, Begam Abdullah, and Sharif Education for Girls at Aligarh," in *Modernization and Social Change among Muslims in India*, ed. Imtiaz Ahmad (New Delhi: Manohar, 1982), 228ff; Minault, foreword to Kazim, *A Woman of Substance*, x.

38. Kazim, *A Woman of Substance*, 108.

39. Lambert-Hurley, *Muslim Women, Reform and Princely Patronage*, 156, 160–61.

40. Minault, *Secluded Scholars*, 286.

41. Qamar Azad Hashmi, *The Fifth Flame*, 73.

42. Hafsa Kanjwal, "Placing Kashmir: Gender, Social Status, and Mobility in a Kashmiri Women's Autobiography" (paper presented at the Feminist South Asia Preconference, 41st Annual Conference on South Asia, University of Madison at Wisconsin, October 2012); personal communication from Sughra Mehdi, February 18, 2006; Saiduzzafar, *Autobiography*, 75.

43. On these various permutations of Islam, see Lapidus, *History of Islamic Societies*, 377.

44. Jahanara Habibullah, *Remembrance of Days Past*, 85–9; Mehrunissa, *An Extraordinary Life*, 10.

45. Alam, "Interrupted Stories," 72; Naim, "How Bibi Ashraf Learned to Read and Write," 99; Saliha Abid Hussain, *Silsila-i-Roz o Shab*, 11.

46. Jahanara Imam, *Of Blood and Fire*, 22.

47. On this exogamy, see Theodore P. Wright, Jr., "Muslim Kinship and Modernization: The Tyabji Clan of Bombay," in *Family, Kinship, and Marriage among Muslims in India*, ed. Imtiaz Ahmad (Delhi: Manohar, 1976), 227.

48. Ishvani, *The Brocaded Sari*, 3–7.

49. For a brief biography, see Aparna Basu and Bharati Ray, *Women's Struggle: A History of the All India Women's Conference, 1927–1990* (Delhi: Manohar, 1990), 182.

50. For a theoretical discussion of how autobiography may be used by those "excluded from official discourse" to "talk back," see Sidonie Smith, *Subjectivity, Identity, and the Body*. South Asian examples include: Chakravarti, *Rewriting History*; and Kumar, *Dalit Personal Narratives*.

51. Quoted in Basu, *Abbas Tyabji*, 36–37.

52. Ibid., 37.

53. See, for example, Shaukat Kaifi, *Yad ki Rahguzar*, 81, 95–96, 114, 122.

54. For an account of living and working in Delhi after Independence, see Saeeda Bano Ahmed, *Dagar se hat kar*, 136ff. Other autobiographers who lived and wrote in Delhi include Anis Kidwai, Raihana Tyabji, Qamar Azad Hashmi, Sughra Mehdi, Saliha Abid Hussain, Nafees Bano Shama, and Qurratulain Hyder.

55. Attiya Dawood, *Aine ke Samne*, p. īē.

56. Akhtar Imam, "Amader Shikal," in Nurunnahar Faizunnessa, *Kaler Samukh Bhela*, 18.

57. Seminal writings on language and identity in South Asia include: Paul R. Brass, *Language, Religion, and Politics in North India* (Cambridge: Cambridge University Press, 1974); David Washbrook, "'To Each a Language of His Own': Language, Culture, and Society in Colonial India," in *Language, History, and Class*, ed. Penelope J. Corfield (Oxford: Basil Blackwell, 1991), 179–203; Sudipta Kaviraj, "Writing, Speaking, Being: Language and the Historical Formation of Identities in India," in *Nationalstaat und Sprachkonflikte in Süd- und Südostasien*, ed. D. Hellmann-Rajanayagam and D. Rothermund (Stuttgart: Steiner, 1992), 25–65; and Christopher R. King, *One Language, Two Scripts: The Hindi Movement in Nineteenth Century North India* (New Delhi: Oxford University Press, 1994).

58. Barbara D. Metcalf, "Urdu in India in the 21st Century: A Historian's Perspective," *Social Scientist* 31, nos. 5/6 (May–June 2003): 30–31.

59. On this process, see Francesca Orsini, ed., *Before the Divide: Hindi and Urdu Literary Culture* (New Delhi: Orient Blackswan, 2010).

60. For evidence from Old Delhi, see Rizwan Ahmad, "Shifting Dunes: Changing Meanings of Urdu in India" (PhD diss., University of Michigan, 2007).

61. Ghulam Fatima Shaikh, *Footsteps in Time*, xxi.

62. Hafsa Kanjwal, "Placing Kashmir."

63. See, for example, contributions by Khorshedi Alam, Moslema Khatun, Hamida Rahman, and Begam Makshuda in Nurunnahar Faizunnessa's edited collection, *Kaler Samukh Bhela*, 102, 118, 191–92, and 220; and Jobeda Khanam, *Jiban Khatar Pataguli*, 89–90.

64. Jobeda Khanam, *Jiban Khatar Pataguli*, 89.

65. Ibid., 91.

66. Ibid., 92.

67. Jobeda Khanam's other works include: *Chotadera Ekankika* (Dhaka: Bangla Ekadami, 1963); *Ananta Pipasa* (Dhaka: Naoroja Kitabistana, 1967); *Ekati Surera Mrtyu* (Dhaka: Adila Bradarsa, 1974); and *Mahasamudra* (Dhaka: Bangladesh Shishu Academy, 1977).

68. C. H. Payne, Translator's preface to Sultan Jahan Begam, *An Account of My Life (Gohur-i-Ikbal)*, v. Italics added.

69. Marlen Karlitzky, "The Tyabji Clan—Urdu as a Symbol of Group Identity," *Annual of Urdu Studies* 17 (2002): 189.

70. Shaukat Kaifi, *Kaifi and I* (New Delhi: Zubaan, 2010), 111. This paragraph on India and Pakistan is not included at the end of the same chapter in the Urdu original. See Shaukat Kaifi, *Yad ki Rahguzar*, 153.

71. M. Asaduddin, introduction to Chughtai, *A Life in Words*, xxiii. On *begamati zuban*, also see Shaista Ikramullah, *Dilli ki Khawatin ki Khavaten aur Muhavare* (Karachi: Oxford University Press, 2005); and Gail Minault, "Begamati Zuban: Women's Language and Culture," in *Gender, Language, and Learning: Essays in Indo-Muslim Cultural History* (Ranikhet: Permanent Black, 2009), 116–34.

230   *Notes to Chapter 3*

72. For examples, see Lambert-Hurley and Sharma, *Atiya's Journeys*, chapter 4, "Narrating the Everyday"; and Alam's section "Nazr's Narrative as a History of Everyday Life," in "Interrupted Stories," 78–82.

73. On Raihana and language, see Lambert-Hurley, "The Heart of a Gopi," 577–78.

74. Qurratulain Hyder, "Sada-i-Absharan Az Faraz–i-Kehsar Amad," in Nazr Sajjad Hyder, *Guzashta Barson ki Baraf*, 12–33. Her point was brought home to me by Zakir Husain's great-granddaughter, who, noting that her Urdu was not fluent enough for the original, explained that she had read her grandmother Sayyida Khurshid Alam's personal account of him in the Nagari script. Personal communication from Samina Misra, Delhi, November 22, 2005. For the original text, see Sayyida Khurshid Alam, *Zakir Sahib ki Kahani*.

75. For development of these points, see the essays in Ather Farouqui, ed., *Redefining Urdu Politics in India* (Delhi: Oxford University Press, 2006).

76. See, for example, Anis Kidwai, *Azadi ki Chhaon Mein*, translated into Hindi by Noor Nabi Abbasi (Delhi: National Book Trust, 1978); Ismat Chughtai, *Kaghazi Hai Pairahan*, transliterated into Devanagari by Iftikhar Anjum (Delhi: Rajkamal Prakashan, 1998); Tehmina Durrani, *My Feudal Lord*, translated into Hindi as *Mere Aaka* (Delhi: Vani Prakashan, 2002); and Attiya Dawood, *Aine ke Samne* (New Delhi: Rajkamal Prakashan, 2004).

77. See, for example, Shaista Ikramullah, *Parday say Parliament tak* (Karachi: Oxford University Press, 2004); and Abida Sultaan, *Ek Inqilabi Shahzadi ki Khud Navisht* (Karachi: Oxford University Press, 2007).

78. On English in postcolonial South Asia, see Vasudha Bharadwaj's PhD dissertation "Languages of Nationhood: Political Ideologies and the Place of English in 20th Century India" (University of Rochester, 2010).

79. The editions include: Nawab Sikandar Begum of Bhopal, *A Pilgrimage to Mecca*, trans. Mrs. Willoughby-Osborne (London: Wm. H. Allen, 1870) and (Calcutta: Thacker, Spink, 1906).

80. Ibid., v–vi.

81. Ibid., frontispiece.

82. Shah Jahan Begam of Bhopal, *Taj ul Ikbal Tarikh-i- Bhopal*, vi.

83. See, for example, *Thacker's Indian Directory* (Calcutta: Thacker, Spink, 1885).

84. "Kitab-i-Akhbar-i-Kihim-Yali," May 9, 1898. A parallel could be drawn here with Anglo-Egyptian author Ahdaf Soueif, who, when asked why she writes in English, explained that she had read English literature throughout her childhood and thus considered English her "literary language." "Desert Island Discs," BBC Radio, June 4, 17, 2012, http://www.bbc.co.uk/programmes/b01jwfpz.

85. Masuma Begam, "From Behind the Veil—Into the Mainstream"; Khan, *A Song of Hyderabad*, 64; Minault, *Secluded Scholars*, 196; Vatuk, *"Hamara Daur–i Hayat,"* 166; Shaukat Kaifi, *Yad ki Rahguzar*, 29.

86. Shaukat Kaifi, *Yad ki Rahguzar*, 116.

87. Chughtai, *A Life in Words*, 264.

88. Sadaf Jaffer, "Queer Feminism in Islamicate South Asia: Ismat Chughtai on Social Justice" (paper presented at the Annual Conference on South Asia, University of Wis-

consin at Madison, October 20, 2013). On Urdu literary tradition, see Shamsur Rahman Faruqi, "A Long History of Urdu Literary Culture, Part I: Naming and Placing a Literary Culture," and Frances Pritchett, "A Long History of Urdu Literary Culture, Part II: Histories, Performances, and Masters," in *Literary Cultures in History: Reconstructions from South Asia*, ed. Sheldon Pollock (Berkeley: University of California Press, 2003), 805–63, 864–911.

89. Personal communication from Sughra Mehdi, February 18, 2006.

90. Saliha Abid Hussain, for instance, published *Safar Zindagi ke liye Soj o Saj* (1982) with Maktaba Jamia, while Sughra Mehdi's *Mekhanon ka Pata* (2005) was published by the Urdu Academy in Madhya Pradesh. Sughra Mehdi and Nafees Bano Shama both published their autobiographies with the Urdu specialist, Modern Publishing House, in Delhi, while Qurratulain Hyder first published *Kar-i-Jahan Daraz Hai* (1977) with Fan aur Fankar in Bombay. On Maktaba Jamia's "enormous contributions in the service of the Urdu language" specifically, see Jamia Millia Islamia's website, accessed January 26, 2014, http://old.jmi.ac.in/2000/MaktabaJamia.htm.

91. Basu and Ray, *Women's Struggle*, 182.

92. Danish Khan, "Kulsum Sayani: A 'Rahbar' of Hindusthani," http://twocircles.net /2010may15/kulsum_sayani_rahber_hindustani.html.

93. Kulsum Sayani, "Visit to Branches," *Roshni* 1, no. 8 (September 1946): 27–32; and "The Trials of a Social Worker," *Roshni* (special issue 1946): 87–91.

94. Iqbalunnisa Hussain, *Changing India*, iii.

95. See Iqbalunnisa Hussain, "The Importance of the Modern Tongue," in *Changing India*, 107–12.

96. See Iqbalunnisa Hussain, "Impressions of a Visit to Europe" and "My Experience in an English University," in *Changing India*, 148–51, 152–69.

97. Iqbalunnisa Hussain, *Changing India*, 69; Kulsum Sayani, "Visit to Branches," 32.

98. This summary is based on a survey of *Roshni* from the 1940s and 1950s at the AIWC library in New Delhi.

99. Personal communication from Shikha Sen, February 8, 2006.

100. Shaista Suhrawardy, "Holland ki Sair," *Ismat* 62, no. 5 (May 1939): 345–48. For another example of her early Urdu publications, see "Apna Ghar," *Ismat* 55, no. 4 (October 1935): 298–300.

101. Shaista Ikramullah, From Purdah to Parliament, 16.

102. Ibid., 17, 29.

103. Her thesis was republished recently as: Shaista Akhtar Bano Suhrawardy, *A Critical Survey of the Development of the Urdu Novel and Short Story* (Karachi: Oxford University Press, 2007).

104. Shaista Ikramullah, *Dilli ki Khawatin ki Khavaten aur Muhavare*; and Shaista Ikramullah, *Behind the Veil* (Karachi: Oxford University Press, 1992).

105. Shaista Ikramullah, *From Purdah to Parliament*, xv.

106. A more recent author equally aware of this potential circulation was Benazir Bhutto in *Daughter of the East*.

107. Avantika Chilkoti, "Indian Publishing: The Pressures of English," January 21,

232   *Notes to Chapter 3*

2014, accessed January 24, 2014, http://blogs.ft.com/beyond-brics/2014/01/21/indian
-publishing-the-pressures-of-english/#axzz2r48J4nkg.

108. Shaukat Kaifi, *Kaifi and I*, x.

109. Tehmina Durrani with William and Marilyn Hoffer, *My Feudal Lord: A Devastating Indictment of Women's Role in Muslim Society* (London: Corgi Books, 1995); Mukhtar Mai with Marie-Thérèse Cuny, *In the Name of Honor*; and Malala Yousafzai with Christina Lamb, *I Am Malala*.

110. Amina Yaqin, "Autobiography and Muslim Women's Lives," *Journal of Women's History* 25, no. 2 (Summer 2013): 171–84, especially 174.

111. Durrani, *My Feudal Lord*, cover.

112. "Manuscript Memoirs of Mrs. Safia Jabir Ali," entry for February 22, 1926. For a recent translation of these memoirs, see Salima Tyabji, *The Changing World of a Bombay Muslim Community*, chapter 4, "A Modern Woman: The Journal of Safia Jabir Ali, 1926–1945."

113. "Manuscript Memoirs of Mrs. Safia Jabir Ali," entry for September 22, 1942.

114. See, for example, ibid., entry for October 5, 1942.

115. Ibid.

116. Ibid., entry for October 3, 1942. Also see, for example, her account "Dada Sahib Tyabally's children," begun in the entry for October 5, 1942, but, as noted on October 21, 1942, not completed.

117. "Manuscript Memoirs of Mrs. Safia Jabir Ali," entry for October 21, 1942.

118. Ibid., entry for October 3, 1942.

119. Ibid.

120. Ibid., 112.

121. On intimacy in Safia Jabir Ali's memoirs, see my "To Write of the Conjugal Act," 173–74.

122. "Manuscript Memoirs of Mrs. Safia Jabir Ali," 111.

123. See Salima Tyabji, *The Changing World of a Bombay Muslim Community*, chapter 4, "A Modern Woman: The Journal of Safia Jabir Ali, 1926–1945."

124. Sikandar, *Pilgrimage*, 2.

125. Ibid., chapters 3, 8, 14.

126. Ibid., 36, 107.

127. Eickelman and Piscatori, *Muslim Travellers*, 6.

128. Sikandar, *Pilgrimage*, 119, 127–28. For further exploration of these themes, see my introduction to *A Princess's Pilgrimage*, especially xxiv–lx.

129. Tahera Aftab, An Introduction to Shahr Bano Begam's "Bītī Kahānī" in *A Story of Days Gone By*, 7.

130. "Bītī Kahānī," in Aftab, *A Story of Days Gone By*, 104.

131. Ibid.

132. Barbara Metcalf, "What Happened in Mecca: Mumtaz Mufti's 'Labbaik,'" in *The Culture of Autobiography: Constructions of Self-Representation*, ed. Robert Folkenflik (Stanford, CA: Stanford University Press, 1993), 156–57.

133. "Bītī Kahānī," in Aftab, *A Story of Days Gone By*, 104, 207. A comparison could

be drawn here with Hameeda Akhtar Husain Raipuri's much later *Hamsafar* (1992). As discussed in chapter 1, it also retains the informal and sometimes disjointed character of a conversation after being instigated on this basis by the author's friend Jamil Bhai.

134. "Bītī Kahānī," in Aftab, *A Story of Days Gone By*, 107. Meaning "sister," *bua* is an endearment between female friends.

135. Ibid., 104.

136. Ibid., 105.

137. See, for example, Atiya Fyzee's entries in *Zamana-i-Tahsil* for 1906 (September 16, October 14, November 15, and December 14) and 1907 (January 26, August 9, and September 27); Nazr Sajjad Hyder, *Guzashta Barson Ki Baraf*, 124.

138. See Atiya's entry for December 14, 1906, in *Zamana-i-Tahsil*.

139. For an analysis of these omissions, see Lambert-Hurley and Sharma, *Atiya's Journeys*, chapter 2.

140. Vatuk, "Hamara Daur-i Hayat," 145.

141. Ibid., 150–51.

142. Amina Tyabji, "A Page from the Past: Extracts from the Diary of Amina Binte Badruddin Tyabji," *Roshni*, special issue (1946): 69–73.

143. See, for example, Atiya's entry for February 2, 1907, in *Zamana-i-Tahsil* when she addresses her two sisters, Zehra and Nazli. Also see Lambert-Hurley and Sharma, *Atiya's Journeys*, 175.

144. Nazli, *Sair-i-Yurop*, 1. The translation will be available in an edited and annotated version of this travelogue being prepared by Sunil Sharma and me.

145. Lambert-Hurley and Sharma, *Atiya's Journeys*, 31–32.

146. Sidonie Smith, "Performativity, Autobiographical Practice, Resistance," in Smith and Watson, *Women, Autobiography, Theory*, 108.

CHAPTER 4

1. Naim, introduction to *Zikr-i-Mir*, 16.

2. For the aims of Price's book, see its excellent introduction: Leah Price, *How to Do Things in Victorian Britain* (Princeton: Princeton University Press, 2012), 1–18. On "book history" in India, see Abhijit Gupta and Swapan Chakravorty, eds., *Print Areas: Book History in India* (Delhi: Permanent Black, 2004)—especially the editors' very useful introduction to this type of scholarship, "Under the Sign of the Book," 1–16.

3. Antoinette Burton, "'An Assemblage/Before Me': Autobiography as Archive," *Journal of Women's History* 25, no. 2 (Summer 2013): 187.

4. I develop this idea from my reading of Hansen's *Stages of Life*.

5. Sherrill Grace, "Theatre and the Autobiographical Pact: An Introduction," in *Theatre and Autobiography: Writing and Performing Lives in Theory and Practice*, ed. Sherrill Grace and Jerry Wasserman (Vancouver: Talonbooks, 2006), 13.

6. Kathryn Hansen, "Performing Gender and Faith in Indian Theatre Autobiographies," in Malhotra and Lambert-Hurley, *Speaking of the Self*, 256. Also see Hansen's *Stages of Life*. We build on this discussion of performers and performativity in Malhotra and Lambert-Hurley, introduction to *Speaking of the Self*, 21–22.

234   *Notes to Chapter 4*

7. Vatuk, "Hamara Daur-i Hayat," 152.

8. Masuma Begum, "From behind the Veil—into the Mainstream" and "The Autobiography of Dr. Rahmathunnisa Begam" were both sent to me by Professor Gail Minault, who obtained the first from the author and the second from Professor Geraldine Forbes.

9. Qamar Jahan Ali cites this version in the bibliography of her PhD dissertation (Aligarh Muslim University, 1950), which was later published as *Princess Jahan Ara Begam: Her Life and Works* (Karachi: S. M. Hamid Ali, 1991).

10. The first was published by Muhammad Aslam in *Journal of Research Society of Pakistan* 16, no. 4 and 17, no. 1 (1979). The second was published by Tanvir Alvi in the journal produced by the Anjuman-i-Islam Urdu Research Institute in Bombay, *Nava-i-Adab* (October 1986): 34–51. I am grateful to Afshan Bokhari and Sunil Sharma for sharing these references.

11. Lal, "Historicizing the Harem," 601. The copy in the British Library is MSS. Eur.C.176/221.

12. Naim, *Zikr-i-Mir*, 20–21.

13. See, for example, ibid., 85n.191.

14. For an overview of these journals, see Gail Minault, "Urdu Women's Magazines in the Early Twentieth Century," *Manushi* 48 (September–October 1988): 2–9.

15. See, for example, Nawab Begam of Janjira, "Sair-i-Yurop," *Ismat*, August 1908, 23–38; Shaista Suhrawardy, "Holland ki Sair," 345–48; Zehra Fyzee, "Safarnama-i-Bhopal" and "Safar-i-Badauda," in *Mazamin*, 46–55, 114–30; Smt. Masuma Begum, "A Day in Samarkand," *Roshni* (September 1959): 25; Mumtaz Wadud, "New York-er Bazaar," *Begum* 34, no. 27 (April 4, 1982); Rafia Khan, "Shadure Ja Dekhlam," *Begum* 34, no. 38 (June 20, 1982). Serialized travel accounts in *Begum* also included Nilufer Khanam's "Amrika Smriti," started in 34, no. 44 (August 15, 1982): 10; and Salima Rahman, "Bilet Deshta Matir," started in 34, no. 39 (June 27, 1982): 16.

16. Sohaila Abdulali, "I Fought for My Life . . . and Won," *Manushi* 16 (June–July 1983), 18–19; Amina Sherwani, "Determined Resistance," *Manushi* (May–June 1985), 24; Zubeida Begum, "Relief or Repression?" *Manushi* (September–December 1987): 39–40.

17. See Atiya's entries in issues of *Tahzib un-Niswan* dated January 26, 1907–November 30, 1907.

18. Atiya Fyzee, *Zamana-i-Tahsil*. On *roznamcha* as a literary form, see Lambert-Hurley and Sharma, *Atiya's Journeys*, 7–8.

19. Hijab Imtiaz Ali's diary was serialized in *Tahzib un-Niswan* as "Lail o Nihar" [Day and night] in 1941–42. Nazr Sajjad Hyder began serializing her "Roznamcha" in *Tahzib un-Niswan* 45, no. 32 (August 8, 1942), 514. For further analysis of the latter's form, see Alam, "Interrupted Stories," 73–78.

20. On this forum, see Minault, *Secluded Scholars*, 119.

21. On Muhammadi Begam, see ibid., 111–21.

22. See Atiya's entry for August 19, 1907, in *Zamana-i-Tahsil*.

23. See, for example, Atiya's entries for March 30 and June 27, 1907, in *Zamana-i-Tahsil*.

24. Nazr Sajjad Hyder, *Guzashta Barson ki Baraf*, 124.

25. There are a number of other texts that underwent a similar process. For example,

Saiyida Lutfunnessa serialized a number of her autobiographical essays in *Begum* under the title "Samay Katha Bale/Samay Bahiya Jay" before publishing them together as *Bibortoner Smriticharon*. Similarly, Sughra Mehdi first serialized her autobiography in a Delhi magazine before publishing it in book form as *Hikayat-i-Hasti*. Personal communication from Sughra Mehdi, February 18, 2006.

26. Asaduddin, introduction to *A Life in Words*, x.

27. This letter was reproduced in ibid.

28. Ibid., xi.

29. Ismat Chughtai, *Kaghazi Hai Pairahan* (New Delhi: Publications Division, 1994).

30. Asaduddin, introduction to *A Life in Words*, x.

31. Ibid., x–xi.

32. Vatuk, "The Book of Life."

33. The highly emotive section on her marriage is widely available, having been translated by Mehr Afshan Farooqi in Qaisari Begam, "Excerpts from *Kitab-e Zindagi*," 232–41.

34. Ibid., 232.

35. Ibid.

36. Alam, "Interrupted Stories," 73–78.

37. Saliha Abid Hussain, *Safar Zindagi ke liye Soj o Saj.*

38. Saliha Abid Hussain, *Silsila-i-Roz o Shab*, 8.

39. See, for example, Nurunnahar Faizunnessa's own chapter in her edited volume *Kaler Samukh Bhela*, 122–39. Following a similar format were those short autobiographical pieces commissioned from former pupils or teachers for alumni or centenary volumes associated with individual schools. See, for example, Lulu Rahman's piece on "the greatest days of her life" in a volume compiled by Selina Bahar for the alumni reunion festival of the Vidyamoyee Government Girls' School in Mymensingh, Bangladesh, in 1999: "Jibaner Sarbattam Dinguli," in *Biddamoyee School Praktan Chatri Purnamilan Utsab.*

40. Noorjehan Murshid, "My Experience as an Editor of a Bangla Magazine," in *Infinite Variety: Women in Society and Literature*, ed. Firdous Azim and Niaz Zaman (Dhaka: University Press, 1994), 322–28. For an overview of her life as a whole, see a tribute by her daughter, Nazneen Murshid, titled "Noor Jehan Murshid, or a Power Woman," *Daily Star*, September 1, 2012.

41. See chapters by Sultana Jafri, Shaukat Azmi, and Shabana Azmi in Saif Hyder Hasan, ed., *One Yesterday*, 15–25, 81–88, 89–98, 99–101.

42. The International Auto/Biography Association addressed the theme of "life writing and translations" at its Sixth Biennial Conference in Honolulu, Hawaii, June 23–26, 2008. For a summary of discussions, see the conference report, accessed January, 30, 2014, http://www.theiaba.org/life-writing-and-translations-iaba-conference/.

43. Lal, "Historicizing the Harem," 605–6, 608.

44. Mrs. E. L. Willoughby-Osborne, translator's preface to Sikandar, *Pilgrimage*; Annette S. Beveridge, preface to Gulbadan Begam, *The History of Humāyūn-Humāyūn-nāmā*, vii; Nasreen Rehman, translator's note to Shaukat Kaifi, *Kaifi and I*, 14; Asaduddin, introduction to Ismat Chughtai, *A Life in Words*, xxiv.

236 Notes to Chapter 4

45. Sikandar, *Pilgrimage*, 35, 64.

46. Nasreen Rehman, translator's note to Shaukat Kaifi, *Kaifi and I*, 14.

47. Tahera Aftab, introduction to *A Story of Days Gone By*, 8.

48. I was inspired to think about this issue by Margot Badran's preface to her translation of Huda Shaarawi's *Mudhakirrati*. Here, she explains how she "arranged the account," adding headings and subheadings, deleting "repetitions" or "occasional overelaboration," and "re-ordering" the text to reflect "chronology" and "preserve the natural flow of the narrative." She also saw fit to "weave" the final section of Huda's memoirs, deemed too "fragmentary," into a "historical Epilogue." See her *Harem Years*, 2–3.

49. See, for example, Tyabji, *Changing World*, 256n.57.

50. Metcalf, "The Past in the Present," 127.

51. Tyabji, *Changing World*, 98–107.

52. "Manuscript Memoirs of Mrs. Safia Jabir Ali," 184ff.

53. Perhaps this editing process will continue, since even more recently, Salima's brother, Nasir Tyabji, himself an economic historian, has taken on the challenge of preparing a revised version of her manuscript for publication with Oxford University Press in Delhi. E-mail communications, May 10 and 22, 2015.

54. In cases where a cowriter's name is *not* included, it can be even harder to judge the impact. A relevant example here is Mehrunissa Khan's *An Extraordinary Life*. A mutual acquaintance indicated to me that it was cowritten, but, in the acknowledgments, the author mentions only the "editing help" of various individuals. Mehrunissa Khan, *An Extraordinary Life*, vii; and personal communication from Geraldine Forbes, May 23, 2014.

55. Hasan Altaf offers an intriguing analysis of *I Am Malala*, in which he deduces Christina Lamb's responsibility for "flattening its heroine to the simplest version of herself"—thus creating not a "memoir or biography or even autobiography," but an "autohagiography." See his "Making Martyrs," *Guernica*, April 1, 2014, https://www.guernica mag.com/daily/hasan-altaf-making-martyrs/.

56. Joan L. Erdman, "Foreword: The Voice of Zohra," in Joan Erdman with Zohra Segal, *Stages*, x. On this period of her life when Segal worked with Shankar, see ibid., 74–111. For an example of Erdman's own research and writing, see *Patrons and Performers in Rajasthan: The Subtle Tradition* (Delhi: Chanakya, 1985).

57. Erdman, "Foreword," xii.

58. Ibid., xiii.

59. Ibid., xii.

60. Ibid., xiii.

61. Nasreen Rehman, translator's note to Shaukat Kaifi, *Kaifi and I*, 14.

62. Ibid., 14–15, 158.

63. For a classic expression of this theory on relationality, see Mary G. Mason, "The Other Voice: Autobiographies by Women Writers," in *Autobiography: Essays Theoretical and Critical*, ed. James Olney (Princeton, NJ: Princeton University Press, 1980), 207–35.

64. See, for example, Sultan Jahan Begam of Bhopal, *'Iffat ul-Muslimat* (Agra: Mufid-i-'Am, 1918); and Muhammad Anwarul Haq, *Silsila-i-Sultaniya: Domestik Ikanomi*, 4 parts (Agra: Mufid-i-'Am, 1922).

65. Atiya Fyzee, *Zamana-i-Tahsil*; Zehra Fyzee, *Mazamin*; Sultan Jahan Begam, *Akhtar-i-Iqbal* (Agra: Mufid-i-'Am, 1914).

66. Linda H. Peterson, "Institutionalizing Women's Autobiography: Nineteenth-Century Editors and the Shaping of an Autobiographical Tradition," in *The Culture of Autobiography: Constructions of Self-Representation*, ed. Robert Folkenflik (Stanford, CA: Stanford University Press), 80–103, esp. 91.

67. While OUP Pakistan first published memoirs by Abida Sultaan, Jahanara Habibullah, Bilquis Jahan Khan, Ghulam Fatima Shaikh, and Atiya Dawood, it also re-published or translated earlier works by Sikandar Begam of Bhopal, Shahr Bano Begam of Pataudi, Iqbalunnisa Hussain, Jahan Ara Shahnawaz, and Shaista Ikramullah,

68. This version is referred to in notes as Begum Khurshid Mirza, "The Uprooted Sapling," original mss.

69. This conference was held in Aligarh, November 27–28, 2005.

70. Begum Khurshid Mirza, "The Uprooted Sapling," *Herald* (August 1982–April 1983).

71. Lubna Kazim, *The Making of a Modern Muslim Woman: Begum Khurshid Mirza, 1918–1989* (Lahore: Brite Books, 2003).

72. Kazim, *A Woman of Substance*.

73. Begum Khurshid Mirza, "The Uprooted Sapling," original mss., chapter 2.

74. Kazim, *A Woman of Substance*, 138–39.

75. Ibid., 137.

76. Ibid., 141, 147–48.

77. On these early Muslim actresses, see ibid., 147–48; and Haresh Pandya, "Naseem Banu: First Female Superstar of the Hindi Cinema," *Guardian* (September 4, 2002), https://www.theguardian.com/news/2002/sep/04/guardianobituaries.filmnews.

78. Kazim, *A Woman of Substance*, 141.

79. Ibid., 177–78, 189–94, 203–4, 210–12.

80. On her participation in these plays and serials, see ibid., chapter 14, "Years of Fame."

81. See the image in ibid., 231.

82. Hansen, *Stages of Life*, 30–31.

83. For a recent translation, see Binodini Dasi, *My Story and My Life as an Actress*.

84. Hansen, "Performing Gender and Faith in Indian Theatre Autobiographies," 256.

85. Begum Khurshid Mirza, "The Uprooted Sapling," *Herald* (November and December 1982).

86. Conversation with Lubna Kazim, November 28, 2005.

87. Begum Khurshid Mirza, "The Uprooted Sapling," original ms., 88–125; *The Making of a Modern Muslim Woman* and *A Woman of Substance*, chapters 7–9.

88. Marianne Hirsch, *Family Frames: Photography, Narrative, and Postmemory* (Cambridge, MA: Harvard University Press, 1997); and Linda Haverty Rugg, *Picturing Ourselves: Photography and Autobiography* (Chicago: University of Chicago Press, 1997).

89. Begum Khurshid Murza, "The Uprooted Sapling," *Herald* (August 1982), 88.

90. Kazim, *The Making of a Modern Muslim Woman*, cover.

238   *Notes to Chapter 4*

91. The photographs in *A Woman of Substance* are between pages 19 and 20 and pages 231 and 232.

92. See especially Begum Khurshid Mirza, "The Uprooted Sapling," *Herald* (February, March, and April 1983); and Kazim, *The Making of a Modern Muslim Woman*, chapters 11–15.

93. Begum Khurshid Mirza, "The Uprooted Sapling," *Herald* (August 1982), 98 and (September 1982), 93.

94. Ibid. (August 1982), 89.

95. Gail Minault, foreword to Kazim, *A Woman of Substance*, ix–xxv.

96. Salman Haidar, foreword to Kazim, *The Making of a Modern Muslim Woman*, 3–7; and "Remembering Appi and Daddy," in Kazim, *A Woman of Substance*, 232–36. For comparison with Khurshid Mirza's own portrayal of her marriage, see Kazim, *A Woman of Substance*, 116.

97. Lubna Kazim, preface and afterword to *The Making of a Modern Muslim Woman*, 1–2, 280–95; and *A Woman of Substance*, vi–viii, 237–45.

98. This exact chapter title is from the Zubaan edition, 86. In *The Making of a Modern Muslim Woman*, it is embellished (and transliterated differently) to: "My Renegade Sister, Rasheed Jahan 1905–1952," 103.

99. See, for example, Shadab Bano, "Rashid Jahan's Writings: Resistance and Challenging Boundaries, *Angaare* and Onwards," *Indian Journal of Gender Studies* 19, no. 1 (February 2012): 57–71.

100. Begum Khurshid Murza, "The Uprooted Sapling," original ms., 18. Emphasis my own.

101. Lubna Kazim, preface to Kazim, *The Making of a Modern Muslim Woman*, 2, and Kazim, *A Woman of Substance*, viii. For a brief biography, see the program for the "Count Me In" conference in Kathmandu, April 16–18, 2011, http://www.countmeinconference.org/.

102. Lubna Kazim, preface to Kazim, *The Making of a Modern Muslim Woman*, 2, and Kazim, *A Woman of Substance*, viii.

103. Conversation with Lubna Kazim, November 28, 2005; e-mail conversation with Gail Minault, January 9, 2014.

104. Conversation with Lubna Kazim, November 28, 2005; Lubna Kazim, preface to Kazim, *A Woman of Substance*, viii.

105. Compare Begum Khurshid Mirza, "The Uprooted Sapling," original ms., 39–64; and *A Woman of Substance*, chapter 2 ("Papa Mian"). Also see Lubna Kazim, preface to Kazim, *A Woman of Substance*, vii–viii.

106. Begum Khurshid Mirza, "The Uprooted Sapling," original ms., 25; Kazim, *The Making of a Modern Muslim Woman*, 51; Kazim, *A Woman of Substance*, 35.

107. See, for example, Begum Khurshid Mirza, "The Uprooted Sapling," *Herald* (August 1982), 90; and Kazim, *A Woman of Substance*, 2.

108. Begum Khurshid Mirza, "The Uprooted Sapling," *Herald* (August 1982), 89.

109. Ibid., *Herald* (April 1983), 98.

110. Kazim, *The Making of a Modern Muslim Woman*, cover.

111. Kazim, *A Woman of Substance*, cover.

Notes to Chapter 4   239

112. Begum Khurshid Mirza, "The Uprooted Sapling," original ms., 5.

113. Ibid.

114. Ibid., 92.

115. Ibid.

116. Ibid., 92–93.

117. Kazim, *The Making of a Modern Muslim Woman*, 137; Kazim, *A Woman of Substance*, 116.

118. Begum Khurshid Mirza, "The Uprooted Sapling," original ms., 141; Kazim, *The Making of a Modern Muslim Woman*, 197; Kazim, *A Woman of Substance*, 167. Italics added.

119. Begum Khurshid Mirza, "The Uprooted Sapling," original ms., 143; Kazim, *The Making of a Modern Muslim Woman*, 204; Kazim, *A Woman of Substance*, 172.

120. Begum Khurshid Mirza, "The Uprooted Sapling," original ms., 144.

121. Kazim, *The Making of a Modern Muslim Woman*, 204; Kazim, *A Woman of Substance*, 172.

122. Begum Khurshid Mirza, "The Uprooted Sapling," original ms., 7; Kazim, *The Making of a Modern Muslim Woman*, 13; Kazim, *A Woman of Substance*, 5.

123. Begum Khurshid Mirza, "The Uprooted Sapling," original ms., 7–9.

124. Metcalf, "What Happened in Mecca," 154.

125. Ibid., 152.

126. Begum Khurshid Mirza, "The Uprooted Sapling," original ms., 107–8 Kazim, *The Making of a Modern Muslim Woman*, 149; Kazim, *A Woman of Substance*, 126.

127. Begum Khurshid Mirza, "The Uprooted Sapling," original ms., 108.

128. Kazim, *The Making of a Modern Muslim Woman*, 149; Kazim, *A Woman of Substance*, 127.

129. Begum Khurshid Mirza, "The Uprooted Sapling," original ms., 130; Kazim, *The Making of a Modern Muslim Woman*, 192.

130. Begum Khurshid Mirza, "The Uprooted Sapling," original ms., 102; Kazim, *The Making of a Modern Muslim Woman*, 146; Kazim, *A Woman of Substance*, 124.

131. Begum Khurshid Mirza, "The Uprooted Sapling," original ms., 103; Kazim, *The Making of a Modern Muslim Woman*, 147; Kazim, *A Woman of Substance*, 125.

132. Conversation with Lubna Kazim, November 28, 2005.

133. Begum Khurshid Mirza, "The Uprooted Sapling," original ms., 150.

134. Ibid.

135. Kazim, *The Making of a Modern Muslim Woman*, 219–20.

136. See, for comparison, Dale, "Steppe Humanism," 39.

137. Lambert-Hurley, "To Write of the Conjugal Act," 159.

138. Ibid., 156.

139. Kazim, *A Woman of Substance*, 113, 115.

140. Begum Khurshid Mirza, "The Uprooted Sapling," original ms., 82–83; Begum Khurshid Mirza, "The Uprooted Sapling," *Herald* (October 1982), 88.

141. Philippe Lejeune, *L'autobiographie en France* (Paris: Colin, 1971), 14. This translation is from Folkenflik, *The Culture of Autobiography*, 13.

142. I summarize a point that Anshu Malhotra and I made in our introduction to

240   *Notes to Chapters 4 and 5*

Speaking of the Self, 8. Here, we draw on Roy Porter, ed., *Rewriting the Self: Histories from the Renaissance to the Present* (London: Routledge, 1997).

143. Smith and Watson, *Reading Autobiography*, 11. Also see Philippe Lejeune, "The Autobiographical Pact," in *On Autobiography*, ed. Paul John Eakin and trans. Katherine Leary (Minneapolis: University of Minnesota Press, 1989), 19–21.

144. Smith and Watson, *Reading Autobiography*, 102.

CHAPTER 5

1. I have discussed the auto/biographical tradition within Bhopal in my "Introduction: A Princess Revealed," in Abida Sultaan's *Memoirs of a Rebel Princess*, xxx–xxxiii.

2. On the comparatively lowly status of Mehrunissa and her mother vis-à-vis her stepmother, see her *An Extraordinary Life*, 33.

3. Some of Muneeza Shamsie's autobiographical outputs were discussed in chapter 1, but another from the Pakistan press is "The Discovery of a Pakistani English Literature: A Personal Odyssey," *Dawn*, May 8, 2005. My sincere thanks to the author for presenting me with copies of all of her pieces. See also her daughter's article "Kamila Shamsie on Applying for British Citizenship: 'I Never Felt Safe,'" *Guardian*, March 4, 2014. Muneeza Shamsie has also traced this "matrix" of "matrilineal narratives" within her family in somewhat more detail in her "Discovering the Matrix."

4. On these important relationships, see Hamida Saiduzzafar, *Autobiography*, chapter 3, "My Brother Mahmud"; and chapter 6, "Rashid Jahan"; and also see Kazim, *A Woman of Substance*, chapter 6, "My Sister, Rasheed Jahan 1905–1952."

5. Saliha Abid Hussain, *Silsila-i-Roz o Shab*, 3.

6. Recent editions of these latter works include: Wheeler M. Thackston, ed., *The Baburnama: Memoirs of Babur, Prince and Emperor* (New York: Modern Library, 2002); and Wheeler M. Thackston, ed., *The Jahangirnama: Memoirs of Jahangir, Emperor of India* (New York: Oxford University Press, 1999).

7. See Altaf Husain Hali, "Maulana Hali ki Khud-navisht Sawanih-i-'Umri,'" 344–51.

8. See Mahmuduzzafar Khan, *Quest for Life* (Delhi: People's Publishing House, 1954); and Mohammad H. R. Talukdar, ed., *Memoirs of Huseyn Shaheed Suhrawardy with a Brief Account of His Life and Work* (Dhaka: University Press Limited, 1987).

9. Saliha Abid Hussain, *Silsila-i-Roz o Shab*, 7. Also see Sayyid Abid Hussain, *Hayat-i-Abid: Khudnavisht* (Delhi: Maktaba Jamia, 1984).

10. Saliha Abid Hussain, *Silsila-i-Roz o Shab*, 7.

11. Isha'at Habibullah, "Memories of the British and Feudal India," parts 1–4, *Dawn*, September 1991, 6–27. Also see his "Investing in Pakistan's Future," *Dawn*, February 8, 2011, http://www.dawn.com/news/604702/investing-in-pakistans-future.

12. Hameeda Akhtar Husain Raipuri, *Hamsafar*, 11. In translation, see Hameeda Akhtar Husain Raipuri, *My Fellow Traveller*, xv. Also see Akhtar Husain Raipuri, *Gard-i-rah: Khudnavisht, Mutala'ah, Mushahadah* (Karachi: Maktaba-i-Afkar, 1984). For the English translation, see Akhtar Husain Raipuri, *The Dust of the Road*, trans. Amina Azfar (Karachi: Oxford University Press, 2007).

13. This name represents his own spelling of what, more strictly, would be transliter-

ated as "Tayyib 'Ali ibn Bhai Miyan." According to his grandson Abbas Tyabji, "Tayyab 'Ali" was "too long" for his Parsi and Hindu contemporaries, so they abbreviated it to "Tyabji." Quoted in Asaf A. A. Fyzee, ed., *The Autobiography of Tyabji Bhoymeeah: Merchant Prince of Bombay, 1803–1863* (Bombay: Government Central Press, 1964), 14. Different branches of the clan have different surnames, including Tyabji, Fyzee, Lukmani, Latifi, Hydari, Futehally, Mirza, Abdul Ali, Ahmadi, and Mohammadi.

14. Ibid., i.

15. As evidence, see A. G. Noorani, *Badruddin Tyabji*, Builders of Modern India (Delhi: Publications Division, Ministry of Information and Broadcasting, Government of India, 1969). Badruddin Tyabji is also commemorated with a statue in the vicinity of the Bombay High Court. For a more recent summary of his achievements, see Brown, "Tyabji, Badruddin (1844–1906)."

16. On or by these leading Tyabjis are: Basu, *Abbas Tyabji*; Farhad Daftary, "Professor Asaf A. A. Fyzee (1899–1981)," *Arabica* 31, no. 3 (November 1984): 327–30; Lambert-Hurley and Sharma, *Atiya's Journeys*, 238; Sálim Ali, *The Fall of a Sparrow* (Delhi: Oxford University Press, 1985).

17. On or by these female Tyabjis are: Lambert-Hurley and Sharma, *Atiya's Journeys*; Basu and Ray, *Women's Struggle*, 188; Surayya Tyabji, *Mirch Masala: One Hundred Indian Recipes* (Bombay: Orient Longman, 1985); "Obituary: Kamila Tyabji," *Guardian*, June 15, 2004, http://www.theguardian.com/news/2004/jun/15/guardianobituaries.india; and "Laila Tyabji—The Keeper of Heritage," accessed March 6, 2014, http://www.tehelka.com/laila-tyabji-the-keeper-of-heritage/.

18. "Manuscript Memoirs of Mrs. Safia Jabir Ali," entry for October 21, 1942. On Mirat ul-'Arus, see Minault, *Secluded Scholars*, 34–36.

19. On Tyabji liminality and their attempts to counter it, see my "The Heart of a Gopi," 583–86.

20. Rare marriages outside the clan in the nineteenth and early twentieth centuries included Nazli Fyzee's marriage to the nawab of Janjira in 1886, Shareefah Tyabji's marriage to Hamid Ali in 1908, and Sohaila Tyabji's marriage to Dr. Mohammad Habib in 1927. On these pairings, see Wright, "Muslim Kinship," 227–29. From the mid-twentieth century, marriages outside the clan and even South Asia became increasingly common, with the effect that Tyabji descendants are now dispersed around the world. However, their family "network" is still maintained through the website http://www.tyabji.net/.

21. These originals were preserved by later members of the Tyabji clan. The second version is referenced as "Kitab Akhbari Tayyib Ali, vol. II," 65–87. Other entries in the book confirm that it was copied between April 27 and May 19, 1862. A third manuscript copy was made by Tyabjee's granddaughter Qamarunnisa, in another family notebook, "Kitab Akhbari Shujauddin Tayyibji, vol. I," 1–30. For my analysis here, I have used a later published version of "Sawanih," prepared and annotated by another Tyabji descendant, Asaf A. A. Fyzee in *The Autobiography of Tyabjee Bhoymeeah*, 1–30. According to his preface, this version was originally prepared in 1944, then published in the *Journal of the Asiatic Society of Bombay* (n.s.): 36–37 in 1961–62.

242   *Notes to Chapter 5*

22. "Sawanih," 3. The latter phrase, translated literally here, was used to denote wealth.

23. Ibid., 3. On indeterminacy, see Pascal, *Design and Truth in Autobiography*, 17.

24. See, for example, "Sawanih," 8.

25. Ibid., 15ff.

26. For comparison, see Metcalf, "What Happened in Mecca," 156–57.

27. The editor of the published text, Asaf A. A. Fyzee, usefully notes these linguistic variations in his footnotes to "Sawanih" and "notes on the text," in *The Autobiography of Tyabjee Bhoymeeah*, v–viii.

28. "Sawanih," 20ff.

29. For an account of Fyzee's talks, see Safia Jabir Ali, "Manuscript Memoirs," 88ff.

30. These are now housed in the University of Mumbai's library as part of the Fyzee Collection.

31. Compare "Kitab-i-Akhbar Amiruddin Tyab Ali" and "Kitab-i-Akhbar Shujauddin Tyab Ali," both quoted in Asaf A. A. Fyzee's *The Autobiography of Tyabjee Bhoymeeah* with the later "Kitab-i-Akhbar-i-Kihim-Yali" and "Akhbarnama-i-Ahmadganj-Murud-Jazira." A number of volumes of the latter two series are available in the University of Mumbai's archives and the Fyzee-Rahamin archives at Aiwan-e-Rifat in Karachi.

32. See, for example, Amiruddin Tyabji's opening entry in the "Kitab-i-Amiri," September 1, 1877, and Badruddin Tyabji's opening entry in a new volume of the "Badruddin Akhbar," May 10, 1901. Transcriptions of these volumes made by Safia Jabir Ali in 1958 are available in the Badruddin Tyabji Family Papers 4, in the Nehru Memorial Library and Museum in New Delhi.

33. See the entries of Badruddin Tyabji for December 1887 and Surayya Tyabji for December 1903 in "Badruddin Akhbar."

34. This summary is based on consultation of the akhbar books from Matheran and Mahableshwar relating to the period from 1894 to 1907 at the Nehru Memorial Library and Museum in New Delhi.

35. Amiruddin Tyabji's opening entry in the "Kitab-i-Amiri," September 1, 1877. See also Durrat-al-Vali's first entry in the "Kitab-i-Akhbar-i-Kihim-Yali," June 1, 1892.

36. See, for example, the entries written by Badruddin Tyabji's daughters Hafiza and Surayya, in the "Badruddin Akhbar" in the mid-1880s.

37. See entries by Badruddin Tyabji's wife, Rahat, and their daughters Sakina and Surayya, in the "Badruddin Akhbar," December 1903 and February 1904. For a recent translation, see Tyabji, *Changing World*, 66–77.

38. Sakina's entry in the Mahableshwar book, dated August 30, 1905; and Hadi's entry from May 1906 in "The Chabooka Chronicle Book," 250–47. The declining page numbers reflect the numbering system common to Urdu compositions. The former entry also appears in translation in Tyabji, *Changing World*, 77–81.

39. Tyabji, *Changing World*, 19.

40. Ibid., 79.

41. Hadi, "The Chabooka Chronicle Book," 249–48.

42. For comparison, see von Grunebaum, "Self-Expression."

43. See her entries for November 19, 1894, in the "Akhbar-i-Amiri," and June 29,

1895, in the "Badruddin Akhbar." More recently, they have been reproduced in Tyabji, *Changing World*, 59–63.

44. Tyabji, *Changing World*, 60, 62.

45. Ibid., 62.

46. Ibid.

47. Ibid.

48. Atia H. Fyzee, "Yali" in the "Kitab-i-Akhbar-i-Kihim-Yali," May 9, 1898. It has also been reproduced on "Accessing Muslim Lives," http://www.accessingmuslimlives.org/images/pdfs/Atiya%20Yali.pdf.

49. Ibid.

50. Safia Jabir Ali, for instance, recalled her mother, Rahat, reading Maulana Shibli Nomani's historical works, *al-Mamun* and *al-Farooq*, as well as, with her as a child, Nazir Ahmad's *Mirat ul-'Arus*. See her "Manuscript Memoirs of Mrs. Safia Jabir Ali," entry for October 21, 1942.

51. Tyabji, *Changing World*, 82–89.

52. Ibid., 84.

53. For examples of the former, see Zehra Fyzee, "Safarnama-i-Bhopal" and "Safar-i-Badauda" in *Mazamin*, 46–55, 114–30.

54. See Atiya's entry for September 17, 1906, in her *Zamana-i-Tahsil*. The translation is taken from Lambert-Hurley and Sharma, *Atiya's Journeys*.

55. See Nazli's entry for May 9, 1908, in her *Sair-i-Yurop*. As noted previously, the translation will be available in an edited and annotated version of this travelogue being prepared by Sunil Sharma and me.

56. See Atiya's entry for June 1, 1907, in her *Zamana-i-Tahsil*. The translation is taken from Lambert-Hurley and Sharma, *Atiya's Journeys*.

57. Dale, "Steppe Humanism," 39.

58. See Atiya's entry for August 5, 1907, in her *Zamana-i-Tahsil*. Also see Lambert-Hurley and Sharma, *Atiya's Journeys*, 57.

59. See Nazli's entry for May 18, 1908, in her *Sair-i-Yurop*.

60. For further development of this point, see my "To Write of the Conjugal Act," 160–61.

61. Sunil Sharma, "Delight and Disgust: Gendered Encounters in the Travelogues of the Fyzee Sisters," in *On the Wonders of Land and Sea*, ed. Roberta Micallef and Sunil Sharma (Boston: Ilex Foundation, 2013), 114; Majchrowicz, "Travel, Travel Writing, and the 'Means to Victory' in Modern South Asia," 139.

62. A rare transcript of Amina's speech, handwritten in Urdu for presentation on August 22, 1894, was consulted in the private collection of Rafia Abdul Ali in Mumbai.

63. For this context, see "Manuscript Memoirs of Mrs. Safia Jabir Ali," 111.

64. A transcript of this speech, titled "Address by Mrs Safia Jabir Ali," was consulted in the private collection of her son, Amiruddin Jabir Ali, in Mumbai.

65. Ibid. I have corrected small spelling errors and punctuation in the original typescript.

66. "A Page from the Past," *Roshni*, Special Number 1946, 69–73.

244   *Notes to Chapter 5*

67. "Manuscript Memoirs of Mrs. Safia Jabir Ali," September 22, 1942.

68. Ibid.

69. Sálim Ali, *The Fall of a Sparrow*.

70. Ibid., 1.

71. Ibid., 13, 54, 63.

72. Ibid., chapter 21, "The Books I Wrote," and chapter 22, "Prizes." Also see Sálim Ali, *The Book of Indian Birds* (Bombay: Bombay Natural History Society, 1941).

73. Sálim Ali, *The Fall of a Sparrow*, 171, 219.

74. Ibid., 177.

75. Ibid., 3, 6, 162, 196.

76. Ibid., 93.

77. Ibid., 74–75, 86, 177.

78. Ibid., 170. On modesty in South Asian women's autobiography, see Malhotra and Lambert-Hurley, introduction to *Speaking of the Self*, 12–13.

79. Sálim Ali, *The Fall of a Sparrow*, 228.

80. Ibid., vii.

81. "Manuscript Memoirs of Mrs. Safia Jabir Ali," 56.

82. See, for example, Sálim Ali, *The Fall of a Sparrow*, 110–14, 127–28, 228–33, 240–47.

83. See, for example, ibid., 41–43; "Manuscript Memoirs of Mrs. Safia Jabir Ali," 184ff

84. Sálim Ali, *The Fall of a Sparrow*, 27.

85. Letter from Tehmina to Kamoo, June 23, 1927, quoted in Sálim Ali, *The Fall of a Sparrow*, 48.

86. For comparison, see Qaisari Begam's *Kitab-i-Zindagi*; and Kazim, *A Woman of Substance*, chapter 8, "On Shikar with Akbar."

87. Sálim Ali, *The Fall of a Sparrow*, 17–18.

88. Ibid., 26, 39–40.

89. "Manuscript Memoirs of Mrs. Safia Jabir Ali," March 4, 1943.

90. Sálim Ali, *The Fall of a Sparrow*, 87.

91. Ibid., 242.

92. On Shareefah Hamid Ali's involvement with the AIWC, see Basu and Ray, *Women's Struggle*, 188.

93. Shareefah Hamid Ali, "My Journey to America by Air" and "My Visit to America II."

94. Shareefah Hamid Ali, "Washington Diary III," and "Excursion to Mount Vernon."

95. Shareefah Hamid Ali, "My Journey to America by Air," 26.

96. Shareefah Hamid Ali, "My Visit to America II," 18–20.

97. Ibid., 19.

98. Ibid.

99. Shareefah Hamid Ali, "Excursion to Mount Vernon," 6–7.

100. Shareefah Hamid Ali, "Washington Diary III," 26.

101. For comparison, see Antoinette Burton, *At the Heart of the Empire: Indians and the Colonial Encounter in Late-Victorian Britain* (Berkeley: University of California Press, 1998), 46–47.

Notes to Chapter 5   245

102. Shareefah Hamid Ali, "My Journey to America by Air."

103. Raihana Tyabji, *Suniye Kakasaheb.*

104. Ved Mehta, *Mahatma Gandhi and His Apostles*; Usha Thakkar and Jayshree Mehta, eds., *Understanding Gandhi: Gandhians in Conversation with Fred J Blum* (Delhi: Sage, 2011).

105. I borrow this translation from Basu, *Abbas Tyabji*, ix.

106. Badruddin Tyabji, *Memoirs of an Egoist*, 2 vols. (New Delhi: Roli Books, 1988).

107. See, for example, Badruddin's passing mention of his youngest son in ibid., 23. One exception is his emotive account of the death of his elder brother, Saif, in 1957; ibid., 27.

108. "Part V: 1964–1967: Japan" provides the best evidence of this trend. Ibid., 196–278.

109. *Memoirs of an Egoist*, 86–90, 230–31, 266–68. For comparison, see Sálim Ali, *The Fall of a Sparrow*, 15, 157–58.

110. On political memoir, see George Egerton, ed., *Political Memoir: Essays on the Politics of Memoir* (London: Frank Cass, 1994).

111. "Retroblog of Najm Tyabji," http://nstyabji.wordpress.com/. Najm does quote from Badruddin's *Memoir* in a post titled "A Fling at Gliding and a Bit of Surveying," accessed May 13, 2014, http://nstyabji.wordpress.com/2009/01/18/a-fling-at-gliding-and -a-bit-of-surveying/.

112. Mark Devereux, "About This Blog," accessed May 13, 2014, http://nstyabji.word press.com/about-this-blog/.

113. I contacted the blog's creator to ascertain whether other auto/biographical sources were available, but received no response. According to Najm's sister, Rafia Abdul Ali, there were originally three volumes, but one was lost. Personal communication, December 16, 2005.

114. Salima Tyabji, for instance, proffered the identities of unnamed women in a photograph in a comment made on November 10, 2013, accessed May 13, 2014, http://nstyabji .wordpress.com/2008/11/30/the-tyabji-clan-and-a-bit-of-background/#comment-481.

115. Najm Tyabji, "The Tyabji Clan and a Bit of Background," accessed May 14, 2014, http://nstyabji.wordpress.com/2008/11/30/the-tyabji-clan-and-a-bit-of-background/.

116. Ibid.

117. Ibid.

118. Najm Tyabji, "The Early Tyabji Women," accessed May 14, 2014, http://nstyabji .wordpress.com/2008/12/07/the-early-tyabji-women/.

119. On women's travel writing "documenting the everyday," see Susan Bassnett, "Travel Writing and Gender," in Pete Hulme and Tim Youngs, eds., *The Cambridge Companion to Travel Writing* (Cambridge: Cambridge University Press, 2002), 229–30.

120. Najm Tyabji, "Off to England," "'Miss Knight' and the Motorcycle," "Hamida and Latin Issues," "City and Guilds College plus Summer Vacation (1934)," "A Happy Reunion and the Bavarian Alps," "A Fling at Gliding and a Bit of Surveying," "Yorkshire Pudding and Engineering," "Romantic Summer," and "The End of an Era," accessed May 14, 2014, http://nstyabji.wordpress.com/. For comparison, see Lambert-Hurley and Sharma, *Atiya's Journeys*, chapter 4, "Narrating the Everyday."

246   *Notes to Chapter 5*

121. Najm Tyabji, "'Miss Knight' and the Motorcycle," accessed 14 May 2014, http://nstyabji.wordpress.com/2008/12/21/miss-knight-and-the-motorcycle/.

122. "Manuscript Memoirs of Mrs. Safia Jabir Ali," 112–13. For a fuller translation, see Tyabji, *Changing World*, 138–39. I have discussed Safia Jabir Ali's telling of her marriage in more detail in my "To Write of the Conjugal Act," 173–74.

123. Sálim Ali, *The Fall of a Sparrow*, 33–36.

124. Najm Tyabji, "Hamida and Latin Issues," accessed 14 May 2014, http://nstyabji.wordpress.com/2008/12/25/hamida_and_latin_issues/.

125. Najm Tyabji, "Romantic Summer," accessed May 14, 2014, http://nstyabji.wordpress.com/2009/02/01/romantic-summer/.

126. Ibid.

127. Ibid.

128. Najm Tyabji, "The Journey Home," accessed May 14, 2014, http://nstyabji.wordpress.com/2009/03/22/the-journey-home/.

129. Laila Tyabji, "Amma—Recipes for a Family," in "Second Nature: Women and the Family," *IIC Quarterly* 23, nos. 3 and 4 (Winter 1996): 40–53.

130. Ibid., 41–42, 44–45, 48.

131. Ibid., 45, 49.

132. Ibid., 49.

133. Ibid.

134. Lambert-Hurley and Sharma, *Atiya's Journeys*, 90.

135. Laila Tyabji, "Amma—Recipes for a Family," 43, 52.

136. Ibid., 49.

137. Ibid., 51.

138. Sohaila Abdulali, "I Fought for My Life . . . and Won," *Manushi* 16 (June–July 1983: 18–19.

139. Ibid., 18.

140. Ibid., 19.

141. Sohaila Abdulali, "I Was Wounded; My Honor Wasn't," *New York Times*, January 7, 2013.

142. Ibid.; Sohaila Abdulali, "After I Wrote about My Rape, Again," *Guardian*, July 14, 2013.

143. I draw here on Azadeh Moaveni, who explained in a discussion at the University of Virginia at Charlottesville in October 2012 how despite being a respected journalist, she was still encouraged to pitch her book, *Lipstick Jihad: A Memoir of Growing Up Iranian in America and American in Iran* (New York: PublicAffairs, 2005), on Iran's "rebellious next generation," as a memoir.

144. One exception is the travelogue written by the wife of legal scholar Asaf A. A. Fyzee, Sultana Asaf Fyzee, about her travels in Egypt: *'Urus-i-Nil* (New Delhi: Maktaba Jamia, 1967). More recently, Sohaila Abdulali also received funding from the Ford Foundation to write her own story into a social ethnography of aboriginal women in Karjat, Maharashtra, to be titled *Bye Bye Mati: A Memoir in a Monsoon Landscape*. A short excerpt appears on her website: http://sohailaink.com/mati_excerpt.html. How-

ever, according to a personal communication from the author, the project was never completed.

145. Laila Tyabji retains a high profile in the Indian press, but her best-known book is *Threads and Voices: Behind the Indian Textile Tradition* (Delhi: Marg, 2007). Academic outputs include Yasmeen Lukmani's *The Shifting Worlds of Kiran Nagarkar's Fiction* (New Delhi: Indialog, 2004). Recent novels include Sohaila Abdulali's *The Madwoman of Jogare* (Delhi: HarperCollins India, 1999) and *Year of the Tiger* (Delhi: Penguin, 2010). Her writings for children include the *RangBibi and Langra* series. For food writing, see Surayya Tyabji, *Mirch Masala*.

146. The Tyabji family website is accessible at tyabji.net. For a Tyabji Twitter feed, see Judi Tyabji@JudiTyabji. Laila Tyabji often writes in an autobiographical mode on Facebook. Salima Tyabji was especially interested in earlier writings within the family. See her *The Changing World of a Bombay Muslim Community, 1870–1945*.

147. Conversation with Rafia Abdul Ali at her home in Bombay, December 16, 2005.

148. This label is borrowed from Smith and Watson's introduction to their *Women, Autobiography, Theory*, 18.

149. Jelinek, *Women's Autobiography*, 10.

150. Ibid.; Hansen, *Stages of Life*, 299–314.

151. Jelinek, *Women's Autobiography*, 16–17.

152. Ibid., 15.

153. For a development of this point, see Malhotra and Lambert-Hurley, introduction to *Speaking of the Self*, 13.

154. Pascal, *Design and Truth in Autobiography*, 14.

155. Tucker, "Biography as History," 11.

156. Arnold and Blackburn, introduction to their edited volume, *Telling Lives in India*, 20–21.

CODA

1. This episode is evoked in innumerable books and articles on "women in Islam." Representative is Kumari Jayawardena's *Feminism and Nationalism in the Third World* (London: Zed Books, 1986), 54.

2. Huda Shaarawi, *Harem Years*, 7.

3. This episode is also evoked in Jayawardena's *Feminism and Nationalism*, 72, but the quotation is taken from an article titled "Soraya Tarzi: The Afghan Queen," in the special series "Leading Ladies" in *Dawn*, January 29, 2012, accessed May 25, 2016, http://www.dawn.com/news/691638/leading-ladies-soraya-tarzi-the-afghan-queen.

4. The following is again representative: Jayawardena, *Feminism and Nationalism*, 68–70.

5. Lambert-Hurley, *Muslim Women, Reform and Princely Patronage*, 102.

6. Jahan Ara Shahnawaz, *Father and Daughter*, 56–57.

7. Other female authors pointed to a similar process and set of justifications. Hameeda Akhtar Husain Raipuri, for instance, noted that her father did not want her mother, her, or her sisters to observe purdah, instead expecting them to mix with company and partici-

248   *Notes to Coda*

pate in conversations (*Hamsafar*, 22). Shaukat Kaifi, too, noted that it was at her father's insistence that her mother packed away her burqa on the platform of the Delhi railway station soon after their marriage (*Yad ki Rahguzar*, 27).

8. "Court Circular," *Times* (London), December 12, 1894.

9. Lambert-Hurley and Sharma, *Atiya's Journeys*, 151.

10. Nazli, *Sair-i-Yurop*, 260–62.

11. Lambert-Hurley and Sharma, *Atiya's Journeys*, 151.

12. Ibid., 24–26, 37, 125, 189, 205.

13. Nazli, *Sair-i-Yurop*, 57–58. As noted previously, the translation will be available in an edited and annotated version of this travelogue being prepared by Sunil Sharma and me.

14. Abida Sultaan, *Memoirs of a Rebel Princess*, 63, 72.

15. Milani, *Words, Not Swords*, xix.

16. Arnold and Blackburn, introduction to *Telling Lives in India*, 15.

17. For a development of this point, see Malhotra and Lambert-Hurley, introduction to *Speaking of the Self*, 9–10.

18. Hansen, *Stages*, 300–9.

19. For a development of this point, see Malhotra and Lambert-Hurley, introduction to *Speaking of the Self*, 8.

20. Arnold and Blackburn make the point that it is an assumption "informing much current life-history research" that "these accounts of personal lives reflect *culture-specific* notions of the person or self"; introduction to *Telling Lives in India*, 4. Italics added.

21. I am grateful to Sana Haroon for encouraging me to draw out this point at a seminar at Boston University in April 2013.

22. Jobeda Khanam, *Jiban Khatar Pataguli*, 26–27.

23. The last reference to her observing purdah comes in a section in which she records wearing a burqa while working at two schools in her hometown of Kushtia as a young widow in the early 1940s. Ibid., 48–49.

BIBLIOGRAPHY

I. PERIODICALS
Begum (Dhaka)
Daily Star (Dhaka)
Dawn (Karachi)
Guardian (Manchester)
Hindu (Delhi)
Ismat (Delhi)
Manushi (Delhi)
New York Times
Roshni (Delhi)
Tahzib un-Niswan (Lahore)
Times (London)
Zebunnisa (Lahore)
Zill us-Sultan (Bhopal)

II. WORKS IN SOUTH ASIAN LANGUAGES
Note: Works in South Asian languages are arranged alphabetically according to the full name of the author. Hence, Abida Sultaan's work appears under *A*, not *S*, while Begam Sarbuland Jang's work appears under *S*, rather than *B* or *J*, since "Begam" is a title. "Sayyid," also a title, is treated the same way.

———. "*Akhbar ki Kitab*" from Matheran and Mahabaleshwar (1894–1907). Badruddin Tyabji Family Papers 4. Nehru Memorial Museum and Library, New Delhi, India.

———. "Akhbarnama-i-Ahmadganj-Murud-Jazira." Fyzee-Rahamin Archives, Karachi, Pakistan.

———. "Akhbarnama-i-Qabila-i-Shujauddin Tyabji." Fyzee-Rahamin Archives, Karachi, Pakistan.

———. "Badruddin Akhbar." Badruddin Tyabji Family Papers 4. Nehru Memorial Museum and Library, New Delhi, India.

———. "Kitab-i-Akhbar-i-Kihim-Yali." University of Mumbai Archives, Mumbai, India.

———. "Kitab-i-Amiri." Badruddin Tyabji Family Papers 4. Nehru Memorial Museum and Library, New Delhi, India.

Abid Hussain, Sayyid. *Hayat-i-Abid: Khudnavisht*. Delhi: Maktaba Jamia, 1984.

Abida Sultaan. *Ek Inqilabi Shahzadi ki Khud Navisht*. Karachi: Oxford University Press, 2007.

250   *Bibliography*

Ada Jafri. *Jo Rehi so Bekhabar Rehi: Khudnavisht*. Karachi: Daniyal, 1995.

Akhtar Husain Raipuri. *Gard-i-rah: Khudnavisht, Mutala'ah, Mushahadah*. Karachi: Maktaba-i-Afkar, 1984.

Akhtar Imam. *Amar Jiban Katha*. Dhaka: Unmesh Prakashan, 1993.

———. *Bileter Din Ghulo*. Dhaka: Unmesh Prakashan, 1997.

———. *Eden theke Bethun*. Dhaka: Akhtar Imam, 1990.

———. *Jemon Bhebechhi, Jemon Dekhechhi*. Dhaka: Akhtar Imam, 1981.

———. *Rokeya Halle Bis Bochhor*. Dhaka: Akhtar Imam, 1986.

Altaf Husain Hali, Khwaja. "Maulana Hali ki Khud-navisht Sawanih-i-'Umri." *Ma'arif* 19, no. 5 (May 1927): 344–51.

———. *Bayan-i-Hali*. Panipat: Shaikh M. Ismail Panipati, 1939.

Amina Tyabji. Speech to Akdé Suraya, handwritten in Urdu for presentation on August 22, 1894. Private collection of Rafia Abdul Ali, Mumbai.

Anis Kidwai. *Azadi ki Chhaon Mein*. New Delhi: National Book Trust, 1980.

———. *Azadi ki Chhaon Mein*. Translated by Noor Nabi Abbasi. Delhi: National Book Trust, 1978.

Asghar Husain, Sayyid. *Nurjahan Badshah Begam ki Sawanih-i-'Umri*. Agra: Agra Akhbar, 1903.

Atiya Fyzee. *Zamana-i-Tahsil*. Agra: Mufid-i-'Am, 1921.

Attiya Dawood. *Aine ke Samne*. New Delhi: Rajkamal Prakashan, 2004.

———. *Aine ke Samne: Khudnavisht*. Karachi: Oxford University Press, 2009.

Azra Abbas. *Mere Bachpan*. Karachi: Jadid Klasik Pablisharz, 1994.

Faizunnessa Chaudhurani, Nawab. *Rupjalal*. Edited by Mohammad Abdul Kuddus. Dhaka: Bangla Academy, 2004.

Hameeda Akhtar Husain Raipuri. *Hamsafar*. Karachi: Daniyal, 1992.

Hamida Khanam. *Johora Bokuler Gondho*. Dhaka: Shahitya Prakash, 2001.

Hamida Rahman. *Jiban Smriti*. Dhaka: Naoroze Kitabistan, 1990.

Hijab Imtiaz Ali. "Lail o Nihar." *Tahzib un-Niswan* (1941–42).

Humayun Mirza. *Meri Kahani Meri Zubani*. Hyderabad: Privately published, 1939.

Inam Fatima Habibullah. *Tasirat-i-Safar-i-Yurop*. N.p., n.d.

Inayat Allah. *Panc Mashhur Begamat*. Lahore: Nur Illahi, 1928.

Ismat Chughtai. *Kaghazi Hai Pairahan*. New Delhi: Publications Division, 1994.

———. *Kaghazi Hai Pairahan*. Transliterated into Devanagari by Iftikhar Anjum. Delhi: Rajkamal Prakashan, 1998.

Jahanara Haq. *Aparahner Sanglap*. Dhaka: Agami Prakashani, 1996.

Jahanara Imam. *Anya Jiban*. Dhaka: Dana, 1985.

Janjira, Nawab Begam of. "Sair-i-Yurop." *Ismat*, August 1908, 23–38.

Jobeda Khanam. *Ananta Pipasa*. Dhaka: Naoroja Kitabistana, 1967.

———. *Chotadera Ekankika*. Dhaka: Bangla Ekadami, 1963.

———. *Ekati Surera Mrtyu*. Dhaka: Adila Bradarsa, 1974.

———. *Jiban Khatar Pataguli*. Dhaka: Kathamala Prakashani, 1991.

———. *Mahasamudra*. Dhaka: Bangladesh Shishu Academy, 1977.

Jowshan Ara Rahman. *Smritikatha: Ekti Ajana Meye*. Dhaka: Nabajuga Prokashani, 2005.

Khurshid Alam, Sayyida. *Zakir Sahib ki Kahani: ap ki beti ke zubani*. Delhi: National Book Trust, 1975.

Kishwar Naheed. *Buri 'Aurat ki Katha: Khudnavisht*. New Delhi: Adab Publications, 1995.

Lalitambika Antarjanam. *Atmakathayku Oru Amukham*. Kottayam: Sahitya Pravarthaka Co-operative Society, 1979.

Lulu Rahman. "Jibaner Sarbattam Dinguli." In *Biddamoyee School Praktan Chatri Purnamilan Utsab 1999*, edited by Selina Bahar, 9. Mymensingh: Vidyamoyee School Prakton Chatri Samiti, 1999.

M. Abd al-Aziz, the Mother of. *Mu'avvin-i-Mashurat*. Hardoi: Matba'-i-Muraqqa'-i-'Alam, 1905.

M. Abd al-Qadir. *Sirat ul-Mamduh*. Edited by Maulavi Hidayat Muhayy al-Din. Agra: Mufid-i-'Am, 1906.

Maimoona Sultan. *Siyahat-i-Sultani*. Agra: Muhammad Qadir Ali Khan, n.d.

Masuma Begum. "A Day in Samarkand." *Roshni* (September 1959): 25.

Matia Chowdhury. *Dayal Diye Ghera*. Dhaka: Agami Prakashoni, 1995.

Muhammad 'Ilm al-Din Salih. *Dukhtaran-i-Hind*. Lahore: Malik House, 1935.

Muhammad Amin Zuberi. *Khutut-i-Shibli ba-nam-i-muhtarma Zahra Begum sahiba Faizi va 'Atiya Begum sahiba Faizi*. Bhopal: Zill us-sultan Buk Ejansi, 1930.

Muhammad Anwarul Haq. *Silsila-i-Sultaniya: Domestik Ikanomi*. 4 parts. Agra: Mufid-i-'Am, 1922.

Muhammad Husain Mahvi Siddiqi. *Azvaj ul-Anboya*. Bhopal: Nawab of Bhopal, 1916.

Muhammadi Begam. *Hayat-i-Ashraf*. Lahore: Rifah-i-'Am Press, 1904.

Mumtaz Wadud. "New York-er Bazaar." *Begum* 34 (April 4, 1982): 27.

Nafees Bano Shama. *Jannat se Nikali hui Hawwa: Ap Biti*. New Delhi: Abshar Publications, 1998.

Nalini Jameela. *Oru Laingikathozhilaliyude Atmakatha*. Kottayam: DC Books, 2005.

Nazli Rafia Sultan Nawab Begam Sahiba. *Sair-i-Yurop*. Lahore: Union Steam Press, n.d.

Nazr Sajjad Hyder. *Guzashta Barson ki Baraf*. Edited by Qurratulain Hyder. Delhi: Educational Publishing House, 2007.

———. "Roznamcha." *Tahzib un-Niswan*. Started in 45, no. 32 (August 8, 1942), 514.

Nilambur Ayisha. *Jeevitathinte Arangu*. Trivandrum: Women's Imprint, 2005.

Nilufer Khanam. "Amrika Smriti." Started in 34, no. 44 (August 15, 1982), 10.

Nishatunnisa Begam. *Begam Hasrat Mohani aur unke Khutut va Safarnama*. Delhi: Maulana Hasrat Mohani Foundation, 2015.

Nurunnahar Faizunnessa, ed. *Kaler Samukh Bhela*. Dhaka: Muktodhara, 1988.

Qaisari Begam. *Kitab-i-Zindagi*. Edited by Zahra Masrur Ahmad. Karachi: Fazli Sons, 2003.

Qamar Azad Hashmi. *Panchwan Chirag*. New Delhi: Safdar Hashmi Memorial Trust, 1995.

Qurratulain Hyder. *Kar-i-Jahan Daraz Hai*. Bombay: Fan aur Fankar, 1977.

———. "Sada-i-Absharan Az Faraz-i-Kehsar Amad." Introduction to Nazr Sajjad Hyder, *Guzashta Barson Ki Baraf*, 12–33. Edited by Qurratulain Hyder. Delhi: Educational Publishing House, 2007.

252 Bibliography

Rafia Khan. "Shadure Ja Dekhlam." *Begum* 34, no. 38 (June 20, 1982).

Rahil Begam Sherwani. *Safarnama-i-Bilad-i-Muqaddas* (1929).

———. *Zad us-Sabil* (1923).

Rahmat Ara Hossain. *Smriti*. Dhaka: Usha Art Press, 1996.

Raihana Tyabji. *Suniye Kakasaheb*. Wardha: Hindustani Pracher Sabha, 1954.

Saeeda Bano Ahmed. *Dagar se hat kar*. New Delhi: Sajad Publishing House, 1996.

Safia Jabir Ali. "Manuscript Memoirs of Mrs. Safia Jabir Ali." Badruddin Tyabji Family Papers 6. Nehru Memorial Museum and Library, New Delhi, India.

Saiyida Lutfunnessa. *Bibortoner Smirticharan*. Dhaka: Unmesh Prakashan, 1994.

Saliha Abid Hussain. *Safar Zindagi ke liye Soj o Saj*. New Delhi: Maktaba Jamia, 1982.

———. *Silsila-i-Roz o Shab Khudnavisht*. New Delhi: Maktaba Jamia, 1984.

Salima Rahman. "Bilet Deshta Matir." Started in 34, no. 39 (June 27, 1982), 16.

Salma Tasadduq Husain. *Azadi ki Safar: Tahrik-i-Pakistan aur Muslim Khawatin*. Lahore: Pakistan Study Centre, Punjab University, 1987.

Sarbuland Jang, Begam. *Dunya 'Aurat ki Nazar Mein*. Delhi: Khwaja Baruqi Press, 1910.

Shah Jahan Begam. *Tahzib un-Niswan wa Tarbiyat ul-Insan*. Delhi: Matba'-i-Ansari, 1889.

Shahr Bano Begam. *Bītī Kahāni, Urdu ki Awwālin Niswānī Khud Navisht*. Edited by Moinuddin Aqeel. Hyderabad, Pakistan: Allied Printing Corporation, 1995.

Shaista Ikramullah. *Dilli ki Khawatin ki Khavaten aur Muhavare*. Karachi: Oxford University Press, 2005.

———. *Parday say Parliament tak*. Karachi: Oxford University Press, 2004.

Shaista Suhrawardy. "Apna Ghar." *Ismat* 55, no. 4 (October 1935): 298–300.

———. "Holland ki Sair." *Ismat* 62, no. 5 (May 1939): 345–48.

Shamsun Nahar Khan. *Ekti Nimesh*. Dhaka: Anwar Ali Khan, 1985.

Shaukat Kaifi. *Yad ki Rahguzar*. New Delhi: Star Publications, 2006.

Shibli Nomani, Maulana. *Safarnama-i-Rum o Misr o Sham*. Lucknow: Anvar ul-Matabi', n.d.

Sufia Kamal. *Ekale Amader Kal*. Dhaka: Gyan Prakashani, 1988.

Sufia Khatun. *Jiban Nadir Banke Banke*. Dhaka: Papyrus, 2005.

Sughra Humayun Mirza. *Sair-i-Bhopal o Bengal*. 1914.

———. *Roznamcha-i-Safar-i-Bhopal*. Hyderabad: al-Nisa monthly, 1924.

———. *Safarnama-i-Iraq*. 1915.

———. *Safarnama-i-Yurop*. 2 vols. Hyderabad: 'Azim Press, 1926.

Sughra Mehdi. *Hikayat-i-Hasti: Ap Biti*. New Delhi: Modern Publishing House, 2006.

———. *Mekhanon ka Pata (Safarnama)*. Bhopal: Urdu Akademi, 2005.

———. *Sair Kar Dunya ki Ghafil . . . (Safarnama)*. New Delhi: Nayi Awaz, 1994.

Sultan Jahan Begam. *Akhtar-i-Iqbal*. Agra: Mufid-i-'Am, 1914.

———. "Diary of Sultan Jahan Begam." Unpublished manuscript in private collection of Princess Abida Sultaan of Bhopal, Karachi, Pakistan.

———. *Gauhar-i-Iqbal*. Bhopal: Matba'-i-Sultani, 1913.

———. *Hadiyat uz-Zaujain*. Madras: Weekly Newspaper Press, 1917.

———. *Hayat-i-Qudsi*. Bhopal: Matba'-i-Sultani, 1917.

———. *Hayat-i-Shahjahani*. Agra: Mufid-i-'Am, 1914.

———. *'Iffat ul-Muslimat.* Agra: Mufid-i-'Am, 1918.

———. *Rauzat ur-Riyahin.* Bhopal: Matba'-i-Sultani, 1909.

Sultana Asaf Fyzee. *'Urus-i-Nil.* New Delhi: Maktaba Jamia, 1967.

Taslima Nasreen. *Amar Meyebela.* Kolkata: People's Book Society, 1999.

———. *Ko.* Dhaka: Chardik, 2003.

———. *Sei Sob Ondhokar Din guli.* Kolkata: People's Book Society, 2004.

———. *Utal Hawa.* Kolkata: People's Book Society, 2002.

Tehmina Durrani. *Mere Aaka.* Delhi: Vani Prakashan, 2002.

Tyab Ali [Tyabjee Bhoymeeah]. "Sawanih Tyab Ali bin Bhai Miyan Baqalam Khud." In *The Autobiography of Tyabji Bhoymeeah: Merchant Prince of Bombay, 1803–1863,* 1–30, edited by Asaf A. A. Fyzee. Bombay: Government Central Press, 1964.

Ummat ul-Ghani Nurunnisa. *Safarnama-i-Hijaz, Sham o Misr,* Hyderabad: N.p., 1996.

Umratul Fazl. *Smritikatha Priyadiner Smriti.* Dhaka: Muktadhara, 1987.

Wahhaj al-Din Alvi. *Urdu Khud Navisht.* New Delhi: Maktaba Jamia, 1989.

Zafar Ali, Begam. *Mere Shab o Roz.* Srinagar, 1987.

Zakia Sultana Nayyar. *Bite Lamhe: Yadon ke Chiragh.* New Delhi: Modern Publishing House, 1995.

Zehra Fyzee. *Mazamin.* Agra: Mufid-i-'Am, 1921.

Zubaida Mirza. *Sei Je Amar Nana Ranger Dinguli.* Dhaka: Muktadhara, 1984.

III. AUTOBIOGRAPHICAL WRITINGS IN ENGLISH OR ENGLISH TRANSLATION

Abbas, Azra. *Kicking Up Dust.* Translated by Samina Rehman. Lahore: ASR Publications, 1996.

Abdulali, Sohaila. "After I Wrote about My Rape, Again." *Guardian,* July 14, 2013.

———. "Excerpt from *Bye Bye Mati: A Memoir in a Monsoon Landscape.*" http://sohailaink.com/mati_excerpt.html.

———. "I Fought for My Life . . . and Won." *Manushi* 3, no. 16 (June–July 1983): 18–19.

———. "I Was Wounded; My Honor Wasn't." *New York Times,* January 7, 2013.

Abdulla, Farida. "A Life of Peace and Dignity." In *Speaking Peace: Women's Voices from Kashmir,* edited by Urvashi Butalia, 262–67. Delhi: Kali for Women, 2002.

Aftab, Tahera, trans. and ed. *A Story of Days Gone By. A Translation of Bīti Kahāni: An Autobiography of Princess Shahr Bano Begam of Pataudi.* Karachi: Oxford University Press, 2012.

Afzal-Khan, Fawzia. *Lahore with Love: Growing Up with Girlfriends Pakistani-Style.* Syracuse, NY: Syracuse University Press, 2010.

Ahmed, Salma. *Cutting Free.* Karachi: Sama, 2002.

Ali, Sálim. *The Fall of a Sparrow.* Delhi: Oxford University Press, 1985.

Ali, Shareefah Hamid. "Excursion to Mount Vernon." *Roshni* 2, no. 9 (November 1947): 5–7.

———. "My Journey to America by Air." *Roshni* 2, no. 6 (July 1947): 23–28.

———. "My Visit to America II." *Roshni* 2, no. 7 (August 1947): 16–22.

———. "Washington Diary III." *Roshni* 2, no. 8 (October 1947): 23–26.

254   *Bibliography*

"Attia Hosain—Interview." Accessed January 10, 2010. http://www.harappa.com/attia/growingup.html.

Bano, Hameeda. "A View from Kashmir." In *Speaking Peace: Women's Voices from Kashmir*, edited by Urvashi Butalia, 171–77. Delhi: Kali for Women, 2002.

Bhopal, Nawab Sikandar, Begum of. *A Pilgrimage to Mecca.* Translated by Mrs. Willoughby-Osborne. London: Wm H. Allen, 1870.

———. *A Pilgrimage to Mecca.* Translated by Mrs. Willoughby-Osborne. Calcutta: Thacker, Spink, 1906.

Bhopal, Shah Jahan Begam of. *Taj ul Ikbal Tarikh-i-Bhopal or The History of Bhopal.* Translated by H. C. Barstow. Calcutta: Thacker, Spink, 1876.

Bhopal, Sultan Jahan, Begam of. *An Account of My Life (Gohur-i-Ikbal).* Translated by C. H. Payne. London: John Murray, 1912.

———. *An Account of My Life.* Vol. 1. Translated by C. H. Payne. London: John Murray, 1910.

———. *An Account of My Life.* Vol. 2. Translated by Abdus Samad Khan. Bombay: Times Press, 1922.

———. *Hayat-i-Qudsi: Life of the Nawab Gauhar Begum alias The Nawab Begum Qudsia of Bhopal.* Translated by W. S. Davis. London: Kegan Paul, Trench, Trubner, 1918.

———. *Hayat-i-Shahjehani: Life of Her Highness the Late Nawab Shahjehan Begum of Bhopal.* Translated by B. Ghosal. Bombay: Times Press, 1926.

———. *Muslim Home, Part 1: Present to the Married Couple.* Calcutta: Thacker, Spink, 1916.

———. *The Story of a Pilgrimage to Hijaz.* Calcutta: Thacker, Spink, 1909.

Bhutto, Benazir. *Daughter of Destiny: An Autobiography.* New York: Simon and Schuster, 1989.

———. *Daughter of the East.* London: Simon and Schuster, 1988.

Butenschon, Andrea. *The Life of a Mogul Princess.* London: George Routledge and Sons, 1931; reprint, Lahore: Sang-e-Meel Publications, 2004.

Chaudhurani, Sarala Debi. *The Scattered Leaves of My Life: An Indian Nationalist Remembers.* Translated by Sikata Banerjee. Delhi: Women Unlimited, 2009.

Chughtai, Ismat. "An Excerpt from *Kaghazi Hai Pairahan* (The 'Lihaf' Trial)." Translated by Tahira Naqvi and Muhammad Umar Memon. *Annual of Urdu Studies* 15 (2000): 429–43.

———. *Kaghazi Hai Pairahan [The paper attire].* Translated by Noor Zaheer. Karachi: Oxford University Press, 2016.

———. *A Life in Words: Memoirs.* Translated by M. Asaduddin. Delhi: Penguin Books, 2012.

Dasi, Binodini. *My Story and My Life as an Actress.* Edited by Rimli Bhattacharya. Delhi: Kali for Women, 1998.

Devika, J. *The Autobiography of a Sex Worker.* Chennai: Westland, 2007.

Durrani, Tehmina. *My Feudal Lord.* London: Bantam Press, 1994.

———. *My Feudal Lord: A Devastating Indictment of Women's Role in Muslim Society.* With William and Marilyn Hoffer. London: Corgi Books, 1995.

"The Final Goal Is Justice . . ." *Manushi* 6, no. 36 (September–October 1986): 2–6.

Forbes, Geraldine, and Tapan Raychaudhuri, eds. *The Memoirs of Haimabati Sen: From Child Widow to Lady Doctor*. Delhi: Roli Books, 2000.

Fyzee, Asaf A. A., ed. *The Autobiography of Tyabji Bhoymeeah: Merchant Prince of Bombay, 1803–1863*. Bombay: Government Central Press, 1964.

Fyzee, Atia H. "Yali (1898)." At "Accessing Muslim Lives." http://www.accessingmuslim lives.org/images/pdfs/Atiya%20Yali.pdf.

Goodyear, Sara Suleri. *Boys Will Be Boys: A Daughter's Elegy*. Chicago: University of Chicago Press, 2003.

"A Grand Old Lady of Music—An Interview with Asghari Begum Sagarwali." *Manushi* 3, no. 3 (March–April 1983): 8–10.

Gulbadan Begam. *The History of Humāyūn-Humāyūn-nāma*. Translated by Annette S. Beveridge. London, 1902.

Habib, Anjum Zamrud. *Prisoner No. 100: An Account of My Days and Nights in an Indian Prison*. Delhi: Zubaan, 2011.

Habibullah, Isha'at. "Investing in Pakistan's Future." *Dawn*, February 8, 2011. http://www .dawn.com/news/604702/investing-in-pakistans-future.

———. "Memories of the British and Feudal India." Parts 1–4. *Dawn*, September 1991, 6–27.

Habibullah, Jahanara. *Remembrance of Days Past: Glimpses of a Princely State during the Raj*. Karachi: Oxford University Press, 2001.

Hai, Yasmin. *The Making of Mr Hai's Daughter: Becoming British; A Memoir*. London: Virago, 2008.

Hasan, Saif Hyder, ed. *One Yesterday*. New Delhi: Rupa, 2004.

Hashmi, Qamar Azad. *The Fifth Flame: The Story of Safdar Hashmi*. Translated by Madhu Prasad and Sohail Hashmi. New Delhi: Penguin, 1997.

Hossain, Rokeya Sakhawat. *Sultana's Dream and Padmarag*. Translated by Barnita Bagchi. New Delhi: Penguin, 2005.

Huq, Farida. *Journey through 1971: My Story*. Dhaka: Academic Press and Publishers, 2004.

Hussain, Iqbalunnisa. *Changing India: A Moslem Woman Speaks*. Bangalore: Hossali Press, 1940.

Ikramullah, Shaista. *Behind the Veil*. Karachi: Oxford University Press, 1992.

———. *From Purdah to Parliament*. London: Cressat Press, 1963; Karachi: Oxford University Press, 1998.

Imam, Jahanara. *Of Blood and Fire: The Untold Story of Bangladesh's War of Independence*. Translated by Mustafizur Rahman. Dhaka: University Press, 1998.

"An Irrepressible Spirit—An Interview with Ismat Chughtai." *Manushi* 4, no. 19 (November–December 1983): 2–7.

Ishvani, *The Brocaded Sari*. New York: John Day, 1947.

Jahanara Begam. "Munis al-Arvah." Translated by Carl Ernst. At "Accessing Muslim Lives." http://www.accessingmuslimlives.org.

———. "Risala-i-Sahibiyah." Translated by Sunil Sharma. At "Accessing Muslim Lives." http://www.accessingmuslimlives.org.

256   *Bibliography*

Jameela, Nalini. "The Autobiography of a Sex-Worker." Unpublished manuscript. Translated by J. Devika.

———. *The Autobiography of a Sex Worker.* Translated by J. Devika. Chennai: Westland, 2007.

Kaifi, Shaukat. *Kaifi and I: A Memoir.* Edited and translated by Nasreen Rehman. New Delhi: Zubaan, 2010.

Kazim, Lubna, ed. *The Making of a Modern Muslim Woman: Begum Khurshid Mirza, 1918–1989.* Lahore: Brite Books, 2003.

———, ed. *A Woman of Substance: The Memoirs of Begum Khurshid Mirza.* Delhi: Zubaan, 2005.

———. Untitled speech. Presented at the conference to celebrate Rashid Jahan's birth centenary, Aligarh, November 27–28, 2005. Unpublished manuscript.

Khan, Bilquis Jehan. *A Song of Hyderabad: Memories of a World Gone By.* Karachi: Oxford University Press, 2010.

Khan, Mahmuduzzafar. *Quest for Life.* Delhi: People's Publishing House, 1954.

Kidwai, Anis. *In Freedom's Shade.* Translated by Ayesha Kidwai. Delhi: Penguin, 2011.

Koofi, Fawzia. *The Favored Daughter: One Woman's Fight to Lead Afghanistan into the Future.* With Nadene Ghouri. Basingstoke: Palgrave Macmillan, 2012.

Lambert-Hurley, Siobhan, and Sunil Sharma. *Atiya's Journeys: A Muslim Woman from Colonial Bombay to Edwardian Britain.* Part 2. A Time of Education. Delhi: Oxford University Press, 2010.

Latif, Bilkees. *Her India: The Fragrance of Forgotten Years.* New Delhi: Arnold-Heinemann Publishers (India), 1984.

Mai, Mukhtar. *In the Name of Honor: A Memoir.* With Marie-Thérèse Cuny. New York: Washington Square Press, 2006.

Masuma, Begam. "From behind the Veil—Into the Mainstream." Unpublished manuscript.

Mirza, Begum Khurshid. "The Uprooted Sapling." Unpublished manuscript.

———. "The Uprooted Sapling." *Herald* (August 1982–April 1983).

Moaveni, Azadeh. *Lipstick Jihad: A Memoir of Growing Up Iranian in America and American in Iran.* New York: Public Affairs, 2005.

Murshid, Noorjehan. "My Experience as an Editor of a Bangla Magazine." In *Infinite Variety: Women in Society and Literature,* edited by Firdous Azim and Niaz Zaman, 322–28. Dhaka: University Press, 1994.

Naim, C. M. "How Bibi Ashraf Learned to Read and Write." *Annual of Urdu Studies* 6 (1987): 99–115.

Piro. "Ik Sau Sath Kafian" [One hundred and sixty kafis]. Translated by Anshu Malhotra. At "Accessing Muslim Lives." http://www.accessingmuslimlives.org.

Pukhraj, Malka. *Song Sung True: A Memoir.* Translated by Saleem Kidwai. Delhi: Kali for Women, 2003.

Qaisari Begam. "Excerpts from *Kitab-e Zindagi.*" *Annual of Urdu Studies* 20 (2005): 232–41.

Rahmathunnisa Begam. "The Autobiography of Dr. Rahmathunnisa Begam." Unpublished manuscript.

Raipuri, Akhtar Husain. *The Dust of the Road*. Translated by Amina Azfar. Karachi: Oxford University Press, 2007.

Raipuri, Hameeda Akhtar Husain. *My Fellow Traveller: A Translation of* Humsafar. Karachi: Oxford University Press, 2006.

Rampur, Princess Mehrunissa of. *An Extraordinary Life*. Noida: Brijbasi Art Press, 2006.

Rashid, Sabrina Q. *Hajj: A Wonderful Experience; With a Guide to Hajj*. Dhaka: Islamic Foundation Bangladesh, 2005.

Rasul, Begam Qudsia Aizaz. *From Purdah to Parliament*. Delhi: Ajanta, 2001.

Riaz, Fahmida. *Reflections in a Cracked Mirror*. Translated by Aquila Ismail. Karachi: City Press, 2001.

Saiduzzafar, Hamida. *Autobiography*. Edited by Lola Chatterji. Delhi: Trianka, 1996.

Sayani, Kulsum. "The Trials of a Social Worker." In special issue, *Roshni* (1946): 87–91.

———. "Visit to Branches." *Roshni* 1, no. 8 (September 1946): 27–32.

Shah, Fatima. *Sunshine and Shadows: The Autobiography of Dr. Fatima Shah*. Lahore: Ferozsons, 1999.

Shahnawaz, Jahan Ara. *Father and Daughter: A Political Autobiography*. Lahore: Nigarishat, 1971; reprint, Karachi: Oxford University Press, 2002.

Shaikh, Ghulam Fatima. "The Changing Faith." *Friday Times* (Lahore) 22, no. 49 (January 21–27, 2011), http://www.thefridaytimes.com/21012011/page26.shtml.

———. *Footprints in Time: Reminiscences of a Sindhi Matriarch*. Translated by Rasheeda Husain. Karachi: Oxford University Press, 2011.

Shamsie, Kamila. "Kamila Shamsie on Applying for British Citizenship: 'I Never Felt Safe.'" *Guardian*, March 4, 2014.

Shamsie, Muneeza. "Discovering the Matrix." In *Critical Muslim 04: Pakistan?*, edited by Ziauddin Sardar and Robin Yassin Kassab, 165–76. London: Hurst, 2012.

———. "The Discovery of a Pakistani English Literature: A Personal Odyssey." *Dawn*, May 8, 2005.

———. "My Uncle and Me." Unpublished manuscript.

———. "My Uncle and Me." In *Strategy, Diplomacy, Humanity: Life and Work of Sahabzada Yaqub-Khan*, edited by Anwar Dil, 361. San Diego and Islamabad: Intercultural Forum, Takshila Research University, 2005.

———. "Women's Day speech." Unpublished manuscript, March 1999.

Shepard, Sadia. *The Girl from Foreign: A Search for Shipwrecked Ancestors, Forgotten Histories, and a Sense of Home*. New York: Penguin, 2008.

Sherwani, Amina. "Determined Resistance." *Manushi* 5, no. 28 (May–June 1985): 24.

Suleri, Sara. *Meatless Days*. Chicago: University of Chicago Press, 1987.

Sulima and Hala. *Behind the Burqa: Our Life in Afghanistan and How We Escaped to Freedom*. As told to Batya Swift Yasgur. Hoboken, NJ: Wiley, 2002.

Sultaan, Abida. *Memoirs of a Rebel Princess*. Karachi: Oxford University Press, 2004.

Talukdar, Mohammad H. R., ed. *Memoirs of Huseyn Shaheed Suhrawardy with a Brief Account of His Life and Work*. Dhaka: University Press Limited, 1987.

Thackston, Wheeler M., ed. *The Baburnama: Memoirs of Babur, Prince and Emperor*. New York: Modern Library, 2002.

258   *Bibliography*

———, ed. *The Jahangirnama: Memoirs of Jahangir, Emperor of India*. New York: Oxford University Press, 1999.

Tyabji, Amina. "A Page from the Past: Extracts from the Diary of Amina Binte Badruddin Tyabji." In special issue, *Roshni* (1946): 69–73.

Tyabji, Badruddin. *Memoirs of an Egoist*. 2 vols. New Delhi: Roli Books, 1988.

Tyabji, Laila. "Amma—Recipes for a Family." In "Second Nature: Women and the Family." Special issue, *IIC Quarterly* 23 (Winter 1996): 40–53.

Tyabji, Najm. "Retroblog of Najm Tyabji." http://nstyabji.wordpress.com/.

Tyabji, Raihana. *The Heart of a Gopi*. Poona: Miss R. Tyabji, n.d.

Yousafzai, Malala. *I Am Malala: The Girl Who Stood Up for Education and Was Shot by the Taliban*. With Christina Lamb. London: W&N, 2013.

Yusuf Ali, Abdullah. "The Indian Muhammedans: Their Past, Present and Future." *Journal of the Society of Arts* 55, no. 2825 (January 4, 1907).

Zafar, Shabnam. Untitled speech. Presented at the conference to celebrate Rashid Jahan's birth centenary, Aligarh, November 27–28, 2005. Unpublished manuscript.

Zoya. *Zoya's Story: An Afghan Woman's Struggle for Freedom*. With John Follain and Rita Cristofari. London: Review, 2002.

Zubeida Begum. "Relief or Repression?" *Manushi* (September–December 1987): 39–40.

IV. AUTOBIOGRAPHICAL FILMS

The House on Gulmohar Avenue. Directed by Samina Mishra. New Delhi: Public Service Broadcasting Trust, 2005. Available online at https://www.youtube.com/watch?v=cjvd6bvj2YA.

Shadows of Freedom. Directed by Sabina Kidwai. New Delhi: Public Service Broadcasting Trust, 2004.

V. SECONDARY WORKS

Abdulali, Sohaila. *The Madwoman of Jogare*. Delhi: HarperCollins India, 1999.

———. *Year of the Tiger*. Delhi: Penguin, 2010.

Adak, Hülya. "An Epic for Peace." In *Memoirs of Halidé Edib*, v–xxvii. Piscataway, NJ: Gorgias Press, 2005.

———. "National Myths and Self-Na(rra)tions: Mustafa Kemal's *Nutuk* and Halid Edib's *Memoirs* and *The Turkish Ordeal*." *South Atlantic Quarterly* 102, nos. 2/3 (January 2003): 509–28.

———. "Suffragettes of the Empire, Daughters of the Republic: Women Auto/biographers Narrate National History (1918–1935)." In "Literature and the Nation." Special issue, *New Perspectives on Turkey* 36 (May 2007): 27–51.

Aftab, Tahera. "An Introduction to Shahr Bano Begam's *Bītī Kahānī*." In *A Story of Days Gone By: A Translation of Bītī Kahānī: An Autobiography of Princess Shahr Bano Begam of Pataudi*, translated and edited by Tahera Aftab, 1–94. Karachi: Oxford University Press, 2012.

Ahmad, Riswan. "Shifting Dunes: Changing Meanings of Urdu in India." PhD diss., University of Michigan, 2007.

Ahmed, Leila. "Between Two Worlds: The Formation of a Turn-of-the-Century Egyptian Feminist." In *Life/Lines: Theorizing Women's Autobiography*, edited by Bella Brodzki and Celeste Schenck, 154–74. Ithaca, NY: Cornell University Press, 1989.

Ahmed, Talat. *Literature and Politics in the Age of Nationalism: The Progressive Episode in South Asia, 1932–56* (Delhi: Routledge, 2009).

Akyildiz, Olcay, Halim Kara, and Börte Sagaster. *Autobiographical Themes in Turkish Literature: Theoretical and Comparative Perspectives.* Würtzburg: Orient-Institute Istanbul, 2007.

Alam, Asiya. "Interrupted Stories: Self-Narratives of Nazr Sajjad Hyder." In *Speaking of the Self: Gender, Performance, and Autobiography in South Asia*, edited by Anshu Malhotra and Siobhan Lambert-Hurley, 72–94. Durham, NC: Duke University Press, 2015.

———. "Intimacy against Convention: Marriage and Romance in Syeda Bano's *Dagar se hat kar*." Paper presented at the 40th Annual Conference on South Asia, University of Wisconsin–Madison, October 21–23, 2011.

———. Introduction to Nazr Sajjad Hyder, *Roz-namcha* (1942). At "Accessing Muslim Lives." http://www.accessingmuslimlives.org.

Alavi, Hamza. "Pakistan and Islam: Ethnicity and Ideology." In *State and Ideology in the Middle East and Pakistan*, edited by Fred Halliday and Hamza Alavi, 64–111. New York: Monthly Review Press, 1988.

Ali, Qamar Jahan. *Princess Jahan Ara Begam: Her Life and Works.* Karachi: S. M. Hamid Ali, 1991.

Ali, Sálim. *The Book of Indian Birds.* Bombay: Bombay Natural History Society, 1941.

Altaf, Hasan. "Making Martyrs." *Guernica*, April 1, 2014. https://www.guernicamag.com/daily/hasan-altaf-making-martyrs/.

Amanat, Abbas. "The Changing World of Taj al-Saltana." In *Crowning Anguish: Memoirs of a Persian Princess from the Harem to Modernity*, edited by Abbas Amanat, 9–102. Washington, DC: Mage Publishers, 2003.

Arnold, David. "The Self and the Cell: Indian Prison Narratives as Life Histories." In *Telling Lives in India: Biography, Autobiography, and Life History*, edited by David Arnold and Stuart Blackburn, 29–53. Delhi: Permanent Black, 2004.

Arnold, David, and Stuart Blackburn, eds. *Telling Lives in India: Biography, Autobiography, and Life History.* Delhi: Permanent Black, 2004.

Asha, S. "The Intersection of the Personal and the Political: Huda Shaarawi's *Harem Years* and Leila Ahmed's *A Border Passage*." *IUP Journal of English Studies* 7, no. 2 (June 2012): 31–38.

"Attia Hosain." Accessed September 18, 2013. http://www.open.ac.uk/researchprojects/makingbritain/content/attia-hosain.

Auer, Blain. "Persian Historiography in India." In *Persian Prose outside Iran: The Indian Subcontinent, Anatolia, and Central Asia after Timur*, edited by John Perry and Sunil Sharma. London: I. B. Tauris, forthcoming.

Aziz, K. K. *Ameer Ali: His Life and Work.* Lahore: Publishers United, 1968.

Babayan, Kathryn. "In Spirit We Ate of Each Other's Sorrow: Female Companionship in Seventeenth Century Safavi Iran." In *Islamicate Sexualities: Translations across Temporal*

260   *Bibliography*

Geographies of Desire, edited by Kathryn Babayan and Afsaneh Najmabadi, 239–74. Cambridge, MA: Harvard Middle Eastern Monographs, 2008.

Badran, Margot. "Expressing Feminism and Nationalism in Autobiography: The Memoirs of an Egyptian Educator." In *De/Colonizing the Subject: The Politics of Gender in Women's Autobiography*, edited by Sidonie Smith and Julia Watson, 270–93. Minneapolis: University of Minnesota Press, 1992.

Banerjee, Swapna. *Men, Women, Domestics: Articulating Middle-Class Identity in Colonial Bengal*. Delhi: Oxford University Press, 2004.

Bano, Shadab. "Rashid Jahan's Writings: Resistance and Challenging Boundaries, *Angaare* and Onwards." *Indian Journal of Gender Studies* 19, no. 1 (February 2012): 57–71.

Bassnett, Susan. "Travel Writing and Gender." In *The Cambridge Companion to Travel Writing*, edited by Peter Hulme and Tim Youngs, 225–41.

Basu, Aparna. *Abbas Tyabji*. New Delhi: National Book Trust, India, 2007.

Basu, Aparna, and Bharati Ray. *Women's Struggle: A History of the All India Women's Conference, 1927–1990*. Delhi: Manohar, 1990.

Basu, Aparna, and Malavika Karlekar. *In So Many Words: Women's Life Experiences from Western and Eastern India*. Delhi: Routledge, 2008.

Bauman, Richard. *Story, Performance, and Event: Contextual Studies of Oral Narrative*. Cambridge: Cambridge University Press, 1986.

Benstock, Shari, ed. *The Private Self: Theory and Practice of Women's Autobiographical Writings*. Chapel Hill: University of North Carolina Press, 1988.

Bharadwaj, Vasudha. "Languages of Nationhood: Political Ideologies and the Place of English in 20th Century India." PhD diss., University of Rochester, 2010.

Bloch, Marc. *Apologie pour l'histoire ou métier d'historien*. Paris: Colin, 1974.

Bokhari, Afshan. "Between Patron and Piety: Jahān Ārā Begam's Sufi Affiliations and Articulations in Seventeenth-Century Mughal India." In *Sufism and Society: Arrangements of the Mystical in the Muslim World, 1200–1800*, edited by John J. Curry and Erik S. Ohlander, 120–42. Abingdon: Routledge, 2012.

———. *Imperial Women in Mughal India: The Piety and Patronage of Jahanara Begum*. London: I. B. Tauris, forthcoming.

———. "Masculine Modes of Female Subjectivity: The Case of Jahanara Begam (1614–1681)." In *Speaking of the Self: Gender, Performance, and Autobiography in South Asia*, edited by Anshu Malhotra and Siobhan Lambert-Hurley, 165–202. Durham, NC: Duke University Press, 2015.

Booth, Marilyn. "Locating Women's Autobiographical Writing in Colonial Egypt." In "Women's Autobiography in South Asia and the Middle East." Special issue, *Journal of Women's History* 25, no. 2 (2013): 36–60.

———. *May Her Likes Be Multiplied: Biography and Gender Politics in Egypt*. Berkeley: University of California Press, 2003.

———. "Reflections on Recent Autobiographical Writing in an Arab Feminist Vein." *Middle East Women's Studies Review* 15, no. 4 and 16, no. 1 (Winter/Spring 2001): 8–11.

———. "Who Gets to Become the Liberal Subject? Ventriloquized Memoirs and the

Individual in 1920s Egypt." In *Liberal Thought in the Eastern Mediterranean: Late 19th Century until the 1960s*, edited by Christoph Schumann, 267–92. Leiden: Brill, 2008.

———, ed. "Women's Autobiography in South Asia and the Middle East." Special issue, *Journal of Women's History* 25, no. 2 (Summer 2013).

Bose, Sugata, and Ayesha Jalal. *Modern South Asia: History, Culture, Political Economy*. 1st ed. London: Routledge, 1997.

Brass, Paul R. *Language, Religion, and Politics in North India*. Cambridge: Cambridge University Press, 1974.

Brodzki, Bella, and Celeste Schenk, eds. *Life/Lines: Theorizing Women's Autobiography*. Ithaca, NY: Cornell University Press, 1988.

Brown, F. H., revised by Jim Masselos. "Tyabji, Badruddin (1844–1906)." In *Oxford Dictionary of National Biography*. Oxford: Oxford University Press. Accessed June 23, 2006. http://www.oxforddnb.com/view/article/36600.

Brown, Judith M. "'Life Histories' and the History of Modern South Asia." *American Historical Review* 114, no. 3 (June 2009): 587–95.

Burton, Antoinette. "'An Assemblage/Before Me': Autobiography as Archive." *Journal of Women's History* 25, no. 2 (Summer 2013): 185–88.

———. *At the Heart of the Empire: Indians and the Colonial Encounter in Late-Victorian Britain*. Berkeley: University of California Press, 1998.

———. *Dwelling in the Archive: Women Writing House, Home, and History in Late Colonial India*. Delhi: Oxford University Press, 2003.

Butalia, Urvashi. *The Other Side of Silence: Voices from the Partition of India*. New Delhi: Penguin, 1998.

Chakravarti, Uma. *Rewriting History: The Life and Times of Pandita Ramabai*. Delhi: Kali for Women, 1998.

Chilkoti, Avantika. "Indian Publishing: The Pressures of English," January 21, 2014. Accessed January 24, 2014. http://blogs.ft.com/beyond-brics/2014/01/21/indian-publishing-the-pressures-of-english/#axzz2r48J4nkg.

Conway, Jill Ker. *When Memory Speaks: Exploring the Art of Autobiography*. New York: Vintage, 1998.

Cook, Blanche Weisen. "Biographer and Subject: A Critical Connection." In *Between Women: Biographers, Novelists, Critics, Teachers, and Artists Write about Their Work on Women*, edited by Carol Ascher, Louise de Salvo, and Sara Ruddick, 397–411. Boston: Beacon Press, 1984.

cooke, miriam. "*Ayyam min Hayati*: The Prison Memoirs of a Muslim Sister." *Journal of Arabic Literature* 26, nos. 1–2 (1995): 121–39.

———. *Nazira Zeineddine: A Pioneer of Islamic Feminism*. Oxford: Oneworld, 2010.

Cooper, Joanne E. "Shaping Meaning: Women's Diaries, Journals, and Letters—The Old and the New." *Women's Studies International Forum* 10, no. 1 (1987): 95–99.

Culley, Margo, ed. *American Women's Autobiography: Fea(s)ts of Memory*. Madison: University of Wisconsin Press, 1992.

Daftary, Farhad. "Professor Asaf A. A. Fyzee (1899–1981)." *Arabica* 31, no. 3 (1984): 327–30.

262 Bibliography

Dale, Stephen Frederic. *The Garden of the Eight Paradises: Bābur and the Culture of Empire in Central Asia, Afghanistan, and India, 1483–1530*. Leiden: Brill, 2004.

———. "Steppe Humanism: The Autobiographical Writings of Zahir al-Din Muhammad Babur, 1483–1530." *International Journal of Middle East Studies* 22 (1990): 37–58.

Datla, Kavita. *The Language of Secular Islam: Urdu Nationalism and Colonial India*. Honolulu: University of Hawai'i Press, 2013.

Datta, Amaresh. *Encyclopedia of Indian Literature*. Delhi: Sahitya Akademi, 1988.

Devika, J., ed. *Her-Self: Gender and Early Writings of Malayalee Women*. Kolkata: Stree, 2005.

Devji, Faisal. "Gender and the Politics of Space: The Movement for Women's Reform in Muslim India, 1857–1900." *South Asia* 14, no. 1 (1991): 141–53.

"Dr. Fatima Shah Passes Away." *Dawn*, October 13, 2002.

Egerton, George, ed. *Political Memoir: Essays on the Politics of Memoir*. London: Frank Cass, 1994.

Eickelman, Dale, and James Piscatori, eds. *Muslim Travellers: Pilgrimage, Migration, and the Religious Imagination*. London: Routledge, 1990.

Elahi, Mohsin Maqbool. "Review: A Princess with Taste." *Dawn*, July 18, 2004.

Erdman, Joan L. *Patrons and Performers in Rajasthan: The Subtle Tradition*. Delhi: Chanakya, 1985.

———. *Stages: The Art and Adventure of Zohra Segal*. With Zohra Segal. Delhi: Kali for Women, 1997.

Farouqui, Ather, ed. *Redefining Urdu Politics in India*. Delhi: Oxford University Press, 2006.

Faruqi, Shamsur Rahman. "A Long History of Urdu Literary Culture. Part I: Naming and Placing a Literary Culture." In *Literary Cultures in History: Reconstructions from South Asia*, edited by Sheldon Pollock, 805–63. Berkeley: University of California Press, 2003.

Fay, Mary Ann, ed. *Auto/biography and the Construction of Identity and Community in the Middle East*. New York: Palgrave, 2001.

Finney, Brian. *The Inner I: British Literary Autobiography of the Twentieth Century*. London: Faber, 1985.

Folkenflik, Robert, ed. *The Culture of Autobiography: Constructions of Self-Representation*. Stanford, CA: Stanford University Press, 1993.

Forbes, Geraldine. *Women in Modern India*. Cambridge: Cambridge University Press, 2008.

Ghosh, Anindita, ed. *Behind the Veil: Resistance, Women, and the Everyday in Colonial South Asia*. Ranikhet: Permanent Black, 2006.

Ghosh, Subhasri. "Population Movement in West Bengal: A Case Study of Nadia District, 1947–1951." *South Asia Research* 34, no. 2 (2014): 113–32.

Gilmore, Leigh. "Limit-Cases: Trauma, Self-Representation, and the Jurisdictions of Identity." *Biography* 24, no. 1 (Winter 2001): 128–39.

Golley, Nawar Al-Hassan, ed. *Arab Women's Lives Retold: Exploring Identity through Writing*. Syracuse, NY: Syracuse University Press, 2003.

———. *Reading Arab Women's Autobiographies: Shahrazad Tells Her Story*. Austin: University of Texas Press, 2003.

Grace, Sherrill. "Theatre and the Autobiographical Pact: An Introduction." In *Theatre and Autobiography: Writing and Performing Lives in Theory and Practice*, edited by Sherrill Grace and Jerry Wasserman, 13–29. Vancouver: Talonbooks, 2006.

Green, Anna, and Kathleen Troup. *The Houses of History: A Critical Reader in Twentieth-Century History and Theory*. Manchester: Manchester University Press, 1999.

Gupta, Abhijit, and Swapan Chakravorty, eds. *Print Areas: Book History in India*. Delhi: Permanent Black, 2004.

Gusdorf, Georges. "Conditions and Limits of Autobiography." In *Autobiography: Essays Theoretical and Critical*, edited by James Olney, 28–48. Princeton, NJ: Princeton University Press, 1980.

Hansen, Kathryn. "Performing Gender and Faith in Indian Theatre Autobiographies." In *Speaking of the Self: Gender, Performance, and Autobiography in South Asia*, edited by Anshu Malhotra and Siobhan Lambert-Hurley, 255–80. Durham, NC: Duke University Press, 2015.

———. *Stages of Life: Indian Theatre Autobiographies*. Ranikhet: Permanent Black, 2011.

Hardy, Peter. *Muslims of British India* (Cambridge: Cambridge University Press, 1972).

Hasan, Farhat. "Presenting the Self: Norms and Emotions in Ardhakathanaka." In *Biography as History: Indian Perspectives*, edited by Vijaya Ramaswamy and Yogesh Sharma, 105–22. Hyderabad: Orient Blackswan, 2009.

Hasanat, Fayeza S., ed. *Nawab Faizunnesa's Rupjalal*. Leiden: Brill, 2008.

Heilbrun, Carolyn G. *Writing a Woman's Life*. New York: Ballantine Books, 1988.

Hirsch, Marianne. *Family Frames: Photography, Narrative, and Postmemory*. Cambridge, MA: Harvard University Press, 1997.

Holmes, Richard. *Dr Johnson & Mr Savage: A Biographical Mystery*. Flamingo, 2004.

Holroyd, Michael. "Our Friends the Dead." *Guardian*, June 1, 2002.

Hourani, Albert. *Arabic Thought in the Liberal Age, 1798–1939*. Oxford: Oxford University Press, 1962.

Hulme, Peter, and Tim Youngs, eds. *The Cambridge Companion to Travel Writing*. Cambridge: Cambridge University Press, 2002.

Humphreys, R. Stephen. *Islamic History: A Framework for Inquiry*. Rev. ed. Princeton, NJ: Princeton University Press, 1991.

Jaffer, Sadaf. "Queer Feminism in Islamicate South Asia: Ismat Chughtai on Social Justice." Paper presented at the Annual Conference on South Asia, University of Wisconsin at Madison, October 20, 2013.

Jayawardena, Kumari. *Feminism and Nationalism in the Third World*. London: Zed Books, 1986.

Jeffery, Patricia. *Frogs in a Well: Indian Women in Purdah*. London: Zed Books, 1979.

Jelinek, Estelle, ed. *Women's Autobiography: Essays in Criticism*. Bloomington: Indiana University Press, 1980.

Joshi, Sanjay. *Fractured Modernity: Making of a Middle Class in Colonial North India*. Delhi: Oxford University Press, 2001.

Kanjwal, Hafsa. "Placing Kashmir: Gender, Social Status, and Mobility in a Kashmiri Woman's Autobiography." Paper presented at the Feminist South Asia PreConference,

264 *Bibliography*

41st Annual Conference on South Asia, University of Madison at Wisconsin, October 2012.

Kapur, Jyotsna. "Putting Herself into the Picture: Women's Accounts of the Social Reform Campaign in Maharashtra, Mid Nineteenth to Early Twentieth Centuries." *Manushi* 56 (1990): 28–30.

Karlekar, Malavika. *Voices from Within: Early Personal Narratives of Bengali Women.* Delhi: Oxford University Press, 1993.

Karlitzky, Marlen. "The Tyabji Clan—Urdu as a Symbol of Group Identity." *Annual of Urdu Studies* 17 (2002): 187–207.

Kaviraj, Sudipta. "Writing, Speaking, Being: Language and the Historical Formation of Identities in India." In *Nationalstaat und Sprachkonflikte in Süd- und Südostasien,* edited by D. Hellmann-Rajanayagam and D. Rothermund, 25–65. Stuttgart: Steiner, 1992.

Khan, Danish. "Kulsum Sayani: A 'Rahbar' of Hindusthani." http://twocircles.net/2010 may15/kulsum_sayani_rahber_hindustani.html.

Khan, Farida Abdulla. "Other Communities, Other Histories: A Study of Muslim Women and Education in Kashmir." In *In a Minority: Essays on Muslim Women in India,* edited by Zoya Hasan and Ritu Menon, 149–88. Delhi: Oxford University Press, 2005.

Khan, Razak. "Minority Pasts: The Other Histories of a 'Muslim Locality,' Rampur, 1889–1949." PhD diss., Freie Universität Berlin, 2014.

———. "Purdah Politics: Rethinking Gender and Power in Princely India." Paper presented at the South Asia Conference, University of Wisconsin at Madison, October 20, 2013.

King, Christopher R. *One Language, Two Scripts: The Hindi Movement in Nineteenth Century North India.* New Delhi: Oxford University Press, 1994.

Kramer, Martin, ed. *Middle Eastern Lives: The Practices of Biography and Self-Narrative.* Syracuse, NY: Syracuse University Press, 1991.

Kumar, Raj. *Dalit Personal Narratives: Reading Caste, Nation and Identity.* New Delhi: Orient Blackswan, 2010.

Kumar, Sukrita Paul, and Sadique. *Ismat: Her Life, Her Times.* Delhi: Katha, 2000.

Kumar, Udaya. "Autobiography as a Way of Writing History: Personal Narratives from Kerala and the Inhabitation of Modernity." In *History in the Vernacular,* edited by Partha Chatterjee and Raziuddin Aquil, 418–48. Delhi: Permanent Black, 2008.

Lahiri, Tripti. "By the Numbers: Where Indian Women Work." *IndiaRealTime: Wall Street Journal,* November 14, 2012. http://blogs.wsj.com/indiarealtime/2012/11/14/ by-the-numbers-where-indian-women-work/.

"Laila Tyabji—The Keeper of Heritage." Accessed March 6, 2014. http://www.tehelka .com/laila-tyabji-the-keeper-of-heritage/.

Lal, Ruby. *Domesticity and Power in the Early Mughal World.* Cambridge: Cambridge University Press, 2005.

———. "Historicizing the Harem: The Challenge of a Princess's Memoir." *Feminist Studies* 30, no. 3 (Fall/Winter 2004): 590–616.

Lambert-Hurley, Siobhan. "Forging Global Networks in the Imperial Era: Atiya Fyzee in Edwardian London." In *India in Britain: South Asian Networks and Connections,*

1858–1950, edited by Susheila Nasta, 64–79. Basingstoke: Palgrave Macmillan, 2013.

———. "The Heart of a Gopi: Raihana Tyabji's Bhakti Devotionalism as Self-Representation." *Modern Asian Studies* 48, no. 3 (May 2014): 569–95.

———. *Muslim Women, Reform and Princely Patronage: Nawab Sultan Jahan Begam of Bhopal.* London: Routledge, 2007.

———. "Muslim Women Write Their Journeys Abroad: A Bibliographical Essay." In *Travel Writing in India*, edited by Shobhana Bhattacharji, 28–39. Delhi: Sahitya Akademi, 2008.

———. *A Princess's Pilgrimage: Nawab Sikandar Begum's "A Pilgrimage to Mecca."* New Delhi: Kali for Women, 2007.

———. "To Write of the Conjugal Act: Intimacy and Sexuality in Muslim Women's Autobiographical Writing in South Asia." *Journal of the History of Sexuality* 23, no. 2 (May 2014): 155–81.

Lambert-Hurley, Siobhan, and Sunil Sharma. *Atiya's Journeys: A Muslim Woman from Colonial Bombay to Edwardian Britain.* Delhi: Oxford University Press, 2010.

Lambert-Hurley, Siobhan, with Sunil Sharma and Daniel Majchrowicz, eds. *Anthology of Muslim Women Travelers.* Bloomington: Indiana University Press, forthcoming.

Lapidus, Ira M. *A History of Islamic Societies.* 2nd ed. Cambridge: Cambridge University Press, 2002.

Lejeune, Philippe. *L'autobiographie en France.* Paris: Colin, 1971.

———. *On Autobiography.* Edited by Paul John Eakin and translated by Katherine Leary. Minneapolis: University of Minnesota Press, 1989.

Lelyveld, David. *Aligarh's First Generation: Muslim Solidarity in British India.* Delhi: Oxford University Press, 1996.

Lionnet, Francoise. *Autobiographical Voices: Race, Gender, Self-Portraiture.* Ithaca, NY: Cornell University Press, 1989.

Lisiecka, Julia. "Re-reading Huda Shaarawi's *Harem Years*—Bargaining with Patriarchy in Changing Egypt." *SOAS Journal of Postgraduate Research* (2015): 46–58.

Lukmani, Yasmeen. *The Shifting Worlds of Kiran Nagarkar's Fiction.* New Delhi: Indialog, 2004.

Majchrowicz, Daniel. "Learning Arabic in a Hammam: Cultivating Islamic Sisterhood between Hyderabad and Syria." Paper presented at the Annual Conference on South Asia, University of Wisconsin at Madison, October 22, 2016.

———. "Travel, Travel Writing, and the 'Means to Victory' in Modern South Asia." PhD diss., Harvard University, 2015.

Majeed, Javed. *Autobiography, Travel, and Postnational Identity: Gandhi, Nehru, and Iqbal.* Basingstoke: Palgrave Macmillan, 2007.

Malhotra, Anshu. *Piro and the Gulabdasis: Gender, Sect, and Society in Punjab.* Delhi: Oxford University Press, 2017.

———. "Piro, Ik Sau Sath Kafian" [One hundred and sixty kafis]. At "Accessing Muslim Lives." http://www.accessingmuslimlives.org/images/pdfs/Piro%20160%20Kafis .pdf.

266   *Bibliography*

———. "Telling Her Tale? Unravelling a Life in Conflict in Peero's *Ik Sau Saṭh Kāfiaṅ* [*One hundred and sixty kafis*]." *Indian Economic and Social History Review* 46, no. 4 (2009): 572–73.

Malhotra, Anshu, and Siobhan Lambert-Hurley, eds. *Speaking of the Self: Gender, Performance, and Autobiography in South Asia*. Durham, NC: Duke University Press, 2015.

"Malika Takes a Final Bow." *Dawn*, February 15, 2004.

Mascuch, Michael. *Origins of the Individualist Self: Autobiography and Self-Identity in England, 1591–1791*. Stanford, CA: Stanford University Press, 1997.

Mason, Mary G. "The Other Voice: Autobiographies by Women Writers." In *Autobiography: Essays Theoretical and Critical*, edited by James Olney, 207–35. Princeton, NJ: Princeton University Press, 1980.

McKay, Elaine. "English Diarists: Gender, Geography, and Occupation, 1500–1700." *History* 90, no. 298 (April 2005): 191–212.

McLeod, John. "Marriage and Identity among the Sidis of Janjira and Sachin." In *India in Africa, Africa in India: Indian Ocean Cosmopolitans*, edited by John C. Hawley, 253–72. Bloomington: Indiana University Press, 2008.

Mehta, Ved. *Mahatma Gandhi and His Apostles*. Harmondsworth, Middlesex: Penguin Books, 1976.

Menon, Anasuya. "Courageous Act." *Hindu*, May 31, 2013. http://www.thehindu.com/features/friday-review/theatre/courageous-act/article4765841.ece.

Metcalf, Barbara D. "Islam and Power in Colonial India: The Making and Unmaking of a Muslim Princess." *American Historical Review* 116, no. 1 (February 1, 2011): 1–30.

———. "The Past in the Present: Instruction, Pleasure, and Blessing in Maulana Muhamad Zakariyya's *Aap Biitii*." In *Telling Lives in India: Biography, Autobiography, and Life History*, edited by David Arnold and Stuart Blackburn, 116–43. Delhi: Permanent Black, 2004.

———. "The Pilgrimage Remembered: South Asian Accounts of the Hajj." In *Muslim Travellers: Pilgrimage, Migration, and the Religious Imagination*, edited by Dale Eickelman and James Piscatori, 85–107. London: Routledge, 1990.

———. "Urdu in India in the 21st Century: A Historian's Perspective." *Social Scientist* 31, nos. 5/6 (May–June 2003): 29–37.

———. "What Happened in Mecca: Mumtaz Mufti's 'Labbaik.'" In *The Culture of Autobiography: Constructions of Self-Representation*, edited by Robert Folkenflik, 149–67. Stanford, CA: Stanford University Press, 1993.

Micallef, Roberta. "Identities in Motion: Reading Two Ottoman Travel Narratives as Life Writing." *Journal of Women's History* 25, no. 2 (2013): 85–110.

Middlebrook, Diane Wood. "Postmodernism and the Biographer." In *Revealing Lives: Autobiography, Biography, and Gender*, edited by Susan Groag Bell and Marilyn Yalom, 155–66. Albany: State University of New York Press, 1990.

Milani, Farzaneh. "Iranian Women's Life Narratives." *Journal of Women's History* 23, no. 2 (Summer 2013): 130–52.

———. "Veiled Voices: Women's Autobiographies in Iran." In *Women's Autobiographies in Contemporary Iran*, edited by William Hanaway, Michael Hillman, and Farzaneh

Milani, 1–16. Cambridge, MA: Center for Middle Eastern Studies, Harvard University, 1990.

———. *Veils and Words: The Emerging Voices of Iranian Women Writers.* Syracuse, NY: Syracuse University Press, 1992.

———. *Words, Not Swords: Iranian Women Writers and the Freedom of Movement.* Syracuse, NY: Syracuse University Press, 2011.

Minault, Gail. "Begamati Zuban: Women's Language and Culture." In *Gender, Language, and Learning: Essays in Indo-Muslim Cultural History*, 116–34. Ranikhet: Permanent Black, 2009.

———. "Purdah Politics: The Role of Muslim Women in Indian Nationalism, 1911–24." In *Separate Worlds: Studies of Purdah in South Asia*, edited by Hanna Papanek and Gail Minault, 243–61. Delhi: Chanakya Publications, 1982.

———. *Secluded Scholars: Women's Education and Muslim Social Reform in Colonial India.* Delhi: Oxford University Press, 1998.

———. "Shaikh Abdullah, Begam Abdullah and Sharif Education for Girls at Aligarh." In *Modernization and Social Change among Muslims in India*, edited by Imtiaz Ahmad, 207–36. New Delhi: Manohar, 1982.

———. "Urdu Women's Magazines in the Early Twentieth Century." *Manushi* 48 (September–October 1988): 2–9.

Mortimer, Mildred. "Assia Djebar's Algerian Quartet: A Study in Fragmented Autobiography." *Research in African Literatures* 28, no. 2 (Summer 1997): 102–17.

Murshid, Nazneen. "Noor Jehan Murshid, or a Power Woman." *Daily Star*, September 1, 2012.

Naim, C. M., trans. *Zikr-i-Mir: The Autobiography of the Eighteenth Century Mughal Poet: Mir Muhammad Taqi "Mir."* Delhi: Oxford University Press, 1999.

Najmabadi, Afsaneh. "A Different Voice: Taj os-Saltaneh." In *Women's Autobiographies in Contemporary Iran*, edited by William Hanaway, Michael Hillman, and Farzaneh Milani, 17–32. Cambridge, MA: Center for Middle Eastern Studies, Harvard University, 1990.

Naqvi, Tahira. "Ismat Chughtai—A Tribute." *Annual of Urdu Studies* 8 (1993): 37–42.

Neuman, Shirley, ed. *Autobiography and Questions of Gender.* London: Frank Cass, 1991.

Noorani, A. G. *Badruddin Tyabji.* Builders of Modern India. Delhi: Publications Division, Ministry of Information and Broadcasting, Government of India, 1969.

"Obituary: Kamila Tyabji." *Guardian*, June 15, 2004. http://www.theguardian.com/news/2004/jun/15/guardianobituaries.india.

Oesterheld, Christina. Review of *Mere Bachpan. Annual of Urdu Studies* 18 (2003): 593–600.

Olney, James, ed. *Autobiography: Essays Theoretical and Critical.* Princeton, NJ: Princeton University Press, 1980.

Orsini, Francesca, ed. *Before the Divide: Hindi and Urdu Literary Culture.* New Delhi: Orient Blackswan, 2010.

———. *Print and Pleasure: Popular Literature and Entertaining Fictions in Colonial North India.* Ranikhet: Permanent Black, 2009.

Panikkar, K. N. *Against Lord and State: Religion and Peasant Uprising in Malabar, 1836–1921.* Delhi: Oxford University Press, 1989.

268 *Bibliography*

Papanek, Hannah. "Purdah: Separate Worlds and Symbolic Shelter." *Comparatives Studies in Society and History* 15, no. 3 (June 1973): 289–325.

Pascal, Roy. *Design and Truth in Autobiography.* New York and London: Garland, 1985.

Passerini, Luisa. *Fascism in Popular Memory: The Cultural Experience of the Turin Working Class.* Cambridge: Cambridge University Press, 1987.

Pernau, Margrit. *Ashraf into Middle Classes: Muslims in Nineteenth-Century Delhi.* Delhi: Oxford University Press, 2013.

Peterson, Linda H. "Institutionalizing Women's Autobiography: Nineteenth-Century Editors and the Shaping of an Autobiographical Tradition." In *The Culture of Autobiography: Constructions of Self-Representation,* edited by Robert Folkenflik, 80–103. Stanford, CA: Stanford University Press, 1993.

———. *Traditions of Victorian Women's Autobiography: The Poetics and Politics of Life Writing.* Charlottesville: University Press of Virginia, 1991.

Plumber, Ken. *Telling Sexual Stories: Power, Change, and Social Worlds.* London: Routledge, 1995.

Porter, Roy, ed. *Rewriting the Self: Histories from the Renaissance to the Present.* London: Routledge, 1997.

Price, Leah. *How to Do Things in Victorian Britain.* Princeton, NJ: Princeton University Press, 2012.

Pritchett, Frances. "A Long History of Urdu Literary Culture. Part II: Histories, Performances, and Masters." In *Literary Cultures in History: Reconstructions from South Asia,* edited by Sheldon Pollock, 864–911. Berkeley: University of California Press, 2003.

Raheja, Gloria Goodwin, and Ann Grodzins Gold. *Listen to the Heron's Words: Reimagining Gender and Kinship in North India.* Berkeley: University of California Press, 1994.

Rajan, Rajeswari Sunder. *Real and Imagined Women: Gender, Culture and Postcolonialism.* London: Routledge, 1993.

Ramanujan, A. K. "The Ring of Memory: Remembering and Forgetting in Indian Literatures." In *A. K. Ramanujan: Uncollected Poems and Prose,* edited by Molly Daniels-Ramanujan and Keith Harrison, 83–100. New Delhi: Oxford University Press, 2001.

Ramaswamy, Vijaya. "Muffled Narratives: The Life and Times of Neelambakai Ammaiyar." In Ramaswamy and Sharma, *Biography as History,* 123–51.

Ramaswamy, Vijaya, and Yogesh Sharma, eds. *Biography as History: Indian Perspectives.* Hyderabad: Orient Blackswan, 2009.

Rao, C. Hayavando. *The Indian Biographical Dictionary.* Madras: Pillar, 1915.

Rege, Sharmila. *Writing Caste/Writing Gender: Narrating Dalit Women's Testimonios.* New Delhi: Zubaan, 2006.

Reynolds, Dwight F. *Interpreting the Self: Autobiography in the Arabic Literary Tradition.* Berkeley: University of California Press, 2001.

Robinson, Francis. *Islam and Muslim History in South Asia.* Delhi: Oxford University Press, 2000.

Rodgers, Susan, ed. *Telling Lives, Telling History: Autobiography and Historical Imagination in Modern Indonesia.* Berkeley: University of California Press, 1995.

Roy, Nilanjana S. "Giving a Voice to the Voiceless in India." *New York Times*, July 6, 2010. http://www.nytimes.com/2010/07/07/world/asia/07iht-letter.html.

Rugg, Linda Haverty. *Picturing Ourselves: Photography and Autobiography*. Chicago: University of Chicago Press, 1997.

Said, Edward. *Beginnings*. Baltimore: Johns Hopkins University Press, 1987.

Saksena, S. P., ed. *Indian Autobiographies*. Calcutta: Oxford University Press, 1949.

Sarkar, Mahua. *Visible Histories, Disappearing Women: Producing Muslim Womanhood in Late Colonial India*. New Delhi: Zubaan, 2008.

Sarkar, Tanika. *Words to Win: The Making of* Amar Jiban—*A Modern Autobiography*. New Delhi: Kali for Women, 1999.

Sen, Indrani. "'Cruel, Oriental Despots': Representations in Nineteenth-Century British Colonial Fiction, 1858–1900." In *India's Princely States: People, Princes, and Colonialism*, edited by Waltraud Ernst and Biswamoy Pati, 30–49. London: Routledge, 2007.

Sengupta, Indra, and Daud Ali. *Knowledge Production, Pedagogy, and Institutions in Colonial India*. Abingdon: Palgrave Macmillan, 2011.

Shaarawi, Huda. *Harem Years: The Memoirs of an Egyptian Feminist*. Translated and with an introduction by Margot Badran. London: Virago, 1986.

Sharma, Sunil. "Delight and Disgust: Gendered Encounters in the Travelogues of the Fyzee Sisters." In *On the Wonders of Land and Sea: Persianate Travel Writing*, edited by Roberta Micallef and Sunil Sharma, 114–31. Boston: Ilex Foundation, 2013.

Shastrapani, Mohsin, ed. *Professor Akhtar Imam Reception Volume*. Dhaka: Professor Akhtar Imam Reception Committee, 2001.

Sivaraman, Myththily. *Fragments of a Life: A Family Archive*. New Delhi: Zubaan, 2006.

Smith, Sidonie. *Subjectivity, Identity, and the Body: Women's Autobiographical Practices in the Twentieth Century*. Bloomington: Indiana University Press, 1993.

Smith, Sidonie, and Julia Watson, eds. *Women, Autobiography, Theory: A Reader*. Madison: University of Wisconsin Press, 1998.

———. *Reading Autobiography: A Guide for Interpreting Life Narratives*. 2nd ed. Minneapolis: University of Minnesota Press, 2010.

———, eds. *De/Colonizing the Subject: The Politics of Gender in Women's Autobiography*. Minneapolis: University of Minnesota Press, 1992.

"Soraya Tarzi: The Afghan Queen." Special series, "Leading Ladies," *Dawn*, January 29, 2012. http://www.dawn.com/news/691638/leading-ladies-soraya-tarzi-the-afghan-queen.

Spivak, Gayatri Chakravorty. "Can the Subaltern Speak?" In *Colonial Discourse and Postcolonial Theory: A Reader*, edited by Patrick Williams and Laura Chrisman, 66–111. New York: Harvester Wheatsheaf, 1993.

———. "The Rani of Sirmur: An Essay in Reading the Archives." *History and Theory* 24, no. 3 (1985): 247–72.

Srivastava, Gouri. *The Legend Makers: Some Eminent Muslim Women of India*. Delhi: Concept Publishing, 2003.

Stanley, Liz. *The Auto/biographical I*. Manchester and New York: Manchester University Press, 1992.

270   *Bibliography*

Stark, Ulrike. *An Empire of Books: The Naval Kishore Press and the Diffusion of the Printed Word in Colonial India*. Ranikhet: Permanent Black, 2007.

Steedman, Carolyn. *Dust*. Manchester: Manchester University Press, 2001.

Stoler, Ann Laura. "Colonial Archives and the Arts of Governance." *Archival Science* 2, nos. 1–2 (March 2002): 87–109.

Stover, Johnnie M. *Rhetoric and Resistance in Black Women's Autobiography*. Gainesville: University Press of Florida, 2003.

Suhrawardy, Shaista Akhtar Bano. *A Critical Survey of the Development of the Urdu Novel and Short Story*. Karachi: Oxford University Press, 2007.

Suhrawardy, Shaista Akhtar Banu. *A Critical Survey of the Development of the Urdu Novel and Short Story*. London: Longmans Green, 1945.

———. *Thacker's Indian Directory*. Calcutta: Thacker, Spink, 1885.

Thakkar, Usha, and Jayshree Mehta, eds. *Understanding Gandhi: Gandhians in Conversation with Fred J Blum*. Delhi: Sage, 2011.

Tosh, John. *The Pursuit of History*. 5th ed. Harlow: Pearson, 2010.

Towards Equality: Report of the Committee on the Status of Women in India. Delhi: Ministry of Education and Social Welfare, 1974.

"Tribute to Shaheed Janani." *Daily Star*, May 4, 2012.

Tucker, Judith E. "Biography as History: The Exemplary Life of Khayr al-Din al-Ramli." In *Auto/biography and the Construction of Identity and Community in the Middle East*, edited by Mary Ann Fay, 9–17. New York: Palgrave, 2001.

Tyabji, Laila. *Threads and Voices: Behind the Indian Textile Tradition*. Delhi: Marg, 2007.

Tyabji, Salima. *The Changing World of a Bombay Muslim Community, 1870–1945*. Margao: CinnamonTeal Publishing, 2013.

Tyabji, Surayya. *Mirch Masala: One Hundred Indian Recipes*. Bombay: Orient Longman, 1985.

Vatuk, Sylvia. "The Book of Life: A Collection of Family and Personal Reminiscences by a North Indian Muslim Woman." Paper presented at Women's Autobiography in Islamic Societies: Representation and Identity conference, American University Sharjah, October 29–31, 2011.

———. "Dr Zakira Ghouse: A Memoir." In *Muslim Portraits: Everyday Lives in India*, edited by Mukulika Banerjee, 109–27. New Delhi: Yoda Press, 2008.

———. "Hamara Daur-i Hayat: An Indian Muslim Woman Writes Her Life." In *Telling Lives in India: Biography, Autobiography, and Life History*, edited by David Arnold and Stuart Blackburn, 144–74. Delhi: Permanent Black, 2004.

———. "A Passion for Reading: The Role of Early Twentieth-Century Urdu Novels in the Construction of an Individual Female Identity in 1930s Hyderabad." In *Speaking of the Self*, 33–55.

Venkatachalapathy, A. R. "Making a Modern Self in Colonial Tamil Nadu." In *Biography as History: Indian Perspectives*, edited by Vijaya Ramaswamy and Yogesh Sharma, 30–52. Hyderabad: Orient Blackswan, 2009.

Ivon Grunebaum, Gustave E. "Self-Expression: Literature and History." In *Medieval Islam*. 2nd ed. Chicago: University of Chicago Press, 1952.

Washbrook, David. "'To Each a Language of His Own': Language, Culture, and Society in Colonial India." In *Language, History, and Class*, edited by Penelope J. Corfield, 179–203. Oxford: Basil Blackwell, 1991.

Waterfield, Henry. *Memorandum on the Census of British India, 1871–72*. London: Eyre and Spottiswoode, 1875.

Whitlock, Gillian. *The Intimate Empire: Reading Women's Autobiography*. London: Cassell, 2000.

———. *Soft Weapons: Autobiography in Transit*. Chicago: University of Chicago Press, 2007.

Woolf, Virginia. *A Room of One's Own*. London: Penguin Classics, 2000.

Wright, Jr., Theodore P. "Muslim Kinship and Modernization: The Tyabji Clan of Bombay." In *Family, Kinship, and Marriage among Muslims in India*, edited by Imtiaz Ahmad, 217–38. Delhi: Manohar, 1976.

Yaqin, Amina. "Autobiography and Muslim Women's Lives." *Journal of Women's History* 25, no. 2 (Summer 2013): 171–84.

———. "Intertextuality of Women in Urdu Literature: A Study of Fahmida Riaz and Kishwar Naheed." PhD diss., University of London, 2001.

Young, Shahla Rahman. "Changing Women's Lives: A Study of Government Schools for Girls in Late Colonial Bengal." PhD diss., University of London, 2012.

Youngs, Tim, ed. *Travel Writing in the Nineteenth Century: Filling the Blank Spaces*. London: Anthem, 2006.

Zaidi, Ali Jawad. *A History of Urdu Literature*. Delhi: Sahitya Akademi, 1993.

Zonis, Marvin. "Autobiography and Biography in the Middle East: A Plea for Psychopolitical Studies." In *Middle Eastern Lives: The Practices of Biography and Self-Narrative*, edited by Martin Kramer, 60–88. Syracuse, NY: Syracuse University Press, 1991.

VI. PERSONAL COMMUNICATIONS

Amiruddin Jabir Ali, January 5, 2005.

Arif Zaman, London, April 27, 2007.

Geraldine Forbes, May 23, 2014.

Irfan Husain, London, September 12, 2006.

J. Devika, Trivandrum, December 24, 2005.

Laila Tyabji, Delhi, April 3, 2006.

Lubna Kazim, between Aligarh and Delhi, November 28, 2005.

Muneeza Shamsie, Delhi, April 7, 2006.

Nasir Tyabji, by e-mail, May 10 and 22, 2015.

Nazneen Nizami, Delhi, December 9, 2005.

Neshat Quaisar, Delhi, November, 2005.

Rafia Abdul Ali, Mumbai, December 16, 2005.

Rani Ray, Delhi, March 1, 2006.

Ritu Menon, Delhi, February 1, 2006.

Sabiha Hussain, Delhi, February 6, 2006.

Sakina Hassan, Delhi, February 13, 2006.

Salima Tyabji, Delhi, November 29, 2005, February 3, 2006, and February 10, 2006.

272   *Bibliography*

Samina Misra, Delhi, November 22, 2005.
Shahana Raza, by e-mail, March 15, 2016.
Shahla Haidar, Delhi, December 10, 2005, and April 10, 2006.
Shikha Sen, Delhi, February 8, 2006.
Sohaila Abdulali, by e-mail, September 7, 2015.
Sonia Amin, Dhaka, January 15, 2006.
Sughra Mehdi, Delhi, February 18, 2006.
Yunus Jaffery, Delhi, November 21, 2005, and December 2, 2005.

INDEX

Abbas, Azra *see* Azra Abbas

Abdulali, Sohaila 183–84, 246n144, 247n145

Abid Hussain, Sayyid 156

Abida Sultaan 26, 44, 60, 71, 89, 155, 191–92, 202n43, 211n71, 214n116, 237n67

Ada Jafri 86

Adak, Hülya 20

Afghanistan 12, 58, 60, 189–90

Aftab, Tahera 54, 118, 135

Afzal-Khan, Fawzia 83, 220n104

Agra 33, 110, 138

Ahmed, Salma 61, 65, 89, 227n25

akhbar books 24, 44–45, 120, 159, 160–64, 166, 173, 177, 178, 184, 185, 186, 211n77, 241n21, 242n31, 242n32

Akhtar Husain Raipuri 47, 51, 156

Akhtar Imam 63, 81–82, 106–7, 219n88, 220n104

Alavi, Hamza 93

Ali Jawad Zaidi 40

Ali, Sálim 158, 169–73, 174, 177–78, 180

Ali, Shareefah Hamid *see* Shareefah Hamid Ali

Aligarh 38, 48, 52, 63, 64, 73, 83, 85, 104, 121, 129, 139, 140, 143, 144, 145, 146, 212n80

All Pakistan Women's Association 91, 141

Allahabad 12, 64

All-India Women's Conference 76, 113, 174

Altaf Husain Hali, Khwaja 54, 156

Anand, Mulk Raj 41

Anis Kidwai 50, 62, 88, 228n54

Anjuman-i-Khawatin-i-Islam (All-India Muslim Ladies' Conference) 104

Arabic ix, 15, 35, 113, 207n106

archive, the 21, 25–27, 30, 31–32, 38–9, 39–45, 55, 117, 178, 211n77, 226n15, 242n31

Arnold, David 3, 17, 18, 54, 187, 248n20

Asghari Begum Sagarwali 45

ashraf 63–64, 67, 71, 74, 77, 92–94, 121, 158

Ashrafunnisa Begam 35, 68, 80, 105, 129, 212n80

Atiya Fyzee *see* Fyzee, Atiya

Attia Hossain *see* Hossain, Attia

Attiya Dawood 86, 106, 237n67

Autobiography (Hamida Saiduzzafar) 61, 155

Azadi ki Chhaon Mein (Anis Kidwai) 50, 62

Azmi, Shabana *see* Shabana Azmi

Azra Abbas 86–87

Babur, Zahiruddin Muhammad 3, 14, 15, 156

The Baburnama (Babur) *see* Vaqa'i' (Babur)

Badran, Margot 7, 20, 189, 206n97, 236n48

Bangladesh 1, 6, 9, 12, 23, 25, 26, 40, 51, 57, 62, 71, 75, 81, 82, 86, 88, 92, 99, 101, 105, 108, 134, 194, 210n52, 224n175. *See also* Dhaka

Bano, Hameeda *see* Hameeda Bano

Baroda 65, 79, 97, 102, 103, 106, 163, 168

Begum (Dhaka) 45, 212n80, 235n25

273

274   *Index*

Bengal 1, 9, 11, 19, 35, 54, 61, 62, 63, 64, 65, 69–70, 71, 72, 74, 81–84, 99–100, 102, 108, 133–34, 142, 178, 194, 199n1, 216n33. *See also* Calcutta
Bengal, Nawab Ali Vardi Khan of 35
Bengali ix, 6, 40, 51, 63, 69, 72, 102, 108–9, 122, 129, 134, 200n22, 212n80
Beveridge, Annette 33, 135
bhakti 11, 42, 176
Bhopal 6, 26, 29, 32, 35, 36, 39, 44, 49, 59, 60, 66, 70, 73–74, 76, 77–78, 79, 90, 100, 102–3, 104, 111, 117, 121, 138, 155, 191, 227n25
Bhopal, Nawab Shah Jahan Begam of *see* Shah Jahan Begam
Bhopal, Nawab Sikandar Begam of *see* Sikandar Begam
Bhopal, Qudsia Begam of *see* Qudsia Begam
Bhopal, Sultan Jahan Begam of *see* Sultan Jahan Begam
Bhutto, Benazir 86, 231n106
Bibi Ashraf *see* Ashrafunnisa Begam
Bilquis Jehan Khan 60, 74, 112, 227n29, 237n67
biography 14, 16, 18, 30, 33–36, 38, 49, 51–53, 78, 153, 236n55
Blackburn, Stuart 3, 17, 18, 54, 187, 248n20
Bohra Muslims 42, 105–6, 158, 169, 176–77, 186
Bombay ix, 6, 13, 23, 24, 26, 39, 42, 45, 60, 64, 65, 73, 76, 85, 88, 97, 100, 105–6, 109, 112, 113, 115, 116, 120, 121, 136, 140, 157–61, 163, 169, 172–73, 174, 176, 183–84, 190, 192
Britain 43, 46, 60, 61, 64, 74–75, 126, 130, 163, 167, 191, 220n104. *See also* England
British Library, The 31–32, 34–38, 128
Burma 116, 136, 169, 171–73, 202n43
Burton, Antoinette 16, 27, 30, 32, 39, 41, 44, 126, 176

Butalia, Urvashi 138

Calcutta ix, 4, 6, 54, 64, 69, 72–73, 81–82, 90, 100, 102, 111, 114, 190, 194
Canada 178, 181
Chand Bibi 35
Chughtai, Ismat 41–42, 45, 65, 74, 85, 103, 104, 106, 112, 130–31, 142
Conway, Jill Ker 30, 31
Cooper, Jilly 114
Cooper, Joanne 43

Dagar se hat kar (Saeeda Bano Ahmed) 90
Dale, Stephen F. 15
Dalits 19, 105
dance 12, 74, 89, 90, 91, 137
Dasi, Binodini 142
Dehra Dun 12, 25, 79, 173
Delhi 6, 23, 25, 26, 35, 38, 39, 40, 42, 43, 45, 48, 50, 53, 59, 60, 74, 83, 90, 92, 100, 106, 110, 114, 117, 118, 121, 125, 129, 131, 137, 139, 146, 150, 181, 183, 184, 207n103, 207n104, 228n54
Delhi gang rape case 183–84
Derrida, Jacques 31
Devika, J. 48
Devji, Faisal 5
Dhaka 5, 6, 23, 26, 39, 40, 45, 64, 69, 71, 72, 73, 81–83, 90–91, 100, 101–2, 106, 107, 109, 121, 134
diaries 2, 4, 21, 25, 26, 32, 38, 43–44, 45, 54, 55, 59, 60, 61, 70, 79, 87, 115, 120, 129, 130, 132, 157, 161, 164, 168, 172, 174, 177, 179, 184, 186, 211n76, 222n148, 224n75. *See also roznamcha*
Dunya 'Aurat ki Nazar Mein (Begam Sarbuland Jang) 88
Durrani, Tehmina 115, 136, 172

Edib, Halidé 20, 51
Egypt 3, 7, 20, 35, 58, 189–90, 246n144
Ekale Amader Kal (Sufia Kamal) 62–63
el-Saadawi, Nawal 20

Index   275

England 61, 63, 93, 118, 138, 152, 157, 160, 167, 178, 179, 190–1

English (language) ix, 4, 6, 15, 39, 54, 58, 66, 71, 74, 89, 91, 108, 109, 100–15, 129, 137, 139, 141, 150, 162, 164, 167, 187, 200n22; English translation 33, 47, 48, 54, 108, 109, 111, 114–15, 117, 120, 135, 136, 137–38, 146

Erdman, Joan 136–37

An Extraordinary Life (Princess Mehrunissa of Rampur) 61, 236n54

Faizunnessa Chaudhurani, Nawab 61, 84

The Fall of a Sparrow (Sálim Ali) 169–73, 177, 180

Father and Daughter (Jahan Ara Shahnawaz) 33, 50, 62

Fay, Mary Ann 16

Forbes, Geraldine 234n8

France 152, 163, 165, 202n43

From Purdah to Parliament (Begam Qudsia Aizaz Rasul) 87

From Purdah to Parliament (Shaista Ikramullah) 33, 87, 114

Fyzee, Asaf A. A. 158, 160, 246n144

Fyzee, Atiya 11–12, 43–44, 73, 84, 112, 119, 120, 129–30, 138, 158, 163–66, 179, 190–1

Fyzee, Zehra 44, 73, 84, 104, 138, 191, 222n150, 233n143

Gandhi, Mohandas Karamchand 4, 11, 18, 42, 46, 88, 110, 117, 122, 136, 169, 175, 176–77, 185

Gard-i-rah (Akhtar Husain Raipuri) 156

Germany 74, 167, 177

Ghalib 41–42, 112

Ghouse, Zakira *see* Zakira Ghouse

Ghulam Fatima Shaikh 10–11, 80, 108, 202n43, 237n67

Golley, Nawar al-Hassan 20

Goodyear, Sara Suleri *see* Suleri, Sara

Grace, Sherrill 127

Gujarati ix, 6, 110, 113, 120–1, 158, 160, 187

Gulabdas, Guru 11, 66, 92, 101

Gulbadan Begam 19, 33, 59, 77, 128, 135, 156

Gusdorf, Georges 13–14

Guzashta Barson ki Baraf (Nazr Sajjad Hyder) 110, 132

Habibullah, Isha'at 156

Habibullah, Jahanara 9, 50, 61, 101, 105, 155, 156, 237n67

hajj see pilgrimage

Hali, Khwaja Altaf Husain *see* Altaf Husain Hali, Khwaja

Hamara Daur-i-Hayat (Zakira Ghouse) 18, 67, 127

Hameeda Akhtar Husain 47, 50, 51, 66, 86, 98, 102–3, 156, 202n43, 233n133, 247n7

Hamida Rahman 51, 68–69

Hamida Saiduzzafar 61, 65, 74, 75, 83, 104, 155–6, 220n104

Hamsafar (Hameeda Akhtar Husain) 47, 50, 51, 156, 202n43, 212n85, 233n133, 247n7

Hansen, Kathryn 19, 127, 142, 193

Hasan, Mushirul 41

Hashmi, Qamar Azad 104,

Hashmi, Saleema 86

Hasrat Mohani, Begam *see* Nishatunnisa, Begam Hasrat Mohani

The Heart of a Gopi (Raihana Tyabji) 11, 42–43, 97, 176

Hijab Imtiaz Ali 129, 130, 222n148

Hindi ix, 6, 39, 53, 54, 89, 91, 107, 109, 110–11, 113, 176, 200n22

Hinduism 8, 10–12, 54, 81, 91, 99, 102, 107, 140, 146, 147, 148, 190, 241n13

Hindustani 33, 35, 37, 53, 109–10, 160, 176

Hosain, Attia 40, 44, 46, 62, 74

Hossain, Rokeya Sakhawat *see* Rokeya Sakhawat Hossain

276 *Index*

Hourani, Albert 14
The House on Gulmohar Avenue (film) 50
Huda Shaarawi 20, 58, 189, 236n48
Humphreys, Stephen 14
Hussain, Iqbalunnisa 74, 103, 113, 237n67
Hyder, Qurratulain *see* Qurratulain Hyder
Hyderabad (Deccan) 6, 9, 18, 23, 39, 60,
    64, 65–66, 67, 73–74, 76, 83, 88, 102–3,
    112, 119, 121, 131, 227n25
Hyderabad (Sindh) 10, 80, 101

Ik Sau Sath Kafian (Piro) 11, 66
Ikramullah, Shaista *see* Shaista Ikramullah
Imam, Jahanara *see* Jahanara Imam
Inam Fatima Habibullah 61–62, 87, 155
Indian People's Theatre Association
    (IPTA) 89
Indonesia 17
Iqbal, Muhammad 18, 112, 119, 166
Iran 3, 7, 9, 20, 41, 177, 189–90, 192,
    246n143
Ishvani 13, 105
Ismat (Delhi) 84, 114, 129, 132
Ismat Chughtai *see* Chughtai, Ismat
Istanbul 13

Jahan Ara Shahnawaz *see* Shahnawaz,
    Jahan Ara
Jahanara (Mughal princess) 33, 35, 59,
    128, 156, 221n123
Jahanara Habibullah *see* Habibullah,
    Jahanara
Jahanara Imam 65, 88–89, 105, 224n175
Jahanjir 91, 156
Jameela, Nalini *see* Nalini Jameela
Jamia Millia Islamia 83, 100
Jamia Nagar 22, 26, 100
Jammu and Kashmir 65, 66, 80, 81, 90,
    102, 146
Janjira 43, 60, 102, 103, 104, 191, 241n20
Janjira, Nazli Rafia Sultan Nawab Begam
    Sahiba of *see* Nazli Rafia Sultan Nawab
    Begam Sahiba of Janjira

Jaora 74, 103
Jeevitathinte Arangu (Nilambur Ayisha)
    89–90
Jeffery, Patricia 100, 225n193
Jelinek, Estelle 185–86
Jiban Khatar Pataguli (Jobeda Khanam)
    69, 90, 108
Jiban Smriti (Hamida Rahman) 51
Jobeda Khanam 1–2, 27, 64–65, 69–70,
    75, 81, 82, 90–1, 108–9, 193–94
Jodhpur 65, 102
Jowshan Ara Rahman 91–92

Kabir, Meher *see* Meher Kabir
Kaghazi Hai Pairahan (Ismat Chughtai)
    41–42, 85–86, 112, 130–1
Kaifi and I (Shaukat Kaifi) 110, 135,
    137–38
Kaifi, Shaukat *see* Shaukat Kaifi
Karachi 26, 44, 49, 101, 139, 141, 145,
    146, 184
Kar-i-Jahan Daraz Hai (Qurratulain
    Hyder) 40
Kashmiri (language) 108
Kazim, Lubna 48–49, 52–53, 139, 142,
    144–52, 207n103
Kerala 4, 18, 23, 26, 47–48, 67, 89–90,
    103–4, 228n36
Khan, Bilquis Jehan *see* Bilquis Jehan
    Khan
Khan, Mahmuduzzafar 156
Khan, Razak 103
Khatemanara Begam 6
Khatun (Aligarh) 129, 140, 145
khud navisht 21, 53, 54
Khurshid Mirza, Begum 9, 21, 23, 48, 52,
    63, 74, 89, 104, 127, 139–153, 156,
    207n103
Kidwai, Anis *see* Anis Kidwai
Kidwai, Sabina 50
Kishwar Naheed 65, 86, 226n16
Kishwar, Madhu 45
Kitab-i-Zindagi (Qaisari Begam) 63, 131

Kolkata *see* Calcutta
Kumar, Sukrita Paul 41–42
Kumar, Udaya 4, 18, 44, 104

Lady Hardinge Medical College 92
Lady Irwin College 74
Lahore 35, 45, 66, 73, 80, 84, 90, 101, 119, 129, 137, 140, 148, 150, 190, 207n103
Lal, Ruby 19, 33, 135
Lalitambika Antarjanam 104
Latif, Bilkees 53
Lejeune, Phillipe 127, 152
Lulu Rahman 219n88, 235n39

Mai, Mukhtar 67, 115, 136
Maimoona Sultan 60, 71, 155, 191–92
Majchrowicz, Daniel 94
Majeed, Javed 18
Maktaba Jamia 112, 231n90
Malayalam ix, 6, 18, 48, 90, 108
Malhotra, Anshu 13, 16, 19
Manushi (Delhi) 45, 129, 183
Marathi ix, 6, 187
marriage 27, 37, 49, 76, 77, 89, 90, 102, 114, 116, 122, 131, 134, 142, 147, 148, 151, 158, 160, 161, 178, 179, 180, 186, 192, 227n25, 241n20, 248n7; child-marriage 70, 71, 194; intercommunal 12, 89; polygamous marriage 84
Mary Wigman's Dance School 74
Masuma Begam 65, 74, 88, 112, 113, 127
Matia Chowdhury 224n175
McKay, Elaine 93
Meatless Days (Sara Suleri) 213, 226n16
Mecca 9, 111, 117
Meher Kabir 9
Mehrunissa, Princess, of Rampur 13, 61, 74, 105, 155, 202n44, 236n54
Memoirs of a Rebel Princess (Abida Sultaan) 44, 60, 214n116
Memoirs of an Egoist (Badruddin Tyabji) 177

Mere Bachpan (Azra Abbas) 86
Mere Shab o Roz (Begam Zafar Ali) 80
Metcalf, Barbara 5, 16, 34, 38, 52, 53, 77–78, 107, 118, 149, 214n119
Milani, Farzaneh 7, 20, 192
Minault, Gail 144, 145–46, 234n8
Mir Muhammad Taqi 3, 98, 125
Mirza, Begum Khurshid *see* Khurshid Mirza, Begum
Mirza, Sughra Humayun *see* Sughra Humayun Mirza
Mishra, Samina 50, 226n13
Moaeni, Azadeh 246n143
Mufid-i-'Am (Agra) 138
Muhammad, Prophet 9–10, 16, 34, 68
Muhammadan Anglo-Oriental College 64, 104, 140
Muhammadan Educational Conference 140, 161
Muhammadi Begam 35, 119, 130
Mulk Raj Anand *see* Anand, Mulk Raj
Mumbai *see* Bombay
Mumtaz Mahal (Mughal queen) 35
Murshid, Noorjehan 134
My Fellow Traveller (Hameeda Akhtar Husain) 47
My Feudal Lord (Tehmina Durrani) 115, 136
Mysore 6, 74, 103, 113

Nafees Bano Shama 86, 112, 228n54, 231n90
Naheed, Kishwar *see* Kishwar Naheed
Naim, C. M. 98, 125, 137
Nalini Jameela 10–11, 47–48, 66–67, 75, 92
Nasreen, Taslima 86, 223n160
Nazir Ahmad, Deputy 71, 158, 243n50
Nazli Rafia Sultan Nawab Begam Sahiba of Janjira 43–44, 60, 73, 104, 105, 120, 163, 164–66, 179, 191, 241n20
Nazr Sajjad Hyder 25, 79–80, 84, 104, 105, 129, 130, 132–33

278 *Index*

Nehru Memorial Museum and Library (New Delhi) 38, 39, 44, 117
Nehru, Jawaharlal 4, 18, 46, 88
Nilambur Ayisha 89–90, 103–4
Nishatunnisa, Begam Hasrat Mohani 10, 87
Nizamuddin Dargah 23, 100–1
Nurjahan (Mughal queen) 35, 91
Nurunnahar Faizunnessa 133

oral narratives 2, 17, 30, 32, 45, 47–50, 54–55
Oru Laingikathozhilaliyude Atmakatha (Nalini Jameela) 47–48, 66–67
Ottoman Empire, the 191, 202n43; *also see* Istanbul

Pakistan 1, 6, 12, 13, 18, 23, 25, 33, 43, 46, 47, 48, 54, 57, 66, 67, 75, 81, 82, 83, 86, 88, 89, 90, 91, 92, 99, 101, 106, 107, 108–9, 110–11, 122, 128, 132, 139, 141, 143, 144, 146, 148, 151, 155, 156, 199n1, 229n70, 237n67, 240n3
Partition 6, 25, 40, 41, 43, 50, 62, 90, 99, 101, 102, 104, 107, 132, 141, 148, 174, 177, 199n1
Pascal, Roy 14, 30, 159, 187
Passerini, Luisa 17
Persian 16, 38, 43, 53, 71, 73, 78, 111, 113, 128, 135, 149, 158, 211n71
pilgrimage 5, 9, 12, 38, 111, 117, 129, 135
A Pilgrimage to Mecca (Sikandar Begam) 111, 117, 201n31
Piro 11, 66, 92, 101
Price, Leah 126
princely states 5, 6, 22, 33, 38, 59–61, 64, 65, 73–74, 77–78, 79, 80–81, 100, 101, 102–103, 121, 191. *See also* Baroda, Bhopal, Hyderabad, Jammu and Kashmir, Janjira, Jaora, Jodhpur, Pataudi, Rampur
Pukhraj, Malka 66, 90

Punjabi (language) ix, 6, 66, 108, 113
purdah *see* veiling and seclusion

Qaisari Begam 63, 65, 71, 103, 131, 132, 212n88
Qamar Azad Hashmi *see* Hashmi, Qamar Azad
Qudsia Aizaz Rasul, Begam 60, 61, 87, 88
Qudsia Begam 35,
Qur'an, the 10, 15, 70, 71, 73, 79, 158, 168
Qurratulain Hyder 40–41, 74, 110, 112, 132, 228n54

Rafia Abdul Ali 184, 245n113
Rahamin, Samuel 11
Rahil Begam Sherwani 65, 87, 104
Rahmat Ara Hossain 64, 219n88, 219n104
Rahmathunnisa Begam 60, 73, 80, 83, 103, 113, 127
Raihana Tyabji *see* Tyabji, Raihana
Raipuri, Akhtar Husain *see* Akhtar Husain Raipuri
Raipuri, Hameeda Akhtar Husain *see* Hameeda Akhtar Husain
Rajan, Rajeswari Sunder 30
Rampur 6, 9, 13, 39, 60–1, 101, 102, 103, 105, 121, 155
Rampur, Princess Mehrunissa of *see* Mehrunissa, Princess, of Rampur
rape 67, 129, 181, 183–84, 186, 187
Rassundari Debi 19, 102
Rasul, Begam Qudsia Aizaz *see* Qudsia Aizaz Rasul, Begam
Raziya Sultana 35
Rehman, Nasreen 138
religious festivals 9, 11
Remembrance of Days Past (Jahanara Habibullah) 9, 61, 101, 155
Reynolds, Dwight 13, 15
Riaz, Fahmida 86, 226n16
Risala-i-Sahibiyah (Jahanara) 33, 59, 128, 221n123
Robinson, Francis 5, 34,

Rodgers, Susan 17
Rokeya Sakhawat Hossain 40
Roshni (Delhi) 45, 113, 120, 168, 174, 179
Rousseau, Jean-Jacques 13, 126, 170
roznamcha 24, 38, 44, 55, 79, 129, 132, 164, 176, 177, 179, 186, 222n148
Rupjalal (Nawab Faizunnessa Chaudhurani) 61, 84–85

Saeeda Bano Ahmed 66, 74, 90
Safarnama 38, 55, 84
Safia Jabir Ali 44, 65, 73, 97, 115–17, 127, 135–36, 167–73, 174, 176, 177, 179, 180, 202n43, 242n32, 243n50
Saharanpur 9, 65
Sahitya Akademi 14, 15
Said, Edward 14, 37
Saiduzzafar, Hamida *see* Hamida Saiduzzafar
Sair-i-Yurop (Nazli Rafia Sultan Nawab Begam Sahiba of Janjira) 60, 120, 164–65
Saiyida Lutfunnessa 69, 235n25
Sakhawat Memorial Girls' School 72
Saksena, S.P. 4
Saliha Abid Hussain 84, 95, 105, 112, 133, 156, 228n54, 231n90
Salma Tasadduq Husain 88
Sarbuland Jang, Begam 65, 66, 87–88, 103, 104
Sarkar, Mahua 8
Sarkar, Tanika 19
Sayani, Kulsum 105, 113
Sayyida Khurshid Alam 50, 88, 230n74
Scotland *see* Britain
self, the 2, 4, 5, 7, 8, 11, 14–19, 20–25, 31, 34, 37, 38, 41, 42, 49, 50, 51, 52, 53, 55, 59, 94, 98, 103, 120, 122–3, 126, 127, 148, 149, 151, 152, 153, 154, 163, 168, 170, 171, 174, 184, 185, 186, 187, 192–93; gendered self 2, 7, 126–27, 153–54, 157, 176, 193; self-expression

22, 41, 83, 135, 162, 164; self-narrative 14, 154; self-reflection 15, 93, 132, 152, 160; self-representation 7, 17, 37, 126, 138, 192, 202n37
sexuality 23, 25, 37, 52, 67, 76, 85, 115, 151, 157, 179–83, 186
Shaarawi, Huda *see* Huda Shaarawi
Shabana Azmi 45, 86
Shah Jahan Begam 35, 37, 59, 77–78, 79, 111, 155
Shah, Fatima 33, 92
Shahnawaz, Jahan Ara 33, 50, 62, 88, 113, 190, 237n67
Shahr Bano Begam 54, 59–60, 77, 117–19, 135, 226n15, 237n67
Shaikh, Ghulam Fatima *see* Ghulam Fatima Shaikh
Shaista Ikramullah 33, 65, 87, 88, 114, 156, 237n67
Shamsie, Kamila 155, 240n3
Shamsie, Muneeza 49–50, 155, 215n21, 240n3
Shareefah Hamid Ali 65, 88, 105, 113, 158, 168, 174–76, 241n20
Sharma, Sunil 166
sharif see ashraf
Shaukat Kaifi 65, 86, 89, 106, 110, 112, 114–15, 135, 137–38, 223n58, 248n7
Shia Islam 9–10, 105, 179; *also see* Bohra Muslims
Shibli Nomani, Maulana 11–12, 243n50
Sikhism 66, 92, 101, 107, 148
Silsila-i-Roz o Shab (Saliha Abid Hussain) 84, 95, 112, 133, 156
Sindhi (language) 15, 108
Smith, Sidonie 21, 122–23, 205n86
Song Sung True: A Memoir (Malka Pukhraj) 66,
Spivak, Gayatri 2
Stark, Ulrike 3
Steedman, Carolyn 31
Sufia Kamal 62, 86
Sufism 9, 34, 100–1, 126, 226n12

280   *Index*

Sughra Humayun Mirza 83, 102, 112,
Sughra Mehdi 102, 104, 112, 156,
    228n54, 235n25
Suhrawardy, Huseyn Shaheed 156
Suhrawardy, Shaista Akhtar Bano *see*
    Shaista Ikramullah
Suleri, Sara 13, 83, 202n41, 226n16
Sultaan, Abida *see* Abida Sultaan
Sultan Jahan Begam 26, 29, 35, 37, 44, 59,
    66, 70–1, 75–76, 78, 79, 104, 109, 138,
    155, 221n126
Sultana Asaf Fyzee 246n144
Sultana Jafri 106
Suniye Kakasaheb (Raihana Tyabji) 106,
    110, 176–77

Tahzib un-Niswan (Lahore) 35, 37, 45, 79,
    84, 119, 129–30, 132, 212n80
Tahzib un-Niswan wa Tarbiyat ul-Insan
    (Shah Jahan Begam) 37
Taqi, Mir Muhammad *see* Mir
    Muhammad Taqi
Taslima Nasreen *see* Nasreen, Taslima
Tata, Navajbai 165
Tehmina Durrani *see* Durrani, Tehmina
travel writing 3, 9–10, 12–13, 18, 21, 26,
    29, 32, 37–38, 40, 43–44, 45, 51, 55,
    59, 60, 78, 83–84, 87–88, 94, 102,
    104, 112, 113, 114, 119, 120, 129, 133,
    155, 156, 157, 163–68, 170, 174–76,
    179–81, 184, 185, 190–92, 202n43,
    220n119, 222n150, 223n168, 234n15,
    246n144
Tucker, Judith E. 16, 78, 187
Tuqan, Fadwa 20
Turkey 3; *also see* Ottoman Empire, the
Tyab Ali 116, 157–58, 159–60
Tyabjee Bhoymeeah *see* Tyab Ali
Tyabji clan 24, 26, 42, 45, 60 , 105,
    109–10, 116, 120–21, 157–87, 190–91,
    241n13, 241n21. *See also* Abdulali,
    Sohaila; Fyzee, Atiya; Fyzee, Zehra;
    Nazli Rafia Sultan Nawab Begam

Sahiba of Janjira; Tyabji, Abbas;
    Tyabji, Amina; Tyabji, Badruddin
    (diplomat); Tyabji, Badruddin (law-
    yer); Tyabji, Camruddin; Tyabji, Hadi
    Camruddin; Tyabji, Kamila; Tyabji,
    Laila; Tyabji, Najmuddin; Tyabji,
    Raihana; Tyabji, Surayya; Tyabji,
    Salima; Rafia Abdul Ali; Safia Jabir
    Ali; Shareefah Hamid Ali
Tyabji, Abbas 65, 106, 158, 168, 170, 174,
    241n13
Tyabji, Amina 65, 73, 79, 120, 163, 164,
    166–68, 170, 174, 177, 179
Tyabji, Badruddin (diplomat) 177–78,
    181–82, 245n107, 245n111
Tyabji, Badruddin (lawyer) 44–45, 65, 73,
    116, 157–58, 161, 162, 163, 164, 169,
    174, 178, 179, 181, 241n15, 242n36
Tyabji, Camruddin 140, 162, 179
Tyabji, Hadi Camruddin 162
Tyabji, Kamila 158
Tyabji, Laila 158, 181–83, 247n145,
    247n146
Tyabji, Najmuddin S. 178–181, 184,
    245n111, 245n113
Tyabji, Raihana 11, 42–43, 65, 88, 97, 106,
    110, 176–77, 179, 205n91, 228n54
Tyabji, Salima 117, 136, 207n104,
    245n114, 247n147
Tyabji, Surayya 158, 161, 171, 181

Uday Shankar 89, 137
Ummat ul-Ghani Nurunnisa 9, 65
UNICEF 92
United Nations 174–75, 185
United Provinces, the 46, 61, 65, 87, 105,
    146
United States of America, the 75, 113,
    129, 174–76, 202n43, 202n44, 207n103
Urdu (language) ix, 6, 8, 14–15, 21, 33, 38,
    39, 40, 41, 43, 44, 47, 51, 53–54, 68, 73,
    74, 79, 83, 85, 86, 87, 97, 107–114, 118,
    119, 120–21, 122, 128–29, 130, 132,

135, 136, 137, 138, 140, 141, 146, 149,
158, 160, 161, 162, 164, 165, 166, 167,
168, 187, 200n22, 203n58, 207n106,
211n71, 229n70, 230n74, 231n90,
231n100, 242n38, 243n62

Vanita, Ruth 45
Vaqa'i' (Babur) 3, 14, 15, 156,
Vatuk, Sylvia 18, 119–20
veiling and seclusion ix, 1–2, 5, 7, 24, 29,
87, 89, 91, 95, 104, 117, 119, 161, 122,
161, 179, 187, 189–94, 247–48n7,
248n23; in schools 70, 71, 73, 74, 76, 79
von Grunebaum, Gustave E. 15,

Watson, Julia 21, 42, 153
White, Hayden 30
A Woman of Substance (Begum Khurshid
Mirza)

Yad ki Rahguzar (Shaukat Kaifi) 112, 137,
223n158, 229n70
Youngs, Tim 38
Yousafzai, Malala 75, 115, 136, 236n55

Zafar Ali, Begam 65, 80–81, 227n24
Zafar, Shabnam 48–49, 139
Zaidi, Ali Jawad *see* Ali Jawad Zaidi
Zakira Ghouse 18, 65, 67–68, 74, 76, 103,
112, 119–20, 127
Zamana-i-Tahsil (Atiya Fyzee) ix, 120,
130, 164–65
Zebunnisa (Lahore) 45, 84
Zehra Fyzee *see* Fyzee, Zehra
Zill us-Sultan (Bhopal) 35
Zohra Mumtaz *see* Zohra Segal
Zonis, Marvin 14
Zubaan (Delhi publishing house) 137–38,
139, 143, 144, 146–47, 148

ALSO PUBLISHED IN THE SOUTH ASIA IN MOTION SERIES

Financializing Poverty: Labor and Risk in Indian Microfinance
Sohini Kar (2018)

*Jinnealogy: Time, Islam, and Ecological Thought
in the Medieval Ruins of Delhi*
Anand Vivek Taneja (2017)

Uprising of the Fools: Pilgrimage as Moral Protest in Contemporary India
Vikash Singh (2017)

The Slow Boil: Street Food, Rights, and Public Space in Mumbai
Jonathan Shapiro Anjaria (2016)

*The Demands of Recognition: State Anthropology
and Ethnopolitics in Darjeeling*
Townsend Middleton (2015)

The South African Gandhi: Stretcher-Bearer of Empire
Ashwin Desai and Goolam Vahed (2015)